Advance Praise for

To Whom Belongs the Land?

"The question of the land and of land ownership is a crucial issue in the Hebrew Bible, and also in many modern societies. Ndikho Mtshiselwa contributes to this debate by a careful examination of Leviticus 25, one of the most important biblical text about the question of justice and land. This book offers a very challenging combination of a socio-historical reading of the chapter in its original context and an analysis of this chapter in the context of the present South African society. A must read for every scholar and student interested in contextual reading that is informed by serious historical-critical scholarship."

—*Thomas Römer, Chaire "Milieux bibliques," Vice-Administrateur Collège de France; Professor, Faculty of Theology and Sciences of Religion, University of Lausanne*

"In this study, Ndikho Mtshiselwa recognises that the land question is at the heart of the socio-economic challenges that are currently gripping South Africa. He correctly apportions some of the blame to colonialism and apartheid, which seem to be kept alive through the neo-liberal policies that were adopted by the ruling government of the day. These are the very policies that are the outcome of a negotiated settlement which safeguarded and appeased those who unscrupulously controlled and continue to control the vast economic resources of South Africa. Employing the Jubilee principles as contained in Leviticus 25:8–55, Mtshiselwa starts a conversation on the question of land in South Africa and argues that impetus for such a conversation is informed by the Jubilee principles. The arguments made in this study on the land question and its interaction with the biblical Jubilee principles are clear and lucid. One immediately recognises the immense influence that Black Theology of Liberation has had on the author in the arguments set forth. This study is a thoughtful and in-depth contribution to black theological scholarship in present day South Africa. It is particularly paramount in a time of numerous calls for the Africanization of knowledge production in South Africa. Anyone who is serious about the issues of poverty, the land question in South Africa, the economic disparities between Blacks and Whites in South Africa, among others, must wrestle with this text."

—*Rothney S Tshaka, Director of the School of Humanities and Professor of Theological Ethics and Systematic Theology, University of South Africa*

To Whom Belongs the Land?

Bible & Theology in Africa

Knut Holter
General Editor

Vol. 23

The Bible & Theology in Africa series is part of the Peter Lang Humanities list.
Every volume is peer reviewed and meets
the highest quality standards for content and production.

PETER LANG
New York • Bern • Berlin
Brussels • Vienna • Oxford • Warsaw

Ndikho Mtshiselwa

To Whom Belongs the Land?

Leviticus 25 in an African Liberationist Reading

PETER LANG
New York • Bern • Berlin
Brussels • Vienna • Oxford • Warsaw

Library of Congress Cataloging-in-Publication Data

Names: Mtshiselwa, Ndikho, author.
Title: To whom belongs the land?: Leviticus 25 in an African liberationist reading / Ndikho Mtshiselwa.
Other titles: Bible and theology in Africa ; v. 23.
Description: New York: Peter Lang.
Series: Bible and theology in Africa; v. 23 | ISSN 1525-9846
Includes bibliographical references and index.
Identifiers: LCCN 2017038863 | ISBN 978-1-4331-3893-5 (hardback: alk. paper)
ISBN 978-1-4331-3897-3 (ebook pdf) | ISBN 978-1-4331-3898-0 (epub)
ISBN 978-1-4331-3899-7 (mobi)
Subjects: LCSH: Bible. Leviticus, XXV, 8–55—Criticism, interpretation, etc.
Land tenure—Religious aspects—Christianity.
Land reform—South Africa.
Liberation theology.
Classification: LCC BS1255.6.L28 M77 | DDC 222.1306—dc23
LC record available at https://lccn.loc.gov/2017038863
DOI 10.3726/978-1-4331-3897-3

Bibliographic information published by **Die Deutsche Nationalbibliothek.**
Die Deutsche Nationalbibliothek lists this publication in the "Deutsche Nationalbibliografie"; detailed bibliographic data are available on the Internet at http://dnb.d-nb.de/.

29 Broadway, 18th floor, New York, NY 10006
www.peterlang.com

With love to my mother, Doris (Bhelekazi),

To my spiritual father, the late Reverend Admiral Malixole Dondashe,

To my wife, Pumla Mtshiselwa,

And to all the (grand)sons and (grand)daughters whose (grand)fathers and (grand)mothers lost their productive land in the history of Africa …

Table of Contents

Tables

Acknowledgements

First and foremost, gratitude is due to u*Qamata* the deity of my ancestors. The completion of this study could not have been possible without the inspiration, strength and wisdom from God. Further, I would like to express the word of gratitude to the following persons and institutions:

Mme Motswadi, Prof Madipoane Masenya (ngwan'a Mphahlele), thank you for the meticulous manner and ingenuity with which you have supervised my work. *Ke Leboga kudu* 'Thank you very much'.

Much gratitude goes to Prof Thomas Römer for proof reading Chapter 3 and his support towards the publication of this book.

To the editor of my manuscript, Dr. Funlola Olojede, you are a language editor of class. My profound gratitude goes to you *Sisi*, 'sister' for your excellent work.

To my mother *Bhelekazi*, the profound gratitude to you is well deserved for the manner in which you have taught me the value of education, determination and hard work. Thank you so much *Bhelekazi, Dlambulo, Khuboni, Qunta, Mafu, Langa, Mnomana, Mbutho, Ncwana, noNtanda* [...].

Abbreviations

AFU	Asset Forfeiture Unit
ANC	African National Congress
BCE	Before the Common Era
BEE	Black Economic Empowerment
CC	Covenant Code
CODESA	Convention for a Democratic South Africa
COSATU	Congress of South African Trade Unions
CRDP	Comprehensive Rural Development Programme
D	Deuteronomistic School authors
DA	Democratic Alliance
DAFF	Department of Agriculture, Forestry and Fisheries
Deut	Book of Deuteronomy
DLA	Department of Land Affairs
DRDLR	Department of Rural Development and Land Reform
DH	Documentary Hypothesis
E	Elohist writers
GDP	Gross Domestic Product
GEAR	Growth, Employment and Redistribution
H	Holiness Code
HSRC	Human Sciences Research Council

IMF	International Monetary Fund
J	Yahwist writers
JCI	Johannesburg Consolidated Investments
JSE	Johannesburg Stock Exchange
KJV	Kings James Version
LAPC	Land and Agricultural Policy Centre
MEC	Minerals-Energy Complex
NAIL	New Africa Investments Limited
NASYSEC	National Rural Youth Services Corps
Neo-DH	Neo-Documentary Hypothesis
NIV	New International Version
Non-DH	Non-Documentary Hypothesis
NP	National Party
P	Priestly authors
Pg	Priestly document—"Grundschrift"
RDP	Reconstruction and Development Program
RSA	Republic of South Africa
SACP	South African Communist Party
SARS	South Africa Revenue Service
Stats SA	Statistics South Africa
TEC	Transitional Executive Committee
UN	United Nations

CHAPTER ONE

Introduction

Statement of Problem

Twenty-three years into democratic rule, South Africa is faced with a burning debate on land redistribution in the context of poverty and socio-economic inequality. However, the debate focuses on productive land, that is, land to be used for agricultural purposes, rather than land in general. Poverty in this research is understood as the inability to attain a minimal standard of living measured in terms of basic consumption needs.[1] The problem of the gap between the rich and the poor constitutes inequality in the context of poverty in South Africa.[2] Against the idea of sharing and redistribution of wealth, the concepts of privatization and capitalism have dominated discussions of poverty and inequality. Capitalism has to with the decentralization of decision-making, coordination by a network of markets, predominantly material incentives, and private ownership of land and capital. South Africa currently operates a capitalistic economy. In such an economy, the empowerment of the poor and the alleviation of poverty are viewed as being dependent on the global integration of finance and market.[3] However, privatization and capitalism do not alleviate poverty or redress inequality.[4] The concern here is that capitalism and privatization progress at the cost of sharing and redistribution of wealth, and the empowerment of the poor African South Africans. The phrase African South Africans is employed here to refer to the indigenous (black) peoples of South Africa who are of African descent including the Xhosas, Ndebeles, Sothos, Tswanas, Zulus, Vendas and so forth.[5] The indigenous peoples of South Africa include the Khoi and San peoples, but because they are not included in the phrase 'African South Africans' as employed by Masenya (ngwan'a Mphahlele) in her analysis and given the limited scope of this research, they will not form part of the category, 'African South African' as used in this study. In my view, a discussion of the issue of land in relation to the Khoi and San peoples would require a study of its own. The idea of redistribution of wealth in South Africa is linked to the issue of land to which this discussion now turns.

The issue of 'land' is at the heart of social, political and economic life in most African economies including South Africa's which continues to rely heavily on agriculture and natural resources for a significant share of its Gross Domestic Product (GDP), national food needs, employment and export revenue.[6] The issue of land redistribution is therefore grounded in the context of poverty and socio-economic inequality. Land redistribution could serve several purposes such as farming, mining and housing, among others. It is imperative at this point to present an overview of the issue of land in South Africa which will serve as the framework for the main research question.

In his article titled *Land, class and the Bible in South Africa today*, Mosala states that the land question is at the heart of the struggle for justice and development in South Africa.[7] No doubt, the issue of land is linked to the historical seizure of land in South Africa. Mosala also probes whether the Israelite Jubilee in Leviticus 25:8–55 could speak more profoundly to the deep aspirations of the people especially on the burning question of land restoration.[8] However, he does not try to answer the question nor discuss the issue of land and alleviation of poverty in relation to the Israelite Jubilee. Clearly, poverty is a direct consequence of the land seizure and migratory labor patterns wrought by colonialism and apartheid in South Africa. Therefore, I view the subject of land as integral to the discussion of poverty and inequality; and the history of land in South Africa is critical to the discussion of land and poverty alleviation. It is to this history, that I now turn.

It is on record that colonialism and apartheid sponsored the massive disenfranchisement of indigenous peoples as well as their alienation from their land.[9] In the period of apartheid, the African National Congress Freedom Charter was adopted by the Congress of the People on 26 June 1955.[10] A clause in the Charter reiterated the demands for equality in the spheres of political, social, educational and cultural life, and for land redistribution. A proposal for transferring power and privileges from the white minority to the population as a whole to the benefit of all South African citizens is also embedded in the same clause.[11] The alleviation of poverty and redress of inequality seem to be the fundamental issues that the Charter sought to address.

However, on the issue of agricultural land, in particular, the land reform policy in South Africa prescribed a 'willing-buyer willing-seller' approach coupled with a limited state grant, the protection of private property and compensation based on market value for any expropriated agricultural land. The policy protected privatization and called for the stabilization of the rural economy within the agricultural sector.[12] Privatization attracts investment, productivity and economic development, and it seems to have been the only option for Africa and for South Africa in particular, especially with regard to the land issue. South Africa has continued to promote privatization rather than land redistribution. In addition to generating wealth and developing the economy, private ownership of the agricultural land, in particular, may be viewed as the only way to ensure the development of South Africa.[13]

The issue of land in South Africa has also emerged in the debate on mines, specifically, on the nationalization of mines. Nationalization is defined as the transfer of private ownership of assets to the government with full or partial compensation.[14] The call for the nationalization of mines therefore seeks to centralize the ownership of mines (or land) by shifting ownership to the government for the benefit of all South Africans. The redistribution of wealth is the primary objective of nationalization, which in my view, seems not to have been achieved because of privatization and capitalism. Shivambu argues that the nationalization of mines can alleviate poverty and redress inequality.[15] This view is motivated by the commitment to redress the apartheid legacy of disparities visible within the mining sector. Nonetheless, the efficiency of nationalization in the redistribution and equalization of wealth in a capitalist economy, in particular, has been questioned.[16] The wearing a way of investor confidence and the possible drain on state coffers rather than access to additional capital are some of the reasons behind the skepticism about nationalization.[17] It came as no surprise that the African National Congress (ANC) conference held in Mangaung rejected the proposal for the nationalization of mines.[18] The conference delegates did not reach a consensus on the discussion of poverty and inequality in the context of capitalism, privatization and redistribution of land in South Africa.

On the other hand, the twentieth century has made the Old Testament an African book.[19] Ancient texts have been related to the experiences of Africans. Could the land question and poverty alleviation in South Africa relate in one way or other to the Israelite Jubilee in Leviticus 25:8–55? Before we attempt to answer the question, some remarks about the Israelite Jubilee in Leviticus 25:8–55 will be helpful.

The Israelite Jubilee in Leviticus 25:8–55 is understood in different ways by Old Testament scholars. Thus, the Hebrew masculine singular absolute noun יוֹבֵל translated as Jubilee (Lev 25:10) from which the institution derives its name originally meant a 'ram' or a 'ram's horn'.[20] The ram's horn was used by the Israelites as a sacred tool in the inauguration of a new and happier era for the conquered and dispersed Israel.[21] The horn was also used by the Israelites to proclaim a year of atonement or reconciliation.[22] From the two uses of the horn, the year of Jubilee derived its name and came to be known as the 'year of the Ram's Horn' as shown in Leviticus 25.[23] The term Jubilee comes from the Latin *jubilum* (from *jubilo*), meaning shout for joy.[24] This meaning resonates with the view that the Jubilee year was characterized by great rejoicing as the restoration of the land took its course and liberation was realized.[25]

Liberation subsequently became the distinguishing mark of the year of Jubilee.[26] The restoration of lost land to its former owners or their living next of kin marked the Israelite celebration of liberation, and it is embedded in Leviticus 25:29.[27] The Jubilee was a year when liberty was proclaimed and the Israelites who had been enslaved were released while land and property were returned to their owners.[28] The proclamation of liberty is mentioned in Leviticus 25:10 and the call for the release of slaves[29] is made in vv.41–47. Moreover, the return of land (agricultural) and property to their owners is embedded in vv.29–34. Furthermore, the Israelite Jubilee in its functional form is expected to respond to the needs of the poor. Its meaning is captured in the position which views it as economic restructuring.[30] However, it is questionable whether the institution of the Israelite Jubilee was ever practiced.

The question of whether the Jubilee was ever put into practice in Israel has been posed by a number of biblical scholars.[31] Ringe observes that historical accounts and records have failed to throw light on the mystery surrounding the observance of the Israelite Jubilee.[32] The observance of a Jubilee year in ancient Israel is not mentioned. Fried and Freedman however claim that the Jubilee was a historic institution in biblical Judah.[33] They are of the view that the years 588/587 BCE were the Israelite Jubilee years. This view is based on the observation of Zedekiah's use of the language of Jubilee to proclaim a mass manumission of slaves and of the occasion in which Jeremiah and Hanamel risked their lives to ensure that Jeremiah redeem his ancestral lands.[34] Evidence of the mass manumission of slaves (Jer 34:8) together with Jeremiah's redemption of his ancestral land (Jer 32:6–15), and the use of the Jubilee language (Jer 34:8) support Fried and Freedman's view. It seems the Israelite Jubilee was understood as the proclamation of liberty for slaves and the restoration of land to its rightful owners.

To which period in the development of ancient Israel should the Jubilee legislation and institution therefore be ascribed, and from where did the Jubilee originate? The latter part of the question will be discussed in the literature review section. However, regarding the first part of the question, the establishment of the period and the reconstruction of its setting(s) can unearth the meaning of the institution in the Israelite context. Different periods and life-settings have been proposed by Old Testament scholars. As early as the 1920s, a pre-monarchic setting for the Israelite Jubilee was proposed.[35] In line with the view of the pre-monarchic setting is the view that the Israelite Jubilee legislation surfaced specifically in the settlement period.[36]

Alternatively, the Israelite Jubilee legislation in Leviticus 25:8–55 is regarded as a priestly response to the disruption of the society which was caused by the growth of the monarchy, an urban trade-based economy, and the poverty experienced by the Israelite land-owners.[37] The poverty provoked a priestly response. In the late 1960s, contrary to the view that supports the tribal, pre-monarchic and monarchic periods, North, suggests that the Israelite Jubilee originated during the exilic period.[38] Based on the argument that the priests created the idea of the Israelite Jubilee in the Babylonian exile with the purpose of regaining their land upon their return under Cyrus, it can be presumed that the Israelite Jubilee took into account the issue of land redistribution.

The view that an early pre-exilic date is most probable for the basic outlines of the institution of the Israelite Jubilee and that a later period in Israel's history is probable for the present form of the Israelite Jubilee legislation in Leviticus 25 is supported by recent Old Testament scholarship.[39] Bergsma associates the walled cities in Leviticus 25:29 with the walled cities which are now apparent from the excavations at Tel Zayit which have large-scale Israelite stone architecture for public and private buildings, including defensive walls incorporating enormous (2 m^3 or more) monoliths.[40] He further notes that an inscribed abecedary was found at Tel Zayit, which attests to Israelite literacy in that period (tenth century BCE), and which supports the pre-exilic dating of the Israelite Jubilee. Indeed, the archaeological findings, the tribal or family orientation of Leviticus 25:8–55, and the connection of Leviticus 25:8–55 to ancient Near Eastern practices support an early dating of the Israelite Jubilee legislation to the tribal period.[41]

Consequently, one could assume that the Israelite Jubilee in its original pre-exilic context served to protect the sacredness of the land and prevent the inalienability of the land of poor families. Later in the monarchic period, it seems that the Israelite Jubilee aimed to redress the inequality between the rich and the poor. However, the transforming and empowering possibilities that the Israelite Jubilee offer to the poor in South Africa is missing in Old Testament scholarship. In the light of the above discussion, the issues of land and the alleviation of poverty can be regarded as two of the pertinent themes embedded in the text of Leviticus 25:8–55. The redistribution of land as it pertains to agriculture and property in the Israelite Jubilee and the South African context has the potential to respond to the needs of the poor. Moreover, the redistribution of land is a bid to redress economic inequality, which manifests in the gap between the rich and the poor. Farms or agricultural land and property as well as the sharing of wealth come up in the discussions about both contexts.

One thing that seems certain, at least on the surface, is that a modern day South African reader may not *easily* read the notion of the nationalization of mines into the text about the Israelite Jubilee in Leviticus 25:8–55. However, the issue of mines in the context of land could not have occurred at the time of writing the Israelite Jubilee legislation in Leviticus 25:8–55. Hence, there is no mention of the redistribution or nationalization of mines in the Leviticus text even though both the Israelite Jubilee and the discourse on redistribution or nationalization of mines speak to the idea of redressing socio-economic injustice. The Israelite Jubilee aimed to redress socio-economic inequalities in a bid to alleviate poverty in much the same way as the nationalization of mines in the South African context. In other words, both the Jubilee legislation and the idea of the nationalization of mines emerged in response to the fundamental needs of the poor, and both support the centralization of land ownership. However, the two contexts differ in the sense that in Leviticus 25:23, Yahweh owned the land while in the context of the nationalization of mines, the land is supposed to belong to the government. The sharing of resources and wealth is embedded in the Israelite Jubilee just as the call for the nationalization of mines in South Africa supports the sharing of resources and wealth. This brief comparison of the two contexts suggests the possibility of a connection between the Israelite Jubilee legislation and the redistribution or nationalization of mines in South Africa.

From the studies examined above, it is clear that scholars have begun to apply the Israelite Jubilee laws to contexts in which inequalities abound. In my view however, the arguments are not strong enough to make a difference in the discourse on social transformation. In this research, I would like to take the arguments further by addressing the following question: If re-read from an African liberationist perspective in the context of land redistribution and socio-economic justice in South Africa, could the Israelite Jubilee in the text of Leviticus 25:8–55 offer liberating and empowering possibilities for the poor in South Africa?

Hypothesis Postulation

A hypothesis is a proposition made based on limited evidence as a starting point for further investigation.[42] It is a provisional conjecture that will guide the investigation of the present study. The main question of this research, which focuses on the role of the Old Testament in the South African context, leads to the hypothesis that: The Israelite Jubilee in Leviticus 25:8–55, when re-read from an African liberationist perspective and in the context of the discourse on redistribution of land and socio-economic justice, can contribute positively to the redress of inequality and, consequently, to poverty alleviation in South Africa.

Methodology Employed for the Study

A methodology is a system of method(s) used in a particular field.[43] In the context of the present research, the methodology presents the theoretical and methodological frameworks as well as the procedures that are used to accomplish the research objectives. The theories and methods that are employed to collect and analyse data will be outlined in the present section.

Qualitative Research

This study is based on qualitative rather than quantitative research, which Housier defines as research that is based on measurement and quantification of data.[44] In contrast to quantitative research, a qualitative research is a process of enquiry, which draws data from the context in which events occur in an attempt to describe these occurrences.[45] In the process, perspectives of those participating in the events are determined, and possible explanations of data based on observable facts are derived. Moreover, Bogdan's idea of participant observation has also influenced the choice of method employed in this research. A prolonged period of intense social interaction between the researcher and the subjects defines participant observation.[46] In the course of such an interaction, data in the form of notes are collected and analysed.[47] Participation in research conferences, seminars and workshops in the fields of Old Testament, social sciences and economics forms part of the participant observation followed in the present study. Further, relevant secondary sources such as books, articles from periodicals, internet sources, theses and dissertations are also consulted.

African Liberationist Perspective

The re-reading of the Israelite Jubilee in Leviticus 25:8–55 in the context of land redistribution in South Africa will be done from an African liberationist perspective. A distinction is made between a liberationist and a liberal perspective thus:

> … Third, a liberal largely accepts the current, western dominated world order, whereas a liberationist is anti-western, wants to counter balance the west and strongly identifies

> with the developing world. Fourth, whereas a liberal aspires to deracinate human relations and universal agreement on moral questions, the liberationist sees racial and cultural relations as antagonistic and fraught with hierarchy, power and skewed representations, and motivates an insistence on the equal worth of non-western cultures ...[48]

Based on the above view, South Africa is viewed, in the present study, as one of the countries that forms part of the developing world. The racial, cultural and social class relations in the context of land redistribution will be discussed in order to argue for equality in terms of class, race and gender. Liberationism is viewed as nurturing a spirit of 'freedom fighting' which requires the struggle against oppression, prejudice and discrimination to grow to fruition through the acquisition and exercise of political power.[49] Of course, one could add the issue of the acquisition of economic power. Liberationism was originally a North American theology of black power and a Latin American theology of liberation from oppression.[50] A concern of liberation theology is the truth of liberation itself as defined by the oppressed in their struggle.[51] In the present study, the ordinary South African readers of the ancient text (cf. Lev 25:8–55) and the unequal and poor context within which they exist will be the subject of interpretation.[52]

Ukpong notes that, like black theologians, liberationists believe that a biblical text has a liberating message for Africans in their state of poverty, oppression and exploitation.[53] Hence, in this study, I wish to re-read the Israelite Jubilee legislation in Leviticus 25:8–55 in the context of the theme of land redistribution in South Africa in order to contribute positively to the discourse on redressing inequality and alleviating poverty. An African liberationist perspective is 'Africentric' in orientation in that it operates from the perspective that Africa, South Africa in particular, constitutes the primordial context for human growth and liberation.[54] An African liberationist perspective will empathize with the poor in pursuit of socio-economic justice and liberation in the South African context, and it will be guided by the following structure:

- Historical-critical method;
- Liberating *blackness* from *whiteness* and *Europeanness*;
- The liberationist dimension of an African liberationist approach; and
- African proverbs and liberation songs as hermeneutical tools.

Historical-critical method

Gerald West claims that African biblical scholarship has been shaped by the historical-critical method and the interests of western biblical scholarship.[55] The historical-critical method in the present study includes text criticism, source criticism and redaction criticism. The study also embraces the view that it is unwise and unhelpful to reject western Old Testament scholarship in South African biblical scholarship.[56] The meaning of the ancient text is uncovered through the so-called western Old Testament scholarship. On the one hand, textual criticism will assist the exegete to locate the text of Leviticus 25 within the broader context of its many versions and translations.[57] On the other hand, redaction criticism will focus on the editorial stage(s) that led to the final written form of the passage.[58] Omissions and insertions of verses, words or phrases that were made to the original form of Leviticus 25 will be investigated and explained. Significantly, the historical-critical method in this study will play a critical role in probing the life-setting of the Israelite Jubilee and the importance of the Jubilee in ancient Near Eastern communities. In order for the methodology to be relevant to the South African context, the historical-critical approach will be used within the theoretical and methodological framework of an African liberationist paradigm. As will be elaborated below, this study will draw on Mosala's approach to historical-critical methods as he is critical of their Euro-American roots.[59] Before relating the African liberationist approach to Leviticus 25:8–55 and the black biblical hermeneutics of liberation as well as on post-colonial biblical scholarship, it is important that we mention some of the concerns about the apparent dominance of *whiteness* and *Europeanness* in biblical scholarship.

Liberating blackness from whiteness and Europeanness

Responding to Perkinson's argument about confronting white privilege in terms of socio-economic frameworks, personal power and cultural habits, Snyman argues that 'in South Africa, *whiteness* has lost its political dominance, but not its cultural and economic domination':

> I may be white, male, middle class and thus advantaged on an economical *(sic)* level. However, on a socio-political level, I am not, as I do not have political power any longer in terms of *whiteness*. Moreover, in terms of political transformation my *whiteness* and maleness pose obstacles to others who want to be advanced, thus pushing me down to the lower steps of the socio-political ladder.[60]

Given the economic privilege associated with *whiteness* in South Africa, which is evident in the disproportionate benefit from land ownership and use, a discussion of *whiteness* is fitting. If an African liberationist reading of Leviticus 25:8–55 would be liberative and relevant to the South African context, it is important to consider the economic privileges attributed to *whiteness* in the country.

How can a discussion of *blackness* unlock the liberative reading of the social location of the poor in South Africa? In terms of a liberated[61] oriented definition of *blackness*, Vellem holds that *blackness* does not refer to the pigmentation of the skins of black people in South Africa.[62] Instead, *blackness* mainly refers to the cultural values, ideological concepts and realities of black people who are of African descent. It has been argued elsewhere that, in South Africa, *blackness* can unlock the meaning of an ancient text, which is not shaded by *whiteness and Europeanness*.[63] In other words, *blackness* needs to be liberated from the dominance of *whiteness* and *Europeanness* that often silences the views of black people in biblical interpretation. Since the present study is based on an African liberationist reading, it supports the preceding argument.

However, the concepts of *whiteness*, *Europeanness* and *blackness* need to be defined at this point. *Whiteness* is a location of structural advantage of privileges enjoyed by the white race; a gaze on society made by white people; and a set of cultural practices of white people that are usually unmarked and unnamed.[64] Snyman confirms that *whiteness* often functions from a position of invisible power where it remains an unreflected norm in biblical interpretation.[65] For Shome, *whiteness* refers to practices of colonialism and neo-colonialism which privilege and sustain global dominance of white and Eurocentric worldviews.[66] In the context of biblical studies, an interpretation or epistemology that is distinctively characterized by cultural practices of white people constitutes *whiteness*. Additionally, in a situation in which there is evident dominance of the distinctive worldviews of white people which in most cases differ from those of black people *whiteness* could manifest, for instance, that the dominance of the worldviews of the white race in biblical interpretation constitutes *whiteness*.

Snyman also argues that historical and literary criticisms are influenced by Eurocentric worldviews and they reflect a Eurocentric reading.[67] In other words, the influence and dominance of Eurocentric worldviews in biblical interpretation result in the imperialism of *Europeanness*. The employment of a particular epistemology namely the construction and nature of knowledge that may be identified with *Europeanness* in that it espouses values which caricatures elements of a European culture and worldview encourages *Europeanness*. However, *blackness* is at odds with both *whiteness* and *Europeanness*.

When a black person's views are grounded or rooted in certain values that are not borrowed from Europe or America, the manifestation of such values constitutes *blackness*. For instance, if one accepts the view that black people generally practice being considerate towards each other, such a practice would then define their *blackness*.[68] For Mtshiselwa, because the Xhosa proverb *Umntu ngumntu ngabantu*, 'A person is a person through other persons' defines who a Xhosa person is, communalism thus constitute *blackness*.[69] Thus, in the context of Old Testament studies, *blackness* would refer to the cultural identity and values that are embedded in themes such as communalism and good neighbourliness, among others. In the context of biblical interpretation, an interpretation of ancient texts which is sympathetic to *blackness* would treat cultural identity and values of black people as the point of reference.

From the understanding of *whiteness*, *Europeanness* and *blackness* above, one would argue for the liberation of *blackness* from imperialistic *whiteness and Europeanness*. Mtshiselwa has shown that 'in the process of colonization, *whiteness* and *Europeanness* were universalized as a norm, legitimizing a particular form of biblical interpretation that has been imposed on African scholarship'.[70] As such, a normative status was given to both *whiteness* and *Europeanness*. Snyman notes that 'The consequence of European normativity was that a western interpretation of Christ was imposed on the missionary subjects inhabiting a world outside of Europe'.[71] His view is supported by Mtshiselwa who notes that there is a persistent influence and dominance of *whiteness* and *Europeanness* in South African biblical scholarship.[72] However, he adds that such dominance and influence should be avoided when re-reading ancient texts among black people.

Subsequently, it might be helpful to probe whether the present interpretations of Leviticus 25:8–55 that will be outlined in Chapter 3 of this study are dominated and influenced by *whiteness* and *Europeanness*. If such interpretations were found to silence values and views that are attractive to black people in South Africa, then, *blackness* would in all probability need to be liberated from *whiteness and Europeanness*. For instance, if communalism, a value which is important to black people, is silenced in the diachronic and synchronic interpretation of Leviticus 25:8–55, one would then be compelled to elevate it, thereby, elevating the liberated orientation of *blackness* that is set against the worldview of individualism which constitutes *whiteness* and *Europeanness*.[73]

It is appropriate to consider an indigenous South African (Xhosa) biblical scholarship, that is, one that highlights hermeneutical tools that are relevant to black people. However, one does not intend to interpret Leviticus 25:8–55 from an indigenous (Xhosa) point of view. Instead, a similar approach that considers the indigenous people of South Africa as a hermeneutical lens is viewed as a model on which an African liberationist reading could be partly based. With such an approach, one also seeks to use values of African South Africans that constitute *blackness* which are embedded in African proverbs and liberation songs to unlock the meaning of Leviticus 25:8–55. The reasoning is that such an interpretation will naturally offer a preferential option for the poor as it aims to offer empowering and liberating possibilities to poor African South Africans. Subsequently, a discussion of the liberationist dimension of an African liberationist approach proposed in this study is warranted.

The liberationist dimension of an African liberationist approach

With respect to the liberationist dimension of an African liberationist approach to Leviticus 25:8–55 we partly draw on Mosala's 'black biblical hermeneutics of liberation'. In his thesis, *Biblical Hermeneutics and Black Theology in South Africa*, Mosala employs the historical-critical methods even though he is well aware of their Euro-American origins with a view to identify and locate a particular layer of strata within the biblical context.[74] He locates the strata in the power dynamics of the society in order to show the variant voices and interests of the class sectors in ancient Israel. Mosala further shows that the ideologies of the composers and redactors of biblical texts were either oppressive or liberative. On that point, his black biblical hermeneutics of liberation insists that 'the task of the biblical cultural worker involved in the struggle for freedom from poverty is to liberate the Bible so that the Bible can liberate us'.[75] What this means is that the liberating possibilities of the text need to be teased out by highlighting the oppressive ideologies of the dominant class at the time of the production of ancient texts. In this task, Mosala's black biblical hermeneutics of liberation demands of the modern reader of the Bible to pay attention to the struggle of the exploited working-class people or the poor.

Interestingly, Mosala's black biblical hermeneutics of liberation is linked to the black theology of liberation. Black theology of liberation reveals that God tends to intervene decisively against forms of oppression and exploitation in favour of the poor.[76] This intervention is often expressed as the preferential option for the poor.[77] Thus, the black theology of liberation calls for the solidarity with the oppressed people in the margins of society.[78] With respect to the black theology of liberation in the South African context, of significance is the view that the slogan of 'Africa for Africans' which demanded the return of the land dispossessed to African South Africans around 1970, throws light to the context from which the black theology of liberation emerged.[79] It therefore comes as no surprise that Mofokeng uses the anecdote: '… after the prayer, the white man had the land and we had the Bible' in his theological reflection on the issue of land.[80] In this instance, not only does the black theology of liberation highlight the view that the colonial and apartheid systems dispossessed African South Africans of their land, as Mosala has correctly noted, but it also calls for land redistribution and socio-economic justice.[81] The fact that Mosala's theoretical framework is also rooted in the black theology of liberation, specifically with regards to the preferential option for the poor as well as to the calls for land redistribution and socio-economic justice, makes his 'black biblical hermeneutic of liberation' attractive.

Mosala's black biblical hermeneutic of liberation is guided by the theoretical position of historical-materialism, a framework which is associated with Karl

Marx.[82] Not only does the framework give priority to social relations, specifically in terms of class, race and gender both in the biblical text and the modern context but it equally advances the interests of the poor.[83] Marxism, a theoretical framework that Mosala adopts, regards the overthrowing of the imperialistic and capitalistic ruling élites by the proletariat as constituting justice in that it seeks to enforce economic equality.[84] However, Marxism does not seem to be entirely innocent. Marxism does not completely oppose capitalism because it is also a theory that is set to take over power with the aim of centralizing it within the leadership of the proletariats.[85]

In the context of the socio-political discourses, Mosala builds on the views of Cornel West and Terry Eagleton, while in the context of biblical studies, he draws on the liberationist work of Norman Gottwald.[86] It is therefore helpful to examine briefly the works of West, Eagleton and Gottwald in order to appreciate Mosala's black biblical hermeneutics of liberation. On the political implications of Marxism, Mosala notes West's remarks thus:

> For the oppressed colored (black) peoples, the central problem is not only repressive capitalist regimes, but also oppressive European civilizing attitudes. And even Marxists who reject oppressive capitalist regimes often display oppressive European civilizing attitudes toward colored peoples. In this sense, such Marxists, though rightly critical of capitalism, remain captives of the worst of European culture.[87]

It is precisely in the light of the preceding remark that I partly depart from Mosala's black biblical hermeneutics of liberation. A theoretical framework that is based on Marxism also has negative traits. It is puzzling that Mosala continues to base his black biblical hermeneutic of liberation on Marxism even though he is well aware of West's view that Marxism as a theoretical framework is a captive of *Europeanness*, and for this reason, it has been shunned by post-colonial biblical criticism.[88] However, it must be noted that the Marxist theory has offered biblical studies a valuable tool particularly with regard to the understanding of the historical mode of production, which enables us to locate our exegetical work within the socio-historical systems in the world of the text's production.[89]

Mosala also identifies with Eagleton's, 'The Revolt of the Reader'. In this contribution, Eagleton argues:

> That the reader should be forcibly subjected to textual authority is disturbing enough; that they should be insultingly invited to hug their chains, merge into empathetic harmony with their oppressors to the point where they befuddledly cease to recognize whether they are subject or object, worker, boss, or product is surely the ultimate opiate.[90]

Based on Eagleton's argument, Mosala proposes a revolutionary reading of the Hebrew Bible, which is critical of the contributions of the political élites who created the indebtedness of the poor in the history of Israel.[91] In my view, Mosala's proposal is impressive as it demands of a modern reader of the Hebrew Bible to tease out instances in which the poor experienced oppression in the world of the text's production. Furthermore, Mosala's hermeneutic insists that a socially engaged reader of the Bible uncovers cases in which the composers and redactors of the ancient texts showed bias towards the poor. Mosala's black biblical hermeneutic of liberation can be viewed as liberative. Thus, an African liberationist reading of Leviticus 25:8–55, one which stands in continuity with Mosala's liberationist reading of the Hebrew Bible, will not only present the various strata in the text in question as merely different voices but it will also highlight the ideological contestations in the text. It will be argued here that the various strata in the biblical text are in dialogue and contestation with each other.

Mosala also draws on Gottwald's liberationist approach to the Bible which adds a curious dimension to his hermeneutic. For instance, based on 'the reality that economic systems cannot be "imported" from the Bible to meet our needs,' Gottwald argues that 'the ethical force of the Bible on issues of economics will have to be perspectival and motivational rather than prescriptive and technical'.[92] Thus, from Gottwald's argument and Mosala's hermeneutic, I submit that in order for an African liberationist re-reading of Leviticus 25:8–55 to be liberative it ought to adopt a hermeneutic suitable for a socio-economic discourse. This approach enables one to re-read the given text in a way that is relevant in the South African context. However, Gottwald cautions us about easily discerning liberative lessons from not-so-liberative texts specifically with regards to the economic relief laws of the Bible as such laws were a project of the kings and priests.[93] Thus, an African liberationist reading of the Israelite Jubilee legislation will take Gottwald's warning seriously, as we inquire, in whose interests was Leviticus 25:8–55 composed and redacted.

Lastly, on the issue of patriarchy, our liberationist reading of Leviticus 25:8–55 also draws on Mosala's black biblical hermeneutic of liberation as it pays attention to 'African women's struggle for liberation'.[94] His liberationist approach is critical of 'the history, the devices, the culture, the ideologies and agendas' of the ancient text.[95] Interestingly, his liberationist approach also appropriates the lessons drawn from the biblical text to the contemporary contexts with a view to offer transformative and liberative possibilities to the oppressed.

Although the African liberationist approach proposed here draws on Mosala's liberationist framework, it departs from his theory and method. West's study, 'Locating "Contextual Bible Study" within Biblical Liberation Hermeneutics and Intercultural Biblical Hermeneutics', shows that a cultural form of biblical hermeneutics reminds contextual readers of the Hebrew Bible of the presence and the importance of cultural resources.[96] Such resources may help with the socio-economic dimensions of both the ancient text and the modern contexts. Building on De Wit's work, West argues that intercultural hermeneutics reminds contextual hermeneutics of the presence of other local contexts within which a socially engaged exegete could read the Bible.[97] No doubt, an African liberationist reading of Leviticus 25:8–55 that draws on Mosala's liberationist approach would benefit from cultural resources, which stand in continuity with post-colonial biblical studies. These cultural resources include indigenous narratives, idioms and proverbs as well as liberation songs.

African proverbs and liberation songs as hermeneutical tools

The focus on indigenous narratives, idioms and proverbs, and liberation songs constitutes an African dimension to our re-reading of Leviticus 25:8–55. This dimension stands in continuity with the post-colonial works of Sugirtharajah, Segovia, Berquist, Dube and Masenya [ngwan'a Mphahlele]. For Sugirtharajah,

> One of the most challenging and exciting aspects of postcolonial criticism has been its rereading of ancient documents and literary texts … it has brought to the fore some of the often neglected and even in some cases unrecognized aspects of well-known texts.[98]

Drawing on Sugirtharajah's approach to ancient texts, we will attempt a re-reading of Leviticus 25:8–55. His main contribution to post-colonial biblical scholarship lies in the way he questions and challenges colonialist discourses to produce a new form of representation of ancient texts.[99] A process of re-reading texts that is inspired by post-colonial studies attempts to produce a new form of interpreting ancient texts which teases out and which is critical of various forms of oppression in the biblical text, particularly with regard to the issue of imperialism and colonialism.

Segovia adds an interesting dimension to post-colonial biblical scholarship with his definition of post-colonialism:

> Postcolonial studies is a model that takes the reality of empire, of imperialism and colonialism, as an omnipresent, inescapable, and overwhelming reality in the world: the world of antiquity, the world of the Near East or of Mediterranean Basin; the world of modernity, the world of Western hegemony and expansionism; and the world of today, of postmodernity, the world of Postcolonialism on the part of the Two-Thirds World and of neocolonialism on the part of the West.[100]

Consequently, a post-colonial approach seeks to bring to light the elements of imperialism in both the biblical text and the modern contexts. At the heart of post-colonial studies is the struggle for liberation and decolonization—a dimension which Mosala does not sufficiently address.[101] However, like the hermeneutics of liberation, the model of post-colonial studies is also ideological as it highlights political experiences of imperialism in the Bible and in modern communities. Thus, a re-reading of Leviticus 25:8–55 will probe the apparent imperialistic tendencies of the Persian Empire in post-exilic Yehud in relation to the South African context. However, the present study departs from Mosala's association of his black biblical hermeneutics of liberation with the Marxist theory. In this regard, Berquist's remark below is worthy of note:

> Functionalist and Marxist sociologies employed alike may focus too much on the activity within a single economic generation, but a Postcolonialism must always focus on the ways in which the populace becomes the colonized, to reproduce the economic relationships of extraction and oppression over multiple generations.[102]

Thus, an African liberationist approach to the text of Leviticus will investigate the persistence of imperialism and abuse of power in Leviticus 25:8–55. As Berquist has also noted, post-colonial studies seek to 'create an interpretation that illuminate the colonial and colonizing tendencies of the text's production and subsequent interpretations, while at the same time such studies seek to suggest contemporary interpretations that have an effect of decolonizing the present world'.[103] Therefore, the present study will consider indigenous narratives, idioms and proverbs as well as liberation songs in order to address the imperialist and colonial ideologies in the Hebrew Bible.

Dube's post-colonial feminist hermeneutics also adds an interesting dimension to post-colonial readings of the Hebrew Bible. Dube[104] outlines certain questions one could ask in carrying out a post-colonial reading of the Bible as follow:

- Does this text take a clear stance against the political imperialism of its time?
- How does imperialism affect men and women of ancient and present times?
- Does the text employ gender representations to construct relationships of subordination and domination? If so, which side am I reading from: the side of the coloniser, the colonised, or the collaborator? If I concentrate on patriarchal analysis of the text, does this translate to a decolonising act?
- How can one re-read a text for relationships of liberating interdependence between genders, and among races and other social categories of our world?

Based on the preceding questions, Dube's hermeneutical approach attempts to analyse biblical texts in a way that brings to the fore instances in which the text approves or shuns the imperialistic tendency to oppress both men and women. Her approach seeks to offer decolonizing possibilities for the modern readers of the ancient biblical text. Worthy of note is the manner in which Dube relates gender issues to the issues of race, class and nationality.[105] Her hermeneutic addresses the issue of oppression in both the ancient text and the modern contexts.

The post-colonial theory of Dube, Berquist and Sugirtharajah is in line with Mosala's approach as it aims to re-read ancient texts with a view to offer transformative possibilities for oppressed people. However, Sugirtharajah and Masenya (ngwan'a Mphahlele) offer an indigenous dimension to the post-colonial theory and African biblical hermeneutics. Indigenous narratives, idioms and proverbs could serve as a point of reference in interpreting ancient texts.[106] Drawing on Masenya (ngwan'a Mphahlele)'s pioneering work of employing indigenous proverbs, it is critical to probe whether certain (South) African proverbs and sayings that are relevant to the socio-economic issues add significant value to the construction of a liberationist framework. Can a cultural or indigenous form of an African liberationist approach relate to the socio-economic dimension of the present study? It is crucial to note that African proverbs and liberation songs that are considered in the formulation of a theoretical framework are those that are relevant to the socio-economic and political issues raised in the present study. On the Xhosa saying *Ubophelele inja enkangeni*, 'He has fastened a dog to a shrub', for instance, Theal comments:

> This saying is used to denote a very greedy person, one who is so greedy as to fasten his dog to a shrub that the animal may not beg for food while he is eating. The shrub denoted is the very common one that is covered with yellow flowers at midsummer.[107]

The saying *Ubophelele inja enkangeni* may be understood as disapproval of greed but which at the same time favours the sharing of resources. Therefore, the saying upholds the idea of equitable sharing of food, which is a resource accruing from the use of productive land. Since we have established the tendency to engage in self-enrichment by the political élites in South Africa, the saying *Ubophelele inja enkangeni*, 'He has fastened a dog to a shrub' discourages greed, and supports the quest for socio-economic justice and equitable sharing of productive land. The saying is relevant in a context where the rich are getting richer and the poor are getting poorer. In fact, as an idiomatic expression, it confirms that neo-liberal capitalism is a problematic system that perpetuates greed and disproportionate ownership of and benefit from the use of productive land in South Africa. The objection to any form of greed becomes a liberationist framework through which one approaches the text of Leviticus 25:8–55 as well as the discourse of socio-economic justice and land redistribution in the country. Instead of encouraging greed, the saying calls for the sharing of resources.

Based on their commendable culture of sharing resources and thus opposing greed and self-enrichment by the élites, Soga describes black people in Xhosa thus: *Ngabantu abebeyifunde nzulu into yokuncedana imihla ngemihla*, 'They are people who deeply learnt the culture of looking after each other on a daily basis'.[108] The statement confirms that African South Africans often took care of one another in various ways including engaging in economic practices that aim at poverty alleviation or in *ukunqomana* which Swartz describes as '… an economic practice of lending a cow to the poor, setting them up for a life of productivity.[109] The cow would be lent to the poor person until it produced a calf on which the assisted household would build their wealth'. As one who was born in apartheid South Africa in the rural setting of Mount Frere, Eastern Cape which is an area dominated by the Xhosa people, the present researcher submits that Swartz's understanding of *ukunqomana* is valid. The *iinkomo enqoma*, 'a cow used for *ukunqomana*' is a resource shared among the people to alleviate poverty and to redress economic disparity. If a member of the community was poor, the one with agricultural resources such as cows would willingly offer a cow to alleviate the poverty of the poor. The value of sharing resources in the form of giving to the poor is considered a model that counteracts socio-economic injustice among African South Africans. This value supports the liberationist framework within which we locate the present discussion of socio-economic justice and land redistribution in the re-reading of Leviticus 25:8–55 in the South African context.

Masenya (ngwan'a Mphahlele) has convincingly employed a Northern Sotho proverb to articulate the indignity of the hunger that is experienced exclusively by the poor. The proverb *Tlala ke a neka phefo ke ja nong*, 'Death, unlike hunger which only chooses the poor, takes the rich who would still be revelling in their riches'.[110] A compelling point within the liberationist framework is that hunger and poverty are forms of indignity experienced in particular by the black masses in South Africa. As such, Masenya (ngwan'a Mphahlele)'s argument that to be poor is to be deprived of human dignity is confirmed by the proverb *Tlala ke a neka phefo ke ja nong*. The need for socio-economic-redress is also implied in the same proverb. In other words, the assumption that the rich continue to revel in their riches whilst the poor experience the scourge of poverty and hunger elevates the need for such redress. Moreover, because economic inequality is problematized, the proverb *Tlala ke a neka phefo ke ja nong* fits into the liberationist framework adopted in this study particularly in the light of the value of sharing of resources.

Masenya (ngwan'a Mphahlele) also argues for the redress of economic inequality. The rich namely people with land (mines, in this instance) and wealth, have a responsibility to share with the poor.[111] This view is confirmed by the proverb *Noka e tlala ka melatswana*, 'A river is filled by other rivers'. In other words, a person is elevated from poverty through the assistance of other people.[112] The proverb corresponds with the Pedi adage *Bana ba motho ba ngwathelana hlogo ya tšie*, 'The siblings share the head of a locust'. That is, the tenor of equitable sharing in the African wise saying advocates for an equal redistribution of wealth that benefits both the poor and the wealthy. Thus, some of the indigenous proverbs point out the indignity of poverty and the need for equitable sharing of resources to counter such indignity.

In Africa, the idea of equitable sharing of resources is also rooted in the view that 'all' human beings are equal children of the deity. The Akan proverb *Nnipa nyinaa ye Onyame mma, obi nye asase ba*, 'All human beings are the children of God, none is a child of the earth' eloquently expresses this view.[113] The preceding proverb, teases out the value of equality and of the interconnectedness of human beings, which demands of human beings, particularly Africans, to care for each other. As such, the idea of equitable sharing of resources forms part of the African liberationist framework.

Significantly, departing from Masenya (ngwan'a Mphahlele) who mainly focuses on African proverbs and her work that stands in continuity with post-colonial biblical scholarship, three African liberation songs are considered as hermeneutical tools for constructing the framework for re-reading the Israelite Jubilee. The songs were originally used during the apartheid period in South Africa. The first song is *Thina sizwe esimnyama*, 'We, the black nation'; the second is *Senzeni na?* 'What have we done?' and the third song is *Lelizwe*, 'This land'. The liberation song *Thina sizwe esimnyama* carries a liberation tenor that is evident in both the struggle against land dispossession and the contestation for the liberation of black people in South Africa. The song is still often sung by many ANC members[114] even in post-apartheid South Africa. For instance, at the funeral service for Nelson Mandela held at Qunu on 15 December 2013, President Jacob Zuma rendered this controversial song, which was sung by African South Africans in the heyday of colonialism and apartheid in the country.[115] The struggle song communicates the cry of the black population over their land, which was confiscated by white people who then ushered in poverty and economic inequality. The lyrics of the song are outlined in Table 1.1:

First, this section will investigate whether the poor have continued to voice their discontent in the present democratic South Africa. The cry over the disproportionate benefits from the ownership and use of land remains apparent in South Africa. Therefore, it is necessary to probe the relevance of the liberation songs sung by the ANC masses in a quest to set a framework for the liberation of many African South Africans from poverty and socio-economic injustice especially in relation to the issue of land distribution. The main purpose of engaging with this

Table 1.1. *Thina sizwe esimnyama*, "We, the black nation"

Verse lines	Nguni version	English translation
1	*Thina sizwe esimnyama,*	We, the black nation,
2	*sikhalela izwe*[116] *lethu,*	are crying for our land,
3	*elathathwa ngabamhlophe.*	which was taken by white people.
4	*Mabawuyeke umhlaba wethu.*	They must leave our land alone.
5	*Abantwana be Afrika,*	Children of Africa,
6	*bakhalela izwe labo,*	are crying for their land,
7	*elathathwa ngabamhlophe.*	which was taken by white people.
8	*Mabawuyeke umhlaba wethu.*	They must leave our land alone.

song is to determine whether the liberation tenor embedded in it have implications for an African liberationist re-reading of Leviticus 25:8–55.

Verse line 1 seems to focus on the needs of black rather than white South Africans. As will be noted below, the observation that black people of South African descent experience the scourge of poverty more than white people is worth restating here. However, this does not suggest that some members of other races namely the Indians, coloureds and whites do not experience the challenges of socio-economic injustice that are predominantly encountered by the majority of African South Africans. Since the struggle for socio-economic justice takes place mainly among African South Africans, an African liberationist reading advocated by the present research will consider mainly the needs of poor African South Africans.

The expression *Thina sizwe* 'We, the nation' is communal and collective rather than individualistic in character. The plural pronoun confirms its communal and collective character. As such, the challenge of land dispossession, if understood primarily in the light of the history of black people in South Africa, becomes a communal and collective challenge. In other words, since the history of African South Africans shows that the whole community benefited from land use, then, it is reasonable to assume that the challenge of dispossession affected the community as a whole rather than individuals.

The African wise saying *Umntu ngumntu ngabantu*, 'A person is a person through other persons' confirms the element of communalism in the worldview of African South Africans. Thus, the issue of land dispossession instigated by the Land Act of 1913 as well as the ensuing poverty and economic inequality may be viewed as a challenge facing the entire nation.[117] Thus, this liberation song in particular embraces the African element and value of communalism. Notably, the expression *Thina sizwe*, 'We, the nation' portrays the collective distress of and the protest by African South Africans against the historical land dispossession and the persistent state of landlessness.

A critical factor in the history of land ownership in South Africa is the distress that land dispossession caused among black people, which is confirmed by verse line 2 *sikhalela izwe lethu*, 'are crying for our land'. The allusion to land dispossession in verse line 3 explains the distress as well as the protest against land dispossession and subsequent poverty and economic inequality. Wilson has digitalized an interesting version *Elathathwa ngamabhulu*, 'It was taken by the Boers' which is different from the version sung by President Zuma *elathathwa ngabamhlophe*, 'which was taken by white people'. The word *ngamabhulu*, 'by the Boers' in the digitalized version refers to the apartheid rule in which the Afrikaners had power, while the word *ngabamhlophe* alludes to the period of colonialism when the white English speaking people were in power. Thus, in order to redress the historical challenge of socio-economic injustice, it would be vital to redistribute the land that was dispossessed in both eras, that is, during the colonial and apartheid periods. Verse line 3 *Elathathwa ngabamhlophe* supposedly refers to the entrenchment of land dispossession and poverty among the blacks during the colonial and apartheid regimes. The liberation tenor that underpins the song *Thina sizwe esimnyama*, 'We, the black nation' which is a critique of socio-economic injustice in South Africa calls for the redress of land dispossession that was initiated by both the colonial and apartheid regimes.

On the one hand, the instructive statement *Mabawuyeke umhlaba wethu*, 'They must leave our land alone' in verse line 4 refers to land dispossession. On the other hand, the statement calls for an end to land dispossession and the redistribution of such land. Thus, the call *Mabawuyeke umhlaba wethu* supports the inference that will be made in Chapter 2 that productive land was certainly seized from African South Africans. In his indigenous Xhosa poem *Zemnk' iinkomo magwalandini*, 'Away go your cattle you cowards', Chief Rubusana recounted that black South Africans were dispossessed of their productive land and livestock by white people.[118] Mpola also explains that *ukumka kwenkomo*, 'the going away of cattle' was derived from the period when white people exploited the Xhosa ethnic group and took their cattle.[119] For instance, in the 1860s, the land and the cattle belonging to the Hlubi people (mostly referred to as Hlubi boys) were expropriated by white farmers.[120]

Furthermore, (South) African literature particularly that which relates to the Xhosa ethnic group contains records of the protest against the dispossession of productive land and livestock. From Julius Malema's argument, which is considered below, such literature highlights the view that white people in the colonial and apartheid eras were thieves. Ngqobe, in verse line 10 of his song *Latshon' emini kwelama Mpondo*, 'The sun set during the day in Mpondoland' refers to white people as *amadlagusha*, 'those who eat sheep'.[121] The song confirms that during the colonial and apartheid periods, white people were stereotyped as people who came to South Africa merely to 'steal' the people's land and livestock.[122] Thus, an African liberationist reading would understand the history of land dispossession from black people in South Africa.

The song *Thina sizwe esimnyama*, 'We, the black nation', was constructed during the colonial and apartheid eras, and it does not contain explicit references to the restoration of land to black people in post-apartheid South Africa. However, the rhetoric of the song particularly the call *Mabawuyeke umhlaba wethu* 'They must leave our land alone' would carry weight if analysed alongside the political slogan *Mayibuye iAfrika*, 'Let Africa return' used by the black protesters. In fact, when coupled with the song *Thina sizwe esimnyama*, 'We, the black nation' the slogan becomes attractive, as it also campaigns for land redistribution and socio-economic justice.

Since the song *Thina sizwe esimnyama*, 'We, the black nation' originated during the colonial and apartheid eras, the relevance of the song to post-apartheid South Africa is worth probing. The expression *Abantwana be Afrika* 'Children of Africa' in verse line 5 gives the song a generational relevance, that is, it resonates with African South Africans who still experience the effects of colonialism and apartheid. Thus, it is reasonable to view the challenge of land dispossession as inter-generational mainly because of the effects of colonialism and apartheid, which are evident in the post-apartheid South African context, as will be argued in Chapter 2.

Furthermore, it may be said that white people inherited land and wealth from their forebears who dispossessed it from black people. Therefore, it makes sense to argue that *Thina sizwe esimnyama*, 'We, the black nation' is a relevant song as it articulates the act of land dispossession the impact of which continues in post-apartheid South Africa. As we re-read Leviticus 25:8–55 from an African liberationist point of view later in this study, it is important to take note of the hereditary nature of land dispossession which the song *Thina sizwe esimnyama*, 'We, the black nation' brings to light. In other words, the colonial and apartheid histories of South Africa explain the reason white people have land while the majority of black people are landless.

The lyrics of the second liberation song is outlined in Table 1.2.

Table 1.2. *Senzeni na?* "What have we done?"

Verse lines	Nguni version	English translation
1	*Senzeni na*	What have we done? (8x)
2	*Sono sethu ubumnyama*[123]	Our sin is our blackness (4x)
3	*Sono sethu yinyaniso*[124]	Our sin is the truth (4x)
4	*Sono sethu ubulili bethu besifazane*[125]	Our sin is our female sex (4x)
5	*Sibulawayo*[126]	We are being killed (8x)
6	*Sohlangana ezulwini*[127]	We will meet in heaven (4x)
7	*Amabhulu azizinja*[128]	The Boers are dogs (4x)
8	*Babulale bafe bonke*[129]	Kill them so that all of them can die (4x)
9	*Mayibuye iAfrika*[130]	Let Africa return (4x)

Nkoala notes that liberation songs generally serve as the means to articulate injustice in the form of poverty and exploitation.[131] As such, the song *Senzeni na*? 'What have we done?' expresses a similar purpose. This song relates the unjust treatment of African South Africans in both the apartheid and the post-apartheid South Africa. As Nkoala rightly observes, verse line 1 which poses the question, *Senzeni na?* 'What have we done?' shows that the song employs a rhetorical question to expose the perturbing nature of racial injustice.[132] The rhetorical nature of the question suggests that black people complain that they did not deserve the racial injustice meted out by the colonial and apartheid regimes. The complaint appears to be justified mainly because of the difficulty in finding evidence of black people's confiscation of the land belonging to white people. There is also no evidence of the exploitation of white people by black people during the colonial and apartheid regimes.

Masenya (ngwan'a Mphahlele) comments on the statement *Sono sethu ubumnyama*, 'Our sin is our blackness' which shows racial injustice in verse line 2 as follows:

> ... the primary threat was the torture and atrocities which were being perpetrated on them on account of their black skin colour: *isono sethu ubumnyama* (literally, 'their sin is their blackness'). Seemingly, reality dictated that the oppressed channel all their energies into challenging and resisting the racial injustices that were being inflicted by a powerful white minority on a powerless black majority.[133]

It is evident that the white people had a problem with the 'blackness' of the black people. Thus, the statement *Sono sethu ubumnyama* implies that the white

European colonialists portrayed *blackness* in a negative light. Hence, Masenya (ngwan'a Mphahlele) further argues that:

> Foregrounding the positive elements of African cultures gives us a more balanced view of Africa and its peoples, a view far removed from the negative one challenged by Biko during the time of apartheid South Africa. Such a view deviates from the negative one inherited during the colonial and apartheid eras ...[134]

Thus, an African liberationist reading of Leviticus 25:8–55 in the South African context is that which is conscious of the negative portrayal of *blackness*. In addition, such a reading would be concerned about imperialism and the dominance of the white minority over the previously disadvantaged black majority in the country.

In view of the oppression of women during the present post-apartheid rule, Masenya (ngwan'a Mphahlele) also examines verse line 4 *Isono sethu ubulili bethu besifazane*, 'Our sin is our female sex' in the song *Senzeni na*? 'What have we done?'.[135] The reason for such a redactional addition is probably because women experienced various forms of oppression during the colonial and apartheid eras. In general, the forms of oppression experienced by women during these periods included economic disadvantage. Their men on the other hand laboured in the mines and farms of white men.

The statement *Sibulawayo*, 'We are being killed' in verse line 5 reminds one of the statistics that out of the twenty-one thousand people who died due to political violence in South Africa during the apartheid regime (1948–1994), fourteen thousand people died from 1990 to 1994.[136] Although the data appear compelling, one remains skeptical about the figures as it merely accounts for the period between 1948 and 1994 but omits the colonial period. The fact that Tshabalala's sources are not clearly articulated also causes one to doubt whether all the deaths of African South Africans in that period are accounted for. Even though it may be difficult to record the precise number of people who were killed by white people during the colonial and apartheid eras, it is not in doubt that black people were killed in various episodes.

The question of why black protesters labelled their white oppressors as *izinja*, 'dogs' which comes up in verse line 7, should be probed. In the traditional culture of the Xhosa people, for example, a human being is labelled *inja*, 'a dog' if the person is engaged in immoral and unacceptable behaviour.[137] Racial injustice perpetrated by white people under the colonial and apartheid regimes was unacceptable mainly because it inflicted pain on other people in particular on black people. Thus, the song *Senzeni na*? 'What have we done?' is a form of protest against the unacceptable treatment of black people which caused distress and promoted injustice. As Mpola rightly notes, the Nguni phrase *Uyinja mlungu*, 'You are a dog, white man' which is contained in most of the protest songs, is meant to provoke white people.[138] However, one can add that the phrase was not only meant to provoke white people but to express also the frustration of the poor black masses at the injustice inflicted on them as well as at their loss of land.

Mphahlele defines protest poetry as, 'An art that speaks to the people in terms of their feelings and ideas about the world … A protest poet is a being who finds himself immersed in an oppressive situation'.[139] Thus, it is pre-supposed that liberation songs which are actually poetic in character articulate the frustration of black protesters at the injustice entrenched in the oppressive policies and practices of the colonial and apartheid governments. The statement *Uyinja mlungu* is similar to a verse in Ngqobe's *Latshon' emini kwelama Mpondo* 'The sun has set in the afternoon in the Mpondoland'.[140] Mpola notes that verse lines 11 and 13 *Lahlokom' igwijo, uyinja mlungu, uyinja mlungu*, 'A song has vibrated, you are a dog white man, you are a dog white man' articulates the anger of the oppressed at the action of the whites who shot at their people indiscriminately without provocation.[141] In light of the perturbing reality of the socio-economic injustice of the colonial and apartheid governments in South Africa, one could agree with Mpola's interpretation of the statement *Uyinja mlungu* as a protest against such injustice. Thus, an African liberationist reading denounces the socio-economic injustice, which is displayed in the disproportionate ownership of and benefits from the land among South Africans.

Verse line 11 represents the ultimate expectation of the song *Senzeni na?*, which is the restoration of Africa in the words *Mayibuye iAfrika*, 'Let Africa return'. First, this verse line acknowledges that (South) Africa was taken from the black people in the historical land dispossession, as it refutes the injustice(s) caused by such dispossession. Second, the plea for the return of Africa is a cry for political and economic freedom. The tenor underlying the protest song *Mayibuye iAfrika* which is that of the struggle for political and economic liberation enables the liberationist framework to probe the theme of land and socio-economic justice in the re-reading of Leviticus 25:8–55.

The lyrics of the third liberation song *Lelizwe*[142] is outlined in Table 1.3.

The song *Lelizwe* describes the experiences of working-class people in South Africa who serve as domestic workers and gardeners for white people. Interestingly, the song is sung neither by the domestic workers nor the garden workers but by their children. However, the children are also part of the working-class people since they call for unity with the statement *Basebenzi masihlanganeni* 'Working-class people let us unite' (verse lines 10 and 12). In verse line 9, the declaration *Lelizwe ngelethu*, 'This land is ours' expresses a claim to the land by the working-class people. The claim reveals that the younger generation is aware

Table 1.3. *Lelizwe*, "This land"

Verse lines	Nguni version	English translation
1	*Umama wami, ekhishini*	My mother, in the kitchen
2	*Bambiza bani, ekhishini*	Who do they call her, in the kitchen?
3	*Bambiz' uJeyi, ekhishini*	They call her Jeyi, in the kitchen
4	*Bambiz'ugeli, ekhishini*	They call her girl, in the kitchen
5	*Ubaba wami, engadini*	My father, in the garden
6	*Bambiza bani, engadini*	Who do they call him, in the garden?
7	*Bambiz' upikinini, engadini*	They call him Pikinini, in the garden
8	*Bambiz'uboyi, engadini*	They call him boy, in the garden
9	*Lelizwe ngelethu,*	This land is ours
10	*Basebenzi masihlanganeni (6x)*	Working-class people, let us unite (6x)
11	*Kudala sisebenzel' amabhulu,*	We have been working for the Boers far too long
12	*Basebenzi masihlanganeni (6x)*	Working-class people, let us unite (6x)

of the historical land dispossession that was perpetrated through the colonial and apartheid systems. For the working-class people, their experience of injustice is linked to the subject of landlessness. This brings to mind Mosala's claim that the Boers 'dispossessed the Africans of their land and created out of them a wage class with nothing but their labour power to sell'.[143] The claim is supported by the lament *Kudala sisebenzel' amabhulu*, 'We have been working for the Boers far too long' in verse line 11. First, the working-class people undoubtedly lost their land to the Boers; second, they became poor; and third, they were forced by the situation of poverty to work for the Boers.

No doubt, the (South) African proverbs and liberation songs examined above have some implications for the construction of a theoretical and methodological framework especially for an African liberationist reading of Leviticus 25:8–55 in terms of land redistribution and socio-economic justice. Moreover, the liberationist dimension of an African liberationist approach forms part of the framework of the present study.

Relevance of the Research

What is the significance of the present study? The study is relevant because it focuses on current and critical issues in South Africa. Poverty and inequality are some of the critical issues that must be addressed in South Africa today. Almost half of South Africans are living below the poverty line surviving on just over R500 a month.[144] These data are disturbing. It is reported also that only twenty percent of the world's people possess eighty-three percent of the wealth. Therefore, any study such as the present one, which challenges the reality of unequal wealth distribution is significant. The restoration of the dignity of the poor, especially African South African (male and female) and white female South Africans who were disadvantaged by the colonial and apartheid systems, is necessary in achieving the objective of the present study which is how to redress socio-economic inequality and alleviate poverty. The redress of inequality is fundamental and at the centre of democratic governance. Hence, a study that pursues the redress of inequality and the alleviation of poverty is relevant in present day South Africa.

The crucial role of the agricultural sector to the socio-economic life of a state merits a study on the question of land and poverty alleviation. The land question is at the heart of socio-economic justice and economic development in South Africa. The question of land and of alleviation of poverty is relevant as it seeks to offer liberating and empowering possibilities for the poor. An anecdote states that:

> When the white man came to Africa, the African had land and the white man had the Bible. The white man said to the African: 'close your eyes and let us pray.' At the end of the prayer, the white man had the land and the African had the Bible.[145]

In the light of South Africa's colonial and apartheid history, the above anecdote could be seen as a silent cry for land redistribution. It is no wonder that President Zuma prioritized the subject of land reform in his State of the Nation address.[146] Since the question of land and poverty alleviation is critical in South Africa today, so is the present study.

Apparent resemblances in terms of factors, principles and features between the context of the Israelite Jubilee and that of land redistribution in South Africa legitimize the reading of the Jubilee and its application to the debate on the redistribution of land and socio-economic justice. Although the applicability of the Israelite Jubilee has been questioned by a number of Old Testament scholars, this study investigates the merit and the significance of the subject. Evidence of the efficiency of the legislation and the institution of the Jubilee in the Old Testament legitimize its study in the context of land redistribution in South Africa. It is because of the possible efficiency of the Jubilee in its context that the Israelite Jubilee legislation could also be re-read within the South African context.

The Akan proverb which says *Onipa na oma onipa ye onipa*, 'It is a human being who makes another person a human being' confirms the positive contribution of the humanities to society.[147] Put differently, the values that the disciplines of humanities add to the welfare of the society are fundamental. Thus, the present study is relevant to the African context.

Chapter Outline

The current chapter introduces and provides an outline for this study. It highlights the field and sub-fields of the research as well as the statement of research and the research question. At this preliminary stage, the hypothesis, the purpose and objectives of the study are also stated. On the research methodology, the chapter stresses the importance of both the historical-critical method and the African liberationist framework in the interpretation of the Bible. In addition, the relevance and the demarcation of the scope of the research are presented.

Drawing partly on Mosala's work, Chapter 2 provides a detailed socialist—orientated critique of socio-economic injustice and land dispossession in South Africa. It presents the social location, in which an African liberationist reader of the Bible finds him or herself, and highlights the impact of socio-economic injustice on poor African South Africans. Chapter 2 begins with the consideration of the political economy of the transitional and post-apartheid South Africa, which focuses on the subject of land and the political élites. Moreover, the chapter explores the impact of land policies, historically, on the reality of socio-economic injustice in South Africa as well as the idea of the empowerment of the poor through the simultaneous provision of productive land, finance and skills. Thus, a historical overview of the land policies in South Africa will be discussed in order to show that various attempts at land policy reforms have failed the (poor) majority of African South Africans.

In Chapter 3, issues relating to land and the socio-economic policy in Leviticus 25:8–55 are analysed. Employing historical-critical tools, the chapter reviews the debate on the Documentary Hypothesis, Neo-Documentary Hypothesis and the Non-Documentary Hypothesis in order to establish a relevant position for the South African context. In the light of the view that Leviticus 25:8–55 forms a unity with some of the neighbouring texts, the chapter examines the literary context of the text in question. Based on the Non-Documentarian approach, the critical exegetical analysis of the text of Leviticus 25:8–55 are used to reconstruct the theme of land and socio-economic policy in Leviticus 25:8–55. In the light of such an analysis, the strata in the text in consideration will be identified, and drawing on Mosala's black biblical hermeneutic of liberation, the ideological contestations will equally be highlighted. In the end, a diachronic analysis of the *Sitz-im-Leben* of the passage is provided with a view to dating the Israelite Jubilee and probing the life experiences of the addressees of the text. Mosala's two-step process that is first a careful historical-critical analysis and then a diachronic analysis of the *Sitz-im-Leben* that is based on a liberationist sociological and ideological re-reading of the historical findings adds a curious dimension to Chapter 3.[148]

Chapter 4 titled, *An African liberationist reading of Leviticus 25:8–55* is an ideological reading of the strata identified in Chapter 3 and it leads us to the interaction between the *Sitz-im-Leben* of Leviticus 25:8–55 and the South African setting. The oppressive and liberative contestations in the discourse of land in South Africa and in Leviticus 25:8–55 will be brought to the fore. Furthermore, I will attempt to re-read Leviticus 25:8–55 from an African liberationist perspective first by providing an African liberationist critique of the theme of land and socio-economic justice in South Africa. The critique will probe both the oppressive and liberative elements in the discourse of land in South Africa in line with Mosala's approach. Second, the ancient text of Leviticus 25:8–55 will be made to interact with the modern context of South Africa; for instance, an interaction between the *Sitz-im-Leben* of Leviticus 25:8–55 and the South African setting will be presented. Additionally, the theme of land and socio-economic policy in Leviticus 25:8–55 will be explored in the light of the land policies in South Africa.

Chapter 5 serves as the conclusion of the study and provides its summary and findings while also reflecting on the research question and hypothesis. These are followed by an outline of the contributions of the research to the field and subfields of this study as well as the recommendations on land redistribution and the liberating and empowering possibilities for the poor of South Africa. Lastly, in the light of the scope of this present study, the possibilities for future research are highlighted.

Notes

1. World Bank, *World Development Report 1990: Poverty* (New York: Oxford University Press, 1990), 1.
2. Patrick Bond, "War on Poverty in a Quagmire," *Sunday Independent*, August 1, 2010, 15.
3. Meshack M. Khosa, "Empowerment and Transformation in South Africa," in *Empowerment through Economic Transformation*, ed. Meshack M. Khosa (Durban: African Millennium Press, 2001), 4–9.
4. Khosa, "Empowerment and Transformation," 9.
5. Madipoane Masenya (ngwan'a Mphahlele), *How Worthy is the Woman of Worth? Rereading Proverbs 31:10–31 in African-South Africa* (New York: Peter Lang, 2004), 69.
6. Camilla Toulmin, "Securing Land and Property Rights in sub-Saharan Africa: The Role of Local Institutions," *Land Use Policy* 26, no. 1 (2009): 10.
7. Itumeleng J. Mosala, "Land, Class and the Bible in South Africa Today," *Journal of Black Theology in South Africa* 5, no. 2 (1991): 44.

8. Mosala, "Land, Class and the Bible," 44.
9. Mosala, "Land, Class and the Bible," 42; Mark Butler and Graham Philpott, "Land in South Africa: Gift for all or Commodity for a few?," *Studies in World Christianity* 11, no. 2 (2005): 215–235.
10. African National Congress (ANC). "The Freedom Charter." http://www.anc.org.za/show.php?id= 72. (Accessed January 16, 2014).
11. Butler and Philpott, "Land in South Africa," 215–235.
12. Stephen Greenberg, "Land Reform and Transition in South Africa." *Transformation: Critical Perspectives on Southern Africa* 52, no. 1 (2003): 56.
13. Moeletsi Mbeki, "Underdevelopment in Sub-Saharan Africa: The Role of the Private Sector and Political Élites," *Cato Foreign Policy Briefing* 85 (2005): 9.
14. Mikhel Truu, "Nationalisation and Privatisation," in *Wealth or Poverty: Critical Choices for South Africa*, ed. Robert A. Schrire (Cape Town: Oxford University Press, 1992), 274.
15. Floyd Shivambu, "Current Debates on Nationalising the Mines in South Africa," in *Nationalising the Mines in South Africa: Prospects, Challenges and Lessons from the SADC Region*, ed. Southern Africa Resource Watch (Johannesburg: Southern Africa Resource Watch, 2010), 2.
16. Baruch Hirson, "Nationalisation: A Matter of Slogans," *Searchlight South Africa* 3, no. 1 (1992): 82; Ronaldo Munck, "South Africa: The Great Economic Debate," *Third World Quarterly* 15, no. 2 (1994): 210.
17. Nicoli Nattrass, "Politics and Economics in ANC Economic Policy," *African Affairs* 93, no. 372 (1994): 345.
18. African National Congress (ANC). "Nationalisation of mines." http://www.timeslive.co.za/politics/2012/12/19/anc-mangaung-conference-latest-news-day-4. (Accessed February 26, 2013).
19. Knut Holter, *Let my People Stay! Researching the Old Testament in Africa: Report from a Research Project on Africanisation of Old Testament Studies* (Nairobi: Acton, 2006), 2.
20. Stephen Barry, "Year of Jubilee," *In die Skriflig* 45, no. 4 (2011): 874.
21. Barry, "Year of Jubilee," 874.
22. Barry, "Year of Jubilee," 874.
23. Joshua R. Porter, *Commentary on Leviticus* (Cambridge: Cambridge University Press, 1976), 199.
24. Barry, "Year of Jubilee," 874.
25. Anthony G. Hartze, "Theological Perspectives on Land Restoration in Leviticus 25:8–55," PhD diss. (Stellenbosch: University of Stellenbosch, 2006), 17.
26. Porter, *Leviticus*, 199.
27. Hartze, "Theological Perspectives," 16.
28. Paul Mhlanga, Paul. "The Maintenance of Land as Theological-ethical Implication of the Sabbath Year in Leviticus 25: 1–7," PhD diss. (University of Stellenbosch: Stellenbosch, 2007), 153.
29. Hereafter, the word "slave" is deliberately used to refer to people who are forced to labour under adverse and oppressive circumstances.
30. Kurt C. Schaefer and Edd S. Noell. "Contract Theory, Distributive Justice, and the Hebrew Sabbatical," *Faith and Economics* 45 (2005): 11.

31. Sharon H. Ringe, *Jesus, Liberation and the Biblical Jubilee: Images for Ethics and Christology* (Overtures to Biblical Theology 19. Philadelphia: Fortress Press, 1985), 28; Lisbeth S. Fried and David N. Freedman, "Was the Jubilee Year Observed in Preexilic Judah?," In *The Anchor Bible. Leviticus 23–27: A New Translation with Introduction and Commentary*, ed. Jacob Milgrom (New York: Doubleday, 2001), 2257; Derek Tidball, *The Message of Leviticus: Free to be Holy* (Leicester: Inter-Varsity Press, 2005), 300.
32. Ringe, *Jesus, Liberation*, 28.
33. Fried and Freedman, "Jubilee Year," 2257.
34. Fried and Freedman, "Jubilee Year," 2257.
35. Henry Schaeffer, *Hebrew Tribal Economy and the Jubilee as Illustrated in Semitic and Indo-European Village Communities* (Leipzig: J. C. Henrichs, 1922), 64–119.
36. Robert North, *Sociology of the Biblical Jubilee* (Vol. 4. Rome: Pontifical Biblical Institute, 1954), 212; William F. Albright, "Review of Robert J. North, Sociology of the Biblical Jubilee," *Biblica* 37 (1956): 488–490.
37. Jacob Milgrom, *Leviticus 23–27: A New Translation with Introduction and Commentary* (New York: Doubleday, 2001), 2145.
38. Robert North, *The Biblical Jubilee, After Fifty Years*, Vol. 145 (Rome: St. Martin's Press, 2000), 114.
39. Karel Van der Toorn, *Family Religion in Babylonia, Ugarit and Israel: Continuity and Changes in the Forms of Religious Life*, Vol. 7 (Leiden: Brill, 1996), 207; John S. Bergsma, *The Jubilee from Leviticus to Qumran: A History of Interpretation* (Boston, Leiden: Brill, 2007), 56–78.
40. Bergsma, *Jubilee from Leviticus*, 78.
41. Edward Neufeld, "Socio-economic Background of *Yobēl* and *Šemiṭṭa*," *Revista Degli Studi Oriental* 33, no. Fasc. 1/2 (1958): 53–124; Sara. Japhet, "The Relationship between the Legal Corpora in the Pentateuch in Light of Manumission Laws," in *Studies in the Bible*, ed. Sara Japhet, Scripta Hierolymitana 31 (Jerusalem: Magnes, 1986), 77–78; von Waldow, H. Eberhard. "Social Responsibility and Social Structure in Early Israel," *The Catholic Biblical Quarterly* (1970): 182–204; Jacob Milgrom, *Leviticus 17–22: A New Translation with Introduction and Commentary* (New York: Doubleday, 2000), 2241–2245.
42. Judy Pearsall, *Concise Oxford English Dictionary (Revised)* (Oxford: Oxford University Press, 2002), 700.
43. Pearsall, *Dictionary*, 896.
44. Rick A. Housier, *Counselling and Educational Research—Evaluation and Application* (Thousand Oaks: Sage, 1998), 15.
45. Gary E. Gorman and Peter Clayton, *Qualitative Research for the Information Professional: A Practical Handbook* (London: Facet Publishing, 2005), 3.
46. Robert C. Bogdan, *Participant Observation in Organised Group Settings* (New York: Syracuse University Press, 1972), 3.
47. Gorman and Clayton, *Qualitative Research*, 41.
48. Eduard Jordaan, "Fall from Grace: South Africa and the Changing International Order," *Politics* 30, no. 1 Supplement (2010): 83.
49. Lourens M. Du Plessis, "Genesis of the Provisions Concerned with the Application and Interpretation of the Chapter on Fundamental Rights in South Africa's Transitional Constitution," *Journal of South African Law* 19, no. 4 (1994): 708.

50. James H. Cone, *A Black Theology of Liberation* (Maryknoll, New York: Orbis Books, 1990), 30.
51. Juan L. Segundo, *The Liberation of Theology* (New York: Orbis Books, 1976), 26.
52. Justin S. Ukpong, "Developments in Biblical Interpretation in Africa: Historical and Hermeneutical Directions," in *The Bible in Africa: Transactions, Trajectories and Trends*, eds. Gerald O. West and Musa W. Dube (Leiden: Koninklijke Brill NV, 2000), 23; Gerald O. West, "Indigenous Exegesis: Exploring the Interface between Missionary Methods and the Rhetorical Rhythms of Africa-locating Local Reading Resources in the Academy," *Neotestamentica* (2002): 153; Knut Holter, "When Biblical Scholars Talk about 'Global' Biblical Interpretation," in *Global Hermeneutics: Reflections and Consequences* (eds. Knut Holter and Louis C Jonker, Atlanta: Society of Biblical Literature, 2010), 87–92.
53. Justin S. Ukpong, "The Emergence of African Theologies," *Theological Studies* 45, no. 3 (1984): 501.
54. Na'Im Akbar, "Africentric Social Sciences for Human Liberation," *Journal of Black Studies* 14, no. 4 (1984): 404.
55. West, "Indigenous Exegesis," 150–151.
56. Jurie H. Le Roux, "Africa and the Future of our Scholarly Past," in *African and European Readers of the Bible in Dialogue: In Quest of a Shared Meaning*, eds. Hans de Wit and Gerald O. West (Leiden: Brill, 2008), 307–308.
57. John H. Hayes and Carl R. Holladay, *Biblical Exegesis: A Beginner's Handbook*, (Louisville: John Knox Press, 2007), 35.
58. Hayes and Holladay, *Biblical Exegesis*, 101–109.
59. Itumeleng J. Mosala, "Biblical Hermeneutics and Black Theology in South Africa," PhD diss. (Cape Town: University of Cape Town, 1987), xi.
60. Gerrie Snyman, "'Looking into Black Eyes and Feel the Embarrassment.' A Selected and Selective Reading of the Africana Bible," *Old Testament Essays* 24, no. 2 (2011): 464–491; cf. James W. Perkinson, *White Theology: Outing Supremacy in Modernity* (New York: Palgrave Macmillan, 2004), 3–4.
61. This term is used here to indicate a liberated definition of which is not based on the pigmentation of one's skin.
62. Vuyani Vellem, "Interlocution and Black Theology of Liberation in the 21st Century: A Reflection," *Studia Historiae Ecclesiasticae* 38 (2012): 1–9.
63. Ndikho Mtshiselwa, "Towards an Indigenous (Xhosa) South African Biblical Scholarship," *Old Testament Essays* 24, no. 3 (2011): 687.
64. Ruth Frankenberg, *White Women, Race Matters: The Social Construction of Whiteness* (Minneapolis: University of Minnesota Press, 1993), 1.
65. Gerrie Snyman, "African Hermeneutics' 'Outing' of Whiteness," *Neotestamentica* 42, no. 1 (2008): 100.
66. Raka Shome, "Whiteness and the Politics of Location," in *Whiteness: The Communication of Social Identity*, eds. Thomas K. Nakayama and Judith N. Martin (Newbury Park, CA: Sage, 1999), 108.
67. Snyman, "African Hermeneutics," 115.
68. Tiyo B. Soga, *Intlalo kaXhosa* (Alice: Lovedale Press, 1937), 11–22; Moshe E. Ncilashe Swartz, "Restoring and Holding on to Beauty: The Role of Aesthetic Relational Values in Sustainable Development," PhD diss. (Stellenbosch: University of Stellenbosch, 2010), 281.

69. Mtshiselwa, "Biblical Scholarship," 683; cf. Augustine Shutte, *Ubuntu, an Ethic for a New South Africa* (Pietermaritzburg: Cluster Publications, 2001), 12; Madipoane Masenya (ngwan'a Mphahlele), "An African-conscious Female's Reading of Steve Biko," in *The Legacy of Stephen Bantu Biko: Theological Challenges*, ed. Cornelius W. du Toit (Pretoria: Research Institute for Religion and Theology, University of South Africa, 2008), 124; Benjamin E. Winks, "A Covenant of Compassion: African Humanism and the Rights of Solidarity in the African Charter on Human and Peoples' Rights," *African Human Rights Law Journal* 11, no. 2 (2011): 460.
70. Mtshiselwa, "Biblical Scholarship," 671.
71. Snyman, "African Hermeneutics," 114.
72. Mtshiselwa, "Biblical Scholarship," 672.
73. Also see Mtshiselwa, "Biblical Scholarship," 683.
74. Mosala, "Biblical Hermeneutics," x, 38–47.
75. Itumeleng J. Mosala, "Wealth and Poverty in the Old Testament: A Black Theological Perspective," *Journal of black theology in South Africa* 5, no. 1 (1996): 21; cf. Mosala, "Azanian mišpāh□t," 239.
76. Mosala, "Wealth and Poverty," 21; cf. Elliot K. M. Mgojo, "Prolegomenon to the Study of Black Theology," *Journal of Theology for Southern Africa* 21 (1977): 25–32.
77. Dwight N. Hopkins, *Heart and Head: Black Theology, Past, Present and Future* (New York: Palgrave, 2002), 54.
78. James H. Cone, *Black Theology and Black Power: Twentieth Anniversary Edition* (New York: Harper and Row, 1989), 151–152; James H. Cone, *The Blues and the Spirituals* (Maryknoll, New York: Orbis books, 1992), 21, 53; Rothney S. Tshaka, "On Being African and Reformed? Towards an African Reformed Theology Enthused by an Interlocution of those on the Margins of Society," *HTS Theological Studies* 70, no. 1 (2014): 1, 2.
79. Dwight N. Hopkins, *Black Theology USA and South Africa: Politics, Culture and Liberation* (Maryknoll, New York: Orbis books, 1989), 19–20.
80. Takatso Mofokeng, "Black Christians, the Bible and Liberation," *Journal of Black Theology* 2, no. 1 (1988): 34.
81. Mosala, "Land, Class and the Bible," 40; cf. Itumeleng J. Mosala, "Ownership or Non-ownership of Land Forms the Basis of Wealth and Poverty: A Black Theological Perspective," in *An African Challenge to the Church in the Twenty-first Century*, eds. Mongezi Guma and A. Leslie Milton (Cape Town: South African Council of Churches, 1997), 57–58; Tinyiko S. Maluleke, "The Land of the Church of the Land: A Response to the Whole Issue," *Bulletin for Contextual Theology in Africa* 5, no. 3 (1999): 63; Butler and Philpott, "Land in South Africa," 215–235.
82. Mosala, "Biblical Hermeneutics," xi.
83. Mosala, "Ownership or Non-ownership," 57–58.
84. Johannes J. Degenaar, *Marxism-Leninism and Its Implications for South Africa* (Pretoria: H & R Academia (Pty) Ltd, 1982), 11.
85. Degenaar, *Marxism-Leninism*, 27.
86. Norman K. Gottwald, "How does Social Scientific Criticism Shape our Understanding of the Bible as a Resource for Economic Ethics?," *The Hebrew Bible in its social world and in ours* (1993): 345; Norman K. Gottwald, *Tribes of Yahweh: A Sociology of the Religion of Liberated Israel, 1250–1050 BCE* (Vol. 66. A&C Black, 1999), 35.

87. Cornel West, "The North American Blacks," in *The Challenge of Basic Christian Communities: Papers from the International Ecumenical Congress of Theology, February 20–March 2, 1980, São Paulo, Brazil* (eds. Eagleson John, and Sergio Torres, Maryknoll, NY: Orbis Press, 1981), 256; Itumeleng J. Mosala, "The Implications of the Text of Esther for African Women's Struggle for Liberation in South Africa," in *The Postcolonial Biblical Reader*, ed. Rasiah S. Sugirtharajah (Oxford: Blackwell Publishing, 2006), 134–135.
88. Roland Boer, "Remembering Babylon: Postcolonialism and Australian Biblical Studies," in *The Postcolonial Bible*, ed. Rasiah S. Sugirtharajah (Sheffield: Sheffield Academic Press, 1998), 24–48.
89. Gerald O. West, "Tracking an Ancient Near Eastern Economic System: The Tributary Mode of Production and the Temple-state," *Old Testament Essays* 24, no. 2 (2011): 513–514, 529.
90. Terry Eagleton, *Against the Grain: Essays 1975–1985* (London: Verso, 1986), 182.
91. Itumeleng J. Mosala, "The Politics of Debt and the Liberation of the Scripture," in *Tracking "The Tribes of Yahweh": On the Trial of a Classic,* ed. Roland Boer (Sheffield: Sheffield Academic Press, 2002), 84.
92. Gottwald, "Social Scientific Criticism," 345.
93. Gottwald, *Tribes of Yahweh*, 35.
94. Mosala, "Implications of the Text," 137.
95. Mosala, "Implications of the Text," 138; cf. Terry Eagleton, *Walter Benjamin: Or Towards a Revolutionary Criticism* (London: Verso, 1981), 113.
96. Gerald O. West, "Locating 'Contextual Bible Study' within Biblical Liberation Hermeneutics and Intercultural Biblical Hermeneutics," *HTS Theological Studies* 70, no. 1 (2014): 1–10.
97. Hans de Wit, "Intercultural Hermeneutics," in *Through the Eyes of Another: Intercultural Reading of the Bible*, eds. Hans de Wit, Louis Jonker, Marleen Kool, and Daniel Schipani (Amsterdam: Institute of Mennonite Studies, 2004), 481; West, "Locating," 3.
98. Rasiah S. Sugirtharajah, "Charting the Aftermath: A Review of Postcolonial Criticism," in *The Postcolonial Biblical Reader*, ed. Rasiah S. Sugirtharajah (Oxford: Blackwell Publishing, 2006), 27.
99. Sugirtharajah, "Charting the Aftermath," 15.
100. Fernando F. Segovia, "Biblical Criticism and Postcolonial Studies: Toward a Postcolonial Optic," in *The Postcolonial Biblical Reader*, ed. by Rasiah S. Sugirtharajah (Oxford: Blackwell Publishing, 2006), 37.
101. Segovia, "Biblical Criticism," 42.
102. Jon L. Berquist, "Postcolonialism and Imperial Motives for Canonization," in *The Postcolonial Biblical Reader*, ed. by Rasiah S. Sugirtharajah (Oxford: Blackwell Publishing, 2006), 85.
103. Berquist, "Postcolonialism," 88.
104. Musa W. Dube, "Rahab Says Hello to Judith: A Decolonizing Feminist Reading," in *The Postcolonial Biblical Reader*, ed. Rasiah S. Sugirtharajah (Oxford: Blackwell Publishing, 2006), 144.
105. Dube, "Rahab," 149–150.
106. Rasiah S. Sugirtharajah, "Thinking about Vernacular Hermeneutics Sitting in a Metropolitan Study," in *Vernacular Hermeneutics*, ed. Rasiah S. Sugirtharajah (Sheffield:

Sheffield Academic Press, 1999), 100; Madipoane Masenya (ngwan'a Mphahlele), "A *Bosadi* (Womanhood) Reading of Proverbs 31:10–31," in *Other Ways of Reading: African Women and the Bible*, ed. Musa W. Dube (Atlanta and Geneva: Society of Biblical Literature and WCC Publications, 2001), 145–157; cf. Mtshiselwa, "Biblical Scholarship," 671.

107. George M. Theal, *Kaffir Folk-lore: A Selection from the Traditional Tales Current Among the People Living on the Eastern Border of the Cape Colony* (No. 34341. London: S. Sonnenschein, Le Bas & Lowrey, 1886), 191. The use of an old source in this instance serves the purpose of linking this Xhosa proverb to the context of colonial rule by white people in South Africa. The sacred text of the Xhosa people already discouraged greed, which seemed to have manifested at the time that the white people dispossessed African South Africans of their land without making provision for equitable sharing of its resources.
108. Soga, *Intlalo kaXhosa*, 11–22.
109. Ncilashe Swartz "Restoring and Holding," 281.
110. Madipoane Masenya (ngwan'a Mphahlele), "Eating the Louse and its Larva! The Indignity of Poverty as Embedded within Selected African and Old Testament Proverbs," *Scriptura* 111 (2013): 457; cf. Joseph R. D. Rakoma, *Marema-ka-dika: tša Sesotho sa lebowa* (Pretoria: Van Schaik, 1971), 221.
111. Masenya (ngwan'a Mphahlele), "Eating the Louse," 454.
112. Rakoma, *Marema-ka-dika*, 198; cf. Masenya (ngwan'a Mphahlele), "Eating the Louse," 454.
113. Cf. Kofi A. Opoku, "Cooking on Two Stones of the Hearth: African Spirituality and the Socio-cultural Transformation of Africa," *Journal of Christian Thought* 13, no. 1 (2009): 7.
114. Jacob Zuma sang the song at the funeral service for Nelson Mandela. Zuma, Jacob G. "Jacob Zuma sings controversial song at Mandela Funeral, in CNN video. Jacob Zuma sings controversial song at Mandela funeral," http://www.rawstory.com/rs/2013/12/15/south-african-president-jacob-zuma-sings-controversial-song-at-nelson-mandela-funeral/. (Accessed December 15, 2013). Also, for a rendition of the song, see http://www.dailymotion.com/video/x18fdfu_jacob-zuma-sings-at-mandela-funeral_news. This video was posted by CNN International. The digitalisation of the song *Thina sizwe esimnyama* was done by Wilson. See Deborah Wilson, *Freedom Songs* (Johannesburg: Historical Papers, University of the Witwatersrand, 2012), 2. The songs is kept in the archives of the Historical Papers Library of the University of Witwatersrand. However, Wilson is not the composer of the song; the composer remains unknown. Since the song was originally sung in ANC gatherings, the composer was probably an ANC member.
115. Zuma, Jacob G. "Jacob Zuma sings controversial song at Mandela Funeral, in CNN video. Jacob Zuma sings controversial song at Mandela funeral," http://www.rawstory.com/rs/2013/12/15/south-african-president-jacob-zuma-sings-controversial-song-at-nelson-mandela-funeral/. Accessed on 15 December 2013.
116. The word *izwe* is often translated as "land." Cf. Wilson, *Freedom Songs*, 2. However, the word does not allude to productive land but to a country. When referring to productive land, the composer of this song used the word "*umhlaba*" (land), as in verse lines 4 and 8.
117. Leepo Modise and Ndikho Mtshiselwa, "The Natives Land Act of 1913 Engineered the Poverty of Black South Africans: A Historico-ecclesiastical Perspective," *Studia Historiae Ecclesiasticae* 39, no. 2 (2013): 359–378.
118. Walter B. Rubusana, *Zemnk' iinkomo Magwalandini* (Alice: Lovedale Press, 1906), 46.

119. Mavis N. Mpola, "An Analysis of Oral Literary Music Texts in isiXhosa," PhD diss. (Grahamstown: Rhodes University, 2007), 97.
120. Paul Maylam, *A History of the African People of South Africa: From the Early Iron Age to the 1970s* (Cape Town: David Philip, 1986), 87; Modise and Mtshiselwa "Natives Land Act," 362–363.
121. See Mpola, "Oral Literary Music," 117.
122. Mpola, "Oral Literary Music," 117.
123. See lyrics of versions used by Nkoala. See Sisanda M. Nkoala, "Songs that Shaped the Struggle: A Rhetorical Analysis of South African Struggle Songs," *African Yearbook of Rhetoric* 4, no. 1 (2013): 55; Cf. Masenya (ngwan'a Mphahlele), "African-conscious Female," 114.
124. See Nkoala, "Songs," 55.
125. See lyrics in the version used by Masenya (ngwan'a Mphahlele), "African-conscious Female," 114.
126. Find the lyrics used in the recording of the Bangor Community Choir from http://www.youtube.com/watch?v=7sMKm1Ulc0U.
127. Cf. the lyrics of the recording by the Hobart's Sing for Your Life Community Choir from https://www.youtube.com/ watch?v=30AsxD1u1Jw. See also the lyrics used in the recording by the Cape Town Youth Choir https://www.youtube.com/watch?v=5fDU1PYWT8A.
128. The Livingstone Organisation includes this verse line. Livingstone Organisation. "Senzeni na?" http://www.livingston.org/cms/lib4/NJ01000562/Centricity/Domain/813/Senzeni%20na.pdf. (Accessed March 25, 2014). See also Wilson, *Freedom Songs*, 2.
129. Compare the lyrics used in the recording by the Afropean Choir. Cf. The Afropean Choir. "Senzeni na?" https://www.youtube.com/watch?v= QseBak54Ass. (Accessed March 28, 2014).
130. See Wilson, *Freedom Songs*, 2.
131. Nkoala, "Songs," 54.
132. Nkoala, "Songs," 56.
133. Masenya (ngwan'a Mphahlele), "African-conscious Female," 114.
134. Masenya (ngwan'a Mphahlele), "African-conscious Female," 126.
135. Masenya (ngwan'a Mphahlele), "African-conscious Female," 114. When the song *Senzeni na* is sung, the word *sono* instead of *isono* is used (cf. version quoted by Masenya [ngwan'a Mphahlele]). Both words mean "sin." The version cited by Masenya (ngwan'a Mphahlele) does not sound right as the prefix "*i*" in the word "*isono*" prolongs the actual singing of the line. Hence, when one listens to the song it is difficult to pick up the prefix from the lyrics.
136. Tshabalala, Vusile. "How many Blacks Died under Apartheid?" http://south-africa-pig.blogspot.com/2010/10/how-many-blacks-died-under-apartheid.html. (Accessed March 30, 2014).
137. Mpola, "Oral Literary Music," 76.
138. Mpola, "Oral Literary Music," 117.
139. Ezekiel Mphahlele, *The African Image* (London: Faber & Faber, 1974), 197.
140. Ngqobe quoted in Mpola, "Oral Literary Music," 76.
141. Mpola, "Oral Literary Music," 76.

142. The song *Lelizwe* is found in the album "The Best of Amaqabane" which is recorded by the musical group "Amaqabane."
143. Mosala, "Land, Class and the Bible," 40.
144. Sponsored Feature. "Poverty and Inequality in South Africa," http://mg.co.za/article/2011-09-16-poverty-and-inequality-in-south-africa. (Accessed November 6, 2012).
145. Tinyiko S. Maluleke, "Justice in Post-apartheid South Africa: Towards a Theology of Restitution," *Verbum et Ecclesia* 29, no. 3 (2008): 685.
146. Zuma, Jacob G. "State of the Nation Address 2013. Read in parliament on 14 February 2013, Cape Town," http://www.timeslive.co.za/politics/ 2013/02/14/full-text-of-president-jacob-zumas-state-of-the-nation-speech-2013. (Accessed February 26, 2013).
147. Kofi A. Opoku, *West African Traditional Religion* (Accra: FEP, 1978), 162; Kofi A. Opoku "Skinny but Imperishable truth: African Religious Heritage and the Regeneration of Africa," *Studia Historiae Ecclesiasticae* 38, Supplement (2011): 149–150.
148. Mosala, "Biblical Hermeneutics," x, 38–47; Itumeleng J. Mosala, *Biblical Hermeneutics and Black Theology in South Africa* (Grand Rapids: Eerdmans, 1989), 32; Itumeleng J. Mosala, "Reconstructing the Azanian mišpāh□t (clans): Land, Class and Bible in South Africa Today," in *Text and Experience: Towards a Cultural Exegesis of the Bible*, ed. Daniel Smith-Christopher (Sheffield: Sheffield Academic Press, 1995), 239; Mosala, "Wealth and Poverty," 21; Mosala, "Ownership or Non-ownership," 57–58; Mosala, "Implications of the Text," 134–135, 137–138.

References

African National Congress. "The Freedom Charter," http://www.anc.org.za/show.php?id= 72.

African National Congress. 2012. "Nationalisation of Mines." http://www.timeslive.co.za/politics/2012/12/19/anc-mangaung-conference-latest-news-day-4.

Akbar, Na'Im. "Africentric Social Sciences for Human Liberation." *Journal of Black Studies* 14, no. 4 (1984): 395–414.

Albright, William F. "Review of Robert J. North, Sociology of the Biblical Jubilee." *Biblica* 37 (1956): 488–490.

Barry, Stephen. "The Year of Jubilee: A Hermeneutic for Social and Moral Transformation in South Africa." *In die Skriflig* 45, no. 4 (2011): 867–897.

Bergsma, John S. *The Jubilee from Leviticus to Qumran: A History of Interpretation.* Boston, Leiden: Brill, 2007.

Berquist, Jon L. "Postcolonialism and Imperial Motives for Canonization." In *The Postcolonial Biblical Reader*, edited by Rasiah S. Sugirtharajah, 78–95. Oxford: Blackwell Publishing, 2006.

Boer, Roland. "Remembering Babylon: Postcolonialism and Australian Biblical Studies." In *The Postcolonial Bible*, edited by Rasiah S. Sugirtharajah, 24–48. Sheffield: Sheffield Academic Press, 1998.

Bogdan, Robert C. *Participant Observation in Organised Group Settings.* New York: Syracuse University Press, 1972.

Bond, Patrick. "War on Poverty in a Quagmire." *Sunday Independent*, August 1, 2010.
Cone, James H. *Black Theology and Black Power: Twentieth Anniversary Edition*. New York: Harper and Row, 1989.
Cone, James H. *A Black Theology of Liberation*. Maryknoll, New York: Orbis Books, 1990.
Cone, James H. *The Blues and the Spirituals*. Maryknoll, New York: Orbis books, 1992.
Degenaar, Johannes J. *Marxism-Leninism and Its Implications for South Africa*. Pretoria: H & R Academia (Pty) Ltd, 1982.
Department of Land Affairs. *White Paper on South African Land Policy*. Pretoria: Department of Land Affairs, 1997.
de Wit, Hans. "Intercultural Hermeneutics." In *Through the Eyes of Another: Intercultural Reading of the Bible*, edited by Hans de Wit, Louis Jonker, Marleen Kool, and Daniel Schipani, 477–492. Amsterdam: Institute of Mennonite Studies, 2004.
Dube, Musa W. "Rahab Says Hello to Judith: A Decolonizing Feminist Reading." In *The Postcolonial Biblical Reader*, edited by Rasiah S. Sugirtharajah, 142–158. Oxford: Blackwell Publishing, 2006.
Du Plessis, Lourens M. "Genesis of the Provisions Concerned with the Application and Interpretation of the Chapter on Fundamental Rights in South Africa's Transitional Constitution." *Journal of South African Law* 19, no. 4 (1994): 706–733.
Eagleton, Terry. *Walter Benjamin: Or Towards a Revolutionary Criticism*. London: Verso, 1981.
Eagleton, Terry. *Against the Grain: Essays 1975–1985*. London: Verso, 1986.
Frankenberg, Ruth. *White Women, Race Matters: The Social Construction of Whiteness*. Minneapolis: University of Minnesota Press, 1993.
Fried, Lisbeth S., and David N. Freedman. "Was the Jubilee Year Observed in Preexilic Judah?." In *The Anchor Bible. Leviticus 23–27: A New Translation with Introduction and Commentary*, edited by Jacob Milgrom, 2257–2270. New York: Doubleday, 2001.
Gorman, Gary E and Peter Clayton. *Qualitative Research for the Information Professional: A Practical Handbook*. London: Facet Publishing, 2005.
Gottwald, Norman K. "How does Social Scientific Criticism Shape our Understanding of the Bible as a Resource for Economic Ethics?." *The Hebrew Bible in its social world and in ours* (1993): 341–347.
Gottwald, Norman K. *Tribes of Yahweh: A Sociology of the Religion of Liberated Israel, 1250–1050 BCE*. Vol. 66. A&C Black, 1999.
Greenberg, Stephen. "Land Reform and Transition in South Africa." *Transformation: Critical Perspectives on Southern Africa* 52, no. 1 (2003): 42–67.
Hartze, Anthony G. "Theological Perspectives on Land Restoration in Leviticus 25:8–55." PhD diss., Stellenbosch: University of Stellenbosch, 2006.
Hayes, John H., and Carl R. Holladay. *Biblical Exegesis: A Beginner's Handbook*. Louisville: John Knox Press, 2007.
Hirson, Baruch. "Nationalisation: A Matter of Slogans." *Searchlight South Africa* 3, no. 1 (1992): 79–88.
Holter, Knut. *Let my People Stay! Researching the Old Testament in Africa: Report from a Research Project on Africanisation of Old Testament Studies*. Nairobi: Acton, 2006.

Holter, Knut. "When Biblical Scholars Talk about 'Global' Biblical Interpretation." In *Global Hermeneutics: Reflections and Consequences*, edited by Knut Holter and Louis C Jonker, 85–93. Atlanta: Society of Biblical Literature, 2010.

Hopkins, Dwight N. *Black Theology USA and South Africa: Politics, Culture and Liberation*. Maryknoll, New York: Orbis books, 1989.

Hopkins, Dwight N. *Heart and Head: Black Theology, Past, Present and Future.* New York: Palgrave, 2002.

Housier, Rick A. *Counselling and Educational Research—Evaluation and Application*. Thousand Oaks, CA: Sage, 1998.

Japhet, Sara. "The Relationship between the Legal Corpora in the Pentateuch in Light of Manumission Laws." In *Studies in the Bible*, edited by Sara Japhet, 63–89, Scripta Hierolymitana 31. Jerusalem: Magnes, 1986.

Jordaan, Eduard. "Fall from Grace: South Africa and the Changing International Order." *Politics* 30, no. 1 Supplement (2010): 82–90.

Khosa, Meshack M. "Empowerment and Transformation in South Africa." In *Empowerment through Economic Transformation*, edited by Meshack M Khosa, 1–20. Durban: African Millennium Press, 2001.

Le Roux, Jurie H. "Africa and the Future of our Scholarly Past." in *African and European Readers of the Bible in Dialogue: In Quest of a Shared Meaning*, edited by Hans de Wit and Gerald O West, 307–323, Leiden: Brill, 2008.

Livingstone Organisation. Senzeni na? http://www.livingston.org/cms/lib4/NJ01000562/Centricity/Domain/813/Senzeni%20na.pdf.

Maluleke, Tinyiko S. "The Land of the Church of the Land: A Response to the Whole Issue." *Bulletin for Contextual Theology in Africa* 5, no. 3 (1999): 61–64.

Maluleke, Tinyiko S. "Justice in Post-apartheid South Africa: Towards a Theology of Restitution." *Verbum et Ecclesia* 29, no. 3 (2008): 681–696.

Masenya (ngwan'a Mphahlele), Madipoane. "A *Bosadi* (Womanhood) Reading of Proverbs 31:10–31." In *Other Ways of Reading: African Women and the Bible*, edited by Musa W. Dube, 145–157. Atlanta and Geneva: Society of Biblical Literature and WCC Publications, 2001.

Masenya (ngwan'a Mphahlele), Madipoane. *How Worthy is the Woman of Worth? Rereading Proverbs 31:10–31 in African-South Africa*. New York: Peter Lang, 2004.

Masenya (ngwan'a Mphahlele), Madipoane. "An African-conscious Female's Reading of Steve Biko." In *The Legacy of Stephen Bantu Biko: Theological Challenges*, edited by Cornelius W. du Toit, 114–155. Pretoria: Research Institute for Religion and Theology, University of South Africa, 2008.

Masenya (ngwan'a Mphahlele), Madipoane. "Eating the Louse and its Larva! The Indignity of Poverty as Embedded within Selected African and Old Testament Proverbs." *Scriptura* 111 (2013): 452–459.

Maylam, Paul. *A History of the African People of South Africa: From the Early Iron Age to the 1970s*. Cape Town: David Philip, 1986.

Mbeki, Moeletsi. "Underdevelopment in Sub-Saharan Africa: The Role of the Private Sector and Political Élites." *Cato Foreign Policy Briefing* 85 (2005): 1–12.

Mgojo, Elliot K. M. "Prolegomenon to the Study of Black Theology." *Journal of Theology for Southern Africa* 21 (1977): 25–32.

Mhlanga, Paul. "The Maintenance of Land as Theological-ethical Implication of the Sabbath Year in Leviticus 25:1–7." PhD diss., Stellenbosch: Stellenbosch University, 2007.

Milgrom, Jacob. *Leviticus 17–22: A New Translation with Introduction and Commentary*. New York: Doubleday, 2000.

Milgrom, Jacob. *Leviticus 23–27: A New Translation with Introduction and Commentary*. New York: Doubleday, 2001.

Modise, Leepo, and Ndikho Mtshiselwa. "The Natives Land Act of 1913 Engineered the Poverty of Black South Africans: A Historico-ecclesiastical Perspective." *Studia Historiae Ecclesiasticae* 39, no. 2 (2013): 359–378.

Mofokeng, Takatso. "Black Christians, the Bible and Liberation." *Journal of Black Theology* 2, no. 1 (1988): 34–42.

Mosala, Itumeleng J. "Biblical Hermeneutics and Black Theology in South Africa." PhD diss., Cape Town: University of Cape Town, 1987.

Mosala, Itumeleng J. *Biblical Hermeneutics and Black Theology in South Africa*. Grand Rapids: Eerdmans, 1989.

Mosala, Itumeleng J. "Land, Class and the Bible in South Africa Today." *Journal of Black Theology in South Africa* 5, no. 2 (1991): 40–46.

Mosala, Itumeleng J. "Reconstructing the Azanian *mišpāh□t* (clans): Land, Class and Bible in South Africa Today." In *Text and Experience: Towards a Cultural Exegesis of the Bible*, edited by Daniel Smith-Christopher, 238–246. Sheffield: Sheffield Academic Press, 1995.

Mosala, Itumeleng J. "Wealth and Poverty in the Old Testament: A Black Theological Perspective." *Journal of black theology in South Africa* 5, no. 1 (1996): 16–22.

Mosala, Itumeleng J. "Ownership or Non-ownership of Land Forms the Basis of Wealth and Poverty: A Black Theological Perspective." In *An African Challenge to the Church in the Twenty-first Century*, edited by Mongezi Guma, and A. Leslie Milton, 57–64. Cape Town: South African Council of Churches, 1997.

Mosala, Itumeleng J. "The Politics of Debt and the Liberation of the Scripture." In *Tracking "The Tribes of Yahweh": On the Trial of a Classic*, edited by Roland Boer, 77–84. Sheffield: Sheffield Academic Press, 2002.

Mosala, Itumeleng J. "The Implications of the Text of Esther for African Women's Struggle for Liberation in South Africa." In *The Postcolonial Biblical Reader*, edited by Rasiah S. Sugirtharajah, 134–141. Oxford: Blackwell Publishing, 2006.

Mphahlele, Ezekiel. *The African Image*. London: Faber & Faber, 1974.

Mpola, Mavis N. "An Analysis of Oral Literary Music Texts in isiXhosa." PhD diss., Grahamstown: Rhodes University, 2007.

Mtshiselwa, Ndikho. "Towards an Indigenous (Xhosa) South African Biblical Scholarship." *Old Testament Essays* 24, no. 3 (2011): 668–689.

Munck, Ronaldo. "South Africa: The Great Economic Debate." *Third World Quarterly* 15, no. 2 (1994): 205–217.

Nattrass, Nicoli. "Politics and Economics in ANC Economic Policy." *African Affairs* 93, no. 372 (1994): 343–359.

Ncilashe Swartz, Moshe E. "Restoring and Holding on to Beauty: The Role of Aesthetic Relational Values in Sustainable Development." PhD diss., Stellenbosch: University of Stellenbosch, 2010.

Neufeld, Edward. "Socio-economic Background of *Yobēl* and *Šemiṭṭa*." *Revista Degli Studi Oriental* 33, no. Fasc. 1/2 (1958): 53–124.

Nkoala, Sisanda M. "Songs that Shaped the Struggle: A Rhetorical Analysis of South African Struggle Songs." *African Yearbook of Rhetoric* 4, no. 1 (2013): 51–61.

North, Robert. *Sociology of the Biblical Jubilee*. Vol. 4. Rome: Pontifical Biblical Institute, 1954.

North, Robert. *The Biblical Jubilee, After Fifty Years*. Vol. 145. Rome: St. Martin's Press, 2000.

Opoku, Kofi A. *West African Traditional Religion*. Accra: FEP, 1978.

Opoku, Kofi A. "Cooking on Two Stones of the Hearth: African Spirituality and the Socio-cultural Transformation of Africa." *Journal of Christian Thought* 13, no. 1 (2009): 3–9.

Opoku Kofi A. "Skinny but Imperishable truth: African Religious Heritage and the Regeneration of Africa." *Studia Historiae Ecclesiasticae* 38, Supplement (2011): 141–151.

Pearsall, Judy. *Concise Oxford English Dictionary (Revised)*. Oxford: Oxford University Press, 2002.

Perkinson, James W. *White Theology: Outing Supremacy in Modernity*. New York: Palgrave Macmillan, 2004.

Butler, Mark, and Graham Philpott. "Land in South Africa: Gift for all or Commodity for a few?." *Studies in World Christianity* 11, no. 2 (2005): 215–235.

Porter, Joshua R. *Commentary on Leviticus*. Cambridge: Cambridge University Press, 1976.

Rakoma, Joseph R. D. *Marema-ka-dika: tša Sesotho sa lebowa*. Pretoria: Van Schaik, 1971.

Ringe, Sharon H. *Jesus, Liberation and the Biblical Jubilee: Images for Ethics and Christology*. Overtures to Biblical Theology 19. Philadelphia: Fortress Press, 1985.

Rubusana, Walter B. *Zemnk' iinkomo Magwalandini*. Alice: Lovedale Press, 1906.

Schaefer, Kurt C., and Edd S. Noell. "Contract Theory, Distributive Justice, and the Hebrew Sabbatical." *Faith and Economics* 45 (2005): 1–19.

Schaeffer, Henry. *Hebrew Tribal Economy and the Jubilee as Illustrated in Semitic and Indo-European Village Communities*. Leipzig: J. C. Henrichs, 1922.

Segovia, Fernando F. "Biblical Criticism and Postcolonial Studies: Toward a Postcolonial Optic." In *The Postcolonial Biblical Reader*, edited by Rasiah S. Sugirtharajah, 33–44. Oxford: Blackwell Publishing, 2006.

Segundo, Juan L. *The Liberation of Theology*. New York: Orbis Books, 1976.

Shivambu, Floyd. "Current Debates on Nationalising the Mines in South Africa." In *Nationalising the Mines in South Africa: Prospects, Challenges and Lessons from the SADC Region*, edited by Southern Africa Resource Watch, 1–10. Johannesburg: Southern Africa Resource Watch, 2010.

Shome, Raka. "Whiteness and the Politics of Location." In *Whiteness: The Communication of Social Identity*, edited by Thomas K. Nakayama and Judith N. Martin, 107–128. Newbury Park, CA: Sage, 1999.

Shutte, Augustine. *Ubuntu, an Ethic for a New South Africa*. Pietermaritzburg: Cluster Publications, 2001.

Simutanyi, Neo. "Experiences of Nationalisation from Selected Southern African Countries: Lessons for South Africa, Nationalisation in Zambia." In *Nationalising the Mines in South Africa: Prospects, Challenges and Lessons from the SADC Region*, edited by Southern Africa Resource Watch, 27–33. Johannesburg: Southern Africa Resource Watch, 2010.

Snyman, Gerrie. "African Hermeneutics' 'Outing' of Whiteness." *Neotestamentica* 42, no. 1 (2008): 93–118.

Snyman, Gerrie. "'Looking into Black Eyes and Feel the Embarrassment.' A Selected and Selective Reading of the Africana Bible." *Old Testament Essays* 24, no. 2 (2011): 464–491.

Soga, Tiyo B. *Intlalo kaXhosa*. Alice: Lovedale Press, 1937.

Sponsored Feature. "Poverty and Inequality in South Africa," http://mg.co.za/article/2011-09-16-poverty-and-inequality-in-south-africa.

Sugirtharajah, Rasiah S. "Thinking about Vernacular Hermeneutics Sitting in a Metropolitan Study." In *Vernacular Hermeneutics*, edited by Rasiah S. Sugirtharajah, 92–115. Sheffield: Sheffield Academic Press, 1999.

Sugirtharajah, Rasiah S. "Charting the Aftermath: A Review of Postcolonial Criticism." In *The Postcolonial Biblical Reader*, edited by Rasiah S. Sugirtharajah, 7–32. Oxford: Blackwell Publishing, 2006.

The Afropean Choir. "Senzeni na?" https://www.youtube.com/watch?v=QseBak54Ass.

Theal, George M. *Kaffir Folk-lore: A Selection from the Traditional Tales Current Among the People Living on the Eastern Border of the Cape Colony*. No. 34341. London: S. Sonnenschein, Le Bas & Lowrey, 1886.

Tidball, Derek. *The Message of Leviticus: Free to be Holy*. Leicester: Inter-Varsity Press, 2005.

Toulmin, Camilla. "Securing Land and Property Rights in sub-Saharan Africa: The Role of Local Institutions." *Land Use Policy* 26, no. 1 (2009): 10–19.

Truu, Mikhel. "Nationalisation and Privatisation." In *Wealth or Poverty: Critical Choices for South Africa*, edited by Robert A. Schrire, 274–293. Cape Town: Oxford University Press, 1992.

Tshabalala, Vusile. "How many Blacks Died under Apartheid?" http://south-africa-pig.blogspot.com/2010/10/how-many-blacks-died-under-apartheid.html.

Tshaka, Rothney S. "On Being African and Reformed? Towards an African Reformed Theology Enthused by an Interlocution of those on the Margins of Society." *HTS Theological Studies* 70, no. 1 (2014): 1–7.

Ukpong, Justin S. "The Emergence of African Theologies." *Theological Studies* 45, no. 3 (1984): 501–536.

Ukpong, Justin S. "Developments in Biblical Interpretation in Africa: Historical and Hermeneutical Directions." In *The Bible in Africa: Transactions, Trajectories and Trends*, edited by Gerald O. West and Musa W. Dube, 11–28. Leiden: Koninklijke Brill NV, 2000.

Van der Toorn, Karel. *Family Religion in Babylonia, Ugarit and Israel: Continuity and Changes in the Forms of Religious Life*. Vol. 7. Leiden: Brill, 1996.

Vellem, Vuyani. "Interlocution and Black Theology of Liberation in the 21st Century: A Reflection." *Studia Historiae Ecclesiasticae* 38 (2012): 1–9.

von Waldow, H. Eberhard. "Social Responsibility and Social Structure in Early Israel." *The Catholic Biblical Quarterly* (1970): 182–204.

West, Cornel. "The North American Blacks." In *The Challenge of Basic Christian Communities: Papers from the International Ecumenical Congress of Theology, February 20-March 2, 1980, São Paulo, Brazil*, edited by Eagleson John, and Sergio Torres, 255–257. Maryknoll, NY: Orbis Press, 1981.

West, Gerald O. "Indigenous Exegesis: Exploring the Interface between Missionary Methods and the Rhetorical Rhythms of Africa-locating Local Reading Resources in the Academy." *Neotestamentica* (2002): 147–162.

West, Gerald O. "Tracking an Ancient Near Eastern Economic System: The Tributary Mode of Production and the Temple-state." *Old Testament Essays* 24, no. 2 (2011): 511–532.

West, Gerald O. "Locating 'Contextual Bible Study' within Biblical Liberation Hermeneutics and Intercultural Biblical Hermeneutics." *HTS Theological Studies* 70, no. 1 (2014): 1–10.

Wilson, Deborah. *Freedom Songs*. Johannesburg: Historical Papers, University of the Witwatersrand, 2012.

Winks, Benjamin E. "A Covenant of Compassion: African Humanism and the Rights of Solidarity in the African Charter on Human and Peoples' Rights." *African Human Rights Law Journal* 11, no. 2 (2011): 447–464.

World Bank. *World Development Report 1990: Poverty*. New York: Oxford University Press, 1990.

Zuma, Jacob G. "State of the Nation Address 2013. Read in parliament on 14 February 2013, Cape Town," http://www.timeslive.co.za/politics/ 2013/02/14/full-text-of-president-jacob-zumas-state-of-the-nation-speech-2013.

Zuma, Jacob G. "Jacob Zuma sings controversial song at Mandela Funeral, in CNN video. Jacob Zuma sings controversial song at Mandela funeral," http://www.rawstory.com/rs/2013/12/15/south-african-president-jacob-zuma-sings-controversial-song-at-nelson-mandela-funeral/.

CHAPTER TWO

A Critique of Socio-Economic Injustice and Land Ownership in South Africa

Introduction

Masenya (ngwan'a Mphahlele) has added a fresh dimension to African biblical hermeneutics with her use of the folktale of the 'Rabbit and the Lion' in her interpretation of the Hebrew Bible.[1] She points out the place of orality and indigenous narratives in African biblical hermeneutics, an area that stands in continuity with postcolonial work. Her use of the folktale of the 'Rabbit and the Lion' reminds one of the Xhosa folktale of *Intsimi yeenyamakazana*, 'The productive land of the animals' which is employed to frame the land question in the present chapter (see Appendix B for both the Xhosa version and the English translation of the folktale).[2] The folktale is about a group of animals, which left their productive land to eat leaves in the mountains. Whilst the animals were in the mountains, an intruder, identified as a strange animal, arrived and confiscated the productive land that belonged to the group of animals. The animals sent the rabbit and suricate to demand their land back from the intruder but failed. Later, in the struggle for the productive land, the tortoise sacrificed his life and defeated the strange animal. In the end, the group of animals rejoiced because they had regained their land.

Interestingly, African South Africans similarly lost their productive land to the white colonialists. Driven by a desire for self-enrichment, an intruder dispossessed them of their land and subsequently excluded the animals that worked the land. The capitalist tendency reminds one of the issue of capitalism in South Africa, an issue which will be discussed in detail here below. What we have in the narrative is a situation of the minority or a single strange animal contributing to the disparities in land ownership and to socio-economic injustice in the field. The majority of the animals became poor because of land dispossession like the African South Africans. In the end, the redistribution of the productive land to the majority of animals, which lost the land to an intruder, constitutes socio-economic justice. However, the tale differs from the issue of land in South Africa because socio-economic justice is yet to be realised by the poor African South Africans.

The present chapter will pay particular attention to how neo-liberal capitalism hinders land redistribution and to a great extent perpetuates socio-economic injustice. The present chapter will also address missing but critical questions such as: Do the political élites contribute to the present disparities in land ownership and to socio-economic injustice in the country? Further, what kind of impact do South Africa's land policies have on land redistribution and how do these perpetuate poverty among the black citizens? Thus, the present chapter will be structured into two parts:

- Political élites and land—a critique of the South African political economy during and after the negotiations; and
- Neo-liberal economic globalisation and land policies as tools of socio-economic injustice.

Political Élites and Land—A Critique of the Political Economy of the Transitional and Post-apartheid South Africa

In a paper *Architects of Poverty: Why African Capitalism Needs Changing*, Mbeki claims that the challenges associated with socio-economic injustice, in general, lie with the political élites.[3] Mbeki points out a trend in which the political élites enrich their bank accounts at the expense of the poverty that is experienced by the majority of Africans. This trend coupled with the abovementioned élite compromise particularly in the context of the land discourse in South Africa is an area of research that South African scholars have basically ignored that the present study seeks to address. To this end, one could ask whether a critique of the activities of the political élites with reference to land offers any contribution albeit small to the discourse on socio-economic redress. Such a critique is thought-out in the following manner:

- The winner takes all? Compromise(s) between the ANC élites and NP élites;
- Investigating socio-economic injustice caused by the ideological clash and compromise(s) during and after negotiations—ANC, SACP and COSATU;
- The scourge of Black Economic Empowerment—Re-locating the political élites; and
- The rise of malfunctioning capitalism! The political élites and socio-economic injustice.

The Winner Takes All? Compromise(s) Between the ANC Élites and NP Élites

South African scholarship often blames colonial and apartheid structures and systems for the present challenge of socio-economic injustice and the inequitable distribution of benefits accruing from the use of productive land. Rightful as the preceding rhetoric appears to be, it leaves one with some concerns. In fact, ascribing socio-economic injustice solely to the colonial and apartheid past limits us with respect to strategies that could be employed for socio-economic redress. In my view, moving beyond the rhetoric of colonialism and apartheid to investigate the historical compromise in particular between the ANC and the NP élites is important. Such an investigation might show us how the historical compromise intensified socio-economic injustice and inequitable benefits accruing from land ownership in South Africa. It may illustrate also the winner-takes-all scenario.

The political élites—The ANC and the NP versus the economic oligarchs

Before going any further, it is important to understand who the political élites are in relation to the South African economy. Mbeki has pointed out that two classes are dominant in South Africa—the black upper middle class that dominates the political arena; and what he terms the economic oligarchy which mainly includes the white owners and controllers of the productive economy such as the Minerals-Energy Complex (MEC).[4] In this study, the term political élites refers to both black and white individuals of influence and power from the ANC as well as from the NP, who are relatively wealthy compared to the working-class people and the poor in South Africa. Such persons possess absolute level of political power.

The relationship between the political élites and the economic oligarchy was first identified by Terreblanche in his critique of the Convention for a Democratic

South Africa (Codesa). He observes that the first convention, Codesa I, constituted the first negotiations between the political parties for a new democratic dispensation in South Africa, while the second, Codesa II, formed the secret negotiations between the economic oligarchy (as understood by Mbeki) and the political élites.[5] Therefore, the political élites are those who took part in the Codesa negotiations and subsequently shaped the post-apartheid South Africa. It must be admitted that the ANC and NP leaders were not the only political figures involved in the negotiations. Nonetheless, this chapter focuses mainly on the African-South African political élites, which would be conveniently limited to the ANC (with reference to the SACP and COSATU) élites because socio-economic and political decisions are made by them. The fact that the ANC holds 264 seats in parliament while the leading opposition party, the Democratic Alliance (DA) has 67, with others holding less than 30, places the ANC in a position of power and decision making. Thus, it can be said with certainty that, due to its influence and seats in parliament, the ANC with its alliance COSATU and the SACP influences and makes socio-economic and political decisions in South Africa.

Contestations converged within the negotiations, that is, Marxism-Leninism and socialism from the ANC and neo-liberal capitalism and/or economic globalisation from the NP as well as from the white economic oligarchy, prior to the compromise(s). Thus, an African (Swahili) proverb comes to mind, which says, *Wapiganapo tembo nyasi huumia*, 'When elephants fight the grass gets hurt'.[6] Applied to the power relations in the negotiations, this proverb illustrates the fact that the tension between the African-South African political élites and the white political élites results in the suffering of the ordinary poor and the working-class people. This tension can be viewed as a power struggle in which at the end the winner often takes all or an inequitable sharing of resources happens. Moreover, because negotiations include what Collinge terms 'give and take bargaining', it might be helpful to investigate what the ANC élites gave and lost in the negotiations for democracy in South Africa.[7] This leads us to a deeper discussion of the compromise(s) made by the ANC élites in particular.

Land compromise—The NP élites and the white oligarchs retained the land

First and foremost, a critique of Ntsebeza's view of the property clause that is couched in Section 28 of the Interim Constitution of the South Africa of 1993 in his discourse of land is worth noting. On the one hand, the clause protected and still protects the property rights of the landowners. On the other hand, it provisions the expropriation of land that is subject to a payment of compensation. The property clause will be examined in detail in the section on land policies. However, a succinct word on the clause is pertinent at this point mainly because it continues to sustain inequitable ownership and benefit from land use as imbued by the historical compromise.

Ntsebeza points out that the clause offers a portrayal of the compromise between the apartheid NP and the ANC élites, that is, the constitutional protection of the property rights.[8] In the compromise, the NP that represented the interests of the economic oligarchs agreed with the ANC élites not to redistribute land to the previously disadvantaged poor African South Africans without compensation. In addition to the compromise, the legal framework on land which is the 'willing-seller, willing-buyer' formula, and which, according to Ntsebeza, is the property clause, limits possibilities for land reform.[9]

As such, the ANC élites permitted the continuity of ownership and control of productive land by the white economic oligarchs. One could conclude that the sustainability of political liberation through the transfer of political power to the ANC élites was achieved at the cost of the persistent poverty cycle that is experienced by the majority of African South Africans. Furthermore, political liberation was attained at the expense of persistent ownership of land by the white minority, that is, the economic oligarchs. The situation is persistent because many African South Africans are presently faced with the challenge of not having the capital to purchase productive land in order to break free from the alarming cycle of poverty or the capital to sustain farming and/or productivity, should they acquire agricultural land.

Consequently, it is valid to claim that the ANC élites have contributed to the perpetual socio-economic injustice in South Africa. The discourse of the historical compromise in particular the property clause aids such a view. Today, more than twenty years after South Africa's political liberation, the compromise of the property clause and the protection of land ownership against redistribution without compensation is still an impediment to socio-economic redress in terms of land reforms. Therefore, the people who benefited from the protection of property right as provisioned by the property clause won the day. In other words, it is not an exaggeration to say that the NP élites and the white oligarchs won in the negotiations. One can say with a level of certainty that a 'winner takes all' kind of situation is noticeable in South Africa.

Ideological compromise—The demise of the ANC's ideology of Marxism-Leninism and socialism

A second compromise, which is worth examining is that which can be called an ideological compromise. In the negotiations, the ANC élites apparently compromised their economic and political ideologies. How did this compromise happen? Terreblanche has uncovered the secret negotiations between the ANC's core leadership, the leadership of the NP and the American and British pressure groups. It seems that the historical compromise was made during the negotiations. In the 1990s, the ANC core leadership secretly met regularly (at night) with the MEC at Little Brenthurst, Oppenheimer's estate and later, when joined by other corporate leaders (American and British pressure groups), they met at the Development Bank of Southern Africa.[10] However, Van Wyk is not explicit about the secret meetings, but merely presents a trend of such secret meetings. She remarks: 'The outcomes of these sometimes secret meetings were preliminary compromises between the top leaders of elite factions, including the ANC's willingness to commence negotiations, tacit assurances of the accommodation of white élites …'.[11]

Therefore, the secret meetings paved the way for the compromises made by both the ANC and NP élites in dialogue with the white economic oligarchs. On his view of the compromise, Terreblanche notes that 'there can be little doubt that the secret negotiations between the MEC and a leadership core of the ANC were mainly responsible for the ideological "somersault" of the ANC'.[12] This means that during the secret negotiations, the ANC élites were manipulated to shift from the ideologies of Marxism-Leninism and socialism and equitable wealth sharing to that of neo-liberal capitalism and/or economic globalisation. The shift constitutes a compromise. As such, the ANC élites eventually subscribed to neo-liberalism. How did this take shape? Terreblanche's insight in this regard is valuable:

> The TEC decided that South Africa needed a loan of $850 million from the International Monetary Fund (IMF) to help tide the country over balance of payments difficulties. Before the IMF granted the loan to South Africa it requested the TEC to sign a document about the economic policy of the future government. If the 'statement on economic policies' is read carefully, it becomes clear that it was the *non-negotiable* GEAR policy of 1996 in embryo form.[13]

It seems that the conditions attached to the loan request, which is the acceptance of neo-liberal economic globalisation, also played a critical role in the negotiations. The ANC élites were ostensibly left with no other option than to subscribe to neo-liberalism. Taking the loan became a necessity, because the ANC was inheriting a bankrupt economy from the NP government. Thus, it was almost impossible for the ANC government to start governing without the loan.[14] Was bankruptcy a deliberate plan, and was it aimed at compelling the ANC élites to compromise their ideologies? One cannot be certain. However, the necessity for a loan, caused by the white political élites, also led the ANC élites to opt for economic policies and/or principles that were endorsed by the IMF such as the 'willing-seller, willing-buyer' formula.

According to Bond, Robert Christiansen who led the World Bank agricultural team in South Africa and the former Director of the Land and Agricultural

Policy Centre (LAPC) David Cooper who co-authored a secret paper in early 1994 observed that the World Bank often issued loans to developing countries, but as a condition, prescribed policies for such countries to implement.[15]

A pertinent question is did the World Bank prescribe land policies to South Africa at the time of negotiations and the transition to democracy? Certainly yes, if one considers the arguments by Hall, Weideman and Bond. Bond, in particular, observes that in October 1993, the South African Agricultural Union declared that no land would be expropriated or nationalized with the intention to establish small-farmer projects.[16] The declaration necessitated that only land from the homelands within the jurisdiction of tribal authorities or land owned by government should be made available to the previously disadvantaged poor African South Africans. In view of this declaration, preconditioned by the World Bank as it were, it is not surprising that the ANC élites, represented by the then Minister of Land Affairs, Derek Hanekom adopted the 'willing-seller, willing-buyer' formula which will be discussed later in this chapter.

It therefore seems that the ANC élites were compelled to disregard socio-economic redress and land redistribution as they accepted and endorsed neo-liberal economic globalisation. Bond asserts that the ANC élites were tamed to accept neo-liberalism. Thus, in my view, the acceptance of neo-liberal economic globalisation, as manifested also in the land policies, forms part of the historical compromise (which the ANC élites made consciously), and which sustained socio-economic injustice in the country.

From the views of Ntsebeza and Terreblanche, it is clear that the discussion of historical compromise is somewhat vague in terms of the participants in the negotiations and the compromise. The fact that it does not explicitly mention who the American and British pressure groups were as well as who formed part of the ANC and NP core leaderships makes it lack substance. Probing the lack of clarity and substance could reveal the ideologies that the negotiators subscribed to as well as the benefits that the political élites (black, Indian and white) and the economic oligarchs derived from the negotiations and the compromise. Thus, it could be helpful to examine briefly what perpetuates socio-economic injustice in the context of the land discourse.

As Bond has already noted, the voices of the business-oriented thinkers, Clem Sunter, Bob Tucker and Lawrence Schlemmer, respectively, from the Anglo-American group, Nedcor/Old Mutual and Sanlam are important in the discussion of the historical compromise and the South African transition to the democratic dispensation.[17] Prior to the negotiations, Sunter published a book, '*The World and South Africa in the 1990s*,' which discusses public policy from the Anglo-American group point of view.[18] The book offers what Bond refers to as 'fairly accurate projections of South Africa's negotiations politics'.[19] In the projections, not only is the rise of neo-liberalism spelt out but it is presumed that the negotiations take the form of 'give-and-take' on all sides.[20] It is possible that one of the ideologies that Sunter, an influential figure in the negotiations, subscribed to was neo-liberalism which was gaining grounds. In this possible scenario, elements of neo-liberal economic globalisation in the use of land in apartheid South Africa permeated in the negotiations. One of the elements is privatisation.

In the middle of 1990, Sunter convened an eminent group of economists and political thinkers and spent R1.7 million of his institutions' funds on scenario planning brainstorms.[21] It is from these brainstorming sessions that economic options for South Africa were constructed and critiqued. Two options were offered for South Africa: the 'High Road' of negotiations that leads to economic growth, a political settlement and/or compromise; and the 'Low Road' of confrontation, which leads to a civil war, imposing of sanctions and a decline in the South African economy.[22] A compromise within the South African political economy was to lead to economic growth and the supposed alleviation of poverty.

However, given the present state of poverty in the country, the ideal option of the 'High Road' particularly in view of its promises has not entirely materialized. Poverty and economic inequality persist in the country despite choosing the option of the 'High Road' during the negotiations. At least, a positive consequence of that option by the TEC was the avoidance of a civil war. As regards the ideologies that the negotiators subscribed to, the avoidance of civil war and advocacy for economic growth point to the rise of neo-liberalism and the demise of Marxism-Leninism and socialism. To further understand the ideologies that informed the eminent group of economists and political thinkers during the scenario planning particularly Sunter and Tucker, it would be helpful to consider the book *The Mind of a Fox: Scenario Planning in Action* by Ilbury and Sunter. The book does not only demonstrate the dominant ideologies but also those the ideologies favoured.

The winner-takes-all outcome in favour of the NP élites and white oligarchs

Ilbury and Sunter identify three main philosophical ideologies which they regard as the 'rules of the game', and which seemed to play a crucial role in the negotiations and South Africa's transition to democracy.[23] The first ideology is 'No winner-takes-all outcome', and the second rule of the game is 'negotiation transforms individuals' while the third ideology is about 'conditions for a winning nation'. In my view, the first ideology of 'no winner-takes-all outcome' is a mirage. This means that the outcome of no winner-takes-all is somewhat impossible because often in negotiations there is a winning and a losing party. A comparable local example that comes to mind is the pre-democracy negotiations. It could be helpful to investigate who the winners and losers were in the negotiations and the compromises made by either the NP or ANC élites.

First and foremost, if wealth is acquired through ownership of assets or a company and not through employment, then, the merit of the ideology of 'no winner-takes-all outcomes' is questionable.[24] In my view, ownership of productive land as well as of a corporate company places one in a position of a potential winner. Thus, we may argue that the 'no winner-takes-all outcome' is not realistic.

In addition, because South African land is not equitably owned by the citizens in terms of race, it would be absurd to argue that there were no losers and winners in the negotiations. The majority of South Africans, who are black people, do not own productive land, and for them, poverty is a persistent reality. Ilbury and Sunter repeatedly use the terms 'competition' and 'winner/loser', raising doubts that their scenario planning was motivated by socio-economic redress.[25] In my view, had the ideology of equitable sharing of resources and wealth been at the centre of scenario planning and transition rather than that of competition, winner/loser, or accumulation of wealth, one would be convinced that there was a 'no winner-takes-all' outcome.

However, in the light of the absence of the emphasis on equitable sharing of resources, coupled with the present reality of economic inequality, it is reasonable to deduce that there was a winner-takes-all outcome. This point is confirmed by the disproportionate number of the poor who are black and coloured people living in rural areas but do not own productive land. Thus, it appears that the ideologies behind Ilbury and Sunter's scenario planning and the discourse on transition from a pivotal part of the contribution of the political élites and economic oligarchs to the present socio-economic injustice in the country.

To some extent, one would agree with Ilbury and Sunter's second main ideology or rule of the game, which states that 'negotiation transforms individuals'. In general, negotiation leads individuals or parties to a compromise. This situation is clearly visible in the portrait of the negotiations that ushered in South Africa's democratic dispensation.[26] Central to the negotiations is the power dynamics, which drives the parties to either gain or protect their control and power. As Ilbury and Sunter show, decentralisation without losing control is a priority in negotiations.[27] This means that parties seek to protect their control especially when control is viewed as power.[28] Thus, the NP élites together with the economic oligarchs must have approached the negotiation table with the aim of protecting their economic interests and control rather than the intention to hand over power and wealth or land to the ANC élites.

The assumption that the NP élites were out to protect their economic interest would make some sense if understood primarily in the context of the land discourse since the property clause protected control and ownership of productive land. In other words, the owners of productive land enjoyed power and wealth, which implies that the NP élites and the economic oligarchs are winners or beneficiaries in the negotiations. The negotiations did not alter their intention to retain productive land and wealth, as Ilbury and Sunter suggest. Evidently, most of the productive land in the country is still owned predominantly by white South Africans.

Ilbury and Sunter's link of the negotiations to the winner/loser discussion in their engagement with Covey is noteworthy. They motivate the need for negotiations by using Covey's concept of 'win-win' or 'no deal' instead of the 'win-lose' outcome.[29] A situation whereby all parties receive equitable share and benefits from the negotiations is supposed. However, the reality is different. On the one hand, the NP élites and the white oligarchs lost political power to the ANC élites while retaining or winning the economic power, in particular productive land. On the other hand, black South Africans with the exception of the ANC élites lost the opportunity to gain the productive land, which was confiscated from them during the colonial and apartheid era. We shall return to the latter point later.

Given the indisputable reality of what was won and lost in the negotiations, one needs to be cautious about agreeing with Covey or with Ilbury and Sunter that the negotiations led to a win-win or no winner-takes-all outcome. The reality of the disproportionate outcomes of the negotiations—poverty and inequality and inequitable ownership of productive land—makes one to consider that there was a possible win-lose outcome. The outcomes therefore explain the present socio-economic injustice in South Africa.

As aforementioned, the third ideology relates to the 'conditions for a winning nation'. According to Ilbury and Sunter, globalisation is an important prerequisite for a winning nation.[30] In other words, a country such as South Africa needs to participate and function within the spectrum of the global economy for it to develop. As such, globalizing economic policies then becomes an unavoidable option as Ilbury and Sunter would argue. In pursuit of developing and creating a winning nation, the accumulation of capital and attraction of investments[31] would play a critical role.[32]

However, the view that redistribution rather than privatisation of land is detrimental to investments and economic growth has also been expounded.[33] Neo-liberal economic globalisation and economic growth therefore became a bone of contention in the scenario planning and negotiations, and redistribution was ignored. Options which emerged from the scenario planning, and which were presented to the NP and ANC élites by Sunter and Tucker, were unstoppable violence and an inheritance of wasteland; or economic growth.[34] This means that the NP and ANC élites could choose the route of violence, which guaranteed retainment of wasteland or that of peace, which would lead to economic growth.

If one considers the possible outcomes of persistent violence and the inheritance of wasteland, it would be logical to opt for the idea of a winning nation. The option made the NP élites to renounce the apartheid system and the ANC élites to refrain from pursuing the radical redistribution of productive land, which was taken from African South Africans. The ANC élites' deviation from the ideology of redistribution of assets and wealth sustained the scourge of socio-economic injustice, that is, of poverty and economic inequality. The deviation also constitutes a compromise, which in my view was detrimental to poor African South Africans.

Tucker who was at the forefront of the negotiations presented the scenario planning to the Anglo-American group, the ANC core leadership, the ANC Department of Economic Planning, COSATU and the NP core leadership.[35] Tucker and Sunter were co-drivers of the scenario planning, which aimed to formulate public policy that is in line with the ideology of the Anglo-American group. Thus, it might not be out of place to point out the involvement of the Anglo-American group in the negotiations. The Anglo-American group was possibly one of the major companies that formed part of the American pressure group, which Terreblanche alludes to in his discussion of the secret meetings. If that is correct, it is not surprising that the ANC élites were swayed to embrace the American led neo-liberal economic globalisation during the negotiations especially in view of the persuasion by Sunter to consider the ideologies embedded in the scenario planning for the transition into a democratic South Africa.

Moreover, the idea of Black Economic Empowerment (BEE), which will be discussed later, possibly influenced the arguments. The indirect or direct involvement of the Anglo-American group points to a vested interest by a South African company in the negotiation. Thus, it is doubtful that the NP élites and white economic oligarchs would have compromised and given away the control and ownership of land or that they would have compromised and agreed to redistribute land. Such a compromise would have affected their ownership of mines and businesses (wealth accumulation). In fact, the American constructed neo-liberal economic globalisation was central to the negotiations.

As we probe the issues surrounding the negotiations and the historical compromise, with particular reference to the American pressure group and Sunter, it appears that one of the parties imposed the rules of the game and the future on the other.[36] In my view, such imposition is characteristic of negotiations. One party wins while the other loses. One party's anger can be strategically toned down in order to attain a compromise that predominantly benefits the other party while that party and the masses lose. After all, as Ilbury and Sunter assert, negotiations transform individuals. A pertinent question to ask is could it be that the radical approach to end apartheid adopted by some individuals affiliated to the ANC was moderated or changed in the negotiations?

The radical approach of the ANC élites to end apartheid, as exemplified by Ramaphosa, was toned down in casual meetings that included sharing cups of tea arranged by Sunter. Bond cites Sunter's statement that 'it is much easier to try and find a plausible compromise between those conflicting interests if you know the people'.[37] The statement is reportedly credited to Sunter after he had tea with Ramaphosa and Golding. Not only did the initiative by Sunter entrench a personal relationship with Ramaphosa and Golding but it also paved the way for the negotiations. It thus became easier for the white oligarchs and the NP élites to present their terms, the rules of the game, to the ANC élites.

While the white oligarchs, NP and ANC élites, benefited from the negotiations and compromise, as suggested above, the poor masses that the ANC élites represented remain trapped in poverty. The concerns of the poor black masses seem to have been ignored or silenced in the negotiations. The discussion of the compromise between the ANC élites and NP élites reveals that the white oligarchs as well as the political élites are the winners that took all the wealth of the country, leaving the majority of the people poor. How then could the ANC élites disregard the concern of the poor masses for land redistribution and redressing the colonial and apartheid legacy? Could an inquiry into the politics of exclusion explain how and why the ANC élites compromised socio-economic redress in the area of land redistribution? These questions in part set the tone for a detailed discussion of the ideological clash and compromise during and after the negotiations.

Socio-Economic Injustice Caused by Ideological Clash Between the ANC, SACP and COSATU—Compromise(s) During and After the Negotiations

From the information in the preceding discussion, it can be argued with some measure of certainty that compromise was made during and after the negotiations by both the ANC and NP élites. Compromise was also struck within the ANC, SACP and COSATU alliance. Probing the impact that these compromises had on socio-economic injustice is critical, as well as how the views of both COSATU and SACP were ignored and excluded. Furthermore, the ideological outlook of the ANC, SACP and COSATU and their ideological clashes are investigated. Lastly, Fukuyama's theory of the 'end of history' is revisited with the aim of criticising the silencing of other ideological voices and views which could contribute to redressing socio-economic injustice.

Politics of exclusion—Alteration of democracy?

In his outline of the impediments to Africa's development, Kwakye identifies the challenge that comes with the politics of exclusion. The politics of exclusion refers to a tendency by political élites to alienate some politicians and ordinary citizens from decision-making processes and from fully participating in the political process. In his view, the danger with such exclusion is discontentment among the masses, a discontentment which at times is manifested in protests.[38] Excluding other parties from decision-making in political and economic processes disregards the concept of democracy as the government of the people, by the people, for the people.

This view of democracy implies that exclusion defies the very essence of freedom. It would be regrettable therefore if the ANC élites not only actually excluded the poor masses or any party during the negotiations but also ignored the voices of other African South Africans (or the majority of the working class) that were represented by the SACP and COSATU in the negotiations. Policies contrary to neo-liberal globalism such as redistributive policies that sought to redress socio-economic injustice particularly in relation to the legacy of land dispossession were disregarded in the secret negotiations. Thus, Hertz explains that at the rise of neo-liberal capitalism, which was rooted in the ideology of Thatcherism, anything and anyone opposed to capitalism came under attack and experienced exclusion.[39] One can only wonder what the outcome of the secret negotiations would have been, had the voices and the ideology of the SACP and COSATU been dominant and firm. Was the voice of socio-economic redress and land redistribution, which was grounded in communism, taken seriously in such negotiations? A focus on socio-economic redress and land redistribution would have offered both black and white South Africans equitable sharing of the land and the benefits that accrue from land ownership.

On the participation of all in decision-making in politics, Desmond reasons that 'You cannot plan an open society behind closed doors; you cannot build a democratic one by undemocratic means. Democracy entails the participation of all in decision-making; including the one to become a democracy'.[40] It is evident that the masses were not given the opportunity to express their views at Codesa.[41] They could not even choose their representatives in the secret negotiations. Desmond points out that the negotiation process became so élitist and secretive to the extent that possibly only Cyril Ramaphosa and Roelf Meyer were fully aware of the compromises and the deals that were made.[42] It is not surprising therefore that Klein concludes that what was altered in the Codesa negotiations for a democratic South Africa is ultimately the discourse on democracy.[43] Perhaps that is why the document 'Making Democracy Work' became unimportant. In my view, there should have been adequate consultation with the ordinary citizens of South Africa who were simply being notified of the decisions and the compromises made. In other words, prior to the final decisions on land, neo-liberal capitalism and the privatisation of the economy, for example, the ordinary members of the political parties involved (the ANC with its alliance partners, the NP) should have been consulted. However, this was not the case. It was a departure from the present trend in South Africa in which the members of the public have the opportunity to comment on a policy before it is made into a bill (constitutionalized). This trend does not only provide the public an opportunity to participate in the decision-making processes and offer their views but it also allows the government to consult with the ordinary citizens. Such consultations did not exist in the negotiations for a democratic South Africa.

Terreblanche maintains that the voices and views of the poor and landless majority of African South Africans regarding land redistribution and socio-economic redress were ignored.[44] In fact, both the SACP and COSATU were not adequately represented in the secret negotiations. Ntsebeza also points out that there was a possible compromise between the African-South African political élites, the ANC, SACP and COSATU.[45] However, he only briefly refers to the compromise between the conservative capitalist-inclined members and the communists within the alliance. Nonetheless, a compromise between the African-South African political élites seems to be a critical point in that, if addressed, it could explain in part the different ideological positions in the negotiations for democracy in South Africa today.

If indeed at the end of apartheid rule the hands of the ANC élites were tied regarding the land issue because they wanted to avert a civil war, then the insistence that land redistribution should have been carried out at the beginning of ANC's rule could not have been a viable option at all. Consequently, even if the poor masses were given the chance to express their opinions as suggested above, some compromise would still have been needed for the end of apartheid to arrive sooner rather than later. However, the need for compromise does not justify the apparent absence of the participation of all citizens in decision-making processes in the context of democracy. Moreover, the compromise, which seemed necessary to avert a civil war, has done little to address socio-economic injustice in South Africa as poverty and economic inequality persist in the post-apartheid South Africa.

In any political economy where neo-liberal capitalism takes the centre stage, the alteration of democracy is inevitable. If it is understood that democracy should include first and foremost the participation of all citizens in decision-making, enabling the business sector to prescribe economic policies can be viewed as undemocratic, as Desmond argues. In a context where the economic oligarchs prescribe policies to states and political élites, it would be naïve to claim that democracy is embraced. In such a context, economic policies are decided by a few who happen to have vested interests in such policies. For example, it would be highly unlikely that the Anglo-American group would recommend redistribution of land because that would mean handing over their businesses to the poor. In such a case, democracy and the will of the masses would be altered seeing that the poor will naturally seek land redistribution. The privatisation of resources and the protection of land ownership by the rich at the expense of economic inequality, as prescribed by Thatcherism or specifically neo-liberal capitalism, alter democracy. Thus, Hertz argues that the rise of the ideologies of Thatcher and Reagan marked the victory of capitalism and the death of democracy.[46]

Prior to the negotiations, the ANC clearly identified with the ideological inclinations of both the SACP and COSATU, that is, Marxism-Leninism and socialism. While the SACP had Marxism-Leninism as its ideological underpinning, COSATU was ideologically grounded in socialism.[47] It is unlikely however that both the SACP and COSATU agreed with the capitalist-oriented neo-liberal globalism accepted by the ANC during the secret negotiations. Given also the ideological position of the SACP and COSATU, an agreement on the issue of land is doubtful.

Ideological outlook of the ANC, SACP and COSATU

As we probe the impact of the ideological clash and compromise on socio-economic injustice and the land discourse, it would be worthwhile to explore the ideological outlook of the ANC, SACP and COSATU during and post-Codesa negotiations. First, elements of communism and/or socialism in the economic policies of COSATU point to a Marxist ideology.[48] Communism is an ideology, which not only favours a collectivist society in which productive land and capital are owned by the society but it also approves of a society in which the imperialistic tendency of the ruling élites is opposed.[49] As such, a party that espouses communism or socialism rejects capitalism, and both communism and socialism are associated with Marxism. Degenaar views Marxism as,

> [a] theory based on the views of Karl Marx, according to which society is structured according to the basic relationships towards the means of production, dividing society into two classes; the owners and the workers, and resulting in an exploitative and alienated situation which can only be overcome by a revolution in which the state as the coercive instrument of the propertied class is overthrown by the proletariat.[50]

Therefore, for Marxists, overthrowing the imperialistic and capitalistic ruling élites constitutes justice in that it seeks to enforce economic equality. Marxism gives priority to justice in as much as capitalism gives priority to economic growth.

Instead of relegating justice and equitable redistribution as capitalism mostly does, Marxism does the opposite. Degenaar rightly points out that Marxists view South Africa as an unequal society, with inequality originating in the exploitation, dispossession and racial imbalances of the colonial and apartheid past.[51] As such, Marxism in the South Africa context requires negotiations, with the aim of redistributing the land and capital equally. However, could the Marxist ideology be embedded in the economic policies of COSATU?

Grounded in a socialist ideology, which is integral to Marxism, COSATU regarded the redistribution of wealth and resources including land as priority in the negotiations for a new democratic South Africa.[52] It therefore means that, in line with the ideological inclination of COSATU, redistribution of resources is at the heart of liberation. Thus, if one's position were based on the ideology of COSATU, it would be assumed that a transition into democratic rule would not avoid or delay the redistribution of land especially when land redistribution seeks to redress socio-economic injustice, which has roots in the country's historical colonial and apartheid systems. Moreover, the quest for redistribution not only aims at redressing the combination of capitalism and apartheid but also at addressing the privatisation of public sectors and productive land.[53] Privatisation in particular contrasts with the ideology of socialism, which promotes social and collective or communal ownership of land as opposed to individualistic and privatized ownership.[54]

However, it is important to clarify the question of what constitutes social and collective ownership when talking about productive land. According to COSATU, this type of ownership has to do with ownership of assets by the public.[55] Workers co-operate with one another collectively to exercise control over assets and wealth. That understanding of ownership in the context of the land discourse seems to resonate with the Freedom Charter clause which states that 'The land shall belong to those who work it'.[56] The clause would then ensure that the means of production (land) is in the hands of the proletariat (the workers or masses), and not of the elitist minority which only exploit workers to accumulate more money for themselves. Therefore, if COSATU subscribed to Marxism, with a firm grounding on the ideals of communism or socialism during and after the Codesa negotiations, an ideal direction would have been towards land redistribution and socio-economic redress.

On the other hand, as a typical communist party, SACP identifies ideologically with Marxism-Leninism. It combines the scientific socialist concepts theorized by Karl Marx and Friedrich Engels, collectively known as Marxism with the theoretical expansions developed by Vladimir Lenin, collectively known as Leninism. In that fusion, Lenin modified Marx's views. According to Degenaar's interpretation, Marxism-Leninism is a far-left ideology, which is anti-bourgeois, anti-capitalist, anti-imperialist and anti-liberal.[57]

At first glance, it appears that Marxism-Leninism as espoused by the SACP is the best ideological position. However, Degenaar shows that Lenin did not only customize the view of revolution as a dialectical process into a concept of revolution as a linear process that includes inevitable violence but he also introduced élitism in that the revolution is solely led by a party particularly by the dedicated élites.[58] It is because of this element of revolution that the SACP did not oppose violent transition. In terms of the Marxism-Leninism ideology, the democratic process of negotiation is not entirely espoused by its exponents, instead we have a process in which one party claims absolute power by means of a revolution.[59]

Degenaar poses three critical questions. First, how does Marxism-Leninism see South Africa? Second, what would a Marxist-Leninist take-over of South Africa imply? Third, which social groups are likely to defend the capitalist *status quo*? These questions are important because they locate the discourse of Marxism-Leninism in the South African context and also in the period of the country's transition. South Africa is divided primarily into two classes—a ruling class of rich white persons and a working class of impoverished persons of colour.[60] The bourgeois are more likely to defend capitalism than the proletariat. Second, a Marxist-Leninist take-over implies that white people would be stripped of their political, social and economic privileges.[61] This may only happen through a revolution as the white élites would not voluntarily surrender their privileges and power. Third, it would be worthwhile to consider the social groups that, in most likelihood, would defend capitalism.

If the Marxist-Leninist SACP were to take over the government of South Africa, it might also constitute a group of élites who would probably climb the economic ladder at the cost of the underprivileged and who would be incorporated in the capitalistic economic system.[62] Degenaar's interpretation of Marxism-Leninism gives the impression that Marxist-Leninists probably do not completely oppose capitalism because of their ambition to take over power with the aim of centralizing such power within the leadership. Nevertheless, in principle, the SACP presents its Marxism-Leninism as an alternative ideology to capitalism and rejects the exploitation of the black proletariat by the white bourgeois.[63] Such an alternative was not upheld in the negotiations and transition to democracy in South Africa.

The SACP of the negotiation and post-negotiation era failed to redress capitalism. The fact that 20 percent of the citizens of South Africa possess 87 percent of land while 80 percent, African South Africans are apportioned 13 percent of land, attests to that persistent failure.[64] The Marxist-Leninists, as well as the socialists, failed to address socio-economic injustice and disproportionate ownership of and benefits from productive land, and one can safely say that they were swayed to embrace neo-liberal capitalism. As such, the SACP together with COSATU in particular compromised their ideological underpinnings. Thus, an investigation of the ANC's ideological stance is necessary in order to understand the ideological dynamics within the alliance between the ANC, SACP and COSATU.

Hertz is of the view that the Marxist rhetoric of the ANC, prior to the negotiations, espoused redistribution of wealth and productive land as well as social and public spending.[65] In the same vein, the Freedom Charter, which served as an economic policy document of the ANC prior to the Codesa negotiations, reveals an ideological inclination towards Marxism.[66] The establishment of *Umkhonto Wesizwe*, a military wing of the ANC, also revealed elements of Marxism-Leninism in the ideological perspective of the ANC, before and during the negotiations. Based on Marxist-Leninist and Marxist rhetoric, Mandela's commitment to the ideals of the Freedom Charter showed the ANC's intention to redistribute productive land.[67] In my view, shifting its intention, which was clearly grounded in ideology, marks a rejection of land redistribution on the part of the ANC. The question here is to which ideology did the ANC shift?

The ANC élites moved towards Thatcherism during and after the Codesa negotiations.[68] Thatcherism may be viewed as an ideological base that places emphasis on privatisation, reduction in inflation and government spending, and on the idea that people should help themselves rather than rely on the state for help. The shift towards Thatcherism by the ANC élites is evident in the adoption of the policy on privatisation of land ownership and the legal protection of the property rights. Furthermore, given the country's indebtedness to the IMF mentioned earlier, the ANC's aim of reducing government spending as provisioned and grounded in the ideology of Thatcherism is not surprising. Mbeki's rhetoric of '*Vuka Uzenzele*' (arise and help yourself), resonates with the Thatcherist idea that people ought to help themselves instead of relying on government for assistance.

Thus, the move towards Thatcherism marked the rise of neo-liberal capitalism in South Africa. Capitalism began to gain primacy in the ANC's ideological stance during and after the Codesa negotiations. According to Plano and Olton, capitalism promotes private ownership of property and the means of production as well as the absence of governmental restraints on ownership, production and trade.[69] In addition, capitalism is concerned by and large with the maximisation of the return on capital. The emphasis on return on capital has to do with the individualistic accumulation of wealth which is a norm within a neo-liberal capitalistic economic system.

Subsequently, the ideological outlooks of COSATU, the SACP and the ANC seem to conflict with the economic policies of the government such as the neo-liberal land policies which will be examined later in this chapter. Moreover, given the distinctions in their ideologies, it would have been improbable to avoid an ideological clash or compromise between the ANC, SACP and COSATU. If that was the case, did the ideological clashes and compromise during and after the Codesa negotiations entrench or intensify socio-economic injustice in South Africa?

Impact of the ideological clash and compromise of land redistribution

At this point, the aforementioned Swahili proverb, *Wapiganapo tembo nyasi huumia* (When elephants fight the grass gets hurt) again comes to mind. A clash between dominant forces often leaves negative effects, and the ideological clashes and compromise must have produced some negative effects on South Africa. First, we have considered the commitment of the African-South African political élites to land redistribution and socio-economic redress. Subsequently, it would be worthwhile to probe how that commitment which was rooted in socialist ideology was altered in the transitional and post-apartheid South Africa.

According to Klein, Mandela's response to questions about his commitment to the economic transformation of South Africa showed that history was not over just yet.[70] In 1990, Mandela remarked:

> The nationalization of the mines, banks and monopoly industries is the policy of the ANC, and the change or modification of our views in this regard is inconceivable. Black Economic Empowerment is a goal we fully support and encourage, but in our situation state control of certain sectors of the economy is unavoidable.[71]

Not only does this statement mark the commitment to redistribute productive land and nationalize mines but it also reveals that the quest for freedom was intertwined with the pursuit of redistribution of land and wealth, which was still important to the ANC before the negotiations. In other words, there can be no freedom without redistribution of land and wealth, or so the ANC deemed. Accordingly, one can say there can be no freedom without equitable sharing of land and the redress of socio-economic injustice. From an ideological point of view, the latter view brings to light the grounding of the ANC's economic policy in Marxism-Leninism. State control of industry coupled with redistribution of land was also fundamental. One can assume that the act of altering redistribution was and is equivalent to altering socialism, and it therefore compromises one of the main ideals of both COSATU and the SACP.

From a Marxist-Leninist point of view, the ANC's economic policy appears faulty simply because it compromises the needs of the masses and the poor. Some Pan-Africanists questioned why the ANC claimed that South Africa belongs to everyone, black and white. Klein also points out that on the one hand staunch Marxists dismissed the ANC's policy as 'petty bourgeois' as it was not revolutionary enough to divide the ownership of land among all people.[72] On the other hand, the Leninists held on to Lenin's view that private property must be abolished.[73] Thus, it seems that the ANC's shift from its commitment to redistribution of land compromised the ideas and interest of the majority of poor African South Africans. The question is why did the ANC élites compromise on land redistribution and their ideological background?

Meer points out that, by 1991, the ANC was criticized for not having any ideological foundation of its own for it retained the ideology of the SACP. Another point of criticism which in a way became a liability was the dual membership of some of the ANC's leadership in both the ANC and the SACP.[74] Dual membership created an ideological tension, as the ANC élites moved toward Thatcherism which is rooted in the ideals propagated by Thatcher and Reagan.

Typical of Thatcherism, the reduction of government spending and of inflation which to some extent was necessitated by repayment of the debt that was passed on quietly by the apartheid government is worth noting. The situation made it difficult for the government to secure capital for land reform. Besides, the move in the ideological position of the ANC élites towards Thatcherism during and after the negotiations clashed with Marxism-Leninism and socialism. Klein points out that the ANC élites represented by Mandela and Mbeki reportedly submitted the ANC's economic program to Harry Oppenheimer for approval claiming there was no reference to nationalisation and no slogan connecting the government to Marxist ideology.[75] This point also shows that the capitalist and imperialist tendency of the apartheid government to use the white oligarchs such as Oppenheimer the former chairperson of Anglo American and De Beers, to advance their aims continued. The aim was to secure economic power and control.

In 1996, Mbeki is also reported to have quipped, 'Just call me a Thatcherite'.[76] Mbeki was appealing for more privatisation, cutback on government expenditure, labour flexibility, free trade and even looser controls of money flow.[77] It is clear that the ANC had turned towards Thatcherism, which is opposed to the SACP's Marxism-Leninism and COSATU's socialism. Cutting or reducing government expenditure means that the state does not need to allocate capital to advance adequate land reforms. In a neo-liberal capitalistic system where the principle of 'willing-seller, willing-buyer' operates, the acquisition of land by the government for the purpose of redistribution would mean that the government has to set aside capital for such a purpose. If government expenditure is reduced, as is presently the case, it then means that the purpose of redistribution cannot be pursued.

Further, it is important here to offer an illustration of the compromise of ideologies by the ANC élites, and this point will bring us to the question of the independence of the South African Reserve Bank and its implication in the land discourse. The ANC élites' agreement to uphold the independence of the Reserve Bank not only took it away from the control of the ANC élites. The privatisation of the Reserve Bank also compromised the ideal of state or community ownership, which is rooted in the ideology of Marxism-Leninism and of socialism. Both the SACP and the COSATU would have agreed to the control of the Reserve Bank by the state rather than its privatisation and handing over to the NP élites and white oligarchs. Privatisation of the Reserve Bank and the fact that the state had no control over it meant that it could limit the ANC's ability to uphold the ideals of the ANC, SACP and COSATU prior the negotiations.

Had the head of the Reserve Bank during the apartheid era supported socio-economic redress and land redistribution, he could have printed more money to loan capital with low interest to the previously disadvantaged poor African South Africans for the purchase of land, thereby enabling land redistribution. However, it would have been surprising to see the former head of the bank act in favour of land redistribution to the detriment of white people who would lose the land they already occupied.

Furthermore, had the Reserve Bank been under the control of the state, the government would have been able to secure capital for land reforms but this was compromised. Constituting the autonomy of the Reserve Bank was a compromise.[78] The protection of privatisation by the addition of the property rights clause made and still makes land reform virtually impossible.[79] This act of protection also contrasts with the Marxism-Leninism ideology of the SACP as well as COSATU's socialism.

If, based on the SACP's Marxism-Leninism, an ideal outcome of the negotiations would have been a complete take-over of power and control of the NP and the replacement of white supremacy including the take-over of the South African Reserve Bank. However, that was compromised by the ANC élites and it did not happen. The ANC élites yielded the control of the central bank to Chris Stals, who also ran it under the apartheid government while the ministry of finance was headed by Derek Keyes, who also led it during the apartheid regime.[80] The continuity of the power and control of the white bourgeois, that is, the NP élites, over the key economic sectors, is against the ideals of the SACP. Thus, in my view, the ANC élites betrayed the SACP's ideology of Marxism-Leninism.

Marxism-Leninism seeks to regain power and control from imperialistic oppressors. On the surface, it appears that was an outcome of the negotiations, since the former oppressed people have constituted the ruling party. Klein documents one of the questions that emerged from Mandela's office after assuming presidency, viz., 'We've got the state, where's the power'?[81] The question presumes that the ANC did not attain power from the NP élites and the white oligarchs while they were in government. However, there is a direct link between power and land ownership as evident in the structural sequence in Klein's argument.[82]

Immediately after posing the question of where the power is, she asks, 'Want to redistribute land?' Her answer is 'Impossible'. The title of Chapter 10 of her study 'Democracy Born in Chains: South Africa's Constricted Freedom' mainly explains her answer. In an interview with Yasmin Sooka, Klein reports Sooka's comment: 'We'll keep everything and you [the ANC] will rule in name ... You can have political power, you can have the facade of governing, but the real governance will take place somewhere else'.[83]

The control of the key economic sectors, including the Reserve Bank and the ownership of productive land that was protected by the property rights clause kept and still keeps the NP élites and the white oligarchs in a position of power. As such, Marxist-Leninists and socialists could not have been content with such an outcome. In addition, the debt left by the NP élites which the ANC élites agreed to repay as well as the payment of the NP élites' pension fund which ballooned from 30 billion rand in 1989 to more than 300 billion rand in 2004, restricts the economic activity of the ANC élites.[84] That restriction probably caused the NP élites to retain economic power and control of the ANC government. It is doubtful that the Marxist-Leninist SACP is content with the situation. In view of the continuing economic control of the NP élites, it would be a joke to suggest that South Africa is a free country especially because socio-economic injustice in terms of poverty and economic inequality persists.

Rassool Snyman, in an interview with Klein laments that 'They never freed us. They only took the chain from around our neck and put it on our ankles'.[85] The compromise of Marxism-Leninism and socialism as well as the abrupt shift towards Thatcherism, which has affinities to neo-liberal globalism, confirms Snyman's remark. As Klein puts it, political freedom was attained at the cost of economic bondage or constriction and chains. She further states that in the transition, the government of the so-called transitional countries including South Africa is 'given the key to the house, but not the combination to the safe'.[86]

What does that mean? It simply means that the ANC élites received political liberation while the NP élites and white oligarchs remained in control of the economy of the country. Based on the methodological and theoretical framework adopted in this study, a postcolonial biblical exegete may argue that political imperialism seems to have been substituted with economic imperialism. Power shifted from the political arena to the economic field mainly because of the ideological compromise. However, one could ask why the ideological position of the ANC, SACP and COSATU before the negotiations altered. The answer is not so straightforward. However, it does seem that the shift in ideology promoted socio-economic injustice and hindered attempts to redistribute land equitably.

Furthermore, the clash of ideologies is also evident in the reception of the ANC policy which is spelled out in GEAR by both the SACP and COSATU. The policy of GEAR is neo-liberalist and Thatcherite rather than socialist and Marxist-Leninist in that it seeks to foster privatisation, fiscal policies, reduction of government spending and taxes, freeing of trade. Despite the differences between Thatcherism and Marxism-Leninism, and the criticism of neo-liberalism, some of the SACP élites supported GEAR and ANC's Thatcherism.[87] However, within the SACP, the Political Education Secretariat led by Langa Zita, Vishwas Satgar and Dale McKinley rejected GEAR based on ideological differences.[88] The SACP was not the only alliance member, which recognised the clash of ideologies, COSATU with its socialist ideals also registered its disapproval of the GEAR.[89]

In other words, both the COSATU and SACP criticized GEAR, which indicates their dissatisfaction with Thatcherism and neo-liberal globalism. Their dissatisfaction not only reveals the clash between the ANC's Thatcherism, Marxism-Leninism of the SACP and the socialism of COSATU but also the compromise that was reached during the negotiations of South Africa's democratic rule. On the ideological clash regarding the GEAR, Bond notes that by June 1998, Mandela and Mbeki accused COSATU and especially the SACP of disloyalty.[90] Clearly, the ideological clash and compromise resulted in socio-economic injustice and disproportionate benefits from land ownership by South African citizens.

Perhaps the best illustration and measure of the impact of the clash of ideologies and the ANC élites' ideological compromise is the present situation of socio-economic injustice in South Africa. The statistics on poverty and inequality reported in the previous chapter shows the reality of the effects of the ideological shift by the ANC élites. The adoption of Thatcherism as opposed to Marxism-Leninism and socialism did not seem to lead to much progress in terms of poverty alleviation and redress of inequality. Instead, poverty, unemployment and inequality have worsened since South Africa turned to Thatcherism.[91] Furthermore, African South Africans continue to struggle to access productive land, which is largely owned by white South Africans. As Hertz has noted, never has economic inequality been more visible and alarming as in the advent of neo-liberal capitalism, which is grounded in Thatcherism.[92]

In her book titled *The silent takeover: global capitalism and the death of democracy*, Hertz describes the impact of the shift to neo-liberal capitalism. First, she traces the popularity of neo-liberal capitalism to the regime of Margret Thatcher, the United Kingdom Prime Minister (1979–1990) and of Ronald Reagan, the United States President (1981–1989). According to Hertz, both Thatcher and Reagan advocated for an economic system, which would shift the governing power from the state and place it in the hands of the corporation at the expense of democracy and of economic equality.[93] How did this take effect? The policies of privatisation, deregulation and trade liberalisation which are rooted in Thatcherism shifted the governing power.

The effect of the shift of power is also evident in South Africa's economic policies. The 'willing-seller, willing-buyer' principle that liberates trade places power in the hands of the owners of land which in most cases are the corporations. Thus, it becomes challenging and almost impossible for government to redistribute land, and following the regimes of Thatcher and Reagan, the state no longer had a role to play in redistributing wealth based on ideological grounds.[94] As Klein would argue, the corporations have the combination to the safe whilst the state has the house keys.

The ANC élites' shift to Thatcherism reduced the role of the government to that of mainly ensuring an environment in which business can prosper and which is attractive for investment.[95] In light of the aforementioned remark that Mandela went to Oppenheimer for the approval of the ANC's economic policies, Klein confirms that the ideological compromise by the ANC élites to accept Thatcherism resulted in the constriction of government's power to such an extent that any movement toward socio-economic redress in terms of land redistribution became also restricted.[96]

Is it over? Revisiting Fukuyama's theory of the "end of history" in the South African context

Fukuyama is renowned for his theory the 'end of history', which to some extent presumes that the construction of philosophical ideologies that underpin economic policies has come to an end. As inferred above, Klein's interpretation suggests some understanding of Fukuyama's view. If one considers the idea of the end of history as equal to the end of the construction of philosophical ideologies, it would then mean that Thatcherism and neo-liberalism are absolute. If that is the case, the leftist might as well regard their struggle and arguments as pointless. To this end, neo-liberalism which features deregulation of markets within the economic arena coupled with liberal democracy in politics represents what Fukuyama views as 'the end point of mankind's ideological evolution and the final form of human government'.[97]

In this viewpoint therefore, Marxism-Leninism and socialism are seen as out-dated due to the dominance of neo-liberalism. As much as one agrees with Fukuyama's portrayal of the global reality and the dominance of neo-liberalism, such a rightist ideological stance as well as its treatment as absolute, poses challenges to developing countries. His theory of the end of history, if not interpreted as a portrayal of reality and the imperialistic nature of neo-liberalism can be understood as suggesting that the only fundamental and practical ideology is either Thatcherism or neo-liberalism. At this point, we wish to return to Klein's chapter 'Democracy Born in Chains: South Africa's Constricted Freedom'.

Klein presents what she terms 'the most persuasive argument' for abandoning the idea of redistribution on the part of the ANC, SACP and COSATU, which is captured in the statement 'everyone is doing it'.[98] Even though Klein does not link the argument to Fukuyama's theory of the end of history, in my view, it is important to understand the ANC's shift to Thatcherism in the light of Fukuyama's theory. Klein reports that the Western governments, the IMF and the World Bank often argue that 'The world has changed; none of that left stuff means anything anymore; this is the only game in town'.[99] The logic behind this statement is that, because both developed and developing countries are embracing either Thatcherism or neo-liberalism, the ANC ought to realise that the only relevant and practical ideology to adopt is that adopted by the global community.

The logic behind the saying 'follow because everyone is moving' and the argument that if one does not follow neo-liberalism it would be deemed that one is left behind seem to have their origin in Fukuyama's theory.[100] In light of the influential role of Fukuyama in the U.S. State Department, his rhetoric probably informed Western governments, the IMF and the World Bank which in turn convinced the ANC élites to shift from Marxism-Leninism and socialism. Thus, I would suggest that Fukuyama's theory of the end of history as well as the statement about 'the only game in town' are fundamental to understanding the ideological clash and compromise that developed during South Africa's transition to democracy. It seems the ANC élites were convinced that the leftist ideologies of Marxism-Leninism and socialism were no longer relevant, thus, they diverged to Thatcherism. Is this explanation convincing and sufficient to understand the implications of Fukuyama's theory in relation to South Africa's transition?

Furthermore, it is reported that the attention of one of the ANC élites Nelson Mandela was drawn to the fact that the left-wing governments were shifting their ideological views in favour of neo-liberalism.[101] The communists in Vietnam and China[102] had begun to opt for a rightist ideology; Russians were embracing neo-liberalism in the same way as the trade unionists in Poland and Hungary.[103] If the ANC élites had ignored such a persuasion and continued to be committed to Marxism-Leninism and to socialism, it would have meant that the ANC was not progressive and that South Africa was going to lag behind or head for the 'Lower Road', as Sunter would argue. To avoid this, the ANC élites not only compromised its ideologies but also deviated from the ideological principles and inclinations of its alliance members—the SACP and COSATU.

The compromise marked the collapse of communism and the victory of neo-liberal capitalism or economic and political liberalism in South Africa.[104] Since no middle path between capitalism and socialism was an option, should we then argue that there were no 'winner-takes-all' outcomes in the negotiations? There were certain winners in the negotiations. However, it is pertinent to ask whether the people's ideological evolution and the construction of ideological scenarios on how to govern are over. Should we also think of alternative ideologies that could help to formulate economic policies, which accelerate socio-economic redress? Given that socio-economic injustice in terms of perpetual poverty and economic inequality is persistent in the country, irrespective of the ANC élites' commitment to Thatcherism or neo-liberalism, an alternative is needed. However, Fukuyama's vision of 'the end of history' which Hertz calls an 'ideological consensus' or 'the silent takeover' seems to prevail for now.[105]

The triumph of neo-liberalism that left a single world ideology can easily be viewed as an 'ideological consensus', hence, the expression 'Washington consensus'. The Washington consensus comprises of a list of ten economic policy reforms that were widely held in Washington and were needed in most or all Latin American countries as of 1989.[106] According to Williamson, this list includes:

- Budget deficits ... small enough to be financed without recourse to the inflation tax;
- Redirecting [public] expenditure from politically sensitive areas [that] ... receive more resources than their economic return can justify ... toward neglected fields with high economic returns and the potential to improve income distribution, such as primary health and education, and infrastructure;
- Tax reform ... [so as to broaden] the tax base and cut ... marginal tax rates;
- Financial liberalisation, [involving] an ultimate objective ... of market-determined interest rates;
- A unified ... exchange rate ... at a level sufficiently competitive to induce a rapid growth in non-traditional exports;
- Quantitative trade restrictions should be rapidly replaced by tariffs, and these should be progressively reduced until a uniform low rate of 10 [to 20] percent is achieved;

- Barriers impeding the entry of foreign [direct investment] should be abolished;
- Privatisation of state-owned enterprises;
- [Abolition of] regulations that impede the entry of new firms or restrict competition;
- The legal system should provide secure property rights without excessive costs and make these available to the informal sector.

The consensus resembles and marks the entrenchment of neo-liberal capitalism of Thatcher and Reagan which became a dominant global economic ideology. At first glance, the Washington consensus seems plausible in particular when the term 'consensus' is interpreted as an agreement between parties. However, in reality, the so-called Washington consensus and its acceptance by certain countries are a product of the clash of ideologies and of ideological compromise. In the South African context, the ANC élites did not just move from Marxist and Marxist-Leninist rhetoric to Thatcherism or Washington consensus. Rather, they compromised their ideological position. Thus, it is argued that the ANC's economic policy changed from commitment to land redistribution and to the Washington consensus.[107]

Disturbing also is the view that the legacy of neo-liberal capitalism, which has gained primacy in the world, is ineradicable. The view is disturbing partly because neo-liberal capitalism perpetuates socio-economic injustice.[108] Consequently, developing countries including South Africa, which followed Thatcherism and the Washington consensus, continue to experience poverty.[109] Stats SA validates this finding. James Wolfensohn, head of the World Bank, also reportedly contends that economic globalisation proves not to be working at the level of the people.[110] De Soto further outlines the failure of neo-liberal capitalism particularly in developing countries in his book titled '*The mystery of capital: why capitalism triumphs in the West and fails everywhere else*'.[111] Given the apparent failure of neo-liberal capitalism, it would be unwise not to pursue alternative economic systems, which should or can redress socio-economic injustice in South Africa.

On a positive note, the historical compromise ushered in the demise of apartheid and the transition to a constitutional democratic era in South Africa. It also established relations between the political élites and the economic oligarchs, thus creating the ruling class of South Africa. However, the challenge of socio-economic injustice perpetuated through the historical compromise is more disturbing than its positive element. The compromise excluded the possibility of a redistributive policy, which was regarded as unaffordable and non-optional based on the conditions prescribed by the American-led neo-liberal empire (as reflected in the pre-requisite by the IMF on the loan offered to South Africa).

Rather, preference was given to the interests of the white political élites and the economic oligarchs (that is, their economic interests, businesses and land) as well those of ANC élites.[112] An apparent bond between the ANC élites and the economic oligarchs is not without challenges. The challenges are discussed in the following overview of the Black Economic Empowerment (BEE) initiative, which may be considered an integral part of the historical compromise that sustained socio-economic injustice in South Africa.

The Scourge of Black Economic Empowerment—Re-locating the Political Élites

The rise and self-enrichment of the ANC élites seem to be evident in the economic initiative called Black Economic Empowerment (BEE). Thus, a discussion of the BEE program and particularly of the role of the political élites is pertinent here. Mbeki sees the BEE as the creation of the country's economic oligarchs who control South Africa's economy namely the white businessmen and their families.[113] This is a rather bold statement to make, but when understood in light of the historical reference and evidence he puts forward, it makes some sense.

To substantiate his statement, Mbeki refers to the establishment of the New Africa Investments Limited (NAIL) by a white owned company Sanlam in 1993.[114] Sanlam sold a controlling stake in Metropolitan Life to a black consortium, NAIL. However, the share was transferred by the white economic oligarchs to some ANC and Pan-Africanist Congress leaders. Some African South African political élites were thus given a relatively small share while the white owner parted with billions of rands. Thus, the African-South African political élites were patronized by the white economic oligarchs.[115] The arrangement of transferring the seeming ownership of companies and wealth to African-South African political élites is what is now known as the BEE initiative. Mbeki presents reasons for the BEE initiative which include:

> [w]eaning of the ANC from radical economic ambitions ... provision of the oligarchs (white business persons) with prominent and influential seats at the high table of the ANC government's economic policy formulation ... and giving of the oligarchs and their companies the first bite at the government contract that interest them ...[116]

Thus, Mbeki's statement on BEE in an interview by Williams is not surprising. Mbeki reportedly said, 'What is wrong with BEE is that it buys off the politicians, I call it legalized corruption'.[117] If Mbeki's statement is understood, first and foremost, in the context of the agricultural sector, it would mean that the white economic oligarchs can accumulate more productive assets by placing African-South

African political élites at the forefront while parting with a larger share of the wealth. By using the black economic élites, the white economic oligarchs would also have first-hand information of the deal and thus a first bite in emerging business opportunities. That a black person who has no political linkages to the ANC élites is disadvantaged in the present situation constitutes to some extent unjust accumulation of land. Thus, based on this scenario, Mbeki's diagnosis of BEE as legalized corruption makes sense. In addition, considering the historical compromise by the ANC élites during the secret negotiations as well as the restriction on land redistribution policies such as the property clause, the statement that BEE buys off the politicians would become valid.

In the context of the secret negotiations, Terreblanche rightly states that the BEE could be seen as redistributive in nature and as part of the process of rectifying the wrongs of apartheid.[118] The decision to abandon the policy of redistribution particularly that of land redistribution based on the reasoning that BEE would redress the legacy of socio-economic injustice instituted by the colonial and apartheid regime, was a sham. Mbeki's explanation of the reasons for establishing the BEE as well as the NAIL shows that such a decision and compromise was disingenuous and a sham in that it guaranteed the protection of the wealth of the white oligarchs. Subsequently, it sustained the impoverishment of many black South Africans, while only a handful of black ANC élites are beneficiaries.

Mbeki's view that the white economic oligarchs had access to and influenced the formulation of the ANC government's economic policy through the BEE resonates with that of Bond. The fact that the white oligarchs use black faces to gain access to the new government and often pay the African-South African political élites in the form of shares in their companies sheds light on the inappropriateness of the BEE.[119] Unlike Mbeki however, Bond explicitly mentions the ANC members who were given shares in NAIL and their political connections. These include Cyril Ramaphosa (one of the ANC representatives in the negotiations), Nthato Motlana (Soweto civic activist and Nelson Mandela's physician) and Dikgang Moseneke (once a militant 'one-settler, one bullet' Pan Africanist Congress leader) who benefited from the BEE.[120]

Apart from the shares in NAIL and the flirtation with the Anglo-American group's Southern Life, Motlana added the African Merchant Bank and *Theta*'s usury-busting *Theta* micro-lending activities to his financial stable, before acquiring the former mining conglomerate Johnnic, which meant diluted control of Times Media Limited (South Africa's major newspaper publisher) and South African Breweries.[121] Motlana's wealth accumulation can be regarded as one of the examples of the capitalist self-enriching tendency by the African-South African political élites. Like the acquisition of NAIL by the African-South African political élites, the mine company Johannesburg Consolidated Investments (JCI) was bought by a consortium led by Mzi Khumalo the former Robben Island prisoner and *Umkhonto weSizwe* fighter.[122]

In 1999, Ramaphosa's ex-colleagues at NAIL Motlana, Jonty Sandler, Moseneke and Zwelakhe Sisulu gave themselves R35 million each in personal bonuses for good performance.[123] During the period of the massive drop in shares, Sandler and Motlana put in an early retirement, procuring more than R50 million each as parting gifts when they traded in their shares.[124] How many poor African South Africans could have been elevated from poverty with such huge bonuses and parting gifts? Another example of how the ANC élites benefited from the BEE is that of Ramaphosa and Lonmin. According to Steyn, Lonmin extended a $304 million loan to Ramaphosa's Shanduka Group to establish its BEE status,[125] and because of the need for Lonmin to have a BEE partner in order to retain its mining licence, Ramaphosa one of the ANC élites benefited from the BEE. He enjoyed that benefit without sharing his wealth with the poor. Thus, the ANC élites seem to find it difficult to share their wealth with the poor ordinary South Africans who have no political connection that could enable them to acquire productive assets.

Even with his shares in the platinum mining company, Lonmin, Ramaphosa, the former ANC general secretary, former National Union of Mineworkers leader and former lead constitution negotiator during the transition to democracy finds it difficult to share his wealth with the poor. Instead, he has enriched himself with the proceeds from productive land to the point that in 2012, he attempted to purchase a buffalo for R19.5 million. Given the wealth accumulated by the African-South African political élites through the BEE and their political connections, the view that the BEE is a flawed model holds water because through it a few individuals become wealthier while few jobs are created and because it legitimates the capitalist system by generating wealth for few companies.[126] As such, it is logical to assume that the African-South African political élites perpetuate socio-economic injustice in terms of poverty and inequality. However, one wonders whether there are more examples of the generation of wealth by the African-South African political élites through the BEE and their political connections.

McKune and Brümmer reveal that Ms Baleka Mbethe the present chairperson of the ANC and the Speaker of Parliament, the ANC veteran Thandi Shongwe and Limpho Hani the widow of the struggle hero Chris Hani received shares from Gold Fields a mining company, as part of the BEE initiative.[127] Furthermore, Tokyo Sexwale's Mvelaphanda Group is a beneficiary of the Coal of Africa Limited under a BEE deal[128] while Mvelaphanda is a key shareholder in Absa via Batho Bonke the broad-based BEE consortium with a 5 percent shareholding in the bank. These points show that other political élites benefited from the BEE. In addition, Julius Cobbett reveals that Matthew Phosa, the former treasurer of the ANC received about R126 million from RCL Food (formerly Rainbow Chicken) company as part of the BEE initiative.[129] Furthermore, Dunnigan, Fazaeli and Spies[130] give further illustrations of BEE initiatives that benefited only a small number of politically well-connected élites as follow:

- Ernst and Young Management Services reported that in 2003, R42.2 billion (US$6.5 billion) worth of BEE deals were made. However, the beneficiaries of these deals belonged largely to the politically well-connected **élite**. Of the R42.2 billion ($6.5 billion) worth of BEE deals concluded in 2003, 60 percent or R25.3 billion ($3.8 billion) accrued to the companies of two men: Patrice Motsepe and Tokyo Sexwale.
- The largest BEE deal of 2003 illustrates the lack of broad based empowerment. The deal was between ARMGold and Avmin for R10.6 billion. Analysis revealed that at least 72 percent of the total deal value benefited six of the narrow based black consortia (these are consortia with very few politically well-connected beneficiaries) namely ARMGold (60percent owned by Motsepe family trust), Mvelaphanda, Shanduka, Safika, Kagiso and Tiso.

As the number of the BEE deals grew after 1994, it reached 231 in 1998 and according to estimations 10 percent of the Johannesburg Stock Exchange (JSE) was owned by black businesses.[131] This means that the wealth of the country began to be transferred to the black owned companies, that is, to the political élites and those with ANC connections, as illustrated above. As at 2003, Empowerdex, an economic empowerment-rating agency in South Africa, estimated the black ownership of the JSE at 10.05 percent.[132] According to its projections, South African companies in general and not only those in the agriculture sector are expected to move towards achieving 25 percent black ownership by 2014.[133] This projection is yet to be realised. At present, the ownership of wealth in South Africa by black people is less than 25 percent. As reflected in the JSE, the black representation at board level, as directors of companies, increased to 36 percent in 2011 from 33 percent in 2010 and dropped to 10 percent by 2012.[134] What can be deduced from these statistics is that few black individuals besides the political élites as well as those with political connection with the ANC are benefiting from the BEE initiative.

Although the views of both Terreblanche and Mbeki appear plausible, the failure to link BEE to the agricultural sector limits its relevance to the present study. The linkage is pertinent to comprehend the dynamics of the African-South

African political élites and land. However, what one gathers from Mbeki's explanation is that the ANC élites sanctioned the continuity of white supremacy over the economy of South Africa while enriching themselves. Bond and Mbeki in particular reveal that through BEE, not only did the African-South African political élites promote an environment from which they largely benefitted but they also encouraged the perpetuation of economic inequality inherited from the colonial and apartheid eras.

Thus, the observation that the continuation of political dominance and racial capitalism, which undeservedly enriched the white oligarchs while the African South Africans remained poor makes sense.[135] In addition, inequality in the present post-apartheid South Africa exists also among African South Africans in that their political élites accumulate more wealth (though it is incomparable to that of the white economic oligarchs), while poor African South Africans become poorer.[136] This implies that the ANC élites are also responsible for the continuation of the poverty cycle in which the majority of African South Africans are trapped.

Rise of Malfunctioning Capitalism! Political Élites and Socio-economic Injustice

The World Bank reports that Sub-Saharan Africa contains a growing share of the world's absolute poor who in turn have little power to influence the allocation of resources.[137] On the other hand, the political élites have great power and control over the resources. The World Bank report shows that in the South African context, that would mean that the majority of the poor—the African South Africans—have little power to influence socio-economic redress. It also means that at the centre of the possibilities for either redress or perpetuation of socio-economic injustice are the ANC élites.

Consequently, the political liberation of 1994, which was spearheaded by the political élites failed to bring socio-economic-redress. Instead, it promoted poverty and economic inequality. In spite of the liberation, the majority of South Africans remain predominantly poor while the ANC's political élites and white South Africans perpetually enrich themselves. To build on the preceding discussion, this paragraph will examine the possible ways in which the capitalist ANC élites encourage socio-economic injustice in South Africa.

First, Mbeki's claim that the African-South African political élites replaced the former white colonial élites in that they continue to exploit the poor is worth revisiting.[138] According to him, the political élites enrich themselves by transferring vast amounts of economic surpluses generated through agriculture to developed countries as capital flight, while also obtaining vast loans from developed countries.[139] By so doing, the political élites divert savings to finance their consumption and accumulate wealth for themselves. An example of self-enrichment by the political élites in Africa is the uncovering by the United States Senate of vast sums paid by oil companies into the private bank accounts of Equatorial Guinea's Head of State, President Teodoro Obiang Nguema in Washington, DC.[140] In that case, the misappropriation of at least US$35 million of oil revenues was uncovered.

Had such huge amounts been shared equitably among the citizens of Equatorial Guinea, some of the poor citizens could have been elevated from their poverty. Could the situation in Equatorial Guinea be happening in South Africa? Is there any evidence of self-enrichment by the ANC élites, in particular, in the agricultural sector? Thus, it is reasonable to assume that the capitalist political élites enrich their bank accounts and subsequently contribute to the entrenchment of poverty among African South Africans.

In a discussion with the South African Members of Parliament (MPs), South African President Jacob Zuma reveals that thirty cases were investigated which relate to land use and particularly to irregular allocation and administration of land reform grants. Six of the cases were referred to the Directorate of Priority Crime Investigation (Hawks) and AFU with the aim of seizing assets (land) to the value of R86 million.[141] Further, it is estimated that R28 million will be recovered from the investigated cases, but the details were not disclosed at that stage.[142] It is surprising that Zuma chose not to identify those who were being investigated; instead, he gave a somewhat generic report to parliament. However, his mention of the arrest of ANC government officials and a KwaZulu-Natal businessman on fraud and corruption charges relating to the irregular award and administration of land reform grants valued at R51 million, leads us to further reports and media statements.[143]

Both Zuma and Mohoebi, the head of communications for the DRDLR, refrain from disclosing the names of the officials involved in the case.[144] Nonetheless, Ndaliso reports that a KwaZulu-Natal businessman Roshen Sewpersadh and three government officials Promise Phumzile Makhanya, Bhekumuzi Patrick Masoka and Sibusiso Chapi were arrested for irregular allocation and administration of land reform grants and released on bail.[145] In the report, Ndaliso notes that the AFU preserved Sewpersadh's farms including livestock and farming equipment, which were bought for labour tenants by the provincial government. It is alleged that Sewpersadh and those government officials tricked labour tenants to sign forms without knowing what they were for, which subsequently granted ownership of farms to Sewpersadh as the primary owner.[146]

Investigations reveal that the farms were transferred to Sewpersadh who did not qualify as beneficiary in the DRDLR programme of redistribution and restitution. The case affords us yet another glimpse into how the capitalist ANC élites and government officials attempt to secure productive land for themselves. In the end, not only are the poor masses disregarded but they also have no means of escaping the scourge of poverty. Clearly, the ANC élites' corrupt acquisition of land perpetuates socio-economic injustice in terms of poverty and inequality. Irregular award of land reform grants fuels socio-economic injustice in that the poor are robbed of the opportunity to obtain capital that can enable them to purchase and use land. The wealthy ANC élites continue to enrich themselves at the expense of the African South Africans who are perpetually trapped in the poverty cycle.

Probing the self-enriching and capitalistic tendencies by the ANC élites with the aim of uncovering inherent socio-economic injustice against the poor could prove helpful in investigating and documenting land and property owned by the ANC élites. From selected information on the ANC-affiliated MPs' declaration of interest which was documented in the 'Joint Committee on Ethics and Members' Interests: Register of Members' Interest' and prepared by the Parliament of the Republic of South Africa,[147] the following observations can be made:

- Fifteen ANC MPs declared ownership of a farm (between 1 ha and 2,500 ha), with three COPE or former ANC MPs.
- Twelve ANC MPs declared ownership of plots (between 1 ha and 18 ha).
- Thirty-nine ANC MPs declared ownership of property (between 27 sq.m and 8000 sq.m).
- Some MPs are directors in mining and/or agricultural companies, yet no farm or property was declared.
- Some MPs have not disclosed the size of their assets.
- Some MPs have also minimised their ownership of land and other property, for instance, by declaring one property, even though the person is a director in several companies.
- Mninwa Mahlangu, one of the ANC political élites in the CODESA negotiations, received gifts and hospitality from the European Parliament, Russian federation, President of India, President of Rwanda and Chinese diplomats, yet he claims he owns only one property in Middleburg, a coal mining area.
- Two ANC MPs Bongi Ntuli and Dalibhunga Mandela hold shares and directorship in farming companies (at Isibonelo Poultry Farm and Brahmandela Farm, respectively), yet they claim that they do not own any farm or land.
- A significant percentage of ANC MPs have not declared their business interests or assets.

Equally alarming is the fact that some ANC élites have refused to declare their assets. Not only have they failed to disclose the exact size of the land they own but they also minimise their ownership of land. The trend of accumulating more wealth and assets has become typical of capitalist politicians in South Africa. If the declaration of interests by the ANC élites, unaudited as it may be, provides an indication of wealth accumulation by the ANC élites, attempts to hide land ownership by some would be a form of socio-economic injustice. It is also clear that the ANC élites access and accumulate productive assets (land), while ordinary South Africans remain poor. This is best seen in the case of Malema who used his political position to obtain first-hand information on and access to tenders as well as to land available for sale.

Although ANC élites accumulate wealth and land, we find little evidence that poor African South Africans equitably share proceeds from the farms. Thus, socio-economic injustice continues, and irregular allocation of land reform grants does not help to redress socio-economic injustice because not only is capital stolen from the poor but the poor are also deprived of ownership and productive use of agricultural land.

Neo-Liberal Economic Globalisation and Land Policies as Tools of Socio-Economic Injustice

Since the literature on South Africa has not probed the influence of neo-liberal economic globalisation on critical land policies in post-apartheid South Africa, the present section will attempt to answer these questions: What kind of impact have the South African land policies had on the state of intense poverty among the African South Africans? Does the constitution of South Africa foster or restrict land redistribution and socio-economic justice?

Navigating the Influence of Neo-liberal Capitalism on Land Policies

It is assumed here that the elements of neo-liberal capitalism in the country's land policies impede land redistribution and the redress of socio-economic injustice. In other words, neo-liberal globalisation and land policies perpetuate poverty and inequality. As such, critical policies are presented and examined in this section with a view of examining the influence of neo-liberal capitalism, and the ways in which socio-economic justice is inhibited by the South African land policies.

Property clause(s)

Regarding property, Section 28 of the Interim Constitution of the Republic of South Africa 200 of 1993 provides that:

> 28. (1) Every person shall have the right to acquire and hold rights in property and, to the extent that the nature of the rights permits, to dispose of such rights.
> (2) No deprivation of any rights in property shall be permitted otherwise than in accordance with a law.
> (3) Where any rights in property are expropriated pursuant to a law referred to in subsection (2), such expropriation shall be permissible for public purposes only and shall be subject to the payment of agreed compensation or, failing agreement, to the payment of such compensation and within such period as may be determined by a court of law as just and equitable, taking into account all relevant factors, including, in the case of the determination of compensation, the use to which the property is being put, the history of its acquisition, its market value, the value of the investments in it by those affected and the interests of those affected.

According to Van der Walt, Section 28 heralds the beginning of the recognition, development and protection of property rights.[148] Section 28(1) protects ownership of the privately owned productive land.[149] Specifically, Section 28(1) protects private land rights of white South Africans, and it entrenches existing property privileges.[150] Unlike Yanou however, Chaskalson submits that what is more important in Section 28 is the creation of an environment for land restoration instead of the protection of existing property rights.[151] His submission is perhaps informed by Section 28(3), which he prioritizes over Sections 28(1) and 28(2). Subsequently, the issue of access to land is picked up from Section 28.

At first, even though one is impressed by the provision for all citizens to access land, there seems to be a condition attached. Productive land is to be purchased or acquired through compensation. When purchased, the market value for the productive land receives prominence. One cannot but observe the traces of neo-liberal capitalism in Section 28. Elements of privatisation, protection of land rights, purchasing land at market value and the need for capital to buy back land constitute features of neo-liberal capitalism. Thus, with their shift to Thatcherism, which influenced and informed Section 28 of the Interim Constitution of the Republic of South Africa 200 of 1993, it appears that the ANC élites accepted neo-liberal capitalism. The property clause in Section 25 of the 1996 Constitution of the Republic of South Africa is also noteworthy.

Section 25(1) institutes and legitimizes the constitutional principle that state interference with property is inevitable and necessary in the interest of the public.[152] In other words, the government may decide to expropriate productive land within the legal framework. Illegal deprivation of property particularly of productive land is prohibited. In line with Section 28(1) of the interim constitution, Section 25(1) protects property that is privately owned by providing legal framework and parameters. Protection of property right resonates with one of the ten economic policy reforms, that is, securing 'property rights through legal guarantees'.[153]

Given the pressure from the Anglo-American group, the Washington consensus probably also influenced the construction of the South African Constitution particularly of Section 25(1) which protects privately owned property. As such, the influence of privatisation, which is one of the key factors in neo-liberal capitalism, is detectable in the property clause. One could say that the protection of privately owned property implies the protection of privatisation and therefore of neo-liberal capitalism.

According to Van der Walt, Section 25(8) provides for the possibility of expropriation without compensation or with relatively little compensation.[154] In other words, there are exceptional circumstances in which just and equitable expropriation can be achieved without compensation. Section 25(8) states that no provision of the property clause may impede land reforms, which redress socio-economic injustice incurred as a legacy of colonialism and apartheid. Although this clause seems plausible, it is not as straightforward and simple.

Van der Walt further explains that Sections 25(1), 25(2) and 25(3) are an apparent impediment to land reform.[155] The reason is that the protection of privately owned property as provisioned in Section 25(1) as well as the subjection of expropriation to payment of compensation in Sections 25(2) and 25(3) constitutes such an impediment. Clearly, the provision of land reform which seems rather constricted is in fact ideological. The Thatcherist neo-liberal capitalism, which is reflected in the principle of privatisation of property, consideration of market value and investments is in conflict with the provision for redistribution which is Marxist in ideological outlook. Thus, one is inclined to admit that impediment of redistribution and land reform as stated in the property clause is influenced by neo-liberal capitalism or economic globalisation.

As in Section 25(2), one is cautious of the tension between individual rights and public interest.[156] On the one hand, this Section provisions expropriation of productive land in the interest of the public for the purpose of land reform (see also Section 25(4) a). On the other hand, Section 25(2), like Section 28(3) of the Interim Constitution, prevents expropriation of land unless there is compensation.

As such, the principle of 'willing-seller, willing-buyer' is upheld.[157] Given the fact that expropriation and land redistribution are subject to the payment of compensation, possibilities for redistribution do not depend on the state but solely lies in the availability of money, of capital.

Without any doubt, dependence of land expropriation and redistribution on capital for compensation point to the influence of neo-liberal capitalism. A critical question is should compensation be paid immediately and in the form of money? Van der Walt argues that:

> Compensation needs not to be paid in money, nor is it necessary that it be paid immediately. The general principle should be, as in the case of the amount of compensation, that the time and manner of payment should be just and equitable, taking into account all the relevant circumstances.[158]

Could there be exceptional cases in which expropriation without compensation would be just and equitable, thus striking an equitable balance? Van der Walt explains that in a case where the acquisition of property was inequitable in the first place or where the state funded or subsidized the acquisition and development of such property, expropriation without compensation is reasonable.[159] However, considering the unjust manner of acquisition, determining the merit of compensation could be a good way to redress the historical injustice. In view of the unjust land dispossession of black people by white farmers during the colonial and apartheid eras, and the provision for an equitable balance through compensation, is the provision for expropriation with compensation justifiable? If it is not justifiable and if expropriation with no compensation is allowed in certain situations, then, one could argue that Section 25 provides for equitable land redistribution and socio-economic justice.

However, there is no guarantee of a ruling that would support expropriation without compensation. If such a ruling was implemented, progress in land reform would not be as slow as it is presently. The argument that Section 25 provides for equitable land redistribution and socio-economic justice cannot be sustained. After all, priority is given to the property rights owner rather than the public. Thus, payment of compensation is critical. Moreover, priority is placed on individual interest at the expense of the interest of the community. Therefore, preference of individualism to communalism shows the primacy of neo-liberal capitalism over socialism or Marxism.

White Paper on Land Reform of 1991

In 1991, the NP introduced the White Paper on Land Reform so as to abolish the land laws based on racial discrimination.[160] When a White Paper is issued, one anticipates that the legacy of colonialism and apartheid would be redressed and the land lost by many African South Africans would be restored. However, from Weideman's interpretation of Section 2(11), it is gathered that the NP submitted that the restoration of land lost because of past racially discriminatory land laws was 'not feasible'.[161] The infeasibility refers to the fact that productive land was not to be returned to black people without the payment of compensation as provisioned by the White Paper in question. The redistribution of land as couched in this policy document is subject to payment.

Thus, the NP's White Paper stipulates that redistribution would occur in a free-market context.[162] However, what does the stipulation mean for us in our navigation of the influence of neo-liberal capitalism on South Africa's land policies? If the payment of compensation is understood first and foremost in the context of trading, it would then mean that African South Africans have to obtain capital to purchase land. Moreover, the allusion to free-market refers to the principle of 'willing-seller, willing-buyer'. Within that principle, the owner has a right to either sell or retain his or her productive land. In my view, freeing the market and not restricting or obliging the landowners to hand over the land without a payment, resonates with neo-liberal capitalism in the shape of Thatcherism. Therefore, the view that neo-liberal capitalism influenced and informed the formulation of the White Paper on Land Reform of 1991 may not be an exaggeration.

It must be noted that the White Paper features elements of redistribution. In line with Yanou's interpretation of the White Paper, the purpose of land redistribution is to provide the poor access to productive land in order to improve their economic life.[163] Based on these features, one cannot deny that the White Paper on Land Reforms echoes sentiments of redistribution, which is characteristic of the ideology of socialism. As such, one could be tempted to assume that Marxism or socialism influenced the formulation of the present White Paper. Although there are apparent traces of leftist ideology in the White Paper on Land Reform of 1991, rightist ideology is equally detectable.

On the surface, the White Paper seems to be pro-poor. However, the redistributive land reform is based on the 'willing-seller, willing-buyer' ideal, and it provides a basis for reversing the view that it is pro-poor.[164] The previously disadvantaged African South Africans opt to obtain capital to access productive land. Consequently, Weideman rightly observes that the provision was introduced to make poor African South Africans eligible for partial grants from the government to acquire land.[165]

After receiving such grants, African South Africans could then muster the needed capital to purchase the land of their ancestors. Subsequently, productive land would be transferred to private owners. Contained also in the White Paper is the principle of privatisation and acquisition of land for personal use rather than for communal upliftment. However, it appears that the redistribution espoused in the White Paper is market-based since productive land is to be sold at market value. Based on the evident principles, which are characteristic of neo-liberal capitalism, I submit that the White Paper on Land Reform of 1991 was influenced by the principles espoused by Thatcher and Reagan which include privatisation, deregulation and trade liberalisation.

White Paper on Reconstruction and Development of 1994

The wording of the policy the White Paper on Reconstruction and Development of 1994 has the potential of a positive ideological document, which could empower previously disadvantaged poor African South Africans. Section 1.2.7 of the preceding paper stipulates that no political democracy can survive and flourish if the majority of its people remain in poverty, without land, without their basic needs being met and without tangible prospects for a better life. Clearly, this section makes provisions for socio-economic redress and land redistribution, which implies that the present White Paper contains traces of Marxism.

Additionally, the White Paper on Reconstruction and Development aims at redressing historical disparities in ownership and access to both residential and agricultural infrastructure as well as to productive land.[166] Subsequently, when such disparities are redressed, poverty would be alleviated and the gap between the rich and the poor would be narrowed. However, it is also apparent from Yanou's argument (although his view is not grounded in any legislation) that land redistribution was meant to serve particularly those who could not afford to pay compensation.[167] Instead, there are more reasons to support the view that expropriation is market-driven and subject to the payment of compensation. It would be helpful to examine those reasons.

As stipulated in section 3.2.4, economic growth is critical for sustainable improvement in people's incomes. Section 3.3.1 also infers that the government's role is partly to establish an economic environment that is conducive to economic growth. It seems however that the inference gives primacy to the market instead of the government. Economic growth is far more important in terms of the allocation and use of productive land. This calls to mind Sunter's scenario planning in which he claims that the path towards economic growth alters possibilities for redistribution. Primacy of markets and the prioritisation of economic growth rather than redistribution fit well within neo-liberal capitalism, as confirmed by Section 3.4.5. Moreover, economic growth precedes redistribution, which is typical of neo-liberal capitalism. Within the neo-liberal economic framework, it is understood that redistribution of wealth would be achieved only when economic growth is boosted. The traces of neo-liberal capitalism as well as the primacy of economic growth lend credence to the argument that neo-liberal capitalism influenced the White Paper on Reconstruction and Development of 1994.

As noted previously, one of the key features of Thatcherism is the cutting or reduction of government expenditure; and these are echoed in Sections 4.1.2 and 4.1.5. Section 4.1.2 of the White Paper in Reconstruction and Development of 1996 permits the government to direct expenditure to priority areas. The reduction of government expenditure is mainly to stimulate economic growth as iterated in Section 4.2.5.

ARI points out that not only was the original 1999 deadline for the redistribution of 30 percent of agricultural land to African South Africans altered but it has been postponed again from 2014 to 2025. ARI also reports that since 1994 there has been no year when more than one percent of the national budget was earmarked for purchasing land for the purpose of redistribution and redress of socio-economic injustice.[168] It is certain that in line with the provisions of the White Paper on Reconstruction and Development of 1996, the government is cutting expenditure. That act is consistent with the ideals of both Thatcher and Reagan and is a form of neo-liberal capitalism. Consequently, it would be reasonable to argue that neo-liberal capitalism influenced the present White Paper.

Land Reform (Labour Tenants) Act, No. 3 of 1996

As a departure point, it is helpful to ask who is a labour tenant. A labour tenant is a poor South African who renders his or her labour to a white farmer in exchange for residence and land to plough or graze stock.[169] The labour is motivated by a quest for the restoration of one's own or ancestral land. The aim in this section is not to probe extensively into the definition of a labour tenant. Instead, the discussion of the Land Reform (Labour Tenants) Act, No. 3 of 1996 aims at exploring the influence of neo-liberal capitalism on land policies in South Africa.

First and foremost, Section 3 provides for the right to occupy and use land. The protection of existing rights and the access to property rights by the labour tenants is couched in the Land Reform (Labour Tenants) Act, No. 3 of 1996. As such, the protection of property rights, which is one of the key factors and policies in the Washington consensus, is noticeable in the preceding policy. Not only does the policy protect land rights but it also protects the economic interests of the landowner. Noticeable traces of the Washington consensus show the influence of neo-liberal capitalism and/or economic globalisation on this particular land policy. After all, the Washington consensus encouraged neo-liberal economic globalisation. As proven above, the ANC élites moved towards Thatcherism and the Washington consensus in the construction of South Africa's post-apartheid economic policies.

Second, Sections 2(2) and 23(1) stipulate that the owner whose land is being expropriated in terms of the Land Reform (Labour Tenant) Act. No. 3 of 1996 is entitled to a just and equitable compensation. What does this provision reveal about the influence of neo-liberal capitalism in this particular Act? Had the Act not required compensation for land reform, one would easily assume that neo-liberal capitalism did not have any effect on the present Act. However, such is not the case. The demand for the payment of market-value compensation pushes the poor labour tenants to acquire capital to buy back their lost land as well as to commence farming operations. Such a demand is typical of the demands of a neo-liberal capitalist system, which requires of the poor capital to gain access to or buy land that is privately owned in a capitalist system. Thus, the influence of neo-liberal capitalism in the construction of the present Act is certain.

Third, productivity is decisive in determining whether the labour tenant is eligible to continue to labour on a farm and to own the expropriated land. As stated in Section 7(2), failure to provide labour to the owner by a labour tenant or lessee is unacceptable. Furthermore, the fact that one is obliged to use the land productively after a farm is allocated to him or her as provided by the Act shows the importance of productivity. For the purpose of economic stability and growth, the factor of productivity and competitiveness is paramount. Subsequently, one cannot but consider the influence of neo-liberal capitalism on the Act. In the context of neo-liberal economic globalisation, under which the farming sector operates, productivity is fundamental when competing with other farms whether locally or globally to enhance economic growth. Thus, it may be assumed that the rendering of productivity in the Act is informed by pressure from neo-liberal capitalism.

Green Paper on South African Land Reform of 2011

The most recent policy document on land is the Green Paper on South African Land Reform 2011. The Green Paper also advocates for the protection of property rights, which are at the disposal of private companies and individuals. The same point is echoed in Section 3.1.[170] As such, the Green Paper not only embraces privatisation of productive land but it also upholds the Washington consensus on the protection of property rights. The traces of privatisation and protection of property rights in the Green Paper suggest that neo-liberal capitalism or economic globalisation had some influence on the Green Paper on South African Land Reform of 2011.

Section 3.3 stipulates the importance of investments while Sections 4.1 (c), 4.2 and 6.3 stress production and economic growth.[171] Any attempt at or risk of disrupting agricultural productivity is opposed in Section 6.1(a).[172] The elevation of investments and production in order to enhance economic growth at the cost of redistribution is typical of neo-liberal capitalism, which implies that the Green Paper does not oppose neo-liberal capitalism. Furthermore, Section 3.3(b) seeks to avoid or minimise land redistribution and restitution which in the Green Paper is unable to generate sustainable livelihood, employment and income.

In other words, it is assumed that redistribution is unable to alleviate poverty and redress inequality. Avoidance of land redistribution marks the (government's) attempt to distance the policy options from Marxism and socialism. Had there been an inclination towards redistribution in the Green Paper, it could then be argued that Marxism informed and shaped the content of the Paper. However, this was not the case as the avoidance of redistribution particularly the ideology of Marxism shows a tendency towards neo-liberal capitalism.

The idea of probing the influence of neo-liberal capitalism in land policies in the present research does not entail identifying those who shaped the land policies in South Africa, as Weideman has done.[173] Rather, it entails probing and identifying factors, which are grounded in neo-liberal capitalism. As such, traces of some of the key factors and principles of neo-liberal capitalism have been identified and documented. It is therefore reasonable to argue that neo-liberal capitalism influenced South Africa's land policies.

How then do land policies which are based on neo-liberal capitalism inhibit attempts to redress socio-economic injustice; and how do such policies impede the redress of the disproportionate benefits from land ownership and use in South Africa?

Land Policies as Impediment to Land Redistribution and Socio-economic Justice

As shown above, Sections 25(1), 25(2) and 25(3) constitute an apparent setback to land reform.[174] As a result, Van der Walt urges the government to circumvent these sections in order to foster redress.[175] However, as he has rightly observed, bypassing Sections 25(1), 25(2) and 25(3) would subsequently contravene Section 36(1) which stipulates that:

> 36. (1) The rights in the Bill of Rights may be limited only in terms of law of general application to the extent that the limitation is reasonable and justifiable in an open and democratic society based on human dignity, equality and freedom, taking into account all relevant factors, including:
> (a) the nature of the right;
> (b) the importance of the purpose of the limitation;

(c) the nature and extent of the limitation;
(d) the relation between the limitation and its purpose; and
(e) less restrictive means to achieve the purpose.

What are the implications of Section 36(1) in the interpretation of the land reforms particularly if Sections 25(1), 25(2) and 25(3) are set aside? Van der Walt explains that:

> … any deprivation of property which does not take place in terms of law of general application would be directly in contravention of section 36(1), and any law which permits arbitrary deprivations would be contrary to the demands of section 36(1) as well. Departure from section 25(2) and 25(3) might include expropriations not in terms of a law of general application (which contravenes section 36(1)); not for public purpose or in the public interest (which would also be in contravention of section 36(1)); and without compensation as provided in section 25(2) and 25(3).[176]

As with the property clause, the law of general application states that expropriation is subject to the payment of compensation. Anything different from expropriation with compensation is regarded as inconsistent and incongruent with the legislative trend globally.[177] Furthermore, in the context of a democratic society where the values of human dignity, equality and freedom are upheld, expropriation without compensation becomes unfair, unjust and unreasonable. Besides, in terms of general law, payment of compensation is viewed as a just and equitable measure, that is, to the extent that expropriation without compensation or at a lower value would be unconstitutional.[178]

The provision for compensation cannot be bridged just because land reforms need to be advanced. Thus, in view of the implication of and the limitations presented by Section 36(1), one is hesitant to claim that there are no impediments to land reforms in the provisions of Section 25(8). Binswanger rightly shows that the provision for compensation impedes land redistribution to the previously disadvantaged poor African South Africans.[179]

The condition of compensation attached to the expropriation of land causes a setback to land redistribution, as many poor African South Africans have no access to capital to purchase land.[180] Quoted by the Law Society of South Africa, Hernando de Soto asserts in his book *The Mystery of Capital* … that the ability to obtain finance is the key for small farmers to exit the cycle of poverty.[181] However, government has a responsibility and legislative power to introduce an alternative regulatory control over property in the public interest, without entertaining compensation.[182] In other words, it is possible for the government to discontinue the provision that requires payment of compensation in order to accelerate land redistribution.

Van der Walt submits that it is incorrect to say that the constitutional protection of property in Sections 25(1) and 25(2) of the 1996 South African Constitution impedes the promotion of land reform since the government can overrule these Sections and the protection of property.[183] However, the concluding remarks in Van der Walt's book reveal skepticism at the prospect of overruling parts if not the entire property clause. The abolition of the property clause is inseparable with the collapse of the efficacy and credibility of the constitution as well as of the courts.[184] It seems then that concern about tampering with the credibility of the constitution deters any suggestion or attempt to overrule the protection of property rights. If the property clause is regarded as an impediment to land redistribution, then, it is also a hindrance to socio-economic justice.

Subsequently, Van der Walt also reasons that if the protection of property is intended to establish equitable constitutional balance between the interest of individuals and the public interest, it can then be accepted that it is not an impediment to land reform.[185] What does this mean? First, according to Van der Walt, the property clause resurrects and protects the land rights that were undermined during the apartheid era. Second, Section 25 successfully protects the existing rights and promotes land reform at the same time.

In my view, Van der Walt's argument is not entirely on point. Protection of existing land rights defeats the means to land reforms. Protection of land owned by the majority of white people and corporations, which was attained unfairly during the colonial and apartheid eras, impedes land reform. A pertinent question therefore is which land would be redistributed if all land rights are protected by law? Thus, it is rather absurd to argue that protection of land rights does not impede land reform. Although Van der Walt does not admit it, the constitutional property clause actually attempts to insulate existing rights from all changes and from socio-political interference.[186]

Therefore, the protection of existing rights resists attempts to redistribute land to the poor and to redress socio-economic injustice. In this regard, Yanou's reception of Van der Walt's interpretation of a balance between individual rights to property and public interest is also noteworthy. In light of the persistent economic inequality, he argues that Van der Walt's view conceived the failure of land reform because it ignores the history of land dispossession from African South Africans by the colonial and apartheid regimes, and the fact that land reform could not happen while property is protected.[187] Thus, the perception that both the protection of property rights and land reforms can materialize simultaneously appears rather unfounded. In fact, it restrains socio-economic redress and land redistribution.

The protection of existing property rights stipulated in the property clause encumbers land redistribution and socio-economic redress. By protecting white people who acquired land unjustly, the clause sustains the legacy of colonialism and apartheid. Claassens' contribution on this point is noteworthy. She notes, for example, that the land of the *Mfengu* clan in *Tsitsikamma* was taken in 1977 and sold to white farmers at a third of its original value. In that case, the white farmers were granted a 100 percent bond by the government as provided by the Agricultural Credit Act 28 of 1966.[188] White farmers who happen to be holders of most of the existing property rights often obtain such land unjustly. Claassens' illustration is just one case in point. If the legacy of apartheid is sustained in the protection of existing rights which were obtained unjustly, it would be preposterous to think that portions of both the 1993 and the 1996 versions of the South African Constitution do not inhibit socio-economic redress. Thus, the nation's land policies obstruct land redistribution and socio-economic justice.

It has been noted above that Section 25(2) requires payment of compensation for land expropriation and redistribution. However, the challenge with Section 25(2)(b) is that the poor African South Africans who lost their land to white farmers in the colonial and apartheid South Africa can only retain such land by purchasing it back. Given the reality of poverty among the black people who lost their land, expropriation that is subject to payment of compensation does not redress socio-economic injustice. It constitutes an unreasonable expectation. Where would the poor get capital? That means Section 25 does little in terms of socio-economic redress, but it sustains poverty and economic inequality in terms of land ownership and productive land use. At first, one may assume that this section overlooks the fact that the previously disadvantaged African South Africans do not have capital to buy back their land. However, Section(s) 25(5) and 25(8) expect the state to assume responsibility to foster equitable access to land.

In this regard, Van der Walt rightly points out that 'Section 25(5) places a general duty upon the state to take reasonable legislative and other steps, within its available resources, to foster conditions which promote equitable access to land'.[189] In such a situation, the state then needs to have capital to buy back the land in order to share it among the previously disadvantaged poor black people in the country. The question to ask is where would the state get the capital to satisfactorily advance land reforms since the property clause of Section 25 does not permit the state to access money from the Reserve Bank to advance the course of land redistribution? Since the state has no control over the Reserve Bank and it inherited huge debts from the apartheid regime, it becomes difficult for it to take financial steps to redress economic inequality relating to land redistribution especially also because expropriation is subject to payment of compensation in post-apartheid South Africa.

Section 28 of the Interim Constitution of the Republic of South Africa 200 of 1993 is not different from Section 25 of the South African Constitution of 1996 in terms of its restriction on socio-economic redress. Section 28 also inhibits equitable sharing of wealth, which seeks to address poverty and economic inequality.[190] In order to avoid undue repetition of the issues in Section 28, I would now focus on the Land Reform (Labour Tenant) Act, No. 3 of 1996.

Section 16(1)b of the Land Reform (Labour Tenant) Act, No. 3 of 1996 stipulates that only a person or the relative of such a person who has occupied or used land for a period of five years prior to the commencement of the Act is eligible to land redistribution. This condition seems to limit the redress of socio-economic injustice because those who use land outside this time frame are not eligible to and will therefore not benefit from the provision of the Land Reform (Labour Tenant) Act, No. 3 of 1996.

As stated in the Land Reform (Labour Tenants) Act, No. 3 of 1996, the Settlement/Land Acquisition Grant is established to provide capital for those who wish to retain their land due to the enforcement of the Act. According to Section 26(1) of the present Act, the Minister of Land Affairs can grant advances or subsidies to enforce the provision of the Act from funds allocated by Parliament for that purpose. However, the provision raises some concern. First, the availability of capital to purchase land under this Act depends on government's budget and disbursement of the money. If at its discretion and based on its priorities, government resolves that there is no money for land redistribution as recommended by the Act, then, the goal of redressing socio-economic injustice would fail.

Second, the Settlement/Land Acquisition Grant is set at a maximum of R16,000 per beneficiary household, which is to be used for land acquisition or purchasing land from a 'willing-seller'.[191] This amount is far too little to enable the beneficiary to retain sizeable productive land. It would only buy a small portion of land. If the person originally lost several hectares of land, he or she might not be able to recover it based on the provision of the Act. This is one of the reasons for concluding here that the Act hinders the redress of socio-economic injustice.

Since the amount allocated is not sufficient to purchase a commercial farm, it is assumed that the 230,886 African South African farmers who by 2013 have acquired land using the grant do not possess commercial farms.[192] It should be noted, however, that ARI simply documents the figures but it does not explicitly state that the farmers did not acquire commercial productive land. In any case, the Land Reform (Labour Tenant) Act, No. 3 of 1996 does not do justice to the process of redistributing land that was lost by black people in the colonial and apartheid eras.

The land issue has been described broadly as 'only an agenda item'.[193] It is not taken seriously. If it was considered serious and urgent, perhaps the land policies would not have hindered land redistribution and the redress of socio-economic injustice. Rather, the land policies especially the latest Green Paper on South African Land Reform of 2011 fail to outline practical measures that would address existing problems such as poverty and inequality.[194]

If the present land policies impede land redistribution and the redress of socio-economic injustice, then, neo-liberal capitalism as a socio-economic model and as a philosophy is unhelpful in the quest to alleviate poverty in South Africa. As such, an important question that arises is: Which ideology could be a reliable basis for the formulation of the land policies and why? As much as it is pertinent to consider, at this point, an alternative socio-economic model and philosophy which, in my view could contribute to the redress of socio-economic injustice, it is probably too soon. However, the next chapter on the exegesis of Leviticus 25:8–55 as well as the one after it which focuses on an African liberationist reading is critical in formulating a clear socio-economic model for land redistribution and socio-economic redress. At this point, it is important to continue the discussion of land redistribution and the redress of socio-economic injustice.

Does Possession of Agricultural Land Guarantee Poverty Alleviation? Empowering the Poor with Assets, Finance and Skills

In his presidential address at the ANC conference of 1941, Alfred Xuma iterated that 'the fundamental basis of all wealth and power is the ownership and acquisition of freehold title to land'.[195] As such, the view that without land black people would be subjected to poverty emerged. One could sympathise with the view, but one is also sceptical to suggest that possession of land by itself would adequately redress socio-economic injustice in terms of alleviating poverty. In the present chapter, it appears initially that the poor's possession of the land would automatically translate to poverty alleviation. However, does the possession of agricultural land guarantee socio-economic redress in terms of poverty alleviation? Further, in light of the present state of climate change in which the weather is no longer as predictable as it used to be, and in which there may even be unexpected floods or veld fires, does possessing a farm guarantee that one would escape poverty?

As previously noted, in 1977 white farmers were granted a 100 percent loan by the government as provided by the Agricultural Credit Act 28 of 1966.[196] The provision of that credit facility enabled the white farmers to use the land they had acquired productively. It is evident that the white farmers could not escape poverty simply because they had acquired land. The history of white farmers in

South Africa reveals that possession of the land does not automatically translate to poverty alleviation and wealth accumulation. Thus, redistributing the land to the poor emerging African South African farmers without the provision of capital and skills would not adequately address the scourge of poverty.

Emerging Unproductive African-South African Farmers—An Impediment to Poverty Alleviation

According to the ANC, nearly 5,000 farms comprising 4.2 million hectares have been transferred to black people, benefiting over 200,000 families with 500,000 persons.[197] In the light of the statistics that 25 million of the South African population are poor, it means that the African-South African farmers who have benefited from the present slow land redistribution process are only 2 percent of the poor.[198] Such a reality is not only perturbing but it also suggests that there is something not effective in the government's attempt to transfer land to the previously disadvantaged poor black people. Before offering possible reason(s) for the inefficiency of black farms to substantially alleviate people from poverty, a word on the percentage of unproductive African-South African farmers is pertinent at this point.

In 2010, the Minister of Rural Development and Land Reform, Gugile Nkwinti is reported to have claimed that 90 percent of farms redistributed to South Africa's black population from white farmers are not productive.[199] This claim shows that African-South African farmers have become unproductive in their use of land. In this case, the claim that two percent of African-South African farmers contribute towards poverty alleviation in the country is doubtful. Rather, it seems that if 90 percent of farms redistributed to African-South African farmers are not utilized productively, any claim that such land redistribution contributes to the redress of socio-economic injustice in alleviating poverty would be without merit. In fact, it would be misguided. Therefore, unproductive African-South African farmers are an impediment to socio-economic redress; and because of the unproductive use of the redistributed land, the South African government is losing the revenue that had accrued from the use of such farms prior to their redistribution. The government is also not retaining the funds used to purchase the redistributed land from the white farmers, because of the unproductive use of the land. Nevertheless, instead of ascribing the lack of poverty alleviation to the unproductivity of the African-South African farmers, it is proper to probe the probable causes of such unproductiveness, that is, to ask why the redistributed land is not utilised productively. This question as well as a response to it is not new in the South African discourse on land, as the observation by Vumelana Advisory Fund confirms:

> Transferred land becomes unproductive because the newly enfranchised land owners cannot raise the capital or acquire the skills needed to work the land. While much of the land has high economic potential and the newly enfranchised land owners are thus asset rich, they remain cash poor. Because of the value of the land it has investment potential but investors are loathed to take on the complexity of land reform projects. The legislation provides for the provision of grants to new land owners but these are difficult to acquire and on their own are not sufficient to make the land productive.[200]

Based on the observation above, the view that land redistribution by itself without the provision of capital and skills is an impediment to the redress of socio-economic injustice arises. It is clear that in cases where the government offers financial support (grant) to the poor emerging African-South African farmers, the grant is rather insufficient. According to clause 4.7 of the Land White Paper on South African Land Policy, the grant offered by the government is R15,000, and it is meant for the on-farm capital items, investment in internal infrastructure and fencing, among other agricultural necessities. In addition, the Provision of Land and Assistance Amendments Act of 2008, clause 10(b)(iii) provides for financial assistance by way of an advance, subsidy, grant or otherwise to any person for the acquisition, maintenance, planning, development or improvement of property and for capacity building, skills development, training and empowerment.[201] In fact, bearing in mind that in 1977, white farmers were granted a 100 percent loan by the government to enhance their productivity, the grant of R15,000 appears unjust. The challenge of inadequate transfer of skills and insufficient provision of the capital to the emerging African-South African farmers is also attested to by Cyril Ramaphosa in his interview by Justice Malala. On the issue of land, in his response to the question: 'In your (ANC) Manifesto you say we must provide a radical answer to the land question and you go on to say the ANC has such an answer. What is the radical answer?' Ramaphosa said:

> ... The people who got land through this Land Reform process were ill equipped to deal with the land and to work the land. The skills that our people used to have on working the land were lost during the forced removal phase or the land dispossession phase and we needed to embark on schemes to train them, to equip them. Many of our people did not have capital, did not have capital to buy implements, seeds and all that. It was like (you know) giving people the land without the way (with all) or without the skills and that is where we also went wrong ...[202]

Ramaphosa's response re-iterates the plan in the ANC's 2014 Election Manifesto to enhance the government's role in the area of rural development, land and agrarian reform and food security, should it win the elections. The Manifesto stipulates that the party would:

- Increase investment in agricultural infrastructure—including irrigation, storage facilities and fencing—in support of small-holder farmer development, with former homeland communal areas being a priority.
- Strengthen agricultural college education through skills development funds.

From the ANC's Election Manifesto and Ramaphosa's remarks, one gathers that there is indeed a challenge of inadequate provision of financial support to the emerging African-South African farmers. It is also clear that the lack of skills continues to impede attempts to redress socio-economic injustice. Furthermore, the ANC élites appear to have just discovered the impediment that the lack of capital and skills poses to socio-economic redress. In fact, by 2010, the DRDLR was not only aware of the impediment but it also implemented strategies to mitigate it.

Following the statement by Nkwinti that 90 percent of farms redistributed to South Africa's black population from white farmers are not productive, between 2011 and 2012, the DRDLR acquired 392,849.71 hectares of land for the purpose of land reform.[203] As part of the Recapitalisation and Development Programme, 257 farms were recapitalized and the emerging African-South African farmers were assisted to enhance their productivity.[204] In addition, twenty more farmers have been empowered through agricultural training programs between 2011 and 2012 while 3,819 beneficiaries of the Comprehensive Rural Development Programme (CRDP) obtained skills in technical development trades.[205] In addition, 464 community based institutions, comprising of 27 Councils of Stakeholders and 437 co-operatives were empowered.[206] However, one wonders whether the attempts to support African-South African farmers were sufficient to elevate them and their communities from poverty. As Shabane rightly claims, the initiative of empowering the poor is insufficient in South Africa. Nonetheless, he fails to provide a convincing solution to the problem.[207]

In addition, 10,049 employment and job opportunities were created by the National Rural Youth Services Corps (NASYSEC) programme and by the CRDP initiative between 2011 and 2012.[208] Thus, Tshatsinde supports the view that poor African-South African farmers have access to the market skills and have attained employment from the abovementioned programmes.[209] However, if one considers that 25 million African South Africans are poor, the figure of 10,049 employment and job opportunities becomes insignificant. Thus, Tshatsinde's assessment of the progress of the DRDLR, which clearly minimizes the insufficient effort of the department to provide capital and skills, is disappointing. The view that the DRDLR has satisfactorily provided skills and capital to the emerging African-South African farmers in a bid to alleviate poverty is also unconvincing.

The present section has revealed that the farms that were redistributed to the poor previously disadvantaged emerging African South Africans are mostly unproductive. The unproductive state of the farms has become an impediment to attempts at poverty alleviation. However, instead of casually blaming anyone for the unproductiveness of black emerging farmers; it might help to consider the issue of climate change as it affects farming in the South Africa.

Impact of Climate Change on Agriculture—A Challenge for Emerging African-South African Farmers

The view that climate is the main determinant of agricultural productivity has received the support of scholars in the field of agriculture.[210] Thus, it is important to investigate the impact of climate change on land redistribution, agriculture and the attempts to redress socio-economic injustice in South Africa. Since the weather is no longer as predictable as it used to be and because unexpected floods or veld fires sometimes occur, does owning a farm guarantee that one would escape poverty?

In a slight departure from Adams, Hurd, Lenhart and Leary, Hassan examines the critical nature of the climate change discourse in the South African context. He points out that domestic agriculture is the main source of food for the country's population.[211] The inference therefore is that climate change does not only affect agricultural productivity but it also affects food security. Hassan argues that if adaptation strategies to climate change are not considered, the effects of the increased temperatures and decreased rainfall on the dryland farms will be even more.[212] As such, 'the crop net revenue will fall by 1.7–5.3 percent per hectare for the whole of South Africa'.[213] The estimates and Hassan's view on changing temperature are only a projection of future possibilities. South Africa's average rainfall is presently estimated at 450 mm per year, below the expected average of 860 mm.[214] The country's climate is becoming hotter, with average minimum monthly temperature at 138°C and maximum monthly temperature at 260°C.[215] As such, reports of veld fires that are caused by unusual hot temperatures have become common in South Africa. For example, the farm of one of the ANC élites Gwede Mantashe was damaged by fire.[216] It can be stated with a level of certainty that the impact of climate change on the agricultural sector is an unbearable reality and requires fresh strategies to counter the challenge.

The effects of climate change render the discussion of adaptation interventions fundamental to the discourse of productivity of agricultural land.[217] Some of the adaptation interventions that have been suggested and tested by scholars include the diversification of crops, investments in new water management and irrigation infrastructure and the use of fertilizers.[218] Clearly, diversification of crops is important as certain crops cope in different seasons and temperatures. In a situation of scarcity of rain, it is important also that one uses an effective irrigation system. These interventions require capital, as Adams, Hurd, Lenhart and Leary confirm that 'Implementing adaptation often requires local access to financial and physical capital, technical assistance and other inputs such as water and fertilizer. Infrastructure costs are also important'.[219]

Therefore, for South Africa to mitigate the impact of climate change, the availability of funds is essential. Furthermore, Hassan in particular seems to offer a clear answer to the challenge of climate change. He highlights the access to credit, markets and necessary technology as critical tools for responding to climate changes.[220] Like Hassan, Maponya and Mpandeli explain that the access to subsidies and insurance facilities are some of the fundamental interventions used in some parts of South Africa, which in my view ought to be made accessible to all farmers.[221] Two questions further arise: Have all farmers in South Africa especially the emerging African-South African farmers successfully adapted to climate change? Is the ownership of a farm a guarantee that emerging African-South African farmers would escape poverty, that is, without adaptation interventions?

The scope of Maponya and Mpandeli's article 'Climate change and agricultural production in South Africa: impacts and adaptation options', is limited to the Limpopo Province.[222] The limited scope of the article indicates a noticeable trend in the whole of South Africa in which the land policies implemented in the Limpopo Province, for instance, could also be applicable in other provinces of the country. Using a quantitative approach to collect their data, Maponya and Mpandeli find that of the 300 farmers interviewed, seventy-four percent do not receive support to adapt to climate change.[223] Actually, 5.7 percent of the farmers received credit while 6.3 percent obtained insurance and 6.7 percent received subsidies to adapt to climate change. Therefore, if we take the Limpopo Province as a reliable and convincing projection of the whole country, the majority of the farmers in South Africa do not implement adaptation interventions as a strategy to mitigate the disastrous impact of climate change. If climate change has a negative impact on agricultural productivity, it means that many farmers are bound to be less productive. Thus, the earlier view that two percent of the African-South African farmers contribute to efforts to alleviate poverty is therefore not surprising. It is noteworthy though that Maponya and Mpandeli's significant contribution does not specifically mention the emerging African-South African farmers.

Since 90 percent of farms redistributed to South Africa's black population are not productive, it might not be far-fetched to assume that climate change is a contributing factor and in essence, a hindrance to poverty alleviation efforts. In fact, if

African-South African farmers are unproductive it means that they are probably not receiving any adaptation intervention such as adequate infrastructure (irrigation system) and sufficient subsidies or grants (not the paltry R15,000 grant). To make things worse, they do not also obtain sufficient credit facility from the South African Bank including the Land Bank especially when the good credit profile criterion is implemented by the banks. This means that if a client is applying for a loan from the bank, he or she needs to have proven that he or she can manage credit well. Since the emerging farmers have no history of lending money to farms, they are most certainly in a disadvantaged position and they would find it difficult to access adaptation interventions such as credit facilities. Therefore, the emerging African-South African farmers would most likely end up being unproductive due to the challenges posed by climate change as well as the difficulty to obtain adaptation interventions such as the capital to invest in new water management and irrigation infrastructure. Moreover, adaptation interventions are needed to educate farmers on how to diversify crops or access markets, among other things. Lastly, skills to farm under the conditions of climate change are necessary to elevate farmers from unproductive farming.

An investigation has been conducted of the impact of climate change on the South African agricultural sector particularly on black farmers. The findings show that most emerging African-South African farmers do not benefit from any adaptation strategies that mitigate the impact of climate change because they find it difficult to access adaptation interventions such as credit facilities, education and skills, as both the ANC Deputy President, Cyril Ramaphosa and the Minister of DRDLR, Nkwinti have admitted.

We have attempted to show in this section that the possession of agricultural land does not guarantee socio-economic redress in terms of poverty alleviation. Secondly, in light of the present challenges posed by climate change such as unpredictable weather and unexpected floods or veld fires, ownership of a farm does not translate into escape from poverty. The lack of productivity on the part of the emerging African-South African farmers is an impediment to poverty alleviation attempts. As such, not only are the poor becoming poorer but the South African government is also losing the revenue that had accrued from the use of such farms (agricultural land) prior to land redistribution. The funds utilised to purchase farms on behalf of disadvantaged African-South African farmers are subsequently lost as well. Lastly, the considerations of the impact of climate change as well as the adaptation interventions that the farmers ought to confirm that possession of land alone without the necessary capital, infrastructure and skills impedes the redress of socio-economic injustice. Subsequently, *possession of agricultural land does not guarantees poverty alleviation*. In fact, land redistribution should be accompanied by strategies that empower the poor to tackle the impact of climate change. Adaptation interventions should include credit facilities or subsidies that cover the costs of infrastructure as well as means to cater for the diversification of crops and animals. Furthermore, relevant irrigation systems as well as the education and transfer of skills with a view to improve excellence in farming are vital strategies that could be used to empower the poor to adapt to climate change.

However, in order to adapt to climate change, policies aimed at promoting farming need to emphasise the fundamental role of education for emerging farmers as well as the provision of capital and skills to access the market would argue.[224] As such, the policies on land in South Africa need to be re-visited, but before doing so, an exegetical reading of Leviticus 25:8–55 could help in the construction of a better policy which calls for land redistribution and the redress of socio-economic injustice.

Conclusion

The main questions we have attempted to answer in the present chapter are in three parts. Do the political élites contribute to the present disproportionate benefits from land ownership and socio-economic injustice in the country? What kind of impact do the South African land policies have on land redistribution and the perpetuation of poverty among the African South Africans? We have offered a critique of the South African political economy in the transitional and post-apartheid South Africa with reference to the political élites and the issue of land. First, the discussion examines whether the political élites contribute to the present imbalances in the area of land ownership and to socio-economic injustice in the country.

Chapter 2 also shows that the ideological clash and compromise between the ANC, SACP and COSATU in the transitional and post-apartheid South Africa impede the quest for socio-economic redress and land redistribution. A discussion of the politics of exclusion reveals alterations in the principles of democracy during the Codesa negotiations. Concerns about the minimal attempts to redistribute land and redress socio-economic injustice were ignored. What is disturbing also about South Africa's political economy is the apparent rise of a flawed capitalism. At the same time, the trend of self-enrichment by the political élites impedes attempts to redress socio-economic injustice and to redistribute land equitably among the citizens. The chapter also examines Fukuyama's theory of the 'end of history', which implies that neo-liberal capitalism is absolute and that there cannot be an alternative ideological basis for governance. As long as socio-economic injustice in terms of poverty and inequality persists, there is a need for discourse on alternative ideologies and economic policies in South Africa.

Second, the present chapter has investigated the impact of land policies on land redistribution and on poor African South Africans. Elements of neo-liberal capitalism are observed in South Africa's land policies. As such, it is argued that neo-liberal economic globalisation has influenced and continued to shape land policies in South Africa. However, land policies that are rooted in neo-liberal capitalism inhibit socio-economic justice. In particular, South Africa's land policies impede efforts to redistribute land to previously disadvantaged black people who lost it during the colonial and apartheid regimes. Moreover, the possession of land without education, skills and sufficient funds does not guarantee the redress of socio-economic injustice. Rather, it perpetuates poverty and economic inequality even among emerging African-South African farmers.

Could we then find alternative provisions from the Bible that would address the persistent socio-economic injustice and the perpetual disparities in land ownership and benefits? It is assumed in what follows that a re-reading of the Israelite Jubilee in the context of land redistribution and socio-economic justice could offer unique possibilities for the empowerment of the poor in South Africa. This assumption guides us to re-read Leviticus 25:8–55 from an African liberationist perspective in the next chapter.

Notes

1. Madipoane Masenya, "'For Better or for Worse?'—The (Christian) Bible and Africana women," *Old Testament Essays* 22, no. 1 (2009): 126–150.
2. Wilson P. T. E. Ndibongo, N. Ntloko and Ann Walton, *Ezinye Iintsomi Zamaxhosa* (Johannesburg: Varia Books, 1990), 74–75.
3. Moeletsi Mbeki, *Architects of Poverty: Why African Capitalism Needs Changing* (Johannesburg: Picador Africa, 2009), 73ff.
4. Mbeki, *Architects of Poverty*, 73.
5. Sampie J. Terreblanche, *Lost in Transformation: South Africa's Search for a New Future Since 1986* (Johannesburg: KMM Review Publishing Company, 2012), 63; cf. Mbeki, *Architects of Poverty*, 73.
6. Joseph G. Healey, "When Elephants Fight the Grass (Reeds) Gets Hurt—Swahili (Eastern and Central Africa African Proverb of the Month November, 2001)," http://www.afriprov.org/index.php/african-proverb-ofthemonth/27001proverbs/172nov2001.pdf. (Accessed August 27, 2013); Julius K. Nyerere, *Freedom and Unity: Uhuru na Umoja—A Selection from Writings and Speeches, 1952–65* (London: Oxford University Press, 1966), 323; Alfons Loogman, *Swahili Grammar and Syntax* (Pittsburgh: Duquesne University Press, 1965), 205.

7. Jo-Anne Collinge, "Launched on a Bloody Tide: Negotiating the New South Africa," in *South African Review 6: From "Red Friday" to CODESA*, eds. Glenn Moss and Ingrid Obery (Johannesburg: Raven Press, 1992), 15.
8. Lungisile Ntsebeza, "Land Redistribution in South Africa: The Property Clause Revisited," in *The Land Question in South Africa: The Challenge of Transformation and Redistribution*, eds. Lungisile Ntsebeza and Ruth Hall (Cape Town: Human Science Research Council, 2007), 115.
9. Helena Dolny and Heinz Klug, "Land Reform: Legal Support and Economic Regulation," South African Review-SARS 6 (1992): 324.
10. Terreblanche, *Lost in Transformation*, 63; Steve Weissman, "How Big Money, Washington and the IMF Trumped Mandela," http://readersupportednews.org/opinion2/292-151/20898-focus-how-big-money-washington-and-the-imf-trumped-mandela. (Accessed January 15, 2014); Jo-Ansie Van Wyk, *Cadres, Capitalists, Élites and Coalitions: The ANC, Business and Development in South Africa* (Uppsala: Nordiska Afrikainstitutet, 2009), 7, 10, 16; Naomi Klein, "Democracy Born in Chains: South Africa's Constricted Freedom," in *The shock Doctrine: The Rise of Disaster Capitalism*, ed. Naomi Klein (New York: Metropolitan Books, Henry Holt and Company, LLC, 2007), 208.
11. Van Wyk, *Cadres*, 15.
12. Terreblanche, *Lost in Transformation*, 64.
13. Terreblanche, *Lost in Transformation*, 64.
14. Terreblanche, *Lost in Transformation*, 64, 68.
15. Patrick Bond, *Elite Transition: From Apartheid to Neoliberalism in South Africa* (Pietermaritzburg: University of Natal Press, 2000), 132–133; Ruth Hall, "The Politics of Land Reform in Post-apartheid South Africa, 1990 to 2004: A Shifting Terrain of Power, Actors and Discourses," PhD diss. (Oxford: St Antony's College, Oxford University, 2011), 176–183; Marinda Weideman, "Who Shaped South Africa's Land Reform Policy?," *Politikon* 31, no. 2 (2004): 223–224.
16. Bond, *Elite Transition*, 132–133.
17. Bond, *Elite Transition*, 40–42.
18. Clem Sunter, *The World and South Africa in the 1990s* (Cape Town: Human and Rousseau (Pty) Ltd/Tafelberg Publishers, 1990), ii.
19. Bond, *Elite Transition*, 42.
20. Sunter, *World and South Africa*, 105; Collinge, "Bloody Tide," 15.
21. Bond, *Elite Transition*, 43–44.
22. Sunter, *World and South Africa*, 91–111.
23. Chantell Ilbury and Clem Sunter, *The Mind of a Fox: Scenario Planning in Action* (Cape Town: Human & Rousseau (Pty) Ltd, 2001), 123.
24. Ilbury and Sunter, *Mind of a Fox*, 138.
25. Ilbury and Sunter, *Mind of a Fox*, 12, 14, 17, 29, 64–65, 67, 116.
26. Ilbury and Sunter, *Mind of a Fox*, 16, 28, 69.
27. Ilbury and Sunter, *Mind of a Fox*, 18.
28. Ilbury and Sunter, *Mind of a Fox*, 100, 105.
29. Ilbury and Sunter, *Mind of a Fox*, 69; cf. Stephen R. Covey, *The 7 Habits of Highly Effective People: Restoring the Character Ethic* (London: Simon and Schuster, 1989), 213.

30. Ilbury and Sunter, *Mind of a Fox*, 21–22, 65–66.
31. As mentioned above, the European pressure group was one of the groups that took part in the negotiations. Unlike Terreblanche, Bond offers a clue as to the possible identity of the members of the European pressure group. The Afrikaner insurance-based conglomerate sponsored a scenario, "Platform for Investment," which is credited to Sanlam, stockbrokers Frankel Max Pollak Vinderine (headed by Sidney Frankel), accountants Ernst and Young, and the Human Sciences Research Council (HSRC, led by Schlemmer) that specialised in apartheid social engineering. See Frankel Max Pollak Vinderine Inc, Sanlam, Ernst & Young and the Human Sciences Research Council, *Platform for Investment* (Pretoria: Human Sciences Research Council, 1992); cf. Bond, *Elite Transition*, 46–47. The scenario places importance on investments and deviation from anything that threatens investor confidence such as land redistribution.
32. Ilbury and Sunter, *Mind of a Fox*, 93–95, 126.
33. Moeletsi Mbeki, "Underdevelopment in Sub-Saharan Africa: The Role of the Private Sector and Political Elites," *CATO Institute Foreign Policy Briefing* 85 (2005): 9; Patrick Bond, "Basic Infrastructure for Socio-economic Development, Environmental Protection and Geographical Desegregation: South Africa's Unmet Challenge," *Geoforum* 30, no. 1 (1999): 47–48.
34. Ilbury and Sunter, *Mind of a Fox*, 123.
35. Bond, *Elite Transition*, 44, 57.
36. Sunter, *World and South Africa*, 105.
37. Bond, *Elite Transition*, 43.
38. John K. Kwakye, *Africa's Long Road to Development: It is Not Just Economics, But Also History, Geography, Politics, and Leadership* (Accra: Frontiers Printing and Publishing Ltd, 2011), 127.
39 Noreena Hertz, *The Silent Takeover: Global Capitalism and the Death of Democracy* (London: William Heinemann, 2001), 22.
40. C. Desmond, "Overview," in *The Codesa File: Negotiating a Non-racial Democracy in South Africa*, ed. Fatima Meer (Durban: Madiba Publishers, 1993), 15.
41. Desmond, "Overview," 15.
42. Desmond, "Overview," 5.
43. Klein, "Democracy Born in Chains," 196–197.
44. Terreblanche, *Lost in Transformation*, 67; cf. Weideman, "Land Reform Policy," 219, 235.
45. Ntsebeza, "Land Redistribution," 116–117.
46. Hertz, *Silent Takeover*, 7, 19.
47. Fatima Meer, *The Codesa File: Negotiating a Non-racial Democracy in South Africa* (Durban: Madiba Publishers, 1993), 38; Congress of South African Trade Unions, *Economic Policy in COSATU: Report of COSATU Economic Policy Conference 27–29 March 1992.* (Johannesburg: COSATU, 1992), 4, 17.
48. Congress of South African Trade Unions, *Economic Policy*, 3–4, 6–7, 17–18.
49. Johannes J. Degenaar, *Marxism-Leninism and its Implications for South Africa* (Pretoria: H & R Academia (Pty) Ltd, 1982), 10; cf. Jack C. Plano and Roy Olton, *The International Relations Dictionary* (New York: Holt, Rinehart and Winston, 1969), 82.
50. Degenaar, *Marxism-Leninism*, 11.

51. Degenaar, *Marxism-Leninism*, 25.
52. Congress of South African Trade Unions, *Economic Policy*, 4.
53. Congress of South African Trade Unions, *Economic Policy*, 3–4.
54. Congress of South African Trade Unions, *Economic Policy*, 6–7, 17.
55. Congress of South African Trade Unions, *Economic Policy*, 18.
56. African National Congress, "The Freedom Charter," http://www.anc.org.za/show.php?id=72. (Accessed January 16, 2014).
57. In Marxist philosophy, the term bourgeois refers to a social class which owns the means of production such as land. To this class, the value of property and the preservation and accumulation of capital is essential, as it maintains economic supremacy in society. In addition, bourgeois refers to the wealthy stratum of the middle class, while proletariat refers to the industrial working class which possesses neither capital nor means of production. Degenaar, *Marxism-Leninism*, 12, 26–27, 30; cf. John Percy, "The Relevance of the 'Communist Manifesto' Today," *Links International Journal of Socialist Renewal* 10, no. 2 (1998): 20.
58. Degenaar, *Marxism-Leninism*, 12, 26.
59. Degenaar, *Marxism-Leninism*, 18, 26.
60. Degenaar, *Marxism-Leninism*, 26.
61. Degenaar, *Marxism-Leninism*, 27.
62. Degenaar, *Marxism-Leninism*, 27.
63. Degenaar, *Marxism-Leninism*, 30.
64. Degenaar, *Marxism-Leninism*, 27; Ruth Hall, "Transforming Rural South Africa? Taking Stock of Land Reform," in *The Land Question in South Africa: The Challenge of Transformation and Redistribution*, eds. Lungile Ntsebeza and Ruth Hall (Cape Town: Human Science Research Council, 2007), 89; Mercia Andrews, "Struggling for a Life in Dignity," in *The Land Question in South Africa: The Challenge of Transformation and Redistribution*, eds. Lungisil Ntsebeza and Ruth Hall (Cape Town: Human Science Research Council, 2007), 203.
65. Hertz, *Silent Takeover*, 29.
66. African National Congress, "The Freedom Charter," http://www.anc.org.za/show.php?id=72. (Accessed January 16, 2014).
67. Nelson Mandela, "ANC Leader Affirms Support for State Control of Industry," *Times* (London), January 26, 1990, 4; cf. Klein, "Democracy Born in Chains," 195.
68. Mandela, "ANC Leader," 4; cf. Ken Wells, "US Investment in South Africa Quickens," *Wall Street Journal* 6 (1994): 1; Klein, "Democracy Born in Chains," 195, 208–209; William M. Gumede, *Thabo Mbeki and the Battle for the Soul of the ANC* (Cape Town: Zebra Press, 2005), 89; Hein Marais, *South Africa: Limits to Change: The Political Economy of Transition* (Cape Town: University of Cape Town Press, 2001), 122.
69. Plano and Olton, *Dictionary*, 81; cf. Degenaar, *Marxism-Leninism*, 32.
70. Klein, "Democracy Born in Chains," 195; cf. Francis Fukuyama, "The End of History?" *The National Interest* 16 (1989): 3.
71. Mandela, "ANC Leader," 4; cf. Klein, "Democracy Born in Chains," 195.
72. Klein, "Democracy Born in Chains," 196.
73. Klein, "Democracy Born in Chains," 196.

74. Meer, *Codesa File*, 38.
75. Klein, "Democracy Born in Chains," 208; cf. Marais, *South Africa*, 122; Wells, "US Investment," 1.
76. Klein, "Democracy Born in Chains," 209; Gumede, *Thabo Mbeki*, 89.
77. Klein, "Democracy Born in Chains," 209; cf. Hertz, *Silent Takeover*, 21.
78. Bond, *Elite Transition*, 55–56; Klein, "Democracy Born in Chains," 200–202.
79. Klein, "Democracy Born in Chains," 203.
80. Klein, "Democracy Born in Chains," 202.
81. Klein, "Democracy Born in Chains," 203.
82. Klein, "Democracy Born in Chains," 203.
83. Klein, "Democracy Born in Chains," 203–204.
84. Klein, "Democracy Born in Chains," 213.
85. Klein, "Democracy Born in Chains," 203.
86. Klein, "Democracy Born in Chains," 204.
87. Bond, *Elite Transition*, 62.
88. Bond, *Elite Transition*, 62.
89. Bond, *Elite Transition*, 62.
90. Bond, *Elite Transition*, 62.
91. Klein, "Democracy Born in Chains," 215; Hertz, *Silent Takeover*, 8.
92. Hertz, *Silent Takeover*, 8.
93. Hertz, *Silent Takeover*, 4, 10.
94. Hertz, *Silent Takeover*, 20; Peter Riddell, *The Thatcher Era and its Legacy* (Oxford: Blackwell, 1991), 150.
95. Hertz, *Silent Takeover*, 8.
96. Klein, "Democracy Born in Chains," 195–197, 203, 208–209.
97. Fukuyama, "End of History," 3.
98. Klein, "Democracy Born in Chains," 216.
99. Klein, "Democracy Born in Chains," 216.
100. Fukuyama, "End of History," 8; Klein, "Democracy Born in Chains," 183.
101. Klein, "Democracy Born in Chains," 216.
102 It is stated that 'The passing of Marxism-Leninism first from China and then from the Soviet Union will mean its death as a living ideology of world historical significance.' See Fukuyama, "End of History," 15; cf. Hertz, *Silent Takeover*, 26.
103. Klein, "Democracy Born in Chains," 216. Fukuyama claims that, 'in Poland, Marxism-Leninism is dead as a mobilizing ideology: under its banner people cannot be made to work harder, and its adherents have lost confidence in themselves.' Cf. Fukuyama, "End of History," 15.
104. Fukuyama, "End of History," 3; cf. Klein, "Democracy Born in Chains," 182–183; Hertz, *Silent Takeover*, 9.
105. Fukuyama, "End of History," 3; Hertz, *Silent Takeover*, 27–32.
106. John Williamson, "The Washington Consensus as Policy Prescription for Development," in *Development Challenges in the 1990s: Leading Policymakers Speak from Experience*, eds. Timothy Besley and Roberto Zagha (Washington, DC: World Bank and Oxford University Press, 2004), 31–60.

107. Dennis Davis, "From the Freedom Charter to the Washington Consensus," *Development Update* 4, no. 3 (2003): 33; Hertz, *Silent Takeover*, 29.
108. Hertz, *Silent Takeover*, 28–29.
109. Hertz, *Silent Takeover*, 41.
110. Wolfensohn cited in Hertz, *Silent Takeover*, 202.
111. Hernando De Soto, *The Mystery of Capital: Why Capitalism Triumphs in the West and Fails Everywhere Else* (London: Black Swan, 2001), 40.
112. Terreblanche, *Lost in Transformation*, 67.
113. Mbeki, *Architects of Poverty*, 66.
114. Mbeki, *Architects of Poverty*, 66.
115. Mbeki, *Architects of Poverty*, 66, 157.
116. Mbeki, *Architects of Poverty*, 68.
117. Mbeki cited in Stephen Williams, "I do not See the West as Africa's Enemy," *New African* 522 (2012): 22.
118. Terreblanche, *Lost in Transformation*, 70.
119. Bond, *Elite Transition*, 28.
120. Bond, *Elite Transition*, 31–32.
121. Bond, *Elite Transition*, 31.
122. Bond, *Elite Transition*, 31.
123. Bond, *Elite Transition*, 32.
124. Bond, *Elite Transition*, 32.
125. See Lisa Steyn, "Lonmin Unlucky in BEE love," http://mg.co.za/article/2012-12-07-00-lonmin-unlucky-in-bee-love. (Accessed December 7, 2012).
126. Bond, *Elite Transition*, 33; cf. Clive Thomas, "Restructuring of the World Economy and its Implications for the Third World," in *Instability and Change in the World Economy* (eds. Arthur MacEwan and William K. Tabb, New York: Monthly Review, 1989), 335.
127. See Craig McKune and Stefaans Brümmer, "Investigators: 'Gold Fields Bribed Mbete,'" http://mg.co.za/article/2013-09-06-00-investigators-gold-fields-bribed-mbete. (Accessed September 6, 2013).
128. See Stefaans Brümmer and Craig McKune, "Tokyo Sexwale's Prints all over R10-billion Tender," http://mg.co.za/article/2012-03-23-sexwales-prints-all-over-r10bn-tender. (Accessed Mrach 12, 2012).
129. See Julius Cobbett, "Mathews Phosa's Trust in R126m RCL Foods Deal," http://www.moneyweb.co.za/moneyweb-empowerment/mathews-phosas-trust-in-r126m-rcl-foods-deal. (Accessed November 21, 2013).
130. Robert Dunnigan, Kevin Fazaeli and Jaco Spies, "Black Economic Empowerment—Difficulties and Opportunities in Making Right the Wrongs of the Past," http://faculty-course.insead.edu/dutt/emdc/projects/Sep-Oct05/Group_D.pdf. (Accessed January 20, 2014).
131. Black Economic Empowerment Commission, *Black Economic Empowerment Commission Report* (Johannesburg: Skotaville Press, 2001), 24.
132. Empowerdex, "The Effects of BEE on FDI: June 2005," http://www.empowerdex.com/Portals/5/docs/BEE%20and%20FDI%20June%202005.pdf. (Accessed January 20, 2014); cf. Empowerdex, "Appraising our Custodians of Wealth: Economic Empowerment

Ranking of South African Asset Managers 2003," http://www.empowerdex.com/Portals/5/docs/Empowerdex%20Ranking%20of%20Asset%20Managers.pdf. (Accessed on January 20, 2014).

133. Empowerdex, "Interim Progress Report and Sector Comparison 2006," http://www.empowerdex.com/Portals/5/docs/INTERIM%20PROGRESS%20 REPORT%20 AND%20SECTOR%20COMPARISON%202006.pdf. (Accessed January 20, 2014).
134. Empowerdex, "Ownership Cannot be the Only Aspect of Transformation," http://www.empowerdex.com/Portals/5/docs/Research/OwnershipEDIT.pdf. (Accessed January 20, 2014; Empowerdex, "Trailblazers 2012 Report," http://www.empowerdex.com/RESEARCH/Trailblazers/Trailblazersreport2012/tabid/560/Default.aspx. (Accessed January 20, 2014).
135. Terreblanche, *Lost in Transformation*, 67.
136. Mbeki, *Architects of Poverty*, 93; cf. Terreblanche, *Lost in Transformation*, 71.
137. World Bank, *Can Africa Claim the 21st century?*, (Washington, DC: World Bank, 2000), 1.
138. Mbeki, *Architects of Poverty*, 7, 16.
139. Moeletsi Mbeki, *Perpetuating Poverty in Sub-Saharan Africa. How African Political Elites Undermine Entrepreneurship and Economic Development* (London: International Policy Network, 2005), 3; Mbeki, *Architects of Poverty*, 9–10.
140. Mbeki, *Architects of Poverty*, 25.
141. Jacob G. Zuma, *Written Replies by President Zuma Submitted to Parliament: 30 September 2012* (Pretoria: The Presidency, Republic of South Africa, 2012), 2.
142. Zuma, *Written Replies*, 2.
143. Zuma, *Written Replies*, 2.
144. Zuma, *Written Replies*, 2; Eddie Mohoebi, *Forfeiture Unit Seizes 2 KwaZulu-Natal Farms as Department Intensifies its fight Against Fraud and Corruption* (Pretoria: DRDLR, 2011), 1–3.
145 Chris Ndaliso, "Land Fraud Case set for 2012." *The Witness*, October 3, 2011, 1.
146. Ndaliso, "Land Fraud," 1.
147. Parliament of the Republic of South Africa. *Joint Committee on Ethics and Members' Interests: Register of Members' Interest* (Cape Town: Parliament RSA, 2012), 5.
148. Andries J. Van der Walt, *The Constitutional Property Clause: A Comparative Analysis of Section 25 of the South African Constitution of 1996* (Kenwyn: Juta & CO. Ltd, 1997), 153.
149. Andries J. Van der Walt, "The Impact of the Bill of Rights on Property Law," *South African Public Law* 8, (1993): 302; Ruth Hall, "Land Restitution in South Africa: Rights, Development, and the Restrained State," *Canadian Journal of African Studies/La Revue canadienne des études africaines* 38, no. 3 (2004): 654.
150. Michael A. Yanou, *Dispossession and Access to Land in South Africa: An African Perspective* (Mankon, Bamenda: Langaa Research & Publishing Common Initiative Group, 2009), 34, 36; Gretchen Carpenter, "Internal Modifiers and Other Qualifications in Bill of Rights-some Problems of Interpretation," *SA Publiekreg* (1995): 273.
151. Matthew Chaskalson, "Stumbling Towards Section 28: Negotiations over the Protection of Property Rights in the Interim Constitution," *South African Journal on Human Rights* 11 (1995): 224; cf. Ntsebeza, "Land Redistribution," 112.
152. Van der Walt, *Constitutional Property Clause*, 18.
153. Williamson, "Washington Consensus," 31.

154. Van der Walt, *Constitutional Property Clause*, 143.
155. Van der Walt, *Constitutional Property Clause*, 146.
156. Van der Walt, *Constitutional Property Clause*, 19.
157. Hall, "Land Restitution," 654.
158. Van der Walt, *Constitutional Property Clause*, 144–145.
159. Van der Walt, *Constitutional Property Clause*, 144.
160. Weideman, "Land Reform Policy," 220–221.
161. Weideman, "Land Reform Policy," 221.
162. Weideman, "Land Reform Policy," 222.
163. Yanou, *Dispossession*, 77.
164. Yanou, *Dispossession*, 77.
165. Weideman, "Land Reform Policy," 223, 235.
166. Van der Walt, *Constitutional Property Clause*, 152; Bond, *Elite Transition*, 132–133; Yanou, *Dispossession*, 49; Africa Research Institute, "Waiting for the Green Revolution: Land Reform in South Africa," *Briefing Note* 1301 (2013): 3.
167. Yanou, *Dispossession*, 49.
168. Africa Research Institute, "Green Revolution," 2; cf. Ben Cousins, "Land Redistribution: Part of a Wider Agrarian Strategy," *Umhlaba Wethu* 15, (2012): 2.
169. Juanita M. Pienaar, "Labour Tenancy: Recent Developments in Case Law." *Stellenbosch Law Review* 9, no. 3 (1998): 311–325.
170. Department of Rural Development and Land Reform. "Green Paper on Land Reform," *Government Gazette* 34656 (2011): 11.
171. Department of Rural Development and Land Reform. "Green Paper," 11.
172. Department of Rural Development and Land Reform. "Green Paper," 11–12.
173. Weideman, "Land Reform Policy," 223.
174. Van der Walt, *Constitutional Property Clause*, 146; Yanou, *Dispossession*, 43, 47–50.
175. Van der Walt, *Constitutional Property Clause*, 146.
176. Van der Walt, *Constitutional Property Clause*, 146.
177. Yanou, *Dispossession*, 47; also see Albie Sachs, "Towards a Bill of Rights in South Africa," *South African Journal on Human Rights* 6, no. 1 (1990): 7.
178. Van der Walt, *Constitutional Property Clause*, 147.
179. Hans Binswanger, "The Political Implications of Alternative Models of Land Reform and Compensation." In *Agricultural Land Reform in South Africa: Policies, Markets and Mechanisms*, eds. Johan Van Zyl, Johann Kirsten and M. P. Binswanger (Cape Town: Oxford University Press, 1996), 139.
180. Weideman, "Land Reform Policy," 223; cf. Binswanger, "Political Implications," 139; Ben Cousins, "Introduction: Does Land and Agrarian Reform have a Future and, if so, Who will Benefit?," in *At the Crossroads: Land and Agrarian Reform in South Africa into the 21st Century: Papers from a Conference held at Alpha Training Centre, Broederstroom, Pretoria, South Africa, 26–28 July 1999*, ed. Ben Cousins (Braamfontein: Programme for Land and Agrarian Studies (PLAAS), 2000), 2; Edward Lahiff, "Land Reform in South Africa: Is it Meeting the Challenge," *Policy brief* 1 (2001): 5.
181. De Soto, *Mystery of Capital*, 45; Law Society of South Africa. "Comments by the Law Society of South Africa (LSSA) on the Green Paper on Land Reform, 2011," http://www.

lssa.org.za/upload/LSSA%20COMMENTS%20ON%20GREEN%20PAPER%20 LAND%20REFORM%20February%202012.pdf. (Accessed November 5, 2013).

182. Van der Walt, *Constitutional Property Clause*, 162.
183. Van der Walt, *Constitutional Property Clause*, 162.
184. Van der Walt, *Constitutional Property Clause*, 164.
185. Van der Walt, *Constitutional Property Clause*, 163.
186. Van der Walt, *Constitutional Property Clause*, 163.
187. Yanou, *Dispossession*, 38; cf. Aninka Claassens, "Compensation for Expropriation: The Political and Economic Parameters of Market Value Compensation," *South African Journal of Human Rights* 9, (1993): 424; Binswanger, "Political Implications," 139.
188. Claassens, "Compensation," 424; Yanou, *Dispossession*, 70.
189. Van der Walt, *Constitutional Property Clause*, 20; Cf. Yanou, *Dispossession*, 95; Bertus De Villiers, *Land Reform: Issues and Challenges. A Comparative Overview of Experiences in Zimbabwe, Namibia, South Africa and Australia* (Johannesburg: Konrad Adenaue Stiftung, 2003), 56; Binswanger, "Political Implications," 141.
190. Matthew Chaskalson, "The Problem with Property: Thoughts on the Constitutional Protection of Property in the United States and the Commonwealth," *South African Journal on Human Rights* 9 (1993): 389; Yanou, *Dispossession*, 117.
191. Weideman, "Land Reform Policy," 219.
192. Africa Research Institute, "Green Revolution," 3.
193. Africa Research Institute, "Green Revolution," 2; Jospeh Ochieno, "18 Years of Progress but ... Real Freedom Remains Elusive for Blacks in South Africa as the Structure of the Former Apartheid Economy Continues Largely Intact," *New African* 525 (2013): 36.
194. Africa Research Institute, "Green Revolution," 3.
195. Alfred Xuma, "Presidential Address. Paper Read at the ANC Conference on 14 December 1941," http://www.anc.org.za/show.php?id=9358. (Accessed January 21, 2014).
196. Claassens, "Compensation," 424; Yanou, *Dispossession*, 70.
197. African National Congress. *Election Manifesto: A Better Life for All* (Marshalltown: African National Congress, 2014), 30; cf. Statistics South Africa. *GHS Series, Volume IV, Food Security and Agriculture, 2002–2011: In-depth Analysis of the General Household Survey Data* (Pretoria: Statistics South Africa, 2012), 7.
198. Terreblanche, *Lost in Transformation*, 101.
199. BBC News, "South Africa black-owned farms 'failing'," http://news.bbc.co.uk/2/hi/africa/ 8547621.stm. (Accessed January 20, 2014); Brendan Boyle, "Massive Farm Failure in SA," Online: http://www.timeslive.co.za/local/ 2010/03/02/massive-farm-failure-in-sa. (Accessed January 20, 2014).
200. Vumelana Advisory Fund, "Making Transferred Land Productive," http://vumelana.org.za/uploads/media/Vumelana_Advisory_Fund_Prospectus.pdf. (Accessed January 20, 2014).
201. Department of Rural Development and Land Reform. *The Annual Report of the Department of Rural Development and Land Reform 2011/2012* (Pretoria: DRDLR, 2012), 7; cf. Parliament of the Republic of South Africa. *Fast Facts: First Sitting Parliament's National Assembly, 4th Parliament, 6 May 2009* (Cape Town: Parliament RSA. 2009), 3.
202. Cyril Ramaphosa, "ANC Manifesto," http://www.youtube.com/watch?v=WWehBQ91ajg. (Accessed January 14, 2014).

203. Mduduzi Shabane, "Accounting Officer's Overview," in *The Annual Report of the Department of Rural Development and Land Reform 2011/2012* (ed. Department of Rural Development and Land Reform, Pretoria: DRDLR, 2012), 13; Department of Rural Development and Land Reform. *Annual Report*, 34
204. Shabane, "Officer's Overview," 13.
205. Department of Rural Development and Land Reform. *Annual Report*, 34; Gugile Nkwinti, "Minister's Statement in Department of Rural Development and Land Reform," in *The Annual Report of the Department of Rural Development and Land Reform 2011/2012*, ed. Department of Rural Development and Land Reform (Pretoria: DRDLR, 2012), 10.
206. Nkwinti, "Minister's Statement," 10.
207. Shabane, "Officer's Overview," 12.
208. Department of Rural Development and Land Reform. *Annual Report*, 17.
209. Mmakgomo A. Tshatsinde, "Evaluation Studies Conducted 2011/12 Financial Year," in *The Annual Report of the Department of Rural Development and Land Reform 2011/2012*, ed. Department of Rural Development and Land Reform (Pretoria: DRDLR, 2012), 171.
210. Richard M. Adams, Brian H. Hurd, Stephanie Lenhart, and Neil Leary, "Effects of Global Climate Change on Agriculture: An Interpretative Review," *Climate Research* 11, no. 1 (1998): 19; Rashid M. Hassan, "Climate Change and African Agriculture," *Centre of Environment Economics and Policy in Africa, Policy Note* 21 (2006): 1; Phokele Maponya and Sylvester Mpandeli. "Climate Change and Agricultural Production in South Africa: Impacts and Adaptation Options," *Journal of Agricultural Science* 4, no. 10 (2012): 48–49.
211. Hassan, "Climate Change," 1.
212. Hassan, "Climate Change," 5.
213. Hassan, "Climate Change," 5.
214. Maponya and Mpandeli "Climate Change," 48; cf. World Bank, *Africa Rainfall and Temperature Evaluation System (ARTES)* (Washington, DC: World Bank, 2010), 1.
215. Maponya and Mpandeli "Climate Change," 48.
216. Annette Steyn, "Did Mantashe Receive Priority Treatment from DAFF?," http://www.da.org.za/newsroom.htm?action=view-news-item&id=12780. (Accessed January 23, 2014).
217. Rashid M. Hassan, "Implications of Climate Change for Agricultural Sector Performance in Africa: Policy Challenges and Research Agenda," *Journal of African Economies* 19, no. 2 Supplement (2010): 77–105; cf. Adams, Hurd, Lenhart and Leary "Global Climate Change," 19–30; James K. A. Benhin, *Climate Change and South African Agriculture: Impacts and Adaptation Options* (Vol. 21. CEEPA discussion paper, 2006), 5–13, 22, 25–39; Maponya and Mpandeli "Climate Change," 48–59.
218. Adams, Hurd, Lenhart and Leary "Global Climate Change," 22; Benhin, *Climate Change*, 9; Hassan, "Implications," 77–105; Maponya and Mpandeli "Climate Change," 48, 53.
219. Adams, Hurd, Lenhart and Leary "Global Climate Change," 25.
220. Hassan, "Implications," 77–105.
221. Maponya and Mpandeli "Climate Change," 48.
222. Maponya and Mpandeli "Climate Change," 48.
223. Maponya and Mpandeli "Climate Change," 50.
224. Hassan, "Implications," 77–105; Benhin, *Climate Change*, 10.

References

Adams, Richard M., Brian H. Hurd, Stephanie Lenhart, and Neil Leary. "Effects of Global Climate Change on Agriculture: An Interpretative Review." *Climate Research* 11, no. 1 (1998): 19–30.

Africa Research Institute. "Waiting for the Green Revolution: Land Reform in South Africa." *Briefing Note* 1301 (2013): 1–4.

African National Congress. "The Freedom Charter," http://www.anc.org.za/show.php?id= 72. (Accessed January 16, 2014).

African National Congress. *Election Manifesto: A Better Life for All.* Marshalltown: African National Congress, 2014.

Andrews, Mercia. "Struggling for a Life in Dignity." In *The Land Question in South Africa: The Challenge of Transformation and Redistribution*, edited by Lungisil Ntsebeza and Ruth Hall, 202–219, Cape Town: Human Science Research Council, 2007.

BBC News. "South Africa black-owned farms 'failing'," http://news.bbc.co.uk/2/hi/africa/8547621.stm.

Benhin, James K. A. *Climate Change and South African Agriculture: Impacts and Adaptation Options*. Vol. 21. CEEPA discussion paper, 2006.

Binswanger, Hans. "The Political Implications of Alternative Models of Land Reform and Compensation." In *Agricultural Land Reform in South Africa: Policies, Markets and Mechanisms*, edited by Johan Van Zyl, Johann Kirsten, and M. P. Binswanger, 139–146. Cape Town: Oxford University Press, 1996.

Black Economic Empowerment Commission. *Black Economic Empowerment Commission Report.* Johannesburg: Skotaville Press, 2001.

Bond, Patrick. "Basic Infrastructure for Socio-economic Development, Environmental Protection and Geographical Desegregation: South Africa's Unmet Challenge." *Geoforum* 30, no. 1 (1999): 43–59.

Bond, Patrick. *Elite Transition: From Apartheid to Neoliberalism in South Africa.* Pietermaritzburg: University of Natal Press, 2000.

Boyle, Brendan. "Massive farm failure in SA," http://www.timeslive.co.za/local/ 2010/03/02/massive-farm-failure-in-sa.Carpenter, Gretchen. "Internal Modifiers and Other Qualifications in Bill of Rights-some Problems of Interpretation." *SA Publiekreg* (1995): 260–282. Chaskalson, Matthew. "The Problem with Property: Thoughts on the Constitutional Protection of Property in the United States and the Commonwealth." *South African Journal on Human Rights* 9 (1993): 388–411.

Chaskalson, Matthew. "Stumbling Towards Section 28: Negotiations over the Protection of Property Rights in the Interim Constitution." *South African Journal on Human Rights* 11 (1995): 222–241.

Claassens, Aninka. "Compensation for Expropriation: The Political and Economic Parameters of Market Value Compensation." *South African Journal of Human Rights* 9 (1993): 422–427.

Cobbett, Julius. "Mathews Phosa's Trust in R126m RCL Foods Deal," http://www.moneyweb.co.za/moneyweb-empowerment/mathews-phosas-trust-in-r126m-rcl-foods-deal.

Collinge, Jo-Anne. "Launched on a Bloody Tide: Negotiating the New South Africa." In *South African Review 6: From "Red Friday" to CODESA*, edited by Glenn Moss and Ingrid Obery, 1–25. Johannesburg: Raven Press, 1992.

Congress of South African Trade Unions. *Economic Policy in COSATU: Report of COSATU Economic Policy Conference 27–29 March 1992.* Johannesburg: COSATU, 1992.

Cousins, Ben. "Introduction: Does Land and Agrarian Reform have a Future and, if so, Who will Benefit?." In *At the Crossroads: Land and Agrarian Reform in South Africa into the 21st Century: Papers from a Conference held at Alpha Training Centre, Broederstroom, Pretoria, South Africa, 26–28 July 1999*, edited by Ben Cousins, 2–8, Braamfontein: Programme for Land and Agrarian Studies (PLAAS), 2000.

Cousins, Ben. "Land Redistribution: Part of a Wider Agrarian Strategy." *Umhlaba Wethu* 15, (2012): 2–3.

Covey, Stephen R. *The 7 Habits of Highly Effective People: Restoring the Character Ethic.* London: Simon and Schuster, 1989.

Craig, McKune and Stefaans Brümmer, "Investigators: 'Gold Fields Bribed Mbete,'" http://mg.co.za/article/2013-09-06-00-investigators-gold-fields-bribed-mbete.

Davis, Dennis. "From the Freedom Charter to the Washington Consensus." *Development Update* 4, no. 3 (2003): 33–34.

De Soto, Hernando. *The Mystery of Capital: Why Capitalism Triumphs in the West and Fails Everywhere Else.* London: Black Swan, 2001.

De Villiers, Bertus. *Land Reform: Issues and Challenges. A Comparative Overview of Experiences in Zimbabwe, Namibia, South Africa and Australia.* Johannesburg: Konrad Adenaue Stiftung, 2003.

Degenaar, Johannes J. *Marxism-Leninism and its Implications for South Africa.* Pretoria: H & R Academia (Pty) Ltd, 1982.

Department of Rural Development and Land Reform. *The Annual Report of the Department of Rural Development and Land Reform 2011/2012.* Pretoria: DRDLR, 2012.

Desmond, C. "Overview." In *The Codesa File: Negotiating a Non-racial Democracy in South Africa*, edited by Fatima Meer, 5–16. Durban: Madiba Publishers, 1993.

Dolny, Helena and Heinz Klug. "Land Reform: Legal Support and Economic Regulation." *South African Review-SARS* 6 (1992): 322–337.

Dunnigan, Robert, Kevin Fazaeli, and Jaco Spies. "Black Economic Empowerment—Difficulties and Opportunities in Making Right the Wrongs of the Past," http://faculty-course.insead.edu/dutt/emdc/projects/Sep-Oct05/Group_D.pdf.

Empowerdex. "Appraising our Custodians of Wealth: Economic Empowerment Ranking of South African Asset Managers 2003," http://www.empowerdex.com/Portals/5/docs/Empowerdex%20Ranking%20of%20Asset%20Managers.pdf.

Empowerdex. "The Effects of BEE on FDI: June 2005," http://www.empowerdex.com/Portals/5/docs/BEE%20and%20FDI%20June%202005.pdf.

Empowerdex. "Interim Progress Report and Sector Comparison 2006," http://www.empowerdex.com/Portals/5/docs/INTERIM%20PROGRESS%20 REPORT%20AND%20SECTOR%20COMPARISON%202006.pdf.

Empowerdex. "Ownership Cannot be the Only Aspect of Transformation," http://www.empowerdex.com/Portals/5/docs/Research/OwnershipEDIT.pdf.

Empowerdex. "Trailblazers 2012 Report," http://www.empowerdex.com/ RESEARCH/Trailblazers/Trailblazersreport2012/tabid/560/Default.aspx.

Frankel Max Pollak Vinderine Inc, Sanlam, Ernst & Young and the Human Sciences Research Council. *Platform for Investment.* Pretoria: Human Sciences Research Council, 1992.

Fukuyama, Francis. "The End of History?" *The National Interest* 16 (1989): 3–18.

Gumede, William M. *Thabo Mbeki and the Battle for the Soul of the ANC.* Cape Town: Zebra Press, 2005.

Hall, Ruth. "Land Restitution in South Africa: Rights, Development, and the Restrained State." *Canadian Journal of African Studies/La Revue canadienne des études africaines* 38, no. 3 (2004): 654–671.

Hall, Ruth. "Transforming Rural South Africa? Taking Stock of Land Reform." In *The Land Question in South Africa: The Challenge of Transformation and Redistribution*, edited by Lungile Ntsebeza and Ruth Hall, 87–106. Cape Town: Human Science Research Council, 2007.

Hall, Ruth. "The Politics of Land Reform in Post-apartheid South Africa, 1990 to 2004: A Shifting Terrain of Power, Actors and Discourses." PhD diss., Oxford: St Antony's College, Oxford University, 2011.

Harrison, Roland K. *Introduction to the Old Testament.* London: Tyndale Press, 1970.

Harrison, Roland K. *Leviticus: An Introduction and Commentary.* Leicester: Inter-Varsity Press, 1980.

Hartze, Anthony George. "Theological Perspectives on Land Restoration in Leviticus 25:8–55." PhD diss., Stellenbosch: University of Stellenbosch, 2006.

Hassan, Rashid M. "Climate Change and African Agriculture." *Centre of Environment Economics and Policy in Africa, Policy Note* 21 (2006): 1–8.

Hassan, Rashid M. "Implications of Climate Change for Agricultural Sector Performance in Africa: Policy Challenges and Research Agenda." *Journal of African Economies* 19, no. 2 Supplement (2010): 77–105.

Healey, Joseph G. "When Elephants Fight the Grass (Reeds) Gets Hurt—Swahili (Eastern and Central Africa African Proverb of the Month November, 2001)," http://www.afriprov.org/index.php/african-proverb-ofthemonth/27001proverbs /172nov2001.pdf.

Hertz, Noreena. *The Silent Takeover: Global Capitalism and the Death of Democracy.* London: William Heinemann, 2001.

Ilbury, Chantell, and Clem Sunter. *The Mind of a Fox: Scenario Planning in Action.* Cape Town: Human & Rousseau (Pty) Ltd, 2001.

Klein, Naomi. "Democracy Born in Chains: South Africa's Constricted Freedom." In *The Shock Doctrine: The Rise of Disaster Capitalism*, edited by Naomi Klein, 194–217. New York: Metropolitan Books, Henry Holt and Company, LLC, 2007.

Kwakye, John K. *Africa's Long Road to Development: It is Not Just Economics, But Also History, Geography, Politics, and Leadership.* Accra: Frontiers Printing and Publishing Ltd, 2011.

Lahiff, Edward. "Land Reform in South Africa: Is it Meeting the Challenge." *Policy brief* 1 (2001): 1–6.

Law Society of South Africa. "Comments by the Law Society of South Africa (LSSA) on the Green Paper on Land Reform, 2011," http://www.lssa.org.za/upload/LSSA%20COMMENTS%20ON%20GREEN%20PAPER%20LAND%20REFORM%20February%20 2012.pdf.

Loogman, Alfons. *Swahili Grammar and Syntax.* Pittsburgh: Duquesne University Press, 1965.

Mandela, Nelson. "ANC Leader Affirms Support for State Control of Industry." *Times* (London), January 26, 1990.

Maponya, Phokele and Sylvester Mpandeli. "Climate Change and Agricultural Production in South Africa: Impacts and Adaptation Options." *Journal of Agricultural Science* 4, no. 10 (2012): 48–60.

Marais, Hein. *South Africa: Limits to Change: The Political Economy of Transition.* Cape Town: University of Cape Town Press, 2001.

Masenya, Madipoane. "'For Better or for Worse?'—The (Christian) Bible and Africana women." *Old Testament Essays* 22, no. 1 (2009): 126–150.

Mbeki, Moeletsi. "Underdevelopment in Sub-Saharan Africa: The Role of the Private Sector and Political Elites." *CATO Institute Foreign Policy Briefing* 85 (2005): 1–12.

Mbeki, Moeletsi. *Perpetuating Poverty in Sub-Saharan Africa. How African Political Elites Undermine Entrepreneurship and Economic Development.* London: International Policy Network, 2005.

Mbeki, Moeletsi. *Architects of Poverty: Why African Capitalism Needs Changing.* Johannesburg: Picador Africa, 2009.

Meer, Fatima. *The Codesa File: Negotiating a Non-racial Democracy in South Africa.* Durban: Madiba Publishers, 1993.

Mohoebi, Eddie. *Forfeiture Unit Seizes 2 KwaZulu-Natal Farms as Department Intensifies Its Fight Against Fraud and Corruption.* Pretoria: DRDLR, 2011.

Ndaliso, Chris. "Land Fraud Case set for 2012." *The Witness*, October 3, 2011, 1–3.

Ndibongo, Wilson P. T., E. N. Ntloko, and Ann Walton, *Ezinye Iintsomi Zamaxhosa.* Johannesburg: Varia Books, 1990.

Nkwinti, Gugile. "Minister's Statement in Department of Rural Development and Land Reform." In *The Annual Report of the Department of Rural Development and Land Reform 2011/2012*, edited by Department of Rural Development and Land Reform (DRDLR), 10–11, Pretoria: DRDLR, 2012.

Ntsebeza, Lungisile. "Land Redistribution in South Africa: The Property Clause Revisited." In *The Land Question in South Africa: The Challenge of Transformation and Redistribution*, edited by Lungisile Ntsebeza and Ruth Hall, 107–131, Cape Town: Human Science Research Council, 2007.

Nyerere, Julius K. *Freedom and Unity: Uhuru na Umoja—A Selection from Writings and Speeches, 1952–65.* London: Oxford University Press, 1966.

Ochieno, Jospeh. "18 Years of Progress but … Real Freedom Remains Elusive for Blacks in South Africa as the Structure of the Former Apartheid Economy Continues Largely Intact." *New African* 525 (2013): 36–61.

Parliament of the Republic of South Africa. *Joint Committee on Ethics and Members' Interests: Register of Members' Interest.* Cape Town: Parliament RSA, 2012.

Percy, John. "The Relevance of the 'Communist Manifesto' Today." *Links International Journal of Socialist Renewal* 10, no. 2 (1998): 5–28.

Pienaar, Juanita M. "Labour Tenancy: Recent Developments in Case Law." *Stellenbosch Law Review* 9, no. 3 (1998): 311–325.

Plano, Jack C., and Roy Olton. *The International Relations Dictionary.* New York: Holt, Rinehart and Winston, 1969.

Ramaphosa, Cyril. "ANC Manifesto," http://www.youtube.com/watch?v=WWehBQ91ajg.

Riddell, Peter. *The Thatcher Era and its Legacy*. Oxford: Blackwell, 1991.

Sachs, Albie. "Towards a Bill of Rights in South Africa." *South African Journal on Human Rights* 6, no. 1 (1990): 1–24.

Shabane, Mduduzi. "Accounting Officer's Overview." In *The Annual Report of the Department of Rural Development and Land Reform 2011/2012*, edited by Department of Rural Development and Land Reform, 12–14. Pretoria: DRDLR, 2012.

Statistics South Africa. *GHS Series, Volume IV, Food Security and Agriculture, 2002–2011: In-depth Analysis of the General Household Survey Data*. Pretoria: Statistics South Africa, 2012.

Stefaans, Brümmer and Craig McKune, "Tokyo Sexwale's Prints all over R10-billion Tender," http://mg.co.za/article/2012-03-23-sexwales-prints-all-over-r10bn-tender.

Steyn, Annette. "Did Mantashe Receive Priority Treatment from DAFF?" http://www.da.org.za/newsroom.htm?action=view-news-item&id=12780.

Steyn, Lisa. "Lonmin Unlucky in BEE love," http://mg.co.za/article/2012-12-07-00-lonmin-unlucky-in-bee-love.

Sunter, Clem. *The World and South Africa in the 1990s.* Cape Town: Human and Rousseau (Pty) Ltd/Tafelberg Publishers, 1990.

Terreblanche, Sampie. J. *Lost in Transformation: South Africa's Search for a New Future Since 1986.* Johannesburg: KMM Review Publishing Company, 2012.

Thomas, Clive. "Restructuring of the World Economy and its Implications for the Third World." In *Instability and Change in the World Economy*, edited by Arthur MacEwan and William K. Tabb, 335–349. New York: Monthly Review, 1989.

Tshatsinde, Mmakgomo A. "Evaluation Studies Conducted 2011/12 Financial Year." In *The Annual Report of the Department of Rural Development and Land Reform 2011/2012*, edited by Department of Rural Development and Land Reform, 169–179. Pretoria: DRDLR, 2012.

Van der Walt, Andries J. "The Impact of the Bill of Rights on Property Law." *South African Public Law* 8, (1993): 296–319.

Van der Walt, Andries J. *The Constitutional Property Clause: A Comparative Analysis of Section 25 of the South African Constitution of 1996.* Kenwyn: Juta & CO. Ltd, 1997.

Van Wyk, Jo-Ansie. *Cadres, Capitalists,* Élites *and Coalitions: The ANC, Business and Development in South Africa.* Uppsala: Nordiska Afrikainstitutet, 2009.

Vumelana Advisory Fund. "Making Transferred Land Productive," http://vumelana.org.za/uploads/media/Vumelana_Advisory_Fund_Prospectus.pdf.

Weideman, Marinda. "Who Shaped South Africa's Land Reform Policy?." *Politikon* 31, no. 2 (2004): 219–238.

Weissman, Steve. "How Big Money, Washington and the IMF Trumped Mandela," http://readersupportednews.org/opinion2/292-151/20898-focus-how-big-money-washington-and-the-imf-trumped-mandela.

Wells, Ken. "US Investment in South Africa Quickens." *Wall Street Journal* 6 (1994): 1.Williams, Stephen. "I do not See the West as Africa's Enemy." *New African* 522 (2012): 22.

Williamson, John. "The Washington Consensus as Policy Prescription for Development." In *Development Challenges in the 1990s: Leading Policymakers Speak from Experience*, edited by Timothy Besley and Roberto Zagha, 31–60. Washington, DC: World Bank and Oxford University Press, 2004.

World Bank. *Can Africa Claim the 21st Century?* Washington, DC: World Bank, 2000.

World Bank. *Africa Rainfall and Temperature Evaluation System (ARTES).* Washington, DC: World Bank, 2010.

Xuma, Alfred. "Presidential Address. Paper Read at the ANC Conference on 14 December 1941," http://www.anc.org.za/show.php?id=9358.

Yanou, Michael A. *Dispossession and Access to Land in South Africa: An African Perspective*. Mankon, Bamenda: Langaa Research & Publishing Common Initiative Group, 2009.

Zuma, Jacob G. *Written Replies by President Zuma Submitted to Parliament: 30 September 2012.* Pretoria: The Presidency, Republic of South Africa, 2012.

CHAPTER THREE

Land and Socio-Economic Policy

Analysis of the Israelite Jubilee Legislation in Leviticus 25:8–55

Introduction

The reality of the country's legacy of colonialism and apartheid in the land discourse, which seems to be entrenched by neo-liberal capitalism, is not addressed in Old Testament scholarship. It is assumed here that the analysis of Leviticus 25:8–55 could offer some insights into how socio-economic justice concerns were upheld in the Israelite Jubilee. Such insights could be tapped to empower the poor with regard to the issue of land in South Africa. Thus, an attempt will be made to reconstruct the Israelite land policy and the idea of socio-economic justice in Leviticus 25:8–55.

To relate Chapters 2 and 3 with each other, Mosala's association of the ancient text with the modern context, specifically in his reading of Micah, comes to mind. He argues that there are enough contradictions in the book of Micah that enable eyes that have been trained hermeneutically in the struggle for liberation in modern context(s) to observe the struggles of the oppressed and the exploited of the biblical communities.[1] Drawing on Mosala's hermeneutic of liberation, our reading of Leviticus 25:8–55 in the present chapter employs the tools of historical-critical method within an African liberationist paradigm which has been outlined in Chapter 1 of this study. In other words, the exegesis of the text in consideration is based on the theoretical and methodological framework of the study that has been established in Chapter 1. First, the discussion of the documentary hypothesis as well as the neo-documentary hypothesis enables us to consider various possible dates for the strata of Leviticus 25:8–55 instead of a single date. This also enables us to highlight various ideological contestations in the text in question. The Swahili proverb, *Kimya kiwapo si chema, na maneno hayafai* 'Constant silence is no good, neither is too much talk', refutes the trend of silencing the ideological voices of other people or institutions.[2]

Second, from an ideological point of view, an intertextual reading of the literary context of Leviticus 25:8–55 suggests that the focus of the Israelite Jubilee legislation on the idea that both the people and land belong to YHWH was a call to redress socio-economic injustice.

Third, eyes that have been trained hermeneutically in the struggle for liberation in the South African context would observe the critical exegetical analysis of the text of Leviticus 25:8–55 with the view to uncover the ideological contestations that underlined the Israelite Jubilee law.

Fourth, the compositional and redactional analysis of Leviticus 25:8–55 in this chapter is set to probe the strata of the text in a bid to identify the author(s) and/or redactor(s). The various strata in the text in consideration are uncovered not only to merely highlight the different voices but also to reveal the ideological contestations in Leviticus 25:8–55.

Fifth, we proceed to pose a critical question: In whose interest was the composition and the redaction of Leviticus 25:8–55? To answer this question, the world of the production of the text of Leviticus 25:8–55 is explored alongside the oppressive and liberating tendencies of the text's production in ancient Israel and the subsequent interpretations. In this attempt, we bring to the fore instances in which the text stands either in favour of or against the oppression of the addressees of the Israelite Jubilee law.

From Documentary Hypothesis to Neo-Documentary Hypothesis—Considering the Non-Documentarian Position for (South) Africa

In this section, we shall consider the current state of Pentateuchal studies. First, we shall briefly examine the history of the documentary hypothesis (DH). Second, we shall provide reasons why a non-documentary hypothesis (non-DH) could prove significant in the South African context.

Stackert points out that only few scholars namely Joel Baden, and Richard Freidman among others remain sympathetic to the Graf-Wellhausenian DH.[3]

Julius Wellhausen was responsible for the classic DH, which has dominated Pentateuch scholarship for most of the twentieth century.[4] Wellhausen was informed by Graf's assessment of the relative chronology of P.[5] In terms of the DH particularly with regard to the early oral and written sources, J is dated to 900–850 BCE in the southern Kingdom of Judah; E to around 750 BCE in the northern Kingdom of Israel; while J and E were combined between 700 and 650 BCE to form JE. The dating of D traced to 622 BCE in Jerusalem during the period of Josianic reformation described in 2 Kings 22 while P is dated hypothetically to 500 BCE during the Babylonian exile which lasted for forty-nine years while liberation occurred in the fiftieth year.[6] However, in his study *The Religion of Israel, from Its Beginnings to the Babylonian Exile* Yehezkel Kaufmann argues that the order of the sources should be J, E, P and D.[7] Schwartz also supports Kaufmann's sequence of the sources.[8] The bone of contention with Kaufmann's documentary theory also seems to be the dating of sources, as he defends the theological value of P and dates it to a much earlier period, before the exile.[9]

Recently, the so-called neo-documentary hypothesis (neo-DH), an approach, which is followed by Baden, Stackert and Schwartz, came to the fore.[10] As Stackert rightly comments, this approach modifies the DH because 'the term "neo-documentarian" serves a pragmatic purpose and, properly contextualized, emphasizes both the continuity and the discontinuity of this approach vis-à-vis previous scholarship on the documentary hypothesis'.[11] As such, it is critical that one gives attention to Baden's contribution—particularly in light of the text of Leviticus 25:8–55.

A reading of Leviticus 25:8–55, which is part of the Pentateuch, suggests that the Israelite Jubilee legislation could not have been the product of a single hand but it must have been written by different authors at different times. It may be argued that the identification of various strata, which are in dialogue and contestation with each other, is critical in probing the meaning of the content of the Pentateuch, which is a decisive factor in the analysis of Leviticus 25:8–55. However, it is important to establish the criteria for identifying the strata in Leviticus 25:8–55. Stackert explains that:

> The identification of an H stratum in Priestly texts both within and outside of Lev 17–26 has been undertaken largely on the basis of stylistic and theological criteria, oftentimes accompanied by reconstructed historical contexts for the literary production of these strata.[12]

From the statement above, one ought to investigate the stylistic features, themes and theology that are prominent in the works of the respective author(s) and redactor(s) to identify the strata in the text. Texts can thus be assigned to most likely sources such as H, P, D and E.[13] Critical to the process of assigning strata to sources is the universally accepted scholarly view that the P material is both reliable and decisive.[14] In other words, one can use the original P stratum to identify non-P strata—but as will be shown below, this is predominantly the stance of Western scholars such as Nihan and Otto, among others. This means that if a stratum does not exhibit P features, it can be viewed as non-P, and one can go on to probe whether that stratum can be identified with other authors.

In the most recent debates on the DH, Schmid has correctly noted that Baden is not a classical documentarian as Wellhausen in that he simplifies the traditional Documentarian Hypothesis by reducing it to just the four sources and one compiler.[15] This resonates with Stackert's view of Baden as a 'neo-documentarian', as shown above. Thus, the reduction of the DH to four sources and one compiler may need to be tested with the text of Leviticus 25:8–55. Furthermore, in his response to Baden's position that post-P texts exhibit neither agreement with nor even knowledge of the priestly texts on which they are purportedly based, Schmid reasons:

> Post-priestly texts, as is true for virtually all redactional additions in the Hebrew Bible, usually elaborate, correct, or modify pre-existing texts, be they priestly, or non-priestly, or both. If they were just in agreement with the priestly texts they rely on, then there would have been no need for them to have been written.[16]

In this case, Schmid makes a valid point. Why would a post-priestly author re-write a text with which he or she agrees? If one agrees with Schmid when considering the deconstruction of the DH, the repetition of words and phrases in Leviticus 25:8–55, would be a hint that a non-P author was at work who was not merely repeating past traditions, but who contextualised such traditions and material. Given the nature of redactional texts, which modify pre-existing material, instead of merely repeating them, it would be difficult to prove a post-priestly source in Leviticus 25:8–55, as would be shown below.[17] However, in the case of Leviticus 25:8–55, it would be interesting to read a text particularly from an African perspective of the contextualisation of ancient texts which suggests that the non-priestly author exhibits no trace of directly and repetitively writing P material, but tries to re-read and reuse it in a different context. Further, it is important to ask whether there are post-priestly texts that is, texts that resonate with P material in Leviticus 25:8–55 that presuppose the existence of P (have knowledge of P) and that do not follow other non-priestly texts (that is, do not oppose the P texts). If the answer is in the affirmative, then, Baden's 'neo-documentarian' view could be somewhat appealing.

Furthermore, a critical point made by Schmid, which is set against Baden, is that 'Deuteronomy includes a significant number of textual portions that belong to the exilic and Persian periods'.[18] At issue here is the historical differentiation of texts based on the problem of dating JEDP or JEPD sources; or stated differently, it is important to identify and stress the plausibility of different historical and social locations of the texts and redactional layers in the Pentateuch. That is, in terms of the stratification that will be conducted below on the deconstructed DH, the historical differentiation of texts may show that the DH is not a suitable theory for the interpretation of the Pentateuch in South Africa. This view differs from the dating of the JEDP or JEPD sources by the so-called DH by both Wellhausen and Kaufmann, respectively. The view also contradicts that of 'neo-documentarian' proponents such as Baden and Stackert.

However, before examining Stackert's view, a point of agreement between Baden and Schmid is noteworthy. While Schmid states that 'the compilation of the sources of the Pentateuch was not the last step in its composition', Baden adds that 'The documentary hypothesis does not deny that each source has a history, nor does it deny that the Pentateuch itself has a history after the compilation of the documents'.[19] Schmid appears to be sympathetic to Baden's position making it a 'significant step towards a convergence' between his view and Baden's.[20]

For his part, Stackert discusses not only the disagreements between the non-documentarians and neo-documentarians but also some of the areas of consensus. First, a noteworthy area of agreement is the 'independence of the P document prior to its compilation alongside other Pentateuchal material and the phenomenon of inner biblical exegesis[21] in at least some Pentateuchal composition'.[22] That is, both the non-documentarians and neo-documentarians make a similar point. Second, on the key principle of distinguishing innerbiblical exegetical composition from redaction, both the non-documentarians and neo-documentarians agree that a revised text may stand independent of its source.[23] Put differently, a source and a revised text may be separated and not be combined in a single document. Third, regarding the sources and revisionary text, it is generally accepted that 'H relies upon the historical myth and cultic system of P and cannot be understood apart from it'.[24] That is, H is most viewed as a supplementary text. These areas of agreement will be substantiated further and tested in the discussion of Leviticus 25:8–55 below.

On the areas of disagreement, Stackert correctly refutes the view of the non-documentarians, as he notes that neo-documentarians, for example, Schwartz, 'admit of no revision of non-priestly Pentateuchal material in H'.[25] However, this is not Stackert's main point regarding the scholarly disagreement over the DH. Rather, he focuses on 'the nature of Pentateuchal redaction and its relation to the compositional technique termed "innerbiblical exegesis"'.[26] Like Baden, Stackert argues that a single compiler is responsible for the combination of four Torah sources namely J, E, D and P.[27] It is precisely on this point that one may find the neo-DH problematic, as there are probably hints at a series of redactors in the Pentateuch. Thus, it will be shown below that a series of redactors probably represents several voices and ideological contestations in Leviticus 25:8–55 and that a non-documentarian position could be assumed.

Furthermore, for Stackert, the compiler who is active at the late stage of the formation of the Torah, merely 'makes very few insertions and does so not to advocate a particular theological agenda but solely to harmonize glaring contradictions *at the level of the narrative*'.[28] Evident contradictions may be viewed as ideological contestations. Furthermore, at the stage of the formation of the Torah there are no traces of an innerbiblical exegesis in the form of an 'interpretive revision, reuse, expansion, or application of biblical source material in subsequent biblical compositions'.[29] At issue here is the differentiation between the supplementary and non-supplementary revisions in which the innerbiblical exegetical composition is distinguished from redactional supplementation.[30] In this differentiation, H is generally located at the compositional stage where it augments pre-existing materials. Given the manner in which H supplements P, non-P and D materials, as argued below, the location of H at the innerbiblical exegetical composition stage would be difficult to reject completely. However, a point that is arguable within the neo-DH framework is the idea that 'H only supplements P, resulting in a P + H combination'.[31] Unlike Nihan, for instance, who claims that H used P and other codes especially CC and D, the neo-documentarians hold that H used only P.[32] Instead of discussing the idea that H supplements P with particular reference to Leviticus 26 as Stackert does, one would instead focus on Leviticus 25:8–55. However, before proceeding with the discussion, Schwartz's contribution to the discourse on DH is noteworthy.

On the DH particularly the J, E, P and D sources, Schwartz considers them to have been composed as continuous narrative documents independently of each other—with the exception of D which draws from E.[33] Ultimately, the documents were combined into the Torah-Book. No doubt, Schwartz's point is confirmed by both Baden and Stackert, first, in that the ultimate redactor was mainly a combiner of sources. In fact, both Baden and Stackert follow Schwartz's lead. Second, Schwartz argues that H supplemented P, a point which is corroborated by both Baden and Stackert.[34] In this case, the productivity of the land, that is, the fertility or the bountifulness of the land is consequent to the avoidance of criminal actions and sexual offense a motif typical of P.[35] That H built on P's theme of impurity in the sanctuary, which H appropriated in the discourse of land, is a trend noticeable in Leviticus 25:8–55. Thus, in this case, the argument of the neo-documentarians would be attractive. However, the sequence of the sources in the DH is J, E, P and

D—besides the disproved existence of JE—is a point which is partly accepted by non-documentarians such as Otto. For Otto, the dating of both P and D is debatable, and he comments on the collapse of the DH thus:

> From Julius Wellhausen on there always remained one problem, which W. M. L. De Wette could solve but not Julius Wellhausen and Abraham Kuenen and the myriad of their followers in the 20th century, and which at the end was responsible for the break-down of one hundred years of Wellhausen documentary hypothesis: 'If the Priestly Code (P; Genesis 1–Leviticus 16) was later than the book of Deuteronomy (D), why do we not find P in D, as we find it in Genesis and Exodus, and supplements of P (PS) in Leviticus, even if some try to find P in three or four verses in Deuteronomy 1 and Deuteronomy 34?'[36]

Furthermore, apart from the questionable dating of P and D, Otto argues that 'The next point which needed revision was the position of Deuteronomy in the literary history of the Deuteronomistic History by the insight that there was already a pre-exilic Deuteronomistic History in 1 Samuel 1:1–2 Kings 23:25'.[37] The neo-documentarians would find it difficult to locate D in the pre-exilic period as it is the case with J and E.

Several scholars such as Schmid, Römer and Carr, among others, support the rejection of the DH on the grounds that first, restricting the dating of sources to a given period is problematic.[38] In other words restricting J to around 900–850 BCE; E to around 750 BCE; combination JE to between 700 and 650 BCE; D to around 622 BCE; and P to around 500 BCE is problematic, for reasons that will be discussed below. Second, the idea that a single compiler is responsible for the combination of four Torah sources namely J, E, D and P is difficult to accept particularly when there are apparent hints that a series of redactors must have had a hand in the Pentateuch (cf. Lev 25:8–55). Third, reducing the work of a redactor to just that of compiling and refuting the nature of redactional texts which is that of modifying pre-existing material is also problematic.[39] As indicated above, this section set out to engage briefly with the history of the DH, and given one's social location—South Africa—the reasons for identifying with the non-DH are worth exploring.

A number of South African biblical scholars, have argued that the use of indigenous narratives, idioms and proverbs as a point of reference in interpreting ancient texts resonates with the reading of the Bible in Africa.[40] As such, some Swahili proverbs come to mind. Swahili is an African indigenous language spoken in Tanzania, Kenya, Democratic Republic of Congo, Uganda, Rwanda, and Burundi as well as in parts of Somalia, Zambia, Malawi, Mozambique and the Comoro Islands.[41] The proverb *Kimya kiwapo si chema, na maneno hayafai*

'Constant silence is no good, neither is too much talk' refutes the trend of silencing others or the ideological positions of others.[42] The proverb problematises the constant silencing of certain voices in a way that resonates with the DH's silencing of other different voices by restricting the dating of sources to a given period. The DH's position is set against the view that P is noticeable in the pre-exilic period, for instance. The implication when read from the African point of view is that the ideological position of P in the pre-exilic period would be silenced by the rejection of the pre-exilic dating of P in the neo-DH framework.

In view of the African Swahili proverb above, the challenge with the neo-DH would be that it assigned sources to times or periods suggesting that only a certain source could be found in a given period. Thus, the act of silencing of some sources is inevitable. Against the neo-DH position on dating sources, the deconstruction of the documentary theory, that is, the non-DH presents competing and contradicting voices in a given period instead of silencing them. Such contradictions not only presuppose that there could not have been a singular source or author in a certain period but also provide clues about the existence of ideological contestations among the sources. In other words, as the neo-documentarians have allocated only J + E to the pre-exilic period, the non-documentarians would identify features in the same period that are not necessarily of a J + E hand, as will be argued below. Thus, one may argue that there are several sources in one period. As such, the tenor of not silencing other voices which underlies the proverb *Kimya kiwapo si chema, na maneno hayafai* could come in handy here. In view of one's social location in the South African context, one which is diverse, it would be difficult to support a theory which first, argues for a single author and compiler in a given period and second which refutes the possibility of different competing voices. South Africa has a history in which colonialism and apartheid silenced certain voices. That historical reality prompts one to identify with a theory that acknowledges and embraces competing voices and sources, instead of a hypothesis, which argues for a single voice.

Kalugila and Lodhi also document an interesting proverb *Apendaye kudhulumu, hujidhulumu mwenyewe*, 'One who enjoys oppressing others oppresses himself'.[43] The tenor of the proverb is that the oppression of others is often not helpful as it could be problematic for the oppressor as well. Given the history of oppression in the form of colonialism and apartheid in Africa, an African would be hesitant to accept a hypothesis, which seems to oppress certain voices, as the DH apparently does. In terms of the South African context, Gerald West's view is noteworthy. He argues that:

> The Bible is a collection of ancient texts, each produced in particular socio-historical contexts, and the task of biblical scholarship is 'to hear' the distinctive, ancient voice

> of the text within its own socio-historical context. Before the text can be brought into dialogue with the context, it must be given its own voice. This is done by locating the text historically, using historical-critical tools, and then situating the historical text sociologically, within a particular social context, using sociological tools ...[44]

In view of the fact that contextual interpretation—be it of a modern or biblical context—is embraced in South Africa, the reduction of the work of a Pentateuchal redactor to just that of compilation is problematic. Equally, the rejection of the nature of redactional texts namely the modification of pre-existing material is unconvincing. The nature of redaction, which could be viewed as the contextualisation of pre-existing material, resonates with the ideals of an aspect of South African biblical scholarship, which is the contextualisation of the ancient text in a contemporary context. Thus, it would be reasonable to support the non-DH, as it is set against the neo-DH which reduces the work of reduction to a mere compilation or merger of sources. On Leviticus 25:8–55, the possibility that H as well as the Pentateuch redactor re-read pre-existing material to suit their context, that is, the post-exilic Yehud context would be an interesting probe.

Against both the DH and the neo-DH, the consideration of the non-documentarian position in Pentateuchal studies will be tested through the exegetical study of Leviticus 25:8–55. The move is based solely on the fact that one would choose to highlight other ideological contestations in Leviticus 25:8–55, which could be dated to one period. As such, we now focus on the relationship of Leviticus 25:8–55 to other texts in the Pentateuch.

Intertextual Reading of the Literary Context of Leviticus 25:8–55

To begin, it is worth noting that the text of Leviticus 25:8–55 forms a unity with some of the neighbouring texts. The interconnectedness reminds one of the isiXhosa proverb *Intaka yakha ngoboya benye*, 'A bird builds its nest with the feathers of other birds'.[45] The proverb which opposes individuality and isolation upholds the value of interconnectedness of people, ideas and the cosmology. In the context of scientific research, the proverb would also imply that one's view is connected to the ideas of other scholars. With this proverb in mind, one would consider an intertextual reading of Leviticus 25:8–55 important in the South African context where the theme of interconnectedness is valued. Leviticus 25:8–55 is not an isolated text as it is situated within the so-called 'Holiness Code' (Chapters 17–26) which form the last section in the book of Leviticus. Interestingly, Nihan includes Chapter 27 in this section for reasons, which will be discussed later.[46] Since Leviticus 25:8–55 is part of the

'Holiness Code', it is then critical to probe the intertextual relationship of this text to the surrounding texts (cf. Lev 25:1–7 and Lev 26) as well as to Leviticus 17–27.

On the relation of Leviticus 25:1–7, that is, the Sabbatical Year to the Israelite Jubilee, Nihan remarks:

> Two decisive arguments, in my opinion, are, first, the instruction of v.20–22 which, (a) that the Jubilee falls on the seventh year, and (b) that there is only *one* year without sowing, and not two as would be expected if the seventh Sabbatical Year and the Jubilee were distinct; second, the math of Lev 23:15–16, according to which the interval of *seven* weeks from the day after the Sabbath to the day after the seventh Sabbath is identified as 'fifty days'.[47]

It is difficult to dispute the arguments in the above statement, as the numeral ordinal שְׁבִיעִת 'seven' clearly links vv.1–7 with vv.8–55. In vv.2–7, first, the idea that the seventh year was exclusively set for the rest of the land is borrowed from the CC (Ex 23:10–11), and second, it is refreshed in the Israelite Jubilee by H with the idea that the land is consecrated mainly because it exclusively belongs to YHWH (cf. vv.23–24). Thus, one may agree with Nihan that the idea of seven years of the Sabbatical Year is supplemented in the Israelite Jubilee.[48] Furthermore, the location of the Sabbatical Year (Lev 25:1–7) just before the Israelite Jubilee (Lev 25:8–55, particularly with v.23 in mind) may reasonably be viewed as a concrete reminder that the land belongs to YHWH.[49] Moreover, in the light of the last section of Leviticus 25—the law on slavery (vv.39–55)—the Israelite Jubilee not only reflects the theme that the land belongs to YHWH but also the theme of YHWH's dominion over Israel, that is, the people belong to YHWH.

Interestingly, the intertextual relationship between Leviticus 25:1–7 and Leviticus 25:8–55 particularly v.23 illuminates the ideological position that the land belonged to YHWH. The view that Leviticus 25:8–55 was set to refute the private accumulation of wealth by the rich élites while there was persistent poverty among the poor, in my view, presupposes an ideological tension.[50] Verse 23 refers to the centralisation of land ownership and provides a clue about the ideological position, which opposed the privatisation of the land. Of significance is the point that the ideological position that the land belonged to YHWH appears to have been set to serve the interests of the poor rather than the interests of the rich Jewish élites.

It is also noteworthy that the theme of land is addressed in Leviticus 26 since several scholars agree that Chapters 25 and 26 are closely related to each other.[51] Building on Carroll's view, Meyer notes that Leviticus 26:34, 35, 53 presents the idea of an empty land which probably attracted the élites who were about to return from the Babylonian exile.[52] However, Meyer distances his recent position from the argument he made a decade ago that the close reading of Leviticus 25 and 26 alludes to the Babylonian exile returnees who sought to claim the so-called 'empty land'. Recently, he has argued that given the dating of H to the end of the fifth century the Jubilee 'probably had more to do with some genuine attempt to do something about an unjust distribution of land'.[53] However, his argument appears inconclusive as will be shown later in the discussion of the *Sitz-im-Leben* of Leviticus 25:8–55. Suffice to say, though, is that there is a clear close relationship between Chapters 25 and 26 in terms of the theme of land. If considered in close connection to each other, the idea of the 'empty land' in Leviticus 26 and the 'return of land' in Leviticus 25 would seem appealing since it would be reasonable to assume that H sought the redistribution of land to the initial owners.

Rather than being on the side of the poor, the idea of the 'empty land' in Leviticus 26 and the 'return of land' in Leviticus 25 seem to have served the interests of the rich. The view that Leviticus 26:34, 35, 53 present the idea of an empty land which probably attracted the élites who were about to return from the Babylonian exile presupposes an ideological position which was meant to serve the interests of the rich Jews.[54] Unlike the ideological position that the land belonged to YHWH, the relationship between the idea of the 'empty land' in Leviticus 26 and the 'return of land' in Leviticus 25 was created possibly to establish a situation in which the rich Jews could attain productive land in post-exilic Yehud.

For his part, Nihan argues that Leviticus 25:55 and Leviticus 26:1 are linked with a reminiscent of the Decalogue namely the reference to the exodus which is also reflected in Exodus 20:2 and Deuteronomy 5:6.[55] Both Leviticus 25:55 and Exodus 20:2 refer to being brought out of Egypt while the negative command used to prohibit the Israelites from worshipping idols in Leviticus 26:1 is in a Decalogue formula. In addition, both Grünwaldt and Meyer note that the fact that the Israelites are addressed as people who are already delivered from Egypt resonates with Nihan's view.[56] In my view, the theme of deliverance from Egypt, though originally P's, as will be argued below, has now been re-used by H in both Leviticus 25 and 26. Furthermore, the formula אֲנִי יְהוָה אֱלֹהֵיכֶם 'I am Yahweh, your God' connects chapters 25 and 26. As argued also with regard to the relationship between the 'Sabbatical Year' and the 'Jubilee' above, the idea of the Israelites belonging to YHWH is equally expressed in the connection between Chapters 25 and 26.

Interestingly, there is an apparent link between the opening verse of Chapter 25 and the concluding verse of Chapters 26 and 27. On the one hand, in Leviticus 25:1, Yahweh spoke to Moses at בְּהַר סִינַי 'Mount Sinai' while in Leviticus 26:46; 27:34, Yahweh gave הַתּוֹרֹת 'the Torah' to the Israelites. However, Leviticus 27:34 uses the absolute noun הַמִּצְוֹת 'the commandments'. For Schwartz, the reference to Mount Sinai, which is more critical in the preceding texts, is typical of non-P sources.[57] However, he does not mention the reason for the preceding links, which could have been the legitimisation of the place of the 'Holiness Code' within the Torah. As Nihan also correctly observes, the idea of the Torah is expressed in the early chapters of the Book of Leviticus—the statement 'this is the Torah' is evident in Leviticus 6:2, 7, 18; 7:1, 11.[58] This links the 'Holiness Code' (Leviticus 17–27) to the P material, that is, Leviticus 1–16.

On the relationship between Leviticus 25:8–55 and the rest of the 'Holiness Code', Nihan's view is noteworthy:

> The first part of H, Ch. 17–22, calls Israel to holiness and ends with two exhortations reinterpreting the exodus as a process of consecration of the people to Yahweh (Lev 20:24b–26 and further 22:33a …). The legislation on slavery in Lev 25:39–55 and, more generally, the entire law of 25:8–55 now concretely illustrate the ultimate purpose of this process for the Israelites: to become dependent workers (v.24) on Yahweh's estate, cultivating the land for him.[59]

In other words, if one agrees with Nihan's arguments, then, the intertextual reading of Leviticus 25:8–55 shows that the Israelite Jubilee law stressed the ideological position that both the people and the land belonged to YHWH in a bid to redress socio-economic injustice, as will be argued below. However, the ideological position contradicts the idea of the return to an empty land, which is expressed in the intertextual relationship between Leviticus 26 and Leviticus 25. It seems that the ideological position that both the people and the land belonged to YHWH was meant to serve the interests of the poor whilst the idea of the return to an empty land served the interests of the rich Jews who returned from the Babylonian exile.

Reconstructed Land and Socio-Economic Policy of Leviticus 25:8–55—Testing the Non-Documentarian Approach

The present section first attempts a critical exegetical analysis of the text of Leviticus 25:8–55 before outlining a possible structure of Leviticus 25:8–55. It then tries to identify the strata of Leviticus 25:8–55 and uncover the ideological contestations in the text, which is guided by the theoretical and methodological framework adopted in Chapter 1.

Possible Structure of Leviticus 25:8–55

The present outline of the structure of Leviticus 25:8–55 does not represent a conclusive meaning of the ancient text, but it aims to clarify the meaning of the text.

That is, the manner in which themes are structurally presented throws light on the meaning of the text. Thus, one may reasonably extract the meaning of Leviticus 25:8–55 from the patterns of the major themes, which are structurally articulated in the text. Nihan, for example, assumes that the reconstruction of a possible structure of Leviticus 25:8–55 is helpful in the articulation of the meaning of the Jubilee.[60] In his book *From Priestly Torah to Pentateuch: A Study in the Composition of the Book of Leviticus*, Nihan proposes the following structure for Leviticus 25:8–55:

Verse(s)	Theme
8–22	The Israelite Jubilee
23–24	Introduction of the second part of Leviticus 25
25–28	Indebted fellow Israelite who must sell a portion of his estate
29–34	The sale of a house located inside a walled town
35–38	Borrowing money to subsist
39–46	Poor Israelite sold as a slave to another Israelite
47–54	Poor Israelite sold as a slave to a wealthy non-Israelite
55	Conclusion: reminder of the exodus event and of its meaning

One could identify with the structure above as it is informed by the manner in which certain words, phrases and themes are structurally presented in Leviticus 25:5–88, which will be discussed below. However, one could also differ with Nihan, first, on the construction of themes in Leviticus 25:8–55. As an African, who is socially located within a South African context which experiences a high level of poverty and inequality as noted in Chapter 2 of this study, disagreeing with Nihan on the level of terminology would be understandable. For example, his reading of vv.35–38 as 'Borrowing money to subsist' may be viewed differently in the South African context. That is, with the challenge of poverty in mind, vv.35–38 may be read as 'Debt because of poverty'. Such a reading would not only incorporate Nihan's view but also identify with the poor African South Africans, as it highlights the challenge of poverty. However, Nihan correctly captures the theme of poverty in the unit of vv.39–46 'Poor Israelite sold as a slave to another Israelite' and vv.47–54 'Poor Israelite sold as a slave to a wealthy non-Israelite'. Thus, a reading of Nihan's structure—one which is informed by the South African social location—would identify with the references to poverty in those units.

Furthermore, the captioning of vv.23–24 as 'Introduction of the second part of Leviticus 25' appears inconclusive. Rather than combining the verses, reading them separately might prove helpful. For example, v.23 is about 'Yahweh's entitlement to the land—against the privatisation of land' while v.24, which is unique, may be viewed as the 'Provision for the payment of compensation'. The elevation of these themes, which is not evident in Nihan's analysis, may be compelling to a South African reader. This will be discussed in detail in Chapter 4.

However, it is necessary to present an alternative structure at this stage; one which is informed by the critical exegetical analysis of the text of Leviticus 25:8–55. The analysis does not only help in identifying statements and verses that are related to each other. It also assists in structuring Leviticus 25:8–55. The present discussion will focus on the recognised divergent segments or sections in Leviticus 25:8–55, which are also interrelated. In other words, the overview of the Israelite Jubilee legislation whether from a socio-economic or a theological perspective will be informed by the critical exegetical analysis of the text of Leviticus 25:8–55. Thus, the following structure is suggested for the text under consideration:

Verse(s)	Theme
8–13	Institution of the Israelite Jubilee—Land Policy
14–22	Trading of agricultural products and food security—the Israelite Jubilee
23	Yahweh's entitlement to the land—against the privatisation of land
24	Provision for the payment of compensation
25–28	Loss of land because of poverty
29–34	City property versus rural land and/or élites versus the poor
35–38	Debt because of poverty
39–46	Hard labour—slavery as a result of poverty with the Israelite as an employer
47–54	Hard labour—slavery as a result of poverty with the non-Israelite as an employer
55	Conclusion

In the light of the critical exegetical analysis of the text of Leviticus 25:8–55, one may divide the verses into two units instead of combining vv.8–22 to form one unit which Nihan names 'The Israelite Jubilee'. That is, vv.8–13 would form a unit about the 'Institution of the Israelite Jubilee—Land Policy'. In addition, vv.14–22 would form a unit about the 'Trading of agricultural products and food security—the Israelite Jubilee'. Furthermore, against Nihan's combination of vv.23–24, it makes sense not to combine the verses as they deal with two different issues namely the privatisation of land and the payment of compensation. The separation of the verses is helpful in that such issues would be highlighted independently, even though the subject of land relates vv.23–24. On the structure of the remaining verses, that is, vv.25–28; 29–34; 35–38; 39–46; 47–54 and 55, one would agree with Nihan's classification, as it is supported by the critical exegetical analysis of the text under the present investigation. As such, we now turn to a detailed discussion of the analysis.

Identifying the Strata of Leviticus 25:8–55—Uncovering Ideological Contestations

Given the intensity of research on identifying strata and sources in the Old Testament, the question of the Pentateuchal redactor(s) remains a major area of inquiry for researchers. Hence, the idea of the redactor(s) is also relevant in the study of Leviticus 25:8–55. Otto argues that any interpretation of the Holiness (H) Code in Leviticus 17–26 should take into consideration first and foremost the narrative of the synchronically read Pentateuch and its legal hermeneutics.[61] One finds that the H and Deuteronomistic (D) authors function differently in the Holiness Code, mainly because of their different historical addressees.[62] This is interesting as it would widen the interpretation of Leviticus 25:8–55 and uncover the supplementations made in the production of the Israelite Jubilee legislation. The person(s) responsible for the redaction of the Pentateuch supplemented P's Sinai pericope with Leviticus 17–26, the so-called Holiness Code.[63] This provokes the view that a third-party was involved in the supplementation which was neither P nor H. However, Otto suggests that H played a role in the formation of the Pentateuch, that is, in the redaction of the Pentateuch.[64] Furthermore, as regards H and the Pentateuchal redaction, Otto concludes:

> The diachronic analysis demonstrates that the legal hermeneutics were those of the redaction of the Pentateuch. The legal hermeneutics of the Pentateuch do not give a slightest hint that H was part of the priestly source or that there was an HR redaction between this source and the redaction of the Pentateuch, but they deliver constructive hints that H was part of a coherent concept of the redaction of the Pentateuch.[65]

It is however difficult to agree fully with Otto's claim. If Leviticus 17–26, the so-called Holiness Code, is viewed as a coherent part of the Pentateuchal redaction, then H should be identified as a redactor of the Pentateuch. By identifying H as a redactor of the Pentateuch, not only does one minimise the possibility of the integration of the strata by P, H and D in Leviticus 25:8–55 with the Pentateuch by a third or fourth party, the elevation of distinct claims and features by the traditions, that is by P, H and D, respectively, is subsequently minimised. Thus, the purpose of P, H and D become lost in Otto's view of the Pentateuchal redaction. A closer look at Otto's argument and conclusion could illustrate the point being made here.

In terms of the Pentateuchal redaction, what is more important is the Torah, which is viewed as Yahweh's decisive gift to the Israelites, rather than the land.[66] What then happened to the theme of land that appears prominent in Leviticus 25:8–55? It can be inferred that in a situation where narratives and laws are not read independently but as a whole, that is, in the context of the whole Pentateuch, a coherent interpretation of such laws would be derived. Although Otto's claim that H is part of the conceptualisation of the redaction of the Pentateuch makes sense, the challenge is that some of his theological concepts, views and formulations could be overthrown when viewed within the broader context of the Pentateuch especially because of the dominance of the Torah over the land noted above. An analysis of the strata in Leviticus 25:8–55 in terms of the distinct features and claims of the traditions (P, H and D) could help in identifying distinct addressees, themes and meanings of layers. Thus, it is possible to extract a broader and diverse meaning of the text without losing any of the voices in the interpretation process, as in Otto's view of the land and Torah.

By contrast, Stackert's view that neither H nor P should be identified as a Pentateuchal redactor is more convincing.[67] Like Stackert, Nihan rejects Otto's argument that H is the product of the Pentateuchal redactor or that he can be identified as the redactor.[68] However, it seems neither Stackert nor Nihan seriously consider Otto's views on H and the Pentateuchal redaction. Otherwise, Otto's explicit identification of H with the first edition of the Pentateuch would have emerged.[69] Nonetheless, it would be useful to determine H's reception of P in Leviticus 25:8–55 compared to that of D, as this could lead us to a decisive claim on whether H is a Pentateuchal redactor (that is, either a redactor(s) of the first edition or the final edition of the Pentateuch), as far as the Israelite Jubilee is concerned.

Stackert's comment on the interaction of H with P is noteworthy:

> In its engagement with P, H seeks to supplement and thereby to recast its Priestly forebear. The resulting product, of course, is not thoroughly consistent. It is this observation that makes the separation of P from H possible in the first place. Nevertheless, as several scholars have observed, H is thoroughly informed by and in agreement with the basic historical myth and cultic ideology of P, even in those instances in which H breaks from P.[70]

Since it is evident that H supplements P as will be shown below, it would be difficult to fault Stackert's claim. In view of the noticeable relationship between H and P as well as of the agreements shared by both sources, one can claim that there was a positive reception of P by H. If such a relationship can be demonstrated in Leviticus 25:8–55, then, the preceding claim could be sustained. Given the positive reception of P by H, the compatibility of H and P can further be noted. The fact that P is used by H, distances it (P) from being a Pentateuchal redactor. On the question of H's reception of D, in a case where there are features of both H and D in a single text specifically in a verse as will be shown below, it might be difficult to prove the improbability of the editing of D by H. In other words, we would not be able to prove that H sidestepped the inserted D feature.

Consequently, the view that H revised and supplemented D as a redactor would be sustained. However, in a case where a D text stands on its own, without any feature that suggests dependence on H, then, the presence of H in such a text cannot be postulated. Therefore, someone else other than H inserted an independent D text, which stands alongside an H text. As such, it would be implausible to postulate that H was the Pentateuchal redactor or the redactor of Leviticus 25:29. Furthermore, where H is shown to be incompatible with D, as Stackert does with Numbers 18,[71] it would be implausible to argue for a Pentateuchal redaction by H. In my view, if the absence of H in a D text can be proven, then, the possibility of a non-H redactor of the Pentateuch and of Leviticus 25:8–55 could be assumed, as will be demonstrated below.

Furthermore, in a case where D is irreconcilable with H mainly because of differing ideologies, it can imply by and large that H did not include a D feature in Leviticus 25:8–55, at least in its final form. In some instances, even if H borrowed from D, the ultimate final H text could be in contrast to a distinct D text, as Stackert has demonstrated in his analysis of Number 18.[72] This means that H could differ conspicuously from D even if H used a D text or reference. The difference could be attributed mainly to the fact that the H ideologies are mostly incompatible with those of D, thus, necessitating a drastic transformation of the D text. Unlike P, with which H often agrees, a D reference in H is often transformed instead of being supplemented, as will be illustrated below. Thus, in a case where such transformation is not evident, the insertion of D next to H would most likely be assigned to a non-H redactor.

If one can show the absence of H in D, the incompatibility of H with D as well as H's irreconcilability with D, then, it can be inferred that a non-H author was the redactor of the Pentateuch. Therefore, a Pentateuchal redactor who is not H, P nor D can be assigned to the final form of Leviticus 25:8–55. However, what do we make of instances where D is received positively by H rather than the two being irreconcilable? On this question, Meyer reckons that the argument by both Otto and Nihan that H is a systematic reception of other codes in the Pentateuch such as the Covenant Code (CC), Decalogue, P and the Deuteronomic code is difficult to dispute.[73] Consequently, Meyer finds Otto's hypothesis that H played a role in the redaction of the Pentateuch plausible.

Although Otto identifies H with the redaction of the Pentateuch, he by no means suggests that H is responsible for its final redaction. His main reason is based on the noticeable additions to the Pentateuch such as Genesis 22.[74] If that reasoning is based simply on the additions to the texts, then it bears some resemblance to Schmid's identification of the final redactor(s), which indicates that the final redactor and redactions refer to the formation of the Pentateuch in terms of the reference to the Torah and the awareness of the entire Pentateuch.[75] In fact, if it can be established that H was aware of the additions to the Pentateuch, then, the conclusion that H was responsible for the final redaction of the Pentateuch could be warranted. However, it is rather difficult to prove that claim especially in Leviticus 25:8–55 as will be illustrated below. In addition, if the activity of the Pentateuchal redactor outside the Pentateuch can be linked to H, then, the role of H in the final redaction of the Pentateuch could be proven. However, that activity has to be later than the dating of H. Linking the Pentateuchal redaction to H outside the Pentateuch is difficult particularly with regard to Leviticus 25:8–55. Therefore, I would not identify H with the final redactor(s) of the Pentateuch with reference to the Israelite Jubilee legislation.

The present section will not discuss in detail some of the thematic issues raised, for instance, the institution of the Israelite Jubilee, but it will focus rather on identifying the strata of the text under discussion or the allocation of their sources. The view that the identification of strata is critical to the meaning of the Pentateuchal texts is a decisive factor in the analysis of Leviticus 25:8–55 and this will be stressed later under the role of the *Sitz-im-Leben* in reconstructing the ancient Israelite society. The present section will also refer to specific verse(s) as 'CC', another one 'D', 'P' and so on. This is not meant to suggest that 'sources' were integrated in Lev 25, but is intended to point out that H integrated older texts and traditions in his work.

Institution of the Israelite Jubilee—Land policy (vv.8–13)

It has been argued that the noticeable repetition of numeral cardinal שֶׁבַע 'seven' in vv. 8 and 20 as well as the plural absolute numeral cardinal הַחֲמִשִּׁים 'fiftieth' in vv. 10 and 11 are typically P.[76] Gerstenberger notes the repetitive use of the number seven in the priestly texts such as in Genesis 1:1–2:4a; 17:12; Exodus 12:15ff. and Leviticus 8:33; 14:8; 16:14, 19.[77] From the biblical texts used to support his claim, one is inclined to identify with his assignment of the repetitive use of the numeral cardinal seven to P. As regards the significance of the numeral cardinal fifty, because the fiftieth year is the year that follows the forty-ninth year, which is derived by multiplying the number seven with seven, the repetition of the numeral cardinal seven by P becomes remarkable. If the ascription of the repetitive use of the numerals to P is correct, as I would maintain, vv.8–11 and v.20 then exhibit a P stylistic feature and influence. That is, even though P ends in Leviticus 16 (before the Holiness Code in Lev 17–27), there is evidence of the influence of P in Leviticus 25:8–55 particularly in cases where H supplemented P.

Furthermore, the fact that the repetition of phrases and words is characteristic of P, as some scholars maintain, supports the view that vv.8–11 display a P hand.[78] In particular, in v.9, the musical instrument the שׁוֹפָר 'horn', which signals cultic celebration, is definitely a P feature.[79] This feature points out the theological element of a fundamental cultic relationship between the Israelites and Yahweh. The assignment of the feature to P strengthens the case that v.9 belongs to a P stratum.

In v.10, the absolute nouns דְּרוֹר 'liberty'[80] and יוֹבֵל 'Jubilee' which are related to the absolute noun שְׁמִטָּה 'remission' in Deuteronomy 15:2 point to an element of the liberation of the Israelites. Bartos and Levinson's observation of the synonymous relationship between the nouns liberty, Jubilee and remission in 11QMechizedek 2:6 reveals a connection between Deuteronomy 15:2 and Leviticus 25:10.[81] However, they do not highlight the connection but merely point to the synonymous nouns in 11QMechizedek 2:6. Furthermore, they classify the noun 'Jubilee' as belonging to H and 'remission' as belonging to D.[82] If H used D, as suggested above, then v.10 confirms this point. The D noun שְׁמִטָּה 'remission' is clearly substituted by H's liberty and Jubilee in Leviticus 25:10. Therefore, v.10 exhibits both the features of H and D, because the preceding noun displays an element of H. Moreover, if the repetitive stylistic feature couched in the numeral cardinal fifty in the phrase 'the fiftieth year' is distinctly P then it is possible to assume that in v.10 one finds H, P and D at the same time. If the deduction is correct, then in v.10, H most likely used both P and D, that is, H substituted a D noun and further adopted P's numeral cardinal.

H's substitution of D's noun שְׁמִטָּה 'remission' with the word 'liberty' and 'Jubilee' in Leviticus 25:10 reveals an ideological contestation. Gerstenberger has noted that the notion of liberty mentioned in the Israelite Jubilee was supposed to be comprehensive in that it included both the return of land and the release of debt-slaves.[83] In other words, the Israelite Jubilee was meant to attain liberation for the poor in Israel not only through cancellation of debts and slavery but also through land redistribution. On this point, H contests the ideological position that the liberation of the poor could only be attained through 'remission'. Due to this conflict, the idea of the return of land is coupled with the idea of the release of debt-slaves in the Israelite Jubilee legislation. The land referred to in Leviticus 25:8–55 comprised of agricultural land (vv.18, 20 and 34) and houses (vv.29–34). It was presumed that the land that was lost or sold by the poor to the rich due primarily to their poverty and debts would be regained through the Israelite

Jubilee legislation in Leviticus 25:8–55.[84] Thus, the Israelite Jubilee can be regarded as a legislation that sought to insure and advocate socio-economic freedom for the Israelites particularly the poor class. If one considers the repetition of the negative command in vv.14 and 17, אַל־תּוֹנוּ אִישׁ אֶת־אָחִיו 'you shall not oppress one another' and of the *qal* imperfect third person masculine singular verb יָמוּךְ 'becomes poor' (vv. 25, 35 and 39), then, liberty in Leviticus 25:10 probably implied socio-economic freedom. Since the repetitions form part of the literary context of the absolute common masculine singular noun דְּרוֹר 'liberty', it can be argued that socio-economic freedom in that context was aimed at alleviating poverty and redressing economic inequality.

Regarding v.11, it could be helpful to take a closer look at P's material in view of the contention that P is probably the most reliable source that can be used to identify non-priestly strata.[85] Genesis 1:1–2:4 and Exodus 16 could be examined in this regard particularly in terms of the stratification of Leviticus 25:11 since it is widely ascribed to P by most scholars.[86] Knohl is precise in attributing Gen 1:1–2:4a to P. He observes that a Sabbath work prohibition is omitted by P, which would have been presented in Genesis 2.[87] Further, in Genesis 1:1–2:4 and Numbers 28:9–10 both of which mention Sabbath offering, no work prohibition is stipulated.

However, it is noteworthy that Stackert contends that Knohl's claim that P demanded no Sabbath work cessation and that H sought to re-elevate the honour of the Sabbath, which P had neglected.[88] In my view, the fact that P mentions work prohibitions in the festival offering (Num 28:18, 25–26; 29:1, 7, 12, 35) casts doubt on the possibility that the work prohibition in the Sabbath text emanated from H as Knohl claims. Therefore, based on the presumption that the work prohibition, which presupposes Sabbath can most likely be ascribed to P, one would also assign Leviticus 25:11 to P especially since the Israelite Jubilee formed one of the festivals in the Israelite calendar. The negative commands in the text of Leviticus 25:11, לֹא תִזְרָעוּ 'you shall neither sow'; together with; וְלֹא תִקְצְרוּ אֶת־סְפִיחֶיהָ 'nor reap that which grows of itself in it'; as well as the command וְלֹא תִבְצְרוּ אֶת־נְזִרֶיהָ 'nor gather the grapes of your untended vine' prohibit work during the Israelite Jubilee. If the work prohibition is typical of P, it then means that v.11 can be viewed as a P stratum. It is supposed here that P's work prohibition adds a theological value to the Israelite Jubilee in that the Jubilee as an institution is given a Sabbatical status and no work was to be done during that period.

According to Baden, P is regarded as being free of aetiology, which means that P does not give causes or reasons for his claims.[89] In other words, P does not present an expression with a historical or mythical explanation. Thus, verse 12 כִּי יוֹבֵל 'For it is the Jubilee' could not have belonged to the original stratum of P. In terms of the sentence-type identification in the critical exegetical analysis of the text under consideration. Leviticus 25:8–55, particularly v.12 expresses a reason. Therefore, the evidently etiological element of that verse, which is non-P, renders v.12 as not entirely P.

With reference to Exodus 21:6; 22:4, 6–7; 23:10–11, 16, 19, Baden sees the allusion to the fields as belonging to CC.[90] The combination of the particle preposition מִן 'out of', particle article הַ 'the' with the masculine singular common noun שָׂדֶה 'field' to form מִן־הַשָּׂדֶה 'out of the field' (cf. v.12) points to the motif, fields. If the observation is deemed correct, we may surmise that v.12 is not exclusively P's. However, this may not necessarily mean that v.12 belongs to the author of CC. Moreover, if one follows Baden's ascription of the field motif to CC, then v.12 displays a CC feature. Furthermore, the masculine singular absolute noun קֹדֶשׁ 'holy' (v.12) weakens the possibility of assigning v.12 to J.[91] Thus, v.12 may be assigned to H, since H supplemented P, D and CC. For Milgrom, the term 'holy' is distinctive of the priestly worldview.[92] This means that the holiness motif, which is evident in v.12, is partly typical of P. However, one is careful about ascribing the holiness motif exclusively to P without considering H since Meyer has correctly claimed that the holiness motif may also be ascribed to H, as will be shown below.

Meyer maintains that Leviticus 25:8–55 as a whole has to do with holiness.[93] Thus, the passage is viewed as an integral part of the Holiness Code. The claim that Leviticus 25:8–55 is entirely and exclusively H cannot be sustained because the holiness motif is also distinctively P, as Milgrom has rightfully noted. One could argue however that if Leviticus 25:8–55 is not an exclusive H text, then v.12 is not either. Leviticus 17–26, classified as the Holiness Code (H) appears as a distinct section within the priestly corpus.[94] This means that H is a distinctive set of writing which has been added to the priestly tradition. Meyer reiterates Milgrom and Knohl's position that H is a product of the priestly school, the so-called Holiness School, which comprises of priests who came from a later period than those who crafted the early priestly source known as P.[95] Furthermore, H exhibits features of an interaction with the earlier source, P as well as with E and D.[96] This means that it is possible (perhaps even likely) that H can be viewed, with a degree of certainty, as an inner biblical exegetical composition because it uses, supplements and augments the earlier sources. Since P is earlier than H and is consistent and decisive,[97] the question that arises is what is distinct of H?

For Collins, the noticeable absence of ethical considerations in P, which elevates the concerns about the effects that one's ethical behaviours have on other people, constitutes one of the distinct features of H.[98] In addition, H's concept of holiness is different from P's. On this point, Trevaskis in particular claims that P is distant from the concept of holiness, which gives attention to people and land whereas H relates to holiness.[99] In other words, from the holiness perspective, H is concerned about social justice issues, while P mostly focuses on rituals as will be explained below. That is, P is mostly concerned with priestly or cultic matters. Thus, it seems that H's ideological position that holiness is intrinsically linked to the issues of social justice stands in contestation with P's ideological conceptualisation of holiness as mainly concerned with priestly or cultic matters.

Trevaskis' view, which is plausible, does not only show P's disjuncture from socio-economic concerns such as people and the question of land but it also means that H broadens P's conceptualisation of holiness which focuses mainly on rituals regarding integrity and social justice issues. For instance, regarding the burnt offering in Leviticus 1:3, Trevaskis claims that behind the primary meaning of the requirement that the sacrificial victim be תָּמִים 'without defect', there is a symbolic reference to human blamelessness in the term תָּמִים 'blameless',[100] which describes the life of Noah (Gen 6:9) and of Abraham (Gen 17:1) both of whom offered burnt offerings. Perhaps in H, earlier legal collections are often modified. If that is correct, one might contend that H possibly interpreted older documents hence, the view that H must have been composed as a supplement, revision and expansion of P.[101]

In v.12, the descriptive command הִוא קֹדֶשׁ תִּהְיֶה 'it shall be holy to you' that is distinctive of P does not describe a ritual, as it typically does in P. Rather, it broadens the conceptualisation of holiness to accommodate the Israelite Jubilee, an event that called for social justice. This means that the quest for poverty alleviation and redress of economic inequality was included in the ideological foundation of the Israelite Jubilee. Thus, it is reasonable to consider v.12 as having both P and H features. In other words, v.12 has both the ideological positions of P and H on the concept of holiness, which stand in opposition to each other. In addition to Stackert and Trevaskis' view of H, Leviticus 25:12 represent an instance in which H probably used P in the re-conceptualisation of the holiness motif. Again, if one considers the noticeable field motif, which most likely belongs to CC, it can therefore be assumed that H used both CC and P to reconstruct v.12. Thus, the view that H is a later stratum in the priestly work appears convincing.[102]

On v.13 which belongs to the section on the institution of the Israelite Jubilee (vv.8–13), Römer notes that the trend of permitting people to return to their homeland resembles some of the contents of Cyrus' edict in the book of Chronicles in which Cyrus allowed the Golah community to return home.[103] This edict is helpful in stratifying v.13 since it points to a link between the book of Chronicles particularly the subject of returning to one's own possession or homeland and the possible author of a similar subject in Leviticus 25:12. In his interpretation of the Babylonian exile as a Sabbatical rest, Jonker identifies a link between two

Chronicles 36:21 and Leviticus 26:34–35, together with Leviticus 25:12.[104] The link is made possible by the use of the noun הָאָרֶץ 'the land' in the context of Cyrus' edict, an edict which liberated the Israelites (cf. 2 Chr 36:22–23). The P material therefore becomes evident with the link.[105] If the observation is correct that P reported the subject of the Golah community's return to their homeland, then v.13 exhibits the influence of P.

As Römer has noted, in the Persian period, power belonged to the priestly and scribal élites from the Babylonian exile, who in turn sought to secure productive land on their return to Yehud.[106] The protection of the rights of the Levites to land ownership in vv.32–33 supports the view that the priestly élites sought to return to secure their homeland. Even though the views discussed above (that is, those of Römer, Japhet, Jonker and Meyer) do not necessarily focus on Leviticus 25:12, an interaction with their interpretation of the typical P subject, that is, the return to the homeland, reveals that v.13 most likely belongs to P. That would mark the protection of the rights of the Levites as P's. Further, the repetitive stylistic feature of P, which is also noticeable in the repetition of יֹבֵל 'Jubilee' in vv.10, 12 and 13, points in the same direction, that is, v.13 most likely belongs to P. Thus, from an African liberationist perspective, one can detect with a level of certainty an element of injustice in the writing of the P author(s) because socio-economic inequality in terms of the land owned by the Levites and by the poor ordinary Israelites is noticeable in the P stratum.

Furthermore, the absolute noun רְכֻשׁ 'possession or property' (cf. Gen 15:14) is viewed as a typical P expression.[107] Interestingly, Leviticus 25:13 uses the noun אֲחֻזַּת 'possession or property', which bears the same meaning as the noun in Genesis 15:14. In this instance, a different word is used but with the same meaning as nouns used elsewhere in distinct P texts such as Genesis 12:5; 13:6; 1 Chronicles 29:28; 2 Chronicles 21:14 and Numbers 16:32.[108] Therefore, it could be argued that v.13 exhibits a P feature.

Trading of agricultural products and food security—The Israelite Jubilee (vv.14–22)

If the reference to the field motif in v.12 belongs to CC, as discussed above, then v.15 possibly also exhibits a CC feature. The relation of the absolute noun שָׂדֶה 'field' (v.12) to תְבוּאֹת 'fruits' (v.15) indicates a relationship between v.12 and v.15 hence the assumption that v.15 also exhibits a CC feature. However, the verse may not be influenced completely or exclusively by CC because of the reference to the Jubilee cycle years, which shows an H feature. It appears then that v.15 exhibits both features of CC and of H while in all probability H used CC, at least in this instance. If first and foremost, the field motif is understood in the context of the negative command אַל־תּוֹנוּ אִישׁ אֶת־אָחִיו 'you shall not oppress one another' (v.14) both vv.14 and 15 would become crucial. A statement against oppression in the context of agriculture indicates a rejection of socio-economic injustice. Thus, H's concern for social justice that is detectable in both vv.14 and 15 is commendable from an African liberationist point of view. Of significance is H's ideological position that holiness is linked to the issues of social justice, which opposes the oppression of the poor specifically within the agricultural community of ancient Israel.

Verses 14–17 contain a provision regarding the trading of agricultural products. Of particular interest in that passage is the ideological principle of fairness and justice, which ought to guide trading. The negative command 'therefore you shall not oppress one another' in Leviticus 25:17 points to the ideology of fairness, which should characterise trading of agricultural products. The call for fairness also denotes a call for socio-economic justice in trading agricultural products. Evidently, when fairness and justice are upheld, not only is the exploitation of the poor minimised, the winner-loser outcome in trading agricultural products is also derailed. In the Israelite Jubilee legislation, the minimisation of poverty is supported by a theological rationale in the sense that the command statement וְיָרֵאתָ מֵאֱלֹהֶיךָ 'but you shall fear your Elohim' a dependent clause is attached to the negative command 'Therefore you shall not oppress one another' (cf. v.17). Thus, the motif 'the fear of Elohim' forms a theological and ideological basis for avoiding oppression. Interestingly, this motif shares links with parts of wisdom literature such as Proverbs 1:29 which reads, 'For that they hated knowledge, and did not choose the fear of the LORD' (KJV). Furthermore, the declarative statement 'for I am the Yahweh your Elohim' כִּי אֲנִי יְהוָה אֱלֹהֵיכֶם (v.17) states the reason for fearing Elohim. The conjunction כִּי 'for' does not only link statements in v.17 but it also introduces the reason for fearing Elohim. Although the declarative statement in v.17 provides a theological justification for fearing Elohim, it also identifies Yahweh as one who opposes injustice against the poor.

Furthermore, in vv.14–17, the identification and naming of God as 'Yahweh Elohim' in v.17 contains P's understanding of God as both Yahweh and Elohim. This identification is noticeable in critical sections on the themes of trading of agricultural products (cf. Lev 25:17); debt because of poverty (cf. Lev 25:38); and hard labour in the hands of a non-Israelite employer due to poverty (cf. Lev 25:55). According to Römer, the author of Pg constructed a portrait of God known as 'Elohim' to people in general, 'El Shadday' to Abraham and his descendants, and 'Yahweh' to Moses.[109] This conclusion finds support in Genesis 17:1 and Exodus 6:3, suggesting that the naming of God in vv.17, 38 and 55 most likely belongs to P. The identification and naming of God in v.17 is significant mainly because it gives the Israelite Jubilee a religious approval. This means that the theological identification of socio-economic redress with God lends credence to Leviticus 25:8–55.

Furthermore, Collins distinctively ascribes the formula 'I am Yahweh your Elohim' to H.[110] In Leviticus 25:8–55, this formula is used as a direct address by Yahweh to the Israelites (vv. 17, 38 and 55). Although the formula 'I am Yahweh your Elohim' could be ascribed to H, it also appears to contain an element of Pg. As Römer points out, the declaration 'I am Yahweh' is dominant in priestly texts particularly in the Exodus narratives.[111] For example, Exodus 6:2–8 (specifically vv.2, 6, 7 and 8) contains a repetition of that declaration. Additionally, the fact that the declaration 'I am Yahweh' is presented in a repetitive stylistic manner, supports its ascription to Pg. Therefore, if the declaration belongs to P, its appearance in the formula 'I am Yahweh your Elohim' (vv. 17, 38 and 55) which is ascribed to H is not surprising. The second part of the formula 'your Elohim' appears to be an addition to the declaration 'I am Yahweh'. Thus, it is possible that H supplemented the P declaration in order to direct it emphatically to the Israelites. Verses 17, 38 and 55 provide evidence that H supplemented the work of P.

Furthermore, in v.17 worthy of note is the command statement that reads: וְיָרֵאתָ מֵאֱלֹהֶיךָ 'but you shall fear your Elohim'. This verse echoes the motif 'fear of Elohim' which belongs to neither P nor H which some scholars have assigned to E.[112] Unlike Schmidt, Nihan argues that the *qal* verb in וְיָרֵאתָ 'but you shall fear' is used exclusively for Elohim in the H verses in Leviticus 25:17, 36 and 43.[113] Similarly, the same verb is employed elsewhere in the Holiness Code as in Leviticus 19:14, 32, which contains a similar use of the motif 'fear of Elohim'. Nihan claims that the expression 'the fear of Elohim' is found in H. However, this claim is uncertain as the texts embedded in the Holiness Code also belong to non-H materials, that is, to P, D and CC. Since the fear of a deity is a universal concept in many religions, it would be difficult to rule out Nihan's claim completely in as much as one may also not refute the observation that the 'fear of Elohim' is noticeable in the non-H materials.

Unlike Schmidt and Nihan, Baden argues that the fear of the deity is embedded in Exodus 20 and Deuteronomy 5. While Exodus 20:12 is an E text according to the neo-documentarians and Deuteronomy 5:16 a D text, D follows up on E since E is its primary source.[114] However, rather than assigning Exodus 20:12 to E, given the argument on DH above, it would make sense to assign this text to non-P sources. On the motif of the 'fear of Elohim', he argues that in D, the giving of the law (the Decalogue) which originates from E is echoed with a particular emphasis on the fear of Elohim.[115] Thus, Baden agrees with Schmidt's claim that the motif 'fear of Elohim' has its origins in E. However, Baden further identifies the motif in a D text. In view of the presence of D elsewhere in Leviticus 25:8–55, as shown in vv.29–34, assigning the motif 'fear of Elohim' in v.17 to D would not be unmerited. Thus, I find more plausible Baden's assignment of the motif to D who borrowed from E than assigning it to H as Nihan does. If the command 'but you shall fear your Elohim' belongs to D, then, v.17 also exhibits features of D as much as those of H, as illustrated above. Furthermore, given the presence of D and H in the same v.17, the Pentateuchal redactor probably juxtaposed both D and H. The field motif under the present theme of agricultural products will be examined further below.

In his article 'From Cult to Community: The Two Halves of Leviticus', Meyer notes a movement from a narrow cultic view (P) of holiness to H's communal perspective in which the land is fundamental.[116] Meyer's observation shows the way P's narrow cultic ideological position is contested by H in favour of the ideological position of prioritising the shared ownership and use of productive land among the poor and the rich Israelites. This does not imply that Meyer does not find cultic views in H. In fact, he maintains that, in H, the cultic views are intertwined, with the land issue remaining in the background.[117] However, a question to ask is how does H address the subject of land? In conversation with Otto, Meyer points out H's trend of using the land, that is, the fields as a carrot to motivate the Israelites to lead a sound ethical life.[118] On this point, Otto remarks:

> *Wer den Geboten folgt, wird leben. Die Völker, die ihnen nicht folgen, bringen sich also um ihr Leben—das Land werde sie ausspeien.* {Those who follow the command will live. The nations who do not follow the commands are killing themselves—the land will spit them out, *own translation*}.[119]

It is difficult not to fault Otto's remark. The text of Leviticus 25:18 stipulates that וַעֲשִׂיתֶם אֶת־חֻקֹּתַי וְאֶת־מִשְׁפָּטַי תִּשְׁמְרוּ וַעֲשִׂיתֶם אֹתָם וִישַׁבְתֶּם עַל־הָאָרֶץ לָבֶטַח 'So you shall do my statutes, and keep my judgments, and do them; and you shall dwell in the land in safety'. If the law is observed, in terms of keeping the judgments and doing the statutes, then, there will be production in the land, as the conditional statement וְנָתְנָה הָאָרֶץ פִּרְיָהּ 'And the land shall yield her fruit' (v. 19) shows. Based on the above, the claim that, for the exilic D, possession of land is inseparable from obedience to the law is not surprising.[120] Although the claim is plausible, it presents v.18 as a perplexing text. If Römer is correct, it means H used D to construct v.18. Therefore, as both Meyer and Römer rightfully observe, H distinctively connects the land to the motif of ethical behaviour, an ideological position or concept of H (that is, H having used D). Thus, one can fittingly assign v.18 to H who used D. In this case, ideologically, food security in the field motif is linked to the motif of ethical behaviour in order to address the issue of poverty.

However, existing literature on the Israelite Jubilee does not clearly shed light on how land redistribution could alleviate poverty. For example, Bellinger merely states that the poor are cared for and granted a mechanism to escape poverty in the

Israelite Jubilee.[121] Although his statement is interesting, one could argue that possession of land is the first and most important step towards alleviating poverty. Only when Israelites possessed productive land could Yahweh bless the land to the point where it would yield fruits. Thus, Bellinger's interpretation of the phrase וְנָתְנָה הָאָרֶץ פִּרְיָהּ 'and the land shall yield her fruit' (v.19) as 'the land will on its own produce an abundance' is worth noting.[122] The land however blessed it may be cannot produce fruit on its own without human labour. Bellinger's interpretation would be valid if the involvement of the Israelites is highlighted in his discussion of how Yahweh enhances the productivity of land.

On the other hand, v.19 could be interpreted as Yahweh making available to the poor a critical resource which when used efficiently would alleviate poverty. That resource is the land. Subsequently, agricultural surplus and productivity become a reality, as promised by Yahweh.[123] In other words, land redistribution that is coupled with Yahweh's blessing on the land and the effective use of the land result in productivity. Productivity then alleviates poverty. As Warner rightly states, the possession of land required that the land be worked for the purpose of production.[124] Therefore, Leviticus 25:8–55 upholds productivity in order to avoid crippling the economy and thereby intensifying poverty.

It is remarkable that food security as well as increase in agricultural production is dependent on adhering to Yahweh's command and legislation in vv.18–22. The conditional statement וְנָתְנָה הָאָרֶץ פִּרְיָהּ 'And the land shall yield her fruit' (v.19) shows literary dependence on וַעֲשִׂיתֶם אֶת־חֻקֹּתַי 'So you shall do my statutes' (v.18). In addition, the conjunctive particle וְ (translated as 'so', 'and' or 'then') links the different parts of vv.18–22. The link between obedience to the command and food security shows that food security could be guaranteed through accelerated production. In other words, a just legislation leads to increase in production and subsequently to food security.

Furthermore, in view of the allusion to the fields belonging to CC as well as the connection between the absolute nouns שָׂדֶה 'field' (v.12) and תְבוּאֹת 'fruits' (v.15), v.19 most likely exhibits an H feature with a CC twist. The masculine singular construct noun that is attached to the third person feminine singular suffix פִּרְיָהּ 'her fruit' is related to the absolute nouns, field and products, and they all have to do with productivity in agricultural activity. Given the relation of the noun 'fruits' to 'field' and 'products', v.19 can fittingly be assigned to H. This verse also demonstrates an instance where H used CC. What is left in this block (vv.18–22) are vv.20 and 21, to which we now focus.

Verses 20 and 21 contain the seventh and sixth year term cycles. Below, we shall assign the six-year term of the servitude time for the slaves to CC. Without delving into the subject of slavery, it is important to consider the reference to six years in order to understand the CC material. Specifically, vv.20 and 21 mention the sixth and the seventh year cycle with reference to agricultural production. The absolute numerals, שְׁבִיעִ 'seventh' in v.20 and שִׁשִּׁי 'sixth' in v.21 indicate this point. The verses reveal an influence of the CC material. If the verses had alluded to a fifty-year term, as will be demonstrated below, they could easily be assigned to H who substituted the seventh-year term with a fifty-year term. Therefore, as vv.20 and 21 stands, it does not seem that they have been revised by H. Thus, one could assume that they exhibit a distinct CC feature, and there is no evidence of revision or redaction by H in vv.20 and 21. The inclusion of these verses is most likely made by a Pentateuchal redactor, who was neither H nor D nor P.

However, unlike in vv.20 and 21, a reference to production in v.22 displays an H feature. Thus, it is fitting to assign v.22 to H. In other words, H probably has a part in the construction of v.22, which belongs to the block of vv.18–22. Yet another proof of H's revision, supplementation and involvement is therefore evident in this block of verses. The theme of 'food security' is related to the earlier discussion on agricultural product and it will be discussed in depth below. In terms of the critical exegetical analysis of the text here under investigation, it seems fitting to highlight the two themes of 'food security' and 'agricultural products' independently, though they are related.

Yahweh's entitlement to the land—Against the privatisation of land (v.23)

First, it is proper to acknowledge Otto's contribution on v.23. He argues that Exodus 19:3b–6 is critical in understanding H's re-conceptualisation of holiness, which relates to Leviticus 25:23.[125] Concerning Exodus 19:3b–6, the reference to P's characteristic features is found in the phrase 'to generations of the Israelites' (v.3b); 'being brought out of Egypt' (v.4); 'to keeping Yahweh's covenant' (v.5); 'to the Israelites as well as the land as being Yahweh's possession' (v.5); and 'to the Israelites as a holy nation' (v.6). Similarly, vv.23, 30, 38, 42, 46, 55 of Leviticus 25 exhibit the characteristic features of H. The reason statement כִּי־לִי הָאָרֶץ 'for the land is mine' (Lev 25:23) which explains Yahweh's entitlement to the land also exhibits an H feature. Moreover, in terms of identifying the sentence type, the reason statement of v.6 exhibits an etiological feature, which is characteristic of a non-P stratum as argued above. One could reasonably deduce that v.23 is a stratum of H even though there could be a different point of view. If v.23 belongs to H, then, it is evident that H did not support the privatisation of land by which the rich took ownership of the land. Thus, H put forward the ideological position of the re-centralisation of the ownership of land to Yahweh; that is, Yahweh is presented as the only owner of the land.

Furthermore, Ross Kinsler and Gloria Kinsler view v.23 as a theological foundation for land redistribution in that God is portrayed as the only owner of the land.[126] In my view however, v.23 can be regarded not only as a theological foundation but also as an ideological contestation, which stands against the privatisation of land in favour of shared ownership of productive land. It is evident that the rationale for the Jubilee, for instance, the proclamation of liberty, was because only Yahweh owned the land. Interestingly, v.23 reads, כִּי־לִי הָאָרֶץ 'for the land is mine'. This statement of entitlement, if credited directly to Yahweh, does not only offer a reason for the Israelite Jubilee but it also opposes the permanent loss of productive land by the poor. By contrast, the construct noun אֲחֻזָּה 'possession' elsewhere refers to 'landed property' (Gen 47:11). Thus, in v.23, Yahweh is the only owner of the land, that is, the land belongs to him, while in v.24, the noun 'possession' is used, and it links the Israelites to the land. However, in v.24, the Israelites are not the owners of land. According to Genesis 47:11, they are given the land by Yahweh the sole owner of the land.

Thus, it seems that the Israelite Jubilee legislation includes both ideological and theological grounds for opposing socio-economic injustice. The Israelites could not claim property rights, lest they contravene the understanding that only Yahweh owned both productive and residential land. The conjunctive particle כִּי 'for' attached to the prepositional suffix לִי 'is mine' in the first person singular to form an interesting phrase כִּי־לִי centralised property rights and exclusively placed them in the hands of Yahweh. Since Yahweh owned the land, the poor should benefit from the wealth that accrued from the use of that land. Therefore, the centralisation of land ownership and property rights in the Israelite Jubilee is encapsulated in v.23. The people's benefit from land use seems to have been rooted in the centralisation of land ownership in which Yahweh is viewed as the owner of land.[127]

It becomes clear that the ideology of economic justice, which is implied in Leviticus 25:8–55, stemmed from the ideological position of centralisation. It is therefore not surprising that private ownership of land by individuals in Israel could not be legislated because of the centralisation of land ownership. The Israelite Jubilee legislation proscribed the permanent ownership of land by a few rich élites. As such, it enabled Israelites to benefit from the wealth generated from the use of the land whose ownership and property rights were reserved for Yahweh. Nonetheless, vv. 24 and 29 also hint at individual ownership of land. Perhaps, it is safe to submit that Yahweh was regarded as the original owner of the land and that individuals were residents in that land. This point is supported by the statement in vv. 23 and 24 that Israelites were not owners of the land. Yahweh is the only owner of the land.

According to Milgrom, the land referred to in v.23 is Canaan.[128] If that observation is correct, Römer's submission that D is featured by the reference of the Promised Land, which is typical of a Canaan material becomes more appealing.[129] Based on this typification of D, it is probable that the verse emanated from D's influence on H. Further, because allusion to the promised land is prominent in the Torah in the final redaction, the inclusion of reference to the land that is typically D is not surprising.[130] Evidence of the prominence of the theme of land in D is found in Deuteronomy 1:8; 6:10; 7:13; 8:1; 9:23; 19:8; 28:11; 31:7, 20–21, hence, the assumption that v.23 also exhibits a D feature. Given the hint of class distinction in D's ideological framework, as will be argued below, the presence of D in v.23 probably shows how the centralisation of land which placed ownership rights in the hand of Yahweh instead of the people sought to redress classism which commoditised and privatised land in favour of the rich.

Could the reference to non-Israelites in vv. 23, 35 and 47 offer a glimpse into the exilic or Assyrian context? The fact that these verses (particularly v.23) appear to be abruptly situated without a clear link to any other verse suggests that they were a later insertion. If that is the case, the verse would then best fit within the Persian period and probably come from D (this deduction is based on a synchronic point of view). The probability is supported by the interpretation of land as the land of Canaan, that is, Canaan understood as D's Promised Land.

Although v.23 exhibits both the features of H and D it is interesting that an element of P is also noticeable in the verse. Exodus 6:4 a distinct P text shows P's conception of the land in which the key construct nouns מְגֻרֵיהֶם 'sojourners' and אֶרֶץ 'the land' are used.[131] On the relation of P's conceptualisation of the land in Exodus 6:4 to Leviticus 25:8–55, Römer points out that 'P's conception of the land comes close to the idea expressed in the Holiness Code: "the land is mine; with me you are but aliens (*gerim*) and tenants"' (Lev 25:23).[132]

Beyond just pointing out that Exodus 6:4 relates to Leviticus 25:23 as Römer has done, I would argue that Leviticus 25:23 shows that H used P's conceptualisation of the land. In v.23, the reason statement כִּי־לִי הָאָרֶץ 'for the land is mine', which exhibits H features is followed by a reason statement כִּי־גֵרִים 'for you are sojourners'. In that sequence, the concepts of land and strangers are combined in the same manner as in Exodus 6:4. Although similar to Römer's analysis, Schmid correctly classifies the absolute plural noun גֵּרִים 'sojourners' as exhibiting a P feature.[133] He does so by referring to P texts, which contain nouns which are similar to those in Exodus 6:4 and Leviticus 25:23 (Gen 17:8; 23:4; 28:4; 35:27; 36:7; 37:1). If P is indeed earlier than H, it then means that the presence of a P feature in v.23 is an instance where H supplemented P. Moreover, if v.23 exhibits a D feature and if one is cautious about the view that H also used D as argued above, then, v.23 provides evidence of how H supplemented both P and D at the same time. Stated differently, it is clear that P's ideological position that land was owned by YHWH is not distant from H's position. However, in v.23, H's ideological standpoint on the centralisation of land opposes the ideological position of classism, which commoditised and privatised land in favour of the rich.

Provision for the payment of compensation (v.24)

Verse 24 reads, וּבְכֹל אֶרֶץ אֲחֻזַּתְכֶם גְּאֻלָּה תִּתְּנוּ לָאָרֶץ 'and in all the land of your possession you shall grant a redemption for the land'. As noted above particularly with regard to identifying the strata of v.13, the noun אֲחֻזַּת 'possession or property' exhibits a P feature. If this argument is sustained in v.24 based on the occurrence of the same noun in the verse, it means that v.24 contains a P element. Nonetheless, one cannot ascertain that v.24 completely and exclusively belongs to P based on that single point. Thus, it is important at this point to further engage with Knohl who identifies v.24 including the payment of redemption with H.[134] However, he does not explain how he arrives at that conclusion. Thus, Kohl fails to identify the strata of v.24. Since v.24 contains a provision for the payment of compensation, it will be helpful to see if similar provisions or themes occur elsewhere in the Pentateuch. The payment of compensation and the payment for a consequence occur frequently in the book of Deuteronomy especially in Deuteronomy 15:2, 15; 19:6; 21:22; 22:28–29; 25:11–12.[135]

To begin with, Deuteronomy 15:2 contains a reference about the release of slaves, a subject typical of D. This reference will be explained below. The release of slaves would occur because Yahweh וַיִּפְדְּךָ 'redeemed' the slaves (Deut 15:15). Therefore, the release of slaves was subject to the payment of compensation. Deuteronomy 19:6 shows how one ought to avenge the death of a friend. In this case, an individual pays for being liable for the murder of another person. Deuteronomy 21:22 also states the consequence of sins worthy of death while Deuteronomy 22:28–29 stipulates that a man must pay compensation for taking a woman forcefully before marrying her. Furthermore, there is a consequence for a woman who attacks a man's genitals in an attempt to save her husband (Deut 25:11–12). The woman's hand is to be cut off.

From the verses on the payment of compensation for the consequence of certain acts, a trend of paying for something becomes evident in the D texts. Subsequently, one can infer that the payment of compensation in Leviticus 25:24 most likely manifests D's influence on H. Knohl's identification of v.24 as H, would then become unconvincing. Furthermore, given the tendency by D to treat land as a commodity and as a private asset, the assignment of v.24 to D would be valid. Such treatment of land as a private asset is not helpful in the attempts to alleviate poverty, that is, in the plight of the poor as the rich élites often utilise assets for their self-interests. That is, the commoditizing of resources particularly of the land in the case of Leviticus 25:24 is preferred to the struggle for equitable sharing.

It is noteworthy that the ideological position detected in Leviticus 25:24, which enjoins the person who lost land to the rich as a result of poverty to pay compensation before regaining the land has received little attention in Old Testament scholarship. In the case of ancient Israel, particularly with regard to the context of Leviticus 25:8–55, poverty was both the cause and the result of the loss of land. That is, in this cycle of poverty, the loss of land as a means of production resulted in poverty. The inability to work the land due to the lack of capital and poverty also resulted in the loss of land. The redistribution of the land to the original owner, subject to the payment of compensation, sought to ensure a fair and equitable transaction.[136] In other words, a person who sold his or her land because of poverty was supposed to offer some payment to regain the land.

At first glance, the command גְּאֻלָּה תִּתְּנוּ לָאָרֶץ 'you shall grant a redemption for the land' appears to be dependent on v.23 because of the use of the feminine singular construct common noun אֶרֶץ 'land' in vv.23 and 24. However, in terms of the content of these verses, v.23 refers to Yahweh's entitlement to the land, which opposes the privatisation of land while v.24 provides for the payment of compensation on land. Verse 24 seems to be an independent command, which is related to v.23; hence, it is located after v.23, which refers to the centralisation of land ownership. The use of absolute nouns in v.24 such as לָאָרֶץ 'for the land' as well as גְּאֻלָּה 'redemption' is noteworthy. The nouns provide a point of focus for the idea of the main clause in v.24, which is the payment of compensation for the land.

Worthy of note also is the ideological position of the payment of compensation shared by P and D, which refutes H's concern for socio-economic justice. As shown above, the demand for the payment of compensation no doubt serves the interests of the rich élites who have the economic resources to pay for productive land. As such, the ideological position in v.24 contradicts the ideological position of H on the redistribution of productive land to the poor Israelites who have no resources to pay compensation for the land. Therefore, the view here is that v.24 relates to both P and D. The statement 'and in all the land of your possession' can be assigned to P while the command 'you shall grant a redemption for the land' can be taken as a D text (cf. v.24). Interestingly, the ideological standpoint of P and D on the payment of compensation for the land mentioned in v.24 opposes H's ideological position on the redistribution of productive land to the poor. In other words, the ideology of both P and D negates H's concern for socio-economic justice. Furthermore, it is important to consider how the poor lose their land mainly because of their poverty.

Loss of land because of poverty (vv.25–28)

Above, it has been argued that H broadens P's conceptualisation of holiness. In other words, H does not merely focus on Israel's cultic life but also on matters of social justice. That point highlights H's distinct concern for social justice. The block of vv.25–28 is introduced by the expression of that concern. Verse 25 includes a conditional clause כִּי־יָמוּךְ אָחִיךָ 'If your brother becomes poor'. If that clause is taken primarily as an expression of concern for social justice, it can only be fitting to assign it (v.25) to H. Furthermore, if the noun 'possession' is assigned to P, v. 25 would then fit well with P. However, the noun is used with reference to the activity of 'selling' (a possession) which most likely belongs to D. In that case one could argue that v.25 וּמָכַר מֵאֲחֻזָּתוֹ 'and has sold some of his possession' exhibits features of both P and D. Furthermore, the last two conditional statements in v.25 are most likely from D and as noted above, references to the payment of redemption or to compensation belong to D. Thus, one can reliably accept the *qal* perfect verb גָּאַל 'to redeem' (v.25) as typically D, and v.25 as manifesting H, P and D features.

Based on the above conclusion that P does not provide causes or reasons for something, one can eliminate v.26 from P. The other option is to assign the verse to either H or D. The presence of the *qal* verb גָּאַל 'to redeem' would therefore point us in the direction of D. However, what further complicates the assignment of v.26 to a particular stratum is the style of repeating words and phrases which is distinctly P and also noticeable in the verse. The verb 'to redeem' is repeated in both vv.26 and 25. The dilemma perhaps hints at the presence of a different writer who was most likely familiar with P and D, that is, H.

By ascribing the repetitive use of the numerals to P above, v.27 could also then be assigned to P. The reference to the counting of years in the fifty-year term of Jubilee, which is a P feature becomes conspicuous. Additionally, the purpose statement וְשָׁב לַאֲחֻזָּתוֹ 'that he may return to his possession' (v.27) shows a feature of P. As argued above, the reference to returning to one's possession is typical of P. Therefore, in view of the absence of traces of other sources and the decisiveness of P, one can deduce with a level of certainty that v.27 is typical of P. In the statement on returning to one's possession is an indication that P espoused the notion of redistributive justice.

Interestingly, v.28 is introduced by a conditional clause וְאִם לֹא־מָצְאָה יָדוֹ דֵּי הָשִׁיב לוֹ 'But if he does not have enough (money) to restore it to himself'. At first glance, the reference to money particularly to the payment of compensation, points one to a D handwriting in v.28. However, this verse mostly reveals a concern for the poor who were clearly the ones who had no money. Thus, the conditional clause in v.28 וְאִם לֹא־מָצְאָה יָדוֹ דֵּי הָשִׁיב לוֹ can be regarded as H because concern for justice is presupposed in it. As earlier noted, H is distinctly concerned about social justice particularly in terms of redressing poverty. The remaining statements which are obviously P allow for the return of possessions in the Jubilee year. Therefore, v.28 exhibit distinct features of both P and H. In this instance, concern for social justice characterises both P and H in the same verse.

Given the presence of D, P and H in vv.25–28, the observation of the presence of ideological contestations is in order. In a situation where the person who lost land because of poverty did not have a next-of-kin to pay compensation for such land, as ideologically contested by D, then, the land could only be returned without compensation in the Jubilee year in accordance with H's ideological position on socio-economic justice. Perhaps, when the payment of compensation was not possible because of persistent poverty, the Israelite Jubilee allowed for land redistribution without payment of compensation. Thus, balance is maintained between capitalism and communism in the Israelite Jubilee.[137] One would agree with Harrison on this point because the provision for both redistribution, which is subject to the payment of compensation and redistribution without compensation are equally upheld by the land policy in Leviticus 25:8–55. Furthermore, it becomes clear that a compromise between H (with respect to the ideological position on socio-economic justice) and D (with regard to ideological standpoint on the payment of compensation) is reached in the Leviticus 25:8–55.

Philpott and Butler rightfully assert that the Israelite Jubilee affirms the redistributive nature of Yahweh's commitment to the poor that seeks to ensure just and equitable access to land and economic resources.[138] The poor are mentioned three times in Leviticus 25:8–55—in vv.25, 35 and 39. It may be assumed that the Israelite Jubilee legislation shows some concern for the poor. Sharing wealth and land as stipulated in vv.25, 35 and 39 aimed at addressing poverty and socio-economic inequality. It is therefore reasonable to argue that the Israelite Jubilee was instituted to redress socio-economic injustice. The injustice is implied in the poverty and inequality, which are expressed by the third person masculine singular *qal* imperfect verb מוּךְ 'become poor' in vv.25, 35 and 39. Hence, the view that the Israelite Jubilee could have been a solution to the problems of exploitation, poverty and marginalisation is plausible.[139] That solution was achieved through the redistribution of land to all Israelite families.

In my view, therefore, the Jubilee legislation in Leviticus 25:8–55 not only served as a legal document to redress disproportional benefits from the use of productive land in Israel but it also offered alternative ideological positions and a mechanism to alleviate poverty. There seems to be a clear preferential option and regard for the poor; otherwise, there would not have been a link between poverty and the loss of land in vv.25–28. The reference to poverty in the introduction of vv.25–28 links the subsequent content of vv.26–28 (loss of land) which is dependent on v.25 to poverty. Therefore, the loss of land was not only caused by poverty but it was also sustained by socio-economic injustice.

In addition, socio-economic oppression informed by the noticeable trend in which the rich became richer and the poor became poorer was rooted in the practice of usury, the private accumulation of land, and slavery in Leviticus 25:8–55.[140] In v.25, the poor lose their מֵאֲחֻזָּתוֹ 'possession' to the rich in their quest to escape conspicuous and inevitable poverty. Thus, Leviticus 25:8–55 makes provision for redressing socio-economic inequality in a bid to address the issue of the accumulation of more wealth by the rich élites at the expense of the poor Israelites (cf. v.47).

The Israelite Jubilee legislation also sought to prevent the private accumulation of wealth by the rich élites while there was persistent poverty among the poor.[141] This sanction is expressed in the use of the negative particle לֹא 'not' which is used to mark negative commands throughout the legislation in Leviticus 25:8–55. The negative command statements suggest that the Israelite Jubilee legislation was made to prevent the gap between a class of few wealthy landowners at the top of the economic scale and the majority of landless Israelites at the bottom. As several biblical scholars have noted, socio-economic injustice that the Israelite Jubilee sought to redress is revealed in the economic inequalities and the disproportionate possession of wealth among the Israelites.[142] Therefore, it could be assumed that Leviticus 25:8–55 is a policy aimed not only at redressing socio-economic inequality but also at addressing the disproportionate benefits from the ownership and use of productive land.

City property versus rural land and the élites versus the poor (vv.29–34)

A striking feature in Leviticus 25:8–55 is the abrupt insertion of vv.29–34, which concern instructions on city property versus rural land as well as the élites versus the poor. The abrupt insertion is noticeable because the sequence from the block on 'Loss of land because of poverty (vv.25–28)' to 'Debt because of poverty (vv.35–38)' is interrupted. The insertion of the block of vv.29–34 in its present location hinders the flow of the points on the causes of poverty. It would have been easier for the reader not to lose the plot and meaning of the text. It is therefore important to make sense of vv.29–34 particularly its abrupt insertion in the passage.

The placing of walls particular city walls to create borders in vv.29–30 is typical of D.[143] If one agrees with Römer's identification of the influence of D who is recognised as a Golah redactor in the reference to city walls, it would also be worthwhile to note the integration of the motif of concerns about the Golah in the Persian period.[144] The Golah élites would be interested in securing the land to which they returned from the Babylonian exile. On the subject of the élites, Römer correctly points out that the Persian ideology of segregation made a distinction between persons based on class and identity.[145] The distinction between the walled cities and village houses in vv.29–34, which clearly marked a distinction between the Golah élites (who returned from the Babylonian exile) and the people of the land (the poor from rural Yehud) is typical of the D of the Persian period. In addition, the evidence of classism in v.29 would fit into D.

Furthermore, v.29 appears to be marginalised by H. This means that it is neither edited nor supplemented by H as there is no evidence of H or P in it. The noticeable absence of H's influence and features in v.29 suggests that D was integrated into Leviticus 25:8–55 by a Pentateuchal redactor. Thus, I presume that v.29 exhibits a D influence on the Pentateuchal redactor.

In v.30 on the other hand, the use of parenesis is worth exploring, as it also presents a decisive criterion for identifying the strata. Baden employs Joosten's definition of parenesis which is the structure of a discourse which not only speaks directly to the addressees but also presents laws that are relevant in different generations.[146] Based on the definition, Baden argues that since in the original P stratum, the laws were addressed to the wilderness generation without any reference to the future generation, the parenesis style therefore does not belong to P.[147] However, it will be helpful to determine whether there is any support for this line of argument outside of Leviticus 25:8–55.

On the one hand, Leviticus 23:20, which is a typical H text, explicitly refers to the future observance of the festival. On the other hand, the unit of Exodus 12:14–20 specifically vv.14 and 17 presents the festival as an institution for all time. However, such a text belongs to H. In view of the frequent use of parenesis in other legal traditions such as H we may thus not regard the parenetic style as distinctively of P origin. That is, the style does not belong to the original P stratum because it is not found anywhere in the stratum. However, in Leviticus 25:8–55, the particle preposition לְ 'throughout', which is affixed to the masculine plural construct noun with a third person masculine singular suffix דֹרֹתָיו 'his generations' eliminates the conditional statement, 'then the house that is in the walled city shall be established for ever to him that bought it throughout his generations' (v.30) from the original P stratum. Consequently, v.30 is not P's handwriting but the verse belongs to the Pentateuchal redactor, as argued below.

Otto's point on H's typical parenetic reference to the generations of the Israelites in a text distinct of H has been noted above. Features of Exodus 19:3b are also noticeable in the Israelite Jubilee legislation in Leviticus 25:8–55. The phrases לְדֹרֹתָיו 'throughout his generations' (v.30), לִבְנֵיכֶם אַחֲרֵיכֶם 'for your sons after you' (v.46), and בְּנֵי־יִשְׂרָאֵל 'the sons of Israel' (v.46) show features of H stratum. This paves way for the assignment of vv.30 and 46 to H. In v.30, the presence of the H feature in the parenetic reference to the generations of Israel does not make the D stratum on walled houses dependent on it. In other words, if one removes H's parenetic reference in v.30, the verse would still make sense. Therefore, one would suppose that the inclusion of the H feature is rather insignificant. Verse 30 ought to be distinguished from v.29, as v.29 exhibits no presence of H, while v.30 shows a minor inclusion of an H feature. Both the absence of H in v.29 and the minimal presence of H in v.30 suggest that H is probably not the redactor of vv.29–30 particularly of v.30.

Furthermore, because v.31 forms an integral part of the distinction between the houses in the city and those in the village, it makes sense to assign it also to D. Therefore, one could say, with a level of certainty, that vv.29–31 belong to D. Certainly, the distinction between the houses in the city and those in the village also reveals an economic disparity which was enforced by D. The Pentateuchal redactor then included vv.29–30 in Leviticus 25:8–55 as a later addition. In other words, the provision for the allocation of land in the cities and in the villages was shaped by classism, that is, it was based on the class and economic status of their inhabitants.

As regards the assets of the Levites, a priestly feature is probably set as the protection of the rights of the Levites in vv.32–33. A study of the Persian period has shown that power was with the priestly and scribal élites from the Babylonian exile, who in turn sought to secure productive land on their return to Yehud.[148] The repetition of the noun 'possession', a typical expression of P's language, also supports the assignment of vv.32–33 to the supplementation of P by H.

However, it is not so easy to assign the stratum of v.34 to a source. On the one hand, the reference to and the motif of the fields, which belong to CC, place v.34 under the authorship of CC. On the other hand, the absolute noun עוֹלָם 'permanent' shows a parenetic feature, which makes reference to the future. The feature is distinctly H. Therefore, v.34 also contains H's handwriting. Further, the presence of the P noun 'possession' worsens the dilemma of assigning strata to sources in v.34. In my view, then, v.34 equally exhibits the features of P, CC and H. However, one can presume that, like the provision regarding land in the cities and in the villages, v.34 supports a preferential treatment of the Levites. Thus, the economic inequality, which sought to place the Levites at an advantageous position in Israel's economic landscape, is evident in the provision of v.34. Such inequality will be addressed below.

From an ideological point of view, the abrupt insertion of vv.29–34 in Leviticus 25:8–55 also reveals an ideological tension. For instance, on the one hand, v.31 stipulates that the houses in the villages be returned to the original owners in the Jubilee. On the other hand, in vv.29–30, the houses in the city were exempted from redistribution in the Jubilee year.[149] The exemption is marked by the negative command לֹא יֵצֵא בַּיֹּבֵל 'it shall not go out in the Jubilee' (v.30) which is dependent on v.29. Provisions for land in the cities are introduced in v.29. Thus, there is a clear inconsistency in terms of the handling of property in the villages versus property in the cities. Such inconsistency could be explained as the result of the later addition and of an ideological contestation.

The view in v.31 that houses in the agricultural area of the villages had greater economic value explains the inconsistency but this explanation is not quite convincing.[150] As will be argued later, the reasons for the inconsistency could be that the edict regarding the Israelite Jubilee was initiated and revised by people who lived in the cities. Thus, the city dwellers were probably trying to protect their property from being redistributed in the Jubilee year. In other words, the interests of the city people were secured through the provisions in vv.29–34, hence, the inconsistency. The insertion of vv.29–34 served the interest of the city people and the Levites and shows that the ideology of classism clashed with socio-economic justice and equality. No doubt, vv.29–34 represents the voice and interests of class sectors namely the ruling class, that is, the professional class, which included the Golah élites as well as the Levites and scribes.

Additionally, the inconsistency reveals an ideology of inequality and segregation based on class. In all likelihood, the villagers were mostly poor while the city dwellers were wealthier. As Römer affirms, there was disparity between those who dwelt in the cities and those in the villages of Yehud.[151] In view of the inconsistency in the administration of land in villages and cities, it is easier to appreciate the abrupt insertion of vv.29–34. If the exploitation of the poor and the outcome of poverty (the loss of land and accumulation of debt) form part of the discussion of poverty in vv.25–38, then, the inconsistency in the administration of land would be justified. The inconsistency that reveals socio-economic inequality in terms of the poor (people from the villages) and the rich (people from the cities—even though not all urbanites were rich) forms an integral part of the challenge of poverty.

Debt because of poverty (vv.35–38)

In Old Testament scholarship, there is no clear stratification of vv.35–38, a block on 'debt because of poverty'. The absolute noun גֵּר 'stranger', which is postulated as distinctly P above, is used in v.35. The relative statement בוֹ גֵּר 'like a stranger' (v.35) points to the use of a distinct P noun. As such, v.35 exhibits a P feature. However, that is not all that is observable in the verse, which also seems to exhibit a feature of H. The concern for the poor, which inspires a social justice consciousness and an ideological position in favour of the poor, exhibits an H influence, as demonstrated above. Thus, it is reasonable to submit that v.35 shows the incorporation of P into a predominantly H text.

Verse 36 stands in contrast to the D element, which requires payment for compensation. The connected negative commands אַל־תִּקַּח מֵאִתּוֹ נֶשֶׁךְ 'take no usury of him' and וְתַרְבִּית 'or interest' signify the rejection of any form of payment (cf. v.36). Thus, these commands cannot be assigned to D. The rejection of payment if understood in the context of the concern for social justice that is evident in v.35 should probably be associated with H. Interestingly, the command וְיָרֵאתָ מֵאֱלֹהֶיךָ 'but fear your Elohim' (v.36) which is dependent on the preceding negative commands that allude to the taking of an interest indicates that D used non-P instead of H, as argued above. In this instance, the motif 'fear of Elohim' can reasonably be assigned to D who borrowed it from non-P. What is therefore remarkable is that the first part of v.36 disputes and rejects a D feature and embraces D in the last part of the same verse. In view of H's concern for social justice and D's motif of the fear of Elohim in v.36, the features of both H and D, which challenge each other can be attested. Similarly, v.37 reveals a concern for social justice, which means that it can also be assigned to H.

The theme of being brought out of Egypt, which is evident in v.38 indicates a P handwriting. On this point, Baden remarks that 'Unlike H, the original stratum of P contained narrative, including, obviously, the story of the Egyptian slavery, plagues and Exodus'.[152] Therefore, a critical question is what is the evidence for Baden's conclusion? Exodus 12:1–13, which is a distinct P text, confirms that the motif of deliverance from Egypt exhibits features of the P stratum. Schmid supports Baden's assignment of the exodus from Egypt to P.[153] The theme of deliverance out of Egypt represents a bone of contention among scholars. On this issue, Baden and Otto are not on the same page. If Exodus 19:3b–6 is key to comprehending H, as concluded above, then the reference to being brought out of Egypt (vv.38, 42 and 55) points in the same direction.[154] In other words, vv.38, 42 and 55 most likely belong to H.

It appears that the way out of Baden and Otto's disagreement lies in the established notion that H used P. Therefore, if H supplemented P, it is highly probable that the theme of exodus from Egypt, as employed in v.38 (by H), originally belonged to the P stratum. Moreover, since the formula, 'I am Yahweh your Elohim' points to H's supplementation of P, as noted above, the declarative statement 'I am Yahweh your Elohim' and the causal statement 'who brought you out of the land of Egypt' can correctly be assigned to H. Thus, it can be assumed with a level of certainty that v.38 shows evidence of H with a P twist, that is, with P features. Unlike the first part of v.38, the later verse line makes reference to אֶת־אֶרֶץ כְּנַעַן 'the land of Canaan'. As concluded above, that reference distinctively belongs to D. Thus, it would be difficult to prove that v.38 was crafted by H alone since the strong presence of D is noticeable. Given the presence of both D and H (as well as a P feature), it can be confidently concluded that v.38 shows evidence of the handwriting of both D and H. In this case, P seems to be supplemented by H since a P feature is not presented firmly as a distinct feature neither is P featured independently; hence, H seems to have supplemented P.

Nihan partly addresses the subject of indebtedness, which is caused by poverty.[155] In fact, he argues that, because of indebtedness, the Israelites were forced by their circumstances to 'sell a portion of his estate'. The textual evidence in vv.25–28 validates the argument. Furthermore, Nihan captions vv.35–38 as 'borrowing money to subsist', as noted above.[156] However, one may also note the idea that poverty led the Israelites, first, to sell their land, as Nihan rightly observes, and second, to indebtedness and further poverty. Again, the proposed structure of Leviticus 25:8–55 by Nihan, hints at the idea that the land issue was related to indebtedness, poverty and subsequent slavery. In fact, as Nihan states, vv.39–54 relate to both the 'poor Israelite sold as a slave to another Israelite' (39–46) and the 'poor Israelite sold as a slave to a wealthy non-Israelite' (vv.47–54).[157] Thus, it may be reasonable to argue that the economic system in ancient Israel was not favourable to the poor, as it resulted in the loss of land, indebtedness and slavery (which will be later re-read as hard labour). As a result, H sought to present the voice and interests of the poor in a bid to attain socio-economic justice. Such a voice rejects the ideology of classism evident in vv.29–34.

In vv.35–38, the Pentateuchal redactor reveals how poverty caused indebtedness among the Israelites, that is, how the poor became poorer and how the rich became richer. Not only does this scenario present the voice and interests of the poor, it further supports the comment on socio-economic injustice, which is embedded in Leviticus 25:8–55. Indebtedness led people to hard labour—slavery—to which we now turn.

Hard labour—Slavery due to poverty with the Israelite as an employer (vv. 39–46)

The established view that H used other sources such as D, among others, to create his material is noteworthy at this point.[158] Leuchter's comment on the subject of slavery is rather significant. He claims that:

> Binding slave manumission to the fifty-year jubilee cycle is a dramatic departure from the D legislature that serves as the author's source, since in D (as well as in the earlier Covenant Code), the slave is given a six-year term of servitude with release in the seventh.[159]

Although Leuchter's claim appears plausible, it should be approached with caution, mainly because he does not provide textual evidence to support his view that

H used both D and the CC. In terms of the CC, Exodus 21:2 spells out a six-year term of servitude, which Leuchter does not mention. Like the CC, D makes reference to the construct noun עֶבֶד 'slave', which points to slavery (Deut 5:15; 15:1,15,17; 21:3; 23:16; 24:22; 34:5). In line with Leviticus 25:39–40, the noun עֶבֶד 'slave' is presented both in an absolute state as well as in the context of a fifty-year Jubilee cycle. In addition, an Israelite is presented as the owner of the slave or an employer. The presentation is in complete contrast to that of the CC and D. Therefore, Leuchter is quite correct to observe H's dramatic departure from the conceptualisation of slavery by CC and D. The verses of Leviticus 25:39–40 express an ideological conflict and a re-conceptualisation of slavery by H, which sought to substitute the six-year term by D and the CC with a fifty-year cycle. However, Baden argues that vv.39–40 point to a trend of joining unrelated years by substituting six with fifty years.[160]

In fact, the rest of the block, that is vv.41–46, belong mostly to H. As demonstrated above, the features of parenesis, which have been assigned to H, are present in vv.41, 45 and 46, which all contain references to inheritance and future generations. Furthermore, in v.42, the theme of exodus from Egypt, which is assigned to H (who used a theme originating from a P stratum) above, is noticeable. Subsequently, the assignment of the exodus theme to H places v.42 with H. Interestingly, the motif of the fear of Elohim integrates v.43 with the block of vv.39–46, and therefore to D who borrowed it from E. Consequently, what we have in v.43 is the insertion of a D text by a Pentateuchal redactor in a block, which is predominantly H.

It is important to note that vv.39–46 are introduced by the conjunctive particle וְ 'and', כִּי 'if' and a third person masculine singular *qal* verb יָמוּךְ 'become poor'. Interestingly, this introductory clause וְכִי־יָמוּךְ 'And if he becomes poor' links vv.35–38 and vv.39–54 with vv.25–28 (the section on loss of land due to poverty) which also contains a similar introductory formation in v.25. One wonders why the author(s) or redactor(s) of Leviticus 25:8–55 linked the challenge of debts and labour to the issue of land. The link could be warranted if the loss of land resulted in debt and slavery. Furthermore, the accumulation of and failure to settle debts most likely resulted in hard labour (slavery) which was probably one of the means by which the poor Israelites paid their debt. Given the fruit of poverty in terms of the sequence of loss of land, debt accumulation and slavery in order to settle debts, it is reasonable to relate vv.35–54 to the land discourse in the Israelite Jubilee. Therefore, the root cause of hard labour or slavery and indebtedness was the loss of land, which the Israelite Jubilee legislation sought to address. The preceding argument presents H's ideological position about slavery.

Hard labour—Slavery due to poverty with the non-Israelite as an employer (vv. 47–54)

First and foremost, the unit of vv.47–54 presents a portrait of slavery which resulted from poverty with the non-Israelite as an employer. The presence of the non-Israelites in this post-exilic setting is indisputable. With regards to the post-exilic context, textual evidence shows that the Persian Empire appointed Persian officials who oversaw the local administration of the province of Judah.[161] Nehemiah 2:7 confirms the influence of the governors of Trans-Euphrates while Nehemiah 3:6–7 shows that the repairs of the Jeshanah Gate were carried out under the authority of a Persian official. Furthermore, the authorisation of the rebuilding of the temple was monitored by Tattenai the governor of Trans-Euphrates and Shethar-Bozenai and by their fellow officials (Ezr 5:3; 6:6). Ezra 8:36 also confirms that the Persian Empire appointed the Persian officials and the governors of Trans-Euphrates to assist the Jews. Such assistance was also financial since the expenses were covered by the Persian officials.[162] Given the strategic appointment of Persian officials to assume oversight of the province of Judah in Ezra-Nehemiah, the argument that Persian officials controlled the Jewish officials makes sense. As such, it appears that the Persian political élites were strategically appointed by the Empire to rule the Jews in the post-exilic period. Thus, the presence of the non-Israelites in the post-exilic setting, in particular, is indisputable.

Noteworthy, verse 47 appears to contain features of both P and H. The conditional statements וְכִי תַשִּׂיג יַד גֵּר 'and if a stranger becomes richer than you' as embedded and עִמָּךְ וּמָךְ אָחִיךָ 'and your brother that dwells by him becomes poor', reveal some concern for social justice. Since that theme had already been assigned to H, v.47 then exhibits an H feature. However, the singular noun that is used in the conditional statement וְתוֹשָׁב 'or a sojourner' by P is dependent on the conditional statement, וְכִי תַשִּׂיג יַד גֵּר. What this implies is that a P statement is dependent on an H text. In this instance, H seems to have taken up a P text. However, in this case H does not dispute P. Therefore, v.47 belongs to H, who in turn used P, based on the dependency of a P text on an H text. Noteworthy is the fact that a non-Israelite (v.47) is presented as the owner of wealth and subsequently as an employer. For H, the non-Israelites feature in the ownership of resources. Interestingly, one observes a different presentation of the employer because in v.47 a non-Israelite is the employer while in v.39 an Israelite is the employer or slave owner. Since both texts belong to H, it is difficult to explain the variation. Perhaps it is due to the difference in time of composition and redaction.

As for vv.48 and 49, the reference to the payment of compensation and an amount for גְּאֻלָּה 'redemption' points to a D feature. Therefore, one can deduce that vv.48–49 exhibit a D feature, since there is no evidence of other sources in the verses. In v.50, the reference to the payment of an amount for the purchase of a slave is most likely a D feature. However, we cannot confidently submit that v.50 belongs entirely to D. The assignment of the reference to the Jubilee cycle years to H shows that v.50 also belongs to H. Thus, it is reasonable to conclude that v.50 exhibits features of both D and H. However, worthy of note is the contestation between D and H. If the non-Israelites in post-exilic Yehud were the Persian authorities, it may be argued that D's ideological feature of the payment of compensation was set to serve the interests of the Persian ruling élites. In opposition with D is H's reference to the Jubilee cycle years. In this case, the fact that H presents the portrait of slavery due to poverty shows that H sought to see the poor Jews being freed from the oppression by the non-Jews who were in the position of economic power in Yehud. On this point, H contests D's requirement of the payment of compensation, rejecting the situation in which the Jews were viewed as part of a business transaction. It must be noted however that the release of slaves is a typical D subject, and H does not reject the subject of release. Rather, H draws on the subject but further contests the element of the payment of compensation.

Unlike v.50, v.51 exhibits the handwriting of both D and a possible Pentateuchal redactor. The reference to the payment of compensation such as the redemption amount in v.51 reveals a D feature. Nonetheless, the conditional statement יָשִׁיב גְּאֻלָּתוֹ מִכֶּסֶף מִקְנָתוֹ 'he shall give again the price of his redemption out of the money that he was bought for'. is dependent on the expression לְפִיהֶן 'according unto them' (cf. v.51). Thus, the reason and causal phrases reveal a non-P etiological style. In v.51, it is also difficult to assign the etiological style to either H or D implying that the etiological style probably belongs to a redactor, who is neither P nor H, nor D. Therefore, one could argue that v.51 exhibits a D feature and possibly a feature of a Pentateuchal redactor.

However, like v.50, one observes in v.52 both H and D features. The reference to the Jubilee cycle years shows H's handwriting and, as stated above, the reference to the payment of compensation is a D element. Thus, v.52 equally exhibits both D and H features. On the other hand, in v.53, the concern for social justice expressed in the negative command לֹא־יִרְדֶּנּוּ בְּפֶרֶךְ לְעֵינֶיךָ 'and the other shall not rule with severity over him in thy sight' exhibits H's handwriting. Thus, we can deduce that v.53 is distinctly H. The provision for liberation in the conditional statement וְיָצָא בִּשְׁנַת הַיֹּבֵל 'then he shall go out in the year of Jubilee' (v.54) also reveals H's concern for social justice. However, since the release of slaves is a typical D subject, as noted above, it can be assumed that H relied mostly on D in his construction of the concern for social justice. Further support for the assignment of v.54 to H is contained in the reference to the Jubilee cycle years, which is typically H. Therefore, v.54 indisputably belongs to H. In the stratum of vv.47–54 is the provision for the release of slaves which fits well with the quest and contestation for redress of socio-economic injustice echoed in Leviticus 25:8–55. The slaves were mostly people who lost their land and became poor as a result. Due to their poverty, they became the slaves of the rich élites. However, their economic condition did not make Yahweh to identify less with them. Slaves also belonged to Yahweh who in turn sought social justice for them, according to H's ideological position.

Conclusion (v.55)

In v.55, stratum that originate from different sources which were juxtaposed by a final redactor of the Pentateuch can be identified. The phrase בְּנֵי־יִשְׂרָאֵל 'the sons of Israel' (v.55) shows a parenetic feature that refers also to future generations. As such, an H feature is recognisable. In v.55, a unique reference to slaves is noticeable, as the verse does not refer to the release of slaves, an ideological position and subject typical of D. Instead, the noun, slave, is used in the context of an entitlement and declarative statement עֲבָדַי הֵם 'they are my slaves' (v.55). In view of this unusual use of the word slave, one is hesitant to assign the verse to what would have been D. In my view, since the entitlement statement, עֲבָדַי הֵם 'they are my slaves' is dependent on the reason, כִּי־לִי בְנֵי־יִשְׂרָאֵל עֲבָדִים 'For to me the sons of Israel are slaves' an H stratum the reference to slavery would fit with H unless a non-H redactor inserted the statement 'they are my slaves' next to an H text ('For to me the sons of Israel are slaves'). In fact, the plural noun 'slaves' is mentioned in preceding statements. Given the fact that H did not employ a repetitive style, it is unlikely that H would present the noun twice. Therefore, v.55 was most likely inserted by a final redactor of the Pentateuch since H does not employ a repetitive style which is evident in this case.

Furthermore, the theme of deliverance from Egypt in v.55, which is employed in v.38 by H, originally belonged to the P stratum. It was inserted in v.55 by H but it exhibits a P feature. The theme is also used in v.55 in a causal statement. This stylistic feature most likely belongs to a non-H redactor, as noted above. Therefore, v.55 exhibits the feature of a redactor who is neither H or P nor D. Interestingly, the declarative and entitlement statement in v.55 is attached to a causal statement making the causal statement to be dependent on the declarative and entitlement statement. In the preceding verse, we have the theme of deliverance from Egypt אֲשֶׁר־הוֹצֵאתִי אוֹתָם מֵאֶרֶץ מִצְרָיִם 'whom I brought forth out of the land of Egypt'. The statement presents both the liberating character of Yahweh and the historic redress of social injustice experienced by the Israelites. Thus, v.55 seems to present the Jubilee legislation as a policy that called for the redress of socio-economic injustice.

Verse 55 ends with the formula אֲנִי יְהוָה אֱלֹהֵיכֶם 'I am Yahweh your Elohim' which has been ascribed correctly to H, but which also appears to contain a feature of P. Consequently, I would submit that the declarative statement אֲנִי יְהוָה אֱלֹהֵיכֶם 'I am Yahweh your Elohim' exhibits the supplementation of P by H. In view of the presence of features of P, H and the Pentateuchal redactor in v.55, it is reasonable to deduce that the final redactor combined such features. In other words, H could not have been the final redactor of Leviticus 25:8–55 since there are verses which exhibit features that belong to neither H nor P and D. Lastly and worthy of note, the declarative statement אֲנִי יְהוָה אֱלֹהֵיכֶם 'I am Yahweh your Elohim' (vv. 55, 17 and 38) is used elsewhere in the Jubilee legislation to conclude the sections on 'trading of agricultural products' (vv.14–17) and 'debt due to poverty' (vv.35–38). It also appears after the section on 'hard labour due to poverty in the hands of the non-Israelite employer' (vv.47–54). If the legislation in Leviticus 25:8–55 provided for an ideological contestation of a legal framework and policy on socio-economic justice, then the declarative statement אֲנִי יְהוָה אֱלֹהֵיכֶם 'I am Yahweh your Elohim' in v.55 served a theological underpinning for the Jubilee. Yahweh is presented as an advocate of the Israelite Jubilee.

Conclusion—Stratification of Leviticus 25:8–55

The main reason for a compositional and redactional analysis of Leviticus 25:8–55 in this chapter is to probe the strata of the text in a bid to identify the author(s) and/or redactor(s). This has not yet been addressed, and though previous studies have analysed Leviticus 25:8–55 as a product of H, it is argued here that the features of other sources are present in the passage. Undoubtedly, H's handwriting is noticeable in Leviticus 25:8–55, but features of P, CC, D and of the Pentateuchal redactor are equally evident in the text. Thus, one would fully agree with non-documentarians such as Otto, Nihan, Schmid, Carr and Römer among others that H supplemented P and other codes especially CC and D against the neo-documentarian view that H only used P.[163] In fact, one finds that the strata of P, D and H were not just combined to form a single narrative and legislation, the Israelite Jubilee, but were also edited by the Pentateuchal redactor. Thus, the non-DH seems convincing, as there are clear hints of redactional additions made by the Pentateuchal redactor, which included elaborating on, correcting or modifying pre-existing texts.[164]

Drawing from Mosala's hermeneutical approach, which probes the ideological motivations behind biblical strata, we have presented various strata in the text in consideration as well as the ideological contestations in Leviticus 25:8–55. Although, one has acknowledged the interests of the composer(s) and redactor(s), we cannot decisively address the question of whose interest the composition and the redaction of Leviticus 25:8–55 served without investigating the historical contexts of P, H and D, respectively. At this stage, we can attempt to identify both the composer(s) and redactor(s) and the ideological contestations embedded in Leviticus 25:8–55.

A Diachronic Analysis of the *Sitz-Im-Leben* of Leviticus 25:8–55

That biblical scholarship has paid scant attention to the importance of the composition and redaction of Leviticus 25:8–55 in exploring its *Sitz-im-Leben* is noticeable. We shall thus consider the life setting of the Israelite Jubilee given this oversight and the goal of the present chapter to construct the Israelite policy of land and socio-economic justice as outlined in Leviticus 25:8–55. Subsequently, the theological and socio-economic ideologies that influenced the composition and redaction of Leviticus 25:8–55 will be investigated. The life setting of the text could help to shed light on the ancient Israelite society and enable us to reconstruct the identities of the addressees of the Israelite Jubilee. In the light of an African liberationist approach adopted in the present study, we shall highlight instances in Leviticus 25:8–55, which support or oppose the oppression of the addressees of the text under consideration. Bearing in mind the features of H, P, D, CC and non-P writers and of the Pentateuchal redactor(s) as well as ideological contestations in Leviticus 25:8–55, we shall investigate the *Sitz-im-Leben* of the Israelite Jubilee with the focus on the context of both the writers and of the redactor(s).

Dating the Composition and Redaction of Leviticus 25:8–55

In the preceding chapter, I have argued in favour of the view that Leviticus 25:8–55 emanated from the supplementation of P, CC, non-P and D by H and the redactional additions made by the Pentateuchal redactor. As such, the presence of P, CC, non-P, D and the Pentateuchal redactor ought to be considered in dating the compositional and redaction layers of Leviticus 25:8–55.

Pentateuchal redactor

Following both Otto and Nihan, Meyer holds that the creation of the Pentateuch be dated to the second half of the fifth to the fourth century BCE.[165] As such, the redaction of the Torah probably took place around that date. Although Otto claims that the composition of the Holiness Code coincides with the creation of the Pentateuch, it appears however that the redactional additions were made by the Pentateuchal redactor after the composition of H.[166] In other words, if there are hints that the redactional additions to the H text namely Leviticus 25:8–55, were made by the Pentateuchal redactor, one would be reluctant to accept Otto's claim.

Furthermore, the view that H was involved in the redaction of Leviticus 25:8–55 in the capacity of a Pentateuchal redactor has been refuted above. We have also noted the absence of the influence and features of H in certain strata. In vv.17, 20–21, 24, 29, 43, 48–49 and 51, it is difficult to detect any H feature. Thus, one has to consider the possibility of a Pentateuchal redactor; and because of the clear instances in which H used P and D, it may be concluded that H is later than both P and D. If indeed there was a Pentateuchal redactor who was neither H nor P nor D, then such a redactor must have come later. In other words, the Pentateuchal redactor of Leviticus 25:8–55 came on the scene later than D, P and H. Thus, a post-exilic dating is fitting for the Pentateuchal redaction of the text under discussion. However, that redactor would then be later than D, P and H in the post-exilic period.

Holiness Code composer

In his study of Leviticus 25, Meyer discusses the possible socio-historical context of the Israelite Jubilee which entails also an attempt at dating Leviticus 25.[167] In his conclusion, Meyer argues in favour of a post-exilic dating of the final form of Leviticus 25, since he finds attempts to date the text back to the pre-exilic period unconvincing. For Milgrom, the origins of H lie in the eighth century, but Meyer correctly refutes such an idea.[168] Meyer further engages with Joosten and with Knohl who argue for a pre-exilic dating of H based on the view that the exile mentioned in Leviticus 26 was to Assyria and not to Babylonia.[169] As Meyer rightly observes, Knohl's claim is not convincing. Like Joosten, my reluctance to follow Knohl's reasoning is because he ignores the possibility that both Leviticus 25 and 26 could refer to the Babylonian exile, even though the text refers to a liberated people.[170] Meyer does not completely rule out the possibility of a late exilic dating of H (the second half of the sixth century BCE), as proposed by Grünwaldt and by Otto who argue for a later date for H because H used earlier traditions such as P, CC and D.[171] This means that a late exilic or post-exilic dating would make sense if H was familiar with earlier sources, that is, with exilic sources. However, both Meyer and Grünwaldt do not support an exilic dating. Instead, they entertain the possibility of a post-exilic dating for two reasons.

First, based on the relationship between Leviticus 25 and Leviticus 26, both of which form part of the Holiness Code (Chapters 17–26), both Meyer and Grünwaldt draw insight from Leviticus 26:13. The point that the Israelites are addressed as people who are already delivered sways them to consider a post-exilic dating for H.[172] Noteworthy, the clauses אֲשֶׁר הוֹצֵאתִי אֶתְכֶם מֵאֶרֶץ מִצְרַיִם 'who brought you out of the land of Egypt' and וָאֶשְׁבֹּר מֹטֹת עֻלְּכֶם 'and I have broken the bands of your yoke' (Lev 26:13) are said to refer to the deliverance from the Babylonian exile. In my view, the theme of deliverance from Egypt, though originally P, as stated above, has now been re-used by H in both Leviticus 25 and 26. Assigning that theme to H justifies the identification of an implicit reference to the Babylonian exile in both Leviticus 25 and 26. Therefore, the post-exilic dating of H by both Meyer and Grünwaldt could be justified. However, more than a single argument would be needed to prove a post-exilic dating of H.

Second, Meyer sees the fifty years of the Jubilee cycle as an attempt by the élites to counter the loss of land and reclaim it after their liberation from the Babylonian exile.[173] In other words, the view that the Babylonian exile lasted for forty-nine years while liberation occurred in the fiftieth year links the reference to fifty years in the H stratum to the exilic context. As a result, he builds a strong argument on this view. The idea that the returning élites who wanted to reclaim land were the addressees of H in Leviticus 25 prompts Meyer to propose a post-exilic dating for H, of course, in agreement with Grünwaldt.[174] A post-exilic dating of H based on the link of the Jubilee cycle with the forty-nine years in exile makes sense. Thus, I am inclined to support the post-exilic dating of H, as both Meyer and Grünwaldt have convincingly shown. However, I choose to differ with Meyer on the assumption that the final form of Leviticus 25 was constructed uniquely by H. Due to his exclusive focus on dating H, one is left with the impression that the whole of Leviticus 25, be it in its final or original form, is from the post-exilic period. However, that conclusion cannot be sustained because other sources appear in the text. Although I support a post-exilic dating for H, this position does not apply to the whole of Leviticus 25. There is also a need to date other sources, which were supplemented by H namely P, CC and D, which are behind the stratum of Leviticus 25, as demonstrated above.

Priestly composer

It is important to probe the dating of P, first, because of the evidence of P features in Leviticus 25:8–55, and second, because of instances in which P is evident in strata where H is not detected, as noted above. Joosten states that 'today it has become fashionable to date the Pentateuch, more or less, wholesale to the Persian period'.[175] Perhaps his observation refers to the final form of the Pentateuch as will be shown below. Nonetheless, Blenkinsopp also notes a critical consensus in scholarship namely the dating of P after the fall of Jerusalem in 586 BCE, in the second part of the sixth century, and the subsequent deportations.[176] This means that an exilic or early post-exilic dating of P is assumed, that is, a late neo-Babylonian or early Persian period dating. At this point, it is important to consider the alternative dating. Could P indeed be exilic, as scholars such as Schwartz and Brueggemann, among others, claim? Although Schwartz assigns an exilic dating to P, he does not substantiate his position.[177] However, Brueggemann claims that the discourse of land in the P tradition forms part of the critical themes of creation, tabernacle and land, which are exilic.[178] The reason for such claims is that, for P, the subject of land was more critical in the exilic context where the Israelites had already lost their homeland. Thus, to some extent, Brueggemann considers it fitting to assign an exilic dating to P. In order to validate Brueggemann's dating of P based on the discourse of land, it might be helpful to look at the P stratum in Leviticus 25:8–55.

Noteworthy are the two distinctive features of P—the 'repetition of the noun, 'possession'' and the 'repeated subject of the return to the homeland (with the protection of rights of the Levites)'. These features are evident in Leviticus 25:8–55 as shown above and their use in this text suggest an exilic dating. Given that the Israelites lost their land when they were deported to Babylonia, a post-exilic dating of the repeated noun 'possession' by P appears reasonable. Moreover, the most likely discussion of returning to the homeland, which was probably in the late exilic period, just before the actual return, is worth noting in dating P. If the discussion is assigned to P, it therefore makes sense to assign a late exilic dating to P. Based on these P features and their possible dating to the exilic period, I would support an exilic dating of P, which scholars such as Brueggemann and Schwartz have proposed.

Following Nihan and Wöhrle, Meyer argues for a post-exilic dating of P. This dating is dependent on the post-exilic dating of the concept, 'resident aliens'.[179] Nihan argues that the concept is best located in the context in which the Israelites were referred to as 'resident aliens' when they had no political control over the land.[180] However, because the Israelites did not have political control over the land does not exclusively imply that they were in a post-exilic context. A situation could also have arisen in the exilic period when the Babylonians had political control.

However, before concluding whether P is pre-exilic, exilic or post-exilic, it is important to ascertain whether P precedes H. A number of scholars agree that H is a post-P literature, meaning that, H came after P.[181] Thus, it is important to determine also whether H follows P in Leviticus 25:8–55. Above, we have shown the presence of distinct features of P and H in certain individual verses and have argued that H used P to construct these verses. In other words, both P and H occur in the same verse because H was probably aware of and used P. To illustrate the presence of both P and H as well as the possible use of P by H, we shall take a second look at two of the verses in Leviticus 25:8–55. In v.17, the repetitive naming of God, 'Yahweh Elohim', which is a priestly feature is used as a reason statement, כִּי אֲנִי יְהוָה אֱלֹהֵיכֶם 'for I am Yahweh your God'. The statement contains an H formula, 'I am Yahweh your Elohim'. God is named 'Yahweh Elohim' by the composer of the preceding formula. Thus, it is evident that H used P.

Furthermore, P's distinct term 'holy' is used in v.12 within the context of H's concern for social justice. In this instance, it is reasonable to postulate that H used P, and if indeed H used P, as I would argue in the case of Leviticus 25:8–55, then, P should be dated earlier than H[182]. That is, given the view that H used P, if a post-exilic dating can be assigned to H convincingly, as one is inclined to do, we might need to consider a dating earlier than that of H. Thus, an exilic dating of P might sound more reasonable and more convincing. What does one make of a pre-exilic dating of P, which has been proposed by scholars such as Milgrom and Hurvitz? Their position, which has added to the controversy on issues of dating in Old Testament scholarship, is from a linguistic perspective, as will be shown below.

From a linguistic point of view, Blenkinsopp argues that a precondition for determining whether P is pre-exilic is showing that 'a term used consistently in P is never used in texts known to be post-exilic with the exception of those clearly and directly dependent on P'.[183] This means that one has to point out a P term that is completely absent in all the post-exilic texts. To this end, some scholars find it difficult to identify a term that is completely absent in post-exilic texts.[184] Milgrom, for example, claims that the P term עֵדָה 'congregation' is absent after the ninth century BCE.[185] In response to this claim, Meyer sees Milgrom's claim as unconvincing, and correctly points out the use of עֵדָה 'congregation' which he (Meyer) translates as 'assembly' after the ninth century BCE.[186] Given the evidence provided by Meyer, Milgrom's claim of a P term that is not used in older texts is inadequate, showing that the precondition set by Blenkinsopp is rather difficult to meet. Due to the difficulty of showing the absence of the P stratum in post-exilic literature, within or outside of Leviticus 25:8–55, I find the rejection of a pre-exilic dating of P by both Blenkinsopp and Meyer convincing.

Consequently, I fully support the assignment of an exilic or early post-exilic dating to P as Schwartz, Brueggemann and Blenkinsopp have done. That is, they date P to around the sixth century (between 600 and 500 BCE). Meyer's point that a pre-exilic dating of P is not convincing is noteworthy but not convincing, as argued above. Regarding Leviticus 25:8–55, there are two main reasons for identifying with an exilic dating (second half of the sixth century BCE). First, if indeed H used P, then, P should be dated earlier than H, that is, in the exilic period. Second, P's discussion of returning to the homeland fits into the late exilic period, just before the actual return.

Deuteronomistic composer

The contributions of two European scholars, Römer and Otto, among others, are critical to the study of the Deuteronomistic History and its composer. In conversation with Römer, Otto argues that 'If we agree with Römer's perspective that the Deuteronomistic scrolls of the pre-exilic period were originally independent literary units, then the question becomes central how these scrolls grew together and became a literary unit'.[187]

The statement above is useful not because of the question it poses, but its suggestion of a most likely pre-exilic dating of D. The pre-exilic dating is contrary to Noth's position, which does not consider the possibility of D's activity before the exile. Noth posits a late exilic dating for D, that is, the period under the neo-Babylonian reign.[188] The main argument for such a claim is based on the apparent similarity between the end of the Deuteronomistic History and the last book of Kings (2 Kgs 25:27–30). The similarity relates to Jehoiachin's release from the Babylonian exile. However, one cannot rule out the possibility of the revision of D in the late exilic and post-exilic period as Otto claims. Thus, given the possibility of a late exilic and post-exilic dating of the revision of D, Römer's claim of a pre-exilic dating of D could have some merit. He asserts that 'It is clear that Hezekiah's reign constitutes a first climax in the DH. But it is quite difficult to assume that there was a first edition of the DH that ended somewhere in 2 Kings 18–20'.[189]

One of the reasons Römer placed D at the time of Hezekiah's reign is because of 2 Kings 22:5, which states, 'There was no one like him [Hezekiah] among all the kings of Judah after him, or among those who were before him'. This means that, if 2 Kings 22 is a distinct D text, then, there is a clear awareness of Hezekiah's reign (716–687 BCE). Moreover, we know that during the reign of Hezekiah there was intense scribal activity (Prov 25:1). Therefore, one cannot rule out the possibility of dating D to Hezekiah's reign. As for Josiah, his reign is documented in 2 Kings 22–23, which is a D text and which prompts Römer to consider the period of Josiah's rule (640–608 BCE) as a plausible time of D's composition. Both Hezekiah and Josiah ruled in the pre-exilic period. If Römer's dating of D to the time of Hezekiah and Josiah, that is, the pre-exilic period, is correct as I am inclined to assume, dating the features of D that are evident in Leviticus 25:8–55 to that period would make sense. This is because 2 Kings 19:5–7 reports that Hezekiah had slaves, and it would make sense for D to speak against that practice of acquiring slaves by Hezekiah. Moreover, the presence of a typical D noun 'remission' in Leviticus 25:10, which is related to Deuteronomy 15:2 as well as to the noun 'slave' in Leviticus 25:39–40, which advocates the release of slaves, would not be irrelevant to Hezekiah's context. Therefore, I would argue that the presence of D in Leviticus 25:8–55 suggests a pre-exilic dating of the first layer of D; that is, D was probably active during Hezekiah's rule and was later documented at the time of Josiah.

In his article, 'Torah and Prophecy: A Debate of Changing Identities', Otto notes that there was a post-exilic revision and re-statement of the prophetic announcement not of only the catastrophe but also of the deliverance of the exilic period.[190] This Deuteronomistic prophecy of doom associates D with the exilic period. Although one could readily support Otto's dating of the prophecy of doom and deliverance to the post-exilic period, the interest here is in its original context namely the exilic period. If we suppose that the prophecy was about an act which was undesirable to Yahweh, the consequence of which was the deportation to Babylonia and the loss of land, the payment or punishment for the act would be, first, the loss of homeland, and second, the actual exile and observance of Yahweh's law. The punishment would then produce deliverance from the consequence of the act, which was undesirable to Yahweh. Therefore, the principle behind D's prophecy of doom and deliverance was the payment for the consequence of an act, which was undesirable to Yahweh. That consequence was the loss of land by the Israelites.[191]

If Römer's observation regarding the loss of land is correct, an exilic dating of D's motif of payment of compensation in Leviticus 25:8–55 would be warranted. In other words, in view of an exilic dating of D's revision of the prophecy of doom and deliverance, which contains an underlying principle of payment for consequences, it would also make sense to assign an exilic dating to D's motif of payment for compensation to redeem the land that was lost. An exilic dating would then mean that the motif is a revision of a pre-exilic motif. Therefore, D's motif of payment of compensation, in all probability, was originally pre-exilic but was re-iterated later in the exilic period, which implies an exilic dating of D.

On this point, Scheffler's view that the Israelite deportees to Babylonia were the wealthy class who continued to be economically active and stable in the Babylonian exile is noteworthy.[192] Scheffler's argument is based on the evidence of economic activity in exile in Jeremiah 40:9–10 as well in the *Marashu Inscription* discovered at *Nippur*. The view is plausible because if the Israelite exiles in Babylonia were indeed economically active, then, they would have had sufficient capital to pay compensation in order to acquire land. The requirement of the payment of compensation for productive land would not have been required by a composer who was outside Babylonia. That is, the scribe could not have been a poor Israelite who was not one of the Babylonian exiles, but an élite scribe or composer who was probably one of those who were economically active and stable in the Babylonian exile. Given also the assignment of the motif of payment of compensation to D, it would be reasonable to support an exilic dating of D.

D's reference to the Promised Land (Canaan) in Leviticus 25:23 (see also Deut 1:8; 6:10; 9:5; 30:20; 34:40), noted above, is worth revisiting at this point. Locating the reference to the Promised Land at a time when people did not possess land would make sense. In other words, a manifesto that supports the possession of land would be realistic in a context where the Israelites needed land. Hence, I would concur with the presupposition that the promise of land or the reference to the Promised Land would have been of immediate relevance to those who aspired to return to Judah in the late neo-Babylonian or early Persian period.[193] Thus, one could easily accept the dating of D's revision in which he presents the subject of the loss of land to the exilic period by Römer.[194] Therefore, D's reference to the Promised Land (Canaan) in Leviticus 25:23 most likely came from a late exilic and was carried into an early post-exilic period.

In view of the possible post-exilic dating of D, that is, the most likely revision of D, as Römer and Otto have argued, we can probe the dating of a D feature in Leviticus 25:8–55 to the same period. Above, we have noted D's motif of the integration of the Golah concerns in the Persian period based on class such as the disparity between those who dwelt in the cities and those in the villages.[195] Thus, the association of the motif with the Golah community and the view that D was revised in the post-exilic period are probable. In other words, the view that D was also revised in the post-exilic period becomes difficult to dispute.

From the above discussion of the dating of the Deuteronomistic composer, it is clear that D would have been of immediate relevance in the pre-exilic period. Additionally, the exilic and the post-exilic periods most likely witnessed the revision and re-expression of texts belonging to D. Therefore, I would also submit that D was composed in the pre-exilic period and was later revised in the both the exilic and post-exilic periods, as demonstrated above.

Covenant Code and Elohist (non-P) composers

First, we shall consider the possible dating of CC in the context of Leviticus 25:8–55. In his contribution to the discussion of the Covenant Code, Wright notes:

> An early dating of the Covenant Code is also supported by a relatively early date of the laws of Deuteronomy. If the latter date to the eight century, for example, then the Covenant Code may be from the ninth or even tenth century BCE. In addition, several scholars believe that the Covenant Code was included as part of the Elohist—a few say Yahwist—source of the Pentateuch.[196]

Wright's remark above shows no decisive argument on the dating of the CC, perhaps because there are several suggestions about who the composer of the CC was. On the view that the CC was a part of either J or E, Otto like most European biblical scholars concludes that 'The "Yahwist" and with him the "Elohist" are gone'.[197] The conclusion means that J and E never really existed. Although it might not be helpful to pursue Wright's view that the CC belonged to either J or E, it could help to probe whether there was an alternative composer of the CC. To this end, Levinson outlines a four-stage process in the reconstruction of the redactional history of the Covenant Code thus:

> ... (1) The compilation of the Covenant Code either from originally independent subcollections of laws of various origins (family, local courts, cult) or from separate continuous strata; (2) pre-Deuteronomic revision of the Covenant Code by way or reformulation, supplementation, and redrafting; (3) a Deuteronomistic redaction of the Covenant code that brings it into conformity with the theology and social concerns of Deuteronomy and that is responsible for embedding it into the larger Sinai narrative (Exodus 19–24); and (4) a final priestly redaction.[198]

A number of scholars including Levinson and Otto have rejected the possibility that D was responsible for the revision of the CC.[199] Similarly, it is difficult to prove D's revision of the aspects of the CC in Leviticus 25:8–55. Therefore, one is left with the possibility of a P revision. If Wright understands that the priestly redaction refers to the priestly corpus which includes both P and H, then, there is a possibility of the revision of the CC by P. However, it is practical to assume that that revision was not conducted by both P and H but by one of the two. Above, we have established the relationship between CC and H. Their strata are featured in Leviticus 25:8–55 alongside each other.

In vv.12 and 15, the motif of fields which traditionally would be assigned to CC,[200] is featured alongside H's concern for social justice. Further, the motif of fields by CC in v.19 appears alongside the H feature which connects 'fruits' to 'field' and 'products'. In fact, according to the present critical exegetical analysis of the text of Leviticus 25:8–55, the field motif which has been assigned previously to CC is dependent on H clauses. In addition, the sixth and the seventh year cycles in vv.39–40 which would be assigned to the CC traditionally, as demonstrated above, is replaced with fifty years by H. Again, we find a connection between the so-called CC feature and the H stratum. In view of the close relationship between the CC and H features in Leviticus 25:8–55 and the dependence of the CC on H texts, it seems reasonable to suggest that the motif of fields which was assigned to the CC belongs to H. This suggestion is raised at this point mainly because of the present analysis of the dating of sources, the recent argument that J and E probably did not really exist, as well as the supposed connection between the CC and H texts.

On the issue of the features that have been assigned to non-P, in vv.17, 36 and 43, the motif 'fear of Elohim' which is assigned to E traditionally is clearly re-used by H with a legal twist.[201] Therefore, the motif of 'fear of Elohim—God' which is universal in most of the world's religions is used by H, and the argument regarding CC and non-P (formerly E) would then enable us to assign to them the dating of H and D, respectively. One would thus date the features which traditionally have been assigned to CC to the period of H. Similarly, the features which have been assigned to non-P would then fit with D's dating.

Historical Re-construction of Ancient Israelite Society in Leviticus 25:8–55

Scholars such as Kinsler and Kinsler as well as Meyer among others have argued for a post-exilic dating of the Israelite Jubilee, as presented above. As a result, the addressees of Leviticus 25:8–55 would have been the post-exilic community. The problem with the dating and re-construction of the addressees of the Israelite Jubilee is the tendency to restrict these to a single period. If indeed other sources contributed to Leviticus 25:8–55, as argued above, it would be unjustifiable to focus only on a single period such as the post-exilic period. Thus, it is important to re-examine also the pre-exilic and the exilic community which in all probability constituted the addressees of at least some parts or strata of Leviticus 25:8–55. The present discussion will engage in part[202] with studies which have attempted to construct the Judaic community in the pre-exilic, exilic and post-exilic periods. It will ask critical questions about the addressees of the Israelite Jubilee in Leviticus 25:8–55, and about the clues that the study of the composition and redaction of Leviticus 25:8–55 offer regarding the society of ancient Israel. The re-construction of the ancient society will focus on the pre-exilic, exilic and post-exilic periods but more critically, it will be guided by the findings on D, P, H and D, as the situation of the addressees of those sources appeared unique.

The pre-exilic society

(i) Addressees of D

In terms of the dating of sources above, the only source that was presumably active in the pre-exilic period was D. Thus, it is appropriate and imperative to find clues about the community that lived in that period from what we have learnt about D in the above study of the composition and redaction of Leviticus 25:8–55. First, a critical question to ask is: Are there clues about the addressees of the Israelite Jubilee in D's motif of the 'fear of Elohim' in vv.17, 36 and 43?

Actually, the giving of the law, by nature, seeks to prevent injustice. As such, it presupposes that an unjust situation arose which necessitated the construction of the law. In other words, there would have been no need to construct a law had there not been a need. Thus, it appears that there was indeed a situation that instigated the composition of the Israelite Jubilee legislation, that is, in order to prevent injustice, as any law would seek to accomplish in principle. Since the Israelite Jubilee legislation in Leviticus 25:8–55 refers to the issues of land, debts and slavery, it makes sense to suppose that a level of injustice operated in the society at that time. At this point however, we shall not attempt to probe into the specific expression of such injustice.

It has been argued earlier that D's motif of the fear of Elohim constituted a theological rationale for forestalling the oppression and impoverishment of the Israelites. Providing a theological reason for pursuing the redress of oppression and poverty suggests that the addressees were religious people especially with respect to the religious connotation in the provision and the reference to Elohim—God. Therefore, one could say with a level of certainty that the addressees were a religious community who also needed to demonstrate their fear of God. Only the presence of behaviour that was contrary to the values such as those, which inflict harm and distress on others, could have necessitated the demonstration of the fear of Elohim, that is, if the community was religious as the motif the fear of Elohim presupposes.

Furthermore, the increase of the land was conditioned by obedience to Yahweh's commandments and instructions, as noted in the conditional statement 'And the land shall yield her fruit' (v.19) which literary depends on the clause 'So you shall do my statutes' (v.18). This point suggests that the people probably experienced challenges in agricultural production, which resulted in food insecurity. Thus, it appears that the author chose to include the subject of food security and production in the discourse of law and the fear of Elohim because of some threat to food security. The dearth of food production, for any reason, would have resulted in food insecurity.

One of the several factors that could have contributed to food scarcity is drought but there is no evidence of the occurrence of drought in Leviticus 25:8–55. Another factor would be dissatisfaction among the labourers in the fields, which could occur if some or all of them were slaves. In the context of D, which distinctively seeks to address the challenge of slavery, this possibility would make sense. As such, the issue of slavery will be discussed below.

Second, it would be helpful to search for clues about the addressees of the Israelite Jubilee in D's theme of payment of compensation in vv.16, 24–26 and 48–52.

In the context of the prophecies of doom in the narratives of consequences and deliverance, several clues about the pre-exilic society could be sought. To understand a possible *Sitz-im-Leben* behind the motif of payment of compensation in order to regain lost land, first, it is important to consider how people acquired land. For example, the narrative of the Deuteronomistic History during the Omri Dynasty and the rule of Jeroboam II shows that, first, the poor acquired land by inheritance or as birth-right. People inherited the land that was previously owned by their family members, as shown by the Naboth narrative in 2 Kings 21. Furthermore, one could purchase land by paying a certain amount of money as Omri did to obtain his land. Ahab also offered Naboth money to purchase his land. Another way of acquiring land in the pre-exilic period particularly during the monarchical period was by force. The élites sometimes used their power to confiscate land from the owners especially from poor landowners. This trend is evident in the Naboth and Ahab narrative, and Jehu probably followed the same trend after he executed Ahab and his family. He is said to have obtained Naboth's vineyard.[203]

The interest here is in the payment of money for acquiring land especially during the monarchical period and with reference to the Omri dynasty. Omri, for example, was able to offer payment for land primarily because he had money and he was a member of the élite class who had political power, connection and money. Clearly, the people who could pay compensation were not the poor Israelites but the rich élites. Thus, when the provision for the payment of compensation was constituted, it favoured the rich élites. It follows then that in the pre-exilic period, the poor unlike the rich élites who had money found it difficult to acquire productive land under the conditions of the payment of compensation. By implication, the poor were in a position of disadvantage mainly because of their poverty and inability to offer money to recover land.

The Babylonian exilic society

Meyer notes, for instance, that in the light of the occurrence of the root שׁוב 'return' in Leviticus 25:10 which would have resonated within the Babylonian exilic context, an exilic dating of Leviticus 25 would be reasonable.[204] However, instead of dating Leviticus 25:8–55 entirely to the exilic period, we have identified two sources namely P and D in Leviticus 25:8–55, which are dated to the Babylonian exile.

(i) Addressees of P

First, to determine the possible addresses of P, P's distinct use of the liturgical musical instrument the שׁוֹפָר 'horn' in v.9 as well as the theological reason for and situation that triggered it should be considered. It appears that the addressees also belonged to the religious community, as those in the pre-exilic community. The work prohibition, which presumably refers to the Sabbath in v.11, also shows that the addressees knew something about religious laws. That clue may not be sufficient to validate the supposition that the addressees were also a religious community in the Babylonian exile, but P's term 'holy' in v.12 also suggests that the community which was probably addressed by the P author in the Babylonian context was religious. The use of the musical instrument שׁוֹפָר 'the horn' makes it difficult for one to make any other deduction than that the addressees were also religious. Therefore, other clues from the P features will be examined.

Other features that could be associated with the Babylonian context are found in the noun 'possession' and the theme of 'return to the homeland' in vv.13, 24–25, 27–28 and 32–34. If the trend of returning to the homeland is contained in Cyrus' edict, it is possible that the discourse of returning to the homeland began prior to the edict. Therefore, it makes sense to link the discourse of liberation to a situation that requires freedom. In this case, the idea of returning to the homeland was necessary in the situation of captivity. In all probability, the discourse of liberation and of returning to the homeland took place at a time the P Israelite addressees were still in captivity, with no land of their own and no independence.

Verses 32–33 contain the protection of the rights of the Levites to land ownership, as already noted. The obvious protection of the rights of a certain group at the expense of the rights of some other group constitutes unfairness. The preferential option given to the Levites by P appears to create an ideology that was typified by economic inequality and the disproportional distribution of benefits from the use of land. If we assume that P was active in the late exilic period, P's preference and sympathy for the Levites could be regarded only as an ideology, not a practice and one which would then be implemented later by the Levites in the post-exilic period. It would be reasonable to assume that the ideology of protecting the rights of the Levites had already been formulated in the late exilic period, that is, before its implementation in the post-exilic period.

One could also assume that the Levites had already been given land to cultivate in exile even though they could not own the land. Consequently, the preferential treatment of the Levites would perfectly fit with the late exilic period, that is, in the middle of the sixth century BCE. In other words, it would have been in practice in the period of the Babylonian exile. However, it is difficult to prove the agricultural activity of the Levites in exile, which could have confirmed that Levites were already economically favoured in the Babylonian exile.

Earlier, we have shown that the noun 'possession' is feminine in vv.45–46, and from an African liberationist point of view, one could argue that it was not uncommon for men to benefit exclusively from land without any consideration for women. The reference to possession does not highlight equal ownership or benefit from land use by both men and women. However, it appears reasonable to support the claim that there was an unequal distribution of the benefits from land use in the exilic context in terms of gender as in all ancient societies of the ancient Near East.

One cannot rule out the possibility that P's theme of deliverance from Egypt in v.42 was appropriate in the exilic context of captivity. It would have served as a theme of hope for liberation as in the Israelites' liberation from Egypt. Thus, locating P's theme of deliverance from Egypt in the exilic period is justified.

(ii) Addressees of D

In vv.10, 39–40 and 54, the noun 'liberty' which is related to D's reference to 'remission' and to the release of 'slaves' is used. The nouns presuppose a situation of captivity which required remission and release. The concept of release could have been directed to those in authority presumably the exilic élites who were in a position to influence the struggle for liberation. In other words, a discussion of liberation among the poor and the slaves would have been unproductive unless it was among those with power to implement liberation. Thus, the addressees of D who were the recipients of the theme of release of slaves were, in all probability, the exilic élites. The discourse of the release of slaves would also have made sense in the exilic context in which the Israelites needed liberation from the Babylonians.

Furthermore, it seems that the mention of the payment of compensation for land (vv.16, 24–26 and 48–52) described the Babylonian exilic situation. From the discussion above, we have determined that the subject of the payment of compensation is pre-exilic. However, it must have been re-iterated in the exilic period. By nature, the provision of payment of compensation favours the wealthy at the expense of the poor in terms of the equitable sharing of resources. It is unlikely that the idea of the payment of compensation was directed at the poor. If the Israelite deportees to Babylonia were the wealthy class who continued to be economically active in exile, as argued above, it would mean that the reference to the payment of compensation was directed at the exilic wealthy class. This was possibly to assist them to acquire land and protect their interests as they were about to be liberated from the Babylonian captivity.

Therefore, in preparation for the return to their homeland, D could have revised the pre-exilic theme of payment of compensation to suit the needs of the wealthy class in the later exilic situation, in which the wealthy class would need land on their return to the homeland. Just as the idea of payment of compensation would have been relevant in the late exilic period, so also would have been the theme of the Promised Land (Canaan). It is most likely that the theme was revisited and re-iterated in the late exilic period, as argued above.

The post-exilic society

(i) Addressees of P

One of the arguments above shows that in the Persian period, power resided with the priestly and scribal élites from the Babylonian exile who in turn sought to secure productive land on their return to Yehud (their homeland). P's theme of return to the homeland as well as the protection of the rights of the Levites (cf. vv.13, 27–28 and 32–33) seems to fit into the post-exilic period. It appears that the themes were directed at the Levites in order to protect their interests suggesting that the Levites and those in authority were the addressees of P in vv.13, 27–28 and 32–33.

In the post-exilic Yehud, the Levites continued to be the beneficiaries of the agricultural activities. The author of the post-exilic book of Nehemiah writes:

> For the people of Israel and the sons of Levi shall bring the contribution of grain, wine, and oil to the storerooms where the vessels of the sanctuary are, and where the priests that minister, and the gatekeepers and the singers are. We will not neglect the house of our God. (Neh 10:39)

(ii) Addressees of H

An interesting and critical feature of H that appears frequently in Leviticus 25:8–55 is the concern for social justice (cf. vv.12, 14–15, 25, 28, 35–37, 47 and 53) which triggers the question of whether the addressees were faced with issues of socio-economic injustice. The negative command 'you shall not oppress one another' (v.14) suggests that some form of oppression triggered the command. Further, from the structure of Leviticus 25:8–55, it is clear that the command was presented in the context of agricultural activity relating to the use of land. Therefore, there is strong indication that there was some degree of injustice in the handling of the issue of land. Moreover, v.25 shows that there was poverty among the addressees, as expressed in the conditional statement, 'If your brother becomes poor'. therefore, this statement gives us a clue that while some people used land productively, for example, for farming, others experienced poverty.

A critical question to ask at this point is, why did H use the statement 'and the land shall yield her fruit' (v.19)? The conditional statement could have been justified in a situation where the land did not yield her fruit. A situation in which the land was unproductive when farmed would fit the *Sitz-im-Leben* for the conditional statement 'and the land shall yield her fruit'. Furthermore, the relative use of the nouns 'fruits', 'field' and 'products' (vv.19, 22) indicates that the addressees were in all likelihood also farmers. Unfortunately, it seems the farmers' land was unproductive but the cause of the unproductiveness was not stated. It could have been due to drought or lack of resources and capital to farm or to any other reason. It seems that H's addressees were also struggling farmers, and it would help to consider the nature and impact of such a struggle, that is, the cause and effects of their struggle.

Nehemiah 5:4 which is a post-exilic text indicates that the Israelites had to use the money that accrued from farming to pay tax to the Persians: 'We have had to borrow money to pay the king's tax on our fields and vineyards' (Neh 5:4 NIV). The payment of taxes caused a strain on their farming; hence, they eventually struggled to make profit. In Nehemiah 5, there are also clues to the causes of loss of land and poverty. Verses 1–2 show that there was food shortage, and in v.11 Nehemiah advocated for the return of fields, vineyards, olive orchards and houses that belonged to the poor. Thus, it is clear that in the post-exilic period, the Israelites were faced with the challenge of loss of land, indebtedness and poverty. This explains H's concern for social justice or the redress of socio-economic injustice.

Nehemiah 5:1–2 provides a glimpse into the physical and emotional condition of the people. It states that 'The men and their wives raised a great outcry against their Jewish brothers. Some were saying, we and our sons and daughters are numerous, in order for us to live and stay alive, we must get grain'.[205] Nehemiah proceeded to challenge the leadership to restore to the poor people their fields, vineyards, olive orchards, and their houses as well as the interest they had charged on money, grain, wine and oil (Neh 5:11). On the socio-economic realities in post-exilic Yehud implied in both Nehemiah 5 and Leviticus 25:8–55, Nihan remarks:

> The economic situation described in Lev 25 has its closest parallel in the account of Neh 5:1–13—where Judean landowners are forced to sell their ancestral estate and, ultimately, become indentured slaves working on the estate of other, wealthy Judeans. (See Neh 5:8)[206]

Thus, it is reasonable to deduce that the addressees of the Israelite Jubilee in the post-exilic period, that is, in the fifth and the fourth century BCE experienced socio-economic injustice which widened the gap between the poor and the wealthy. Furthermore, Nehemiah 5 is not the only text that throws light on the life of the Jews in the post-exilic period who were probably the addressees of H. Concerning land and poverty, Deuteronomy 15, Jeremiah 32 and Ruth 4 come to mind. Some scholars have recognised a relationship between Leviticus 25 and Deuteronomy

15 especially because of the subject of land and poverty in the two texts.[207] In addition, Carroll and Grünwaldt correctly observe a connection between Jeremiah 32 and Leviticus 25.[208] In this case, the redemption or redistribution of land to a person who once lost it links the two texts. The evidence of the redemption of land and poverty in the book of Ruth also links Leviticus 25 to Ruth 4.[209] These texts sustain the view that in the post-exilic period the Israelites were faced with the challenge of poverty and landlessness. The situation locates the setting in life of the addressees of H in the post-exilic period which necessitated the call for socio-economic justice.

D's call for the payment of compensation and the distinction between the houses in villages and walled cities seem to favour the rich élites instead of the struggling farmers. Interestingly, H differs from D in that H's conditional statement 'But if he does not have enough (money) to restore it to himself' is more concerned about the poor especially the ones with no money. In all probability, H addressed both the poor and the rich but emphasised the plight of the poor. In fact, H rejects D's motif of payment of compensation as reflected in the connected negative commands 'Take no usury of him' (v.10) and 'or interest' (v.10). Thus, it is clear that H's interest focused on the plight of the poor while D's interest was with the rich élites, as will be demonstrated below. For H, poverty led to indebtedness, hence, his concern in v.35 for social justice, which had to be addressed. The verse refers to debt that was likely caused by poverty. Since H addressed both the rich returnees from the Babylonian exile and the poor who were not deported to Babylonia, one could agree with Meyer's claim that the addressees of Leviticus 25 were the wealthy élite returnees from exile who had money and the support of the Persian leadership.[210] However, I would not rule out the presence of the poor people in the post-exilic period as Meyer has done. That is, the addressees of Leviticus 25 were not merely the wealthy élite returnees from exile.

The formula 'I am Yahweh your Elohim' (vv.17 and 55) is also worth examining. I have argued earlier that the declarative statement 'for I am the Yahweh your Elohim' (v.17) provides a reason for fearing Elohim. That reason shows that H's addressees had some religious affiliation. Hence, there is theological justification for the objection to the oppression of others in Leviticus 25:8–55. Moreover, the use of the descriptive command 'it shall be holy to you' (v.12) which is distinctive of P shows the re-conceptualisation of holiness by H to accommodate the Israelite Jubilee. In the re-conceptualisation, a communal point of view is associated with the concept of holiness (cf. v.18). If the concept of holiness were presented in the context of the concern of social justice, it would then appear that the H's addressees were members of a religious community. Second, it would make sense to assume that such a community also faced socio-economic injustice.

On the features that were re-conceptualised by H, one could ask, if P's theme of deliverance from Egypt (vv.42, 55) referred to the captivity that the Babylonian exile embodied, why did H re-use it long after the liberation from exile? Were there other forms of captivity which called for liberation in the post-exilic period, and why would H find it imperative to re-conceptualise 'slavery' (vv.39–40, 44–46) after the Babylonian exile, which was regarded as captivity or slavery? A few scenarios may explain H's re-conceptualisation of exilic concepts. First, as Meyer has argued, H probably only sought to remind the Israelites particularly those who were from the Babylonian exile of their history so that they could preserve it.[211] This first scenario is not appealing enough, as it would not have necessitated the rewriting of that history. The second scenario is that H probably witnessed a situation that was similar to that of the exilic period. In other words, the Israelites encountered other forms of captivity in the post-exilic period which resembled the Babylonian exile. Hence, H re-conceptualised the idea of 'slavery' and the theme of 'deliverance from Egypt'. Could it be that the Judeans in Yehud were not free after the Babylonian exile?

According to Rugwiji, the Judeans were unfortunately not free in Yehud as the recurrence of oppression and poverty in this restored community suggests that liberation and economic stability did not prevail.[212] If this claim is correct, it would mean that H is justified to re-conceptualise the themes of 'slavery' and 'deliverance from Egypt' because the Yehud community continued to experience other forms of captivity. The fact that the Persians did not allow the Judeans to have their own government points out that the Judeans were not free.[213] Biblical evidence also shows that Jewish governors such as Nehemiah (cf. Neh 5:14); Sheshbazzar (cf. Ezra 5:14); Zerubbabel (cf. Hag 1:1, 2:2); and Persian officials (cf. Ezra 5:3, 6:6, 8:36; Neh 2:7, 3:7) were appointed not by the Judeans but by Persians to oversee the local administration of the province of Judah.

Interestingly, Rugwiji argues that slavery continued from Babylonia to Yehud. He claims that the Jews were slaves first in Babylonia, but he also draws evidence from post-exilic literature (cf. Neh 5:3–5; 9:36–37; Ezra 9:7–9) to show that the Judeans were equally treated as slaves by the Persian authorities.[214] Based on the biblical evidence, I would concur with Rugwiji that the Israelites were indeed not a free community in the post-exilic period. A number of scholars also agree that there was a degree of slavery or oppression and poverty in the post-exilic Yehud community.[215] However, unlike Brueggemann, Usue draws his claim from Nehemiah 5:3–5, which points out that indebtedness led to poverty and slavery, that is, the Israelites became debt-slaves under the Persian rule as post-exilic literature shows.

(iii) Addressees of D

The author of vv.29–31 makes a distinction between the provision of the walled cities and of houses in the villages. From an African liberationist perspective, and in line with Römer, the distinction shows the Persian ideology of segregation which is based on class and identity. Thus, it is almost certain that the addressees of vv.29–31 were the Golah community. The provision of vv.29–31 protects the interests of those residing in the walled cities who were probably the élites who returned from the Babylonian exile. It seems both the poor and the rich were the addressees of D in this instance. It is worth noting that the Golah community was faced with the challenge of inequality which is shown in the distinction between the property in the villages and those in the cities. Unfortunately, the D author did not address the inequality. However, the inequality is not surprising because even in the pre-exilic period, the D author who made provision for the payment of compensation had already favoured the rich élites against the poor who remained poor.

Scholars point out that throughout the Monarchic, neo-Assyrian and neo-Babylonian periods and even during the Persian period, large portions of agricultural land which produced wealth were owned by the rich and powerful élites who resided in the cities.[216] Thus, the rich élites most likely lived in cities whose productive land was managed by the poor Israelites. The rich élites resided in the cities but their wealth was generated by the poor. Given the apparent distinction between the ownership of land in the village and in the cities, it becomes clear that D preferred the rich élites to the poor.

Furthermore, it is possible that D's theme of 'slavery' was re-iterated in the post-exilic period especially if considered in the light of the persistence of slavery during the Persian rule. Rugwiji argues that the term '"slavery" … refers to a condition of being under the control of someone who exercises both economic and capitalistic power'.[217] Furthermore, 'Due to greed, the élite among the Judeans did not seem to adhere to the demands of the law on the treatment of the poor as evidenced by practicing the very 'evils' that the Torah prohibited'.[218] In that case, it appears that the rich élites continued to be the perpetuators of socio-economic injustice in the post-exilic period. The evidence of persistent slavery and of the socio-economic injustice, which was perpetuated by the élites shows the situation of the addressees of D.

Oppressive and Liberating Tendencies in Leviticus 25:8–55

Drawing on Mosala's pioneering work, which builds on the work of liberationist biblical scholars such as Gottwald, amongst others, it is critical that we investigate the aspects of Leviticus 25:8–55, which are both oppressive and liberating to its addressees. As Mosala has convincingly argued, the task of a socially engaged interpreter of the Hebrew Bible is to 'liberate the Bible so that the Bible can liberate us'.[219] Mosala's point suggests that the modern reader of the Old Testament needs to illuminate both the oppressive and liberating elements of ancient texts. Since Mosala is critical of 'the history, the devices, the culture, the ideologies and agendas' of ancient texts, his work is liberationist.[220] Gottwald adds a curious dimension to biblical hermeneutics of liberation. As mentioned in Chapter 1, he cautions us about easily discerning liberative lessons from not-so-liberative texts, as certain texts were the project of the élite kings and priests.[221] Therefore, an African liberationist approach adopted here is critical of both the liberative and oppressive lessons drawn from Leviticus 25:8–55. This section presents a liberationist sociological and ideological re-reading of historical-critical findings alongside the discussion of the strata (including the ideological contestations) of Leviticus 25:8–55 and of the historical re-construction of ancient Israelite society in the text in question.

With regard to v.10, H's contestation of the ideological position that the liberation of the poor could be attained not only through 'remission' but also through the release of debt-slave and the return of land to the poor reveals a liberating possibility of Leviticus 25:10 for its addressees. In line with Mosala's Marxist theory which the present study draws on, the argument that the concept of liberty in Leviticus 25:10 hints at socio-economic freedom and suggests the Israelite Jubilee may have offered liberating possibilities to its addressees.

Furthermore, the ideological contestation between H and P on the concept of holiness in vv.8–13 indicates the presence of oppression. In view of socio-economic justice, P's ideological conceptualisation of holiness as mainly concerned with priestly or cultic matters does not offer liberating possibilities to the poor. Rather, P's ideology seems to perpetuate poverty. From a liberationist perspective, the ideological concept of holiness should have covered dimensions that holistically liberate people, especially the oppressed Jews, rather than serving as a palliative to the poor. In terms of P's ideological framework, the ideology of holiness is comforting to the poor addressees of Leviticus 25:8–55, in that it calls the poor to focus mainly on cultic matters even though there were pertinent socio-economic injustice issues that needed to be addressed. Therefore, from African liberationist point of view, P's conceptualisation of holiness is oppressive.

However, H's contestation of P's ideological conceptualisation of holiness offers liberating possibilities as it presents holiness as intrinsically inseparable from issues of socio-economic justice. In other words, the ideological conceptualisation of holiness that ignores the redress of socio-economic injustice may be found wanting by a modern reader of the Bible whose eyes have been trained, hermeneutically, to be conscious of the struggle for liberation in modern context(s) and of the similar struggles of the oppressed and exploited of the biblical communities.[222] As Meyer has correctly perceived, H's cultic views are intertwined with the land issue.[223] However, he does not acknowledge that the link between cultic matters and the issue of land offered liberating possibilities to the poor, specifically, from a liberationist perspective. Interestingly, according to H, the redress of socio-economic injustice produces holiness. Clearly, H's contestation of P's ideological conceptualisation of holiness which led to the re-conceptualisation of holiness to include socio-economic justice appears to be liberating to the poor.

Furthermore, H's ideological position that holiness is linked to the issues of social justice in vv.14–15 offers liberating possibilities to the poor. The link is made by the use of the negative command אַל־תּוֹנוּ אִישׁ אֶת־אָחִיו 'you shall not oppress one another' (v.14) both vv.14 and 15, specifically, in the context of ancient Israelites' agricultural community.

We have earlier noted Bellinger's interpretation of the phrase וְנָתְנָה הָאָרֶץ פִּרְיָהּ 'and the land shall yield her fruit' (v.19) as 'the land will on its own produce an abundance' in v.18.[224] This observation is not liberating as it presumes that when the land is blessed it can produce fruit on its own without human labour. In this case, Bellinger's interpretation supports the persistence of the oppression of the poor as it does not highlight the need for the provision of financial capital and farming skills. However, productive land cannot produce fruits on its own without human labour as well as without the availability of skills and capital to work the land.

In v.19, the ideological view that Yahweh makes available to the poor a critical resource which when used efficiently would alleviate poverty seems to offer liberating possibilities to the poor. As in a situation in which land redistribution is coupled with both YHWH's blessing on the land and the effective use of the land, the inevitable result is productivity.[225] Therefore, it is reasonable to argue that the emphasis on productivity in v.19 bears liberating possibilities in that it upholds productivity with the view to avoid crippling the economy and intensifying poverty.

Another interpretation Leviticus 25:8–55 which is presented by Ross Kinsler and Gloria Kinsler views v.23 as the theological foundation for land redistribution because God is portrayed as the sole owner of the land.[226] On this point, H expresses an ideological position which cedes the re-centralisation of the ownership of land to Yahweh. Against the ideological position of the privatisation of productive land is H's theological and ideological position that YHWH owns the productive land. In this case, H's ideological position is liberating as it rejects a capitalistic tendency that perpetuates self-enrichment on the part of the rich élites. Furthermore, it seems that the people's benefit from land use was rooted in the centralisation of land ownership in which Yahweh is viewed as the owner of the land.[227] This argument supports the ideological position that the centralisation of productive land to YHWH advances the liberating possibility of the Israelite Jubilee legislation in that it refutes the self-enriching tendencies of the ruling élites in the ownership and use of land. As such, it is reasonable to argue that v.23 offers liberating possibilities to the poor. As mentioned above, the ideology of economic justice, which is implied in Leviticus 25:8–55, probably stemmed from the ideological position of centralisation in v.23 which ultimately proscribed the permanent ownership of land by a few rich élites.

Regarding v.23, H's ideological standpoint on the centralisation of land is set to contest the ideology of classism, which commoditised and privatised land in favour of the rich élites, as already noted above. If one considers Mosala's theoretical framework of Marxism, which refutes capitalism, one would appreciate v.23, which upholds the ideology of the centralisation of land against the privatisation of the ownership and use of productive land. From an ideological point of view, v.23 seeks to address poverty that emanates from the ideological position of privatisation of productive land. Thus, v.23 may be viewed as a liberating stratum.

As far as Leviticus 25:24 is concerned, it has been argued that the redistribution of land to the original owners, subject to the payment of compensation, represents a fair and equitable transaction.[228] However, the view that a person who sold his or her productive land because of poverty should offer some payment to regain the land appears to be oppressive to the poor. There is no way that a poor person can afford to pay the compensation money to attain productive land due to the existing state of poverty. Thus, it is clear that the ideological position of the payment of compensation to facilitate the process of transferring productive land to the poor, which P shares with D is oppressive. It is oppressive mainly because it does not provide or advocate for a reasonable process of land redistribution, which would be practical to the poor who do not have the economic resources for the payment of compensation. Furthermore, that the ideological position of the payment of compensation, which is shared by P and D stands in contestation to H's concern for socio-economic justice allows v.24 to be viewed as an oppressive text.

In vv.25–28, although the requirement of the payment of compensation appears to be oppressive to the poor, the idea that land could be returned without compensation in the Jubilee offers liberating possibilities. This means that vv.25–28 offers both liberating and oppressive possibilities to the addressees of the text. D's ideological position on the payment of compensation serves the interests of the rich élites who have financial resources, and it is therefore oppressive to the poor.

However, H's refutal of D's ideological standpoint on the payment of compensation renders vv.25–28 a liberating text especially for the poor. As such, the preferential option for the poor is detected in these verses. Furthermore, the view that the loss of land is not only caused by poverty but also sustained by socio-economic injustice confirms the liberating dimension of vv.26–28. Against the capitalist ideology of individualism, the ideological position of sharing wealth and land that is stipulated in vv.25, 35 and 39 is liberative as it is aimed at addressing poverty and socio-economic inequality.

As mentioned earlier, the unit of vv.29–34 serves the interests of the ruling and professional class which included the Golah élites as well as the Levites and scribes. No doubt, the ideology of economic inequality and segregation, which is based on class reveals an oppressive dimension to vv.29–34. Although the view expressed in these verse protects the rights of the rich people who resided in the cities as well as of the Levites, the ideology of classism and inequality that is upheld in vv.29–34 is oppressive as it perpetuates socio-economic injustice.

Verses 35–55 appear to offer liberating possibilities to the working-class people, except for vv.48 and 49. As observed earlier, D's ideological position on the payment of compensation served the interests of the Persian ruling élites but did not offer liberating possibilities to the poor Jews who experienced oppression from the non-Jews who held economic power in post-exilic Yehud. Additionally, D's requirement of the payment of compensation depicts the Jews as a commodity. Thus, vv.48 and 49 may be viewed as containing oppressive elements.

Conclusion

On the one hand, the present chapter set out to offer a positive contribution to the study of how socio-economic justice was upheld in the Israelite Jubilee in Leviticus 25:8–55. On the other hand, it has attempted to reconstruct the Israelite policy on land ownership and socio-economic justice in Leviticus 25:8–55. First, this research adopted the non-documentary hypothesis as the position in the Pentateuchal studies. The led us to consider various dates for the strata of Leviticus 25:8–55 rather than a single date. Thus, we were able to uncover the various ideological contestations in the text. Second, the chapter examined the literary context of Leviticus 25:8–55. Further, an analysis of the possible structure of the text was followed by a compositional and redactional analysis of the same passage, which was set within the framework of the non-documentarian approach. The *Sitz-im-Leben* of Leviticus 25:8–55 is also considered in the attempt to reconstruct the ancient Israelite society.

Traditionally, Leviticus 25:8–55 is interpreted as a text that belonged to the authors of the Holiness Code, as demonstrated above. If that interpretation is accepted as correct, then the text under discussion is a single unit with a single author, group of addressees and *Sitz-im-Leben*. Interestingly, the critical exegetical analysis of the text under consideration in this study has shown the verses that are dependent on each other as well as those which are independent and unrelated. Subsequently, the revelation of the verses that are not related to each other has led us to the uncovering of the ideological contestations that underlined the Israelite Jubilee law. Furthermore, as a result of the exegetical analysis of the text of Leviticus 25:8–55, with respect to the Jubilee, the composition and the redaction of the text were examined to determine the distinct strata in the Israelite Jubilee legislation. More importantly, the main reason for the compositional and redactional analysis of Leviticus 25:8–55 in this chapter was to probe the strata in the text in order to identify the author(s) or redactor(s) and their addressees. Thus, we have argued that other sources are present in Leviticus 25:8–55. The compositional and redactional analysis of Leviticus 25:8–55 has not only helped to uncover the various strata in the text in order to highlight different voices but it has also exposed the various ideological contestations in Leviticus 25:8–55. Based on the distinct features and ideological positions of sources such as D, P, D and the Pentateuchal redactor present in the text, the dating of the sources as well as the *Sitz-im-Leben* of their addressees were also investigated. The analysis has helped us to understand the Israelite policy of land and issues of socio-economic justice in Leviticus 25:8–55.

Subsequently, the analysis has helped us to determine that the addressees of D in the pre-exilic society were religious people. The provision of a theological reason for redressing oppression and poverty in D's motif of the fear of Elohim suggests that the addressees were religious people. The present chapter has also found that the rich élites used their power to confiscate land from the poor Israelites in the pre-exilic period. Therefore, the policy of Leviticus 25:8–55 sought to address such misuse of power in attaining productive land. However, on the acquisition of land in the pre-exilic period, people purchased land by paying a certain amount of money while the poor also acquired land through inheritance, as the story of Omri's dynasty shows. More importantly, it was noted that the poor found it difficult to acquire or regain productive land under D's condition, which required the payment of compensation, but it was easy for the rich élites because they had the financial capital to do so.

In the exilic period, the addressees of the P author were most likely also religious. P's addressees were captive Israelites in Babylonia who had no land of their own. The author of P also showed that the Levites were probably already favoured economically in the Babylonian period, and in the exilic context, the benefits from the land were unequally distributed in terms of gender. On the other hand, D's addressees in the exilic period were primarily the people in captivity, and D favoured the rich élites in the legislation of the payment of compensation when acquiring land. Therefore, in the exilic context, D elevated the rich élites, who were given privileges to acquire land but relegated the poor with the requirement of the payment of compensation.

Furthermore, it was argued that during the Persian rule, power rested with the priestly and scribal élites from the Babylonian exile whose main interest was to secure productive land on their return to Yehud. It is evident that in the post-exilic period, the Levites continued to be the beneficiaries of the agricultural activities in Yehud. However, unlike the addresses of P, H's addressees in the post-exilic period were faced with the challenge of loss of land, indebtedness and poverty. In fact, H addressed both the poor Judeans and the rich élites, but showed special interest in the plight of the poor. The élites had money and the support of the Persian leadership but unfortunately, the addressees of H were not free in Yehud, as elements of oppression and poverty continued to manifest in the post-exilic period.

The present chapter has pointed out the oppressive and liberating tendencies behind the production of Leviticus 25:8–55 in ancient Israel and its subsequent interpretations. In the process, it has highlighted instances in which the Israelite Jubilee law either supports or challenges the oppression of the addressees of the Israelite Jubilee. In response to the question, 'In whose interest was the composition and the redaction of Leviticus 25:8–55?', we have outlined instances in which the composer(s) and redactor(s) were inclined to affirm either the interests of the poor or those of the rich élites. The world of the production of the text of Leviticus 25:8–55 explored in the present chapter calls for an interaction between the *Sitz-im-Leben* of the Israelite Jubilee and the South African setting. This interaction will be steered by an African liberationist paradigm proposed in this study.

Notes

1. Itumeleng J. Mosala, "Biblical Hermeneutics and Black Theology in South Africa," PhD diss. (University of Cape Town, 1987), 248.
2. Leonidas Kalugila and Abdulaziz Y. Lodhi. *Methali Zaidi za kiSwahili toka Afrika Mashariki: more Swahili Proverbs from East Africa* (Uppsala: Nordiska Afrikainstitutet, 1980), 82.
3. Jeffrey Stackert, "Distinguishing Innerbiblical Exegesis from Pentateuchal Redaction: Leviticus 26 as a Test Case," in *The Pentateuch: International Perspectives on Current Research*, eds. Thomas B. Dozeman, Konrad Schmid, and Baruch J. Schwartz (Tübingen: Mohr Siebeck, 2011), 369.

4. Jacob Milgrom, *Leviticus 1–16: A New Translation with Introduction and Commentary* (New York: Doubleday, 1991), 698; Christophe Nihan, "The Laws about Clean and Unclean Animals in Leviticus and Deuteronomy and their Place in the Formation of the Pentateuch," in *The Pentateuch: International Perspectives on Current Research*, eds. Thomas B. Dozeman, Konrad Schmid, and Baruch J. Schwartz (Tübingen: Mohr Siebeck, 2011), 401; Esias E. Meyer, "Leviticus 11, Deuteronomy 14 and Directionality," *Journal for Semitics* 23, no. 1 (2014): 71.
5. Christophe Nihan, *From Priestly Torah to Pentateuch: A Study in the Composition of the Book of Leviticus* (Tübingen: Mohr Siebeck, 2007), 1.
6. Greg A. King, "The Documentary Hypothesis," *Journal of the Adventist Theological Society* 12, no. 1 (2001): 24–25.
7. Yehezkel Kaufmann, *The Religion of Israel: From its Beginnings to the Babylonian Exile*. Translated by Moshe Greenberg (New York: Schocken Books, 1972).
8. Baruch J. Schwartz, "Reexamining the Fate of the 'Canaanites' in the Torah Traditions," in *Sefer Moshe—The Moshe Weinfeld Jubilee Volume: Studies in the Bible and Ancient Near East, Qumran, and Post-biblical Judaism*, eds. Chaim Cohen, Avi Hurvitz, and Shalom M. Paul (Winona Lake, Indiana: Eisenbrauns, 2004), 153.
9. Esias E. Meyer, "Dating the Priestly Text in the Pre-exilic Period: Some Remarks about Anachronistic Slips and other Obstacles," *Verbum et Ecclesia* 31, no. 1 (2010): 1.
10. Joel S. Baden, "Identifying the Original Stratum of P: Theoretical and Practical Considerations," in *The Strata of the Priestly Writings: Contemporary Debate and Future Directions*, eds. Sarah Shectman and Joel S. Baden (Zürich: Theologischer Verlag Zürich, 2009), 13–30; Jeffrey Stackert, "The Holiness Legislation and its Pentateuchal Sources: Revision, Supplementation, and Replacement," in *The Strata of the Priestly Writings: Contemporary Debate and Future Directions*, eds. Sarah Shectman and Joel S. Baden (Zürich: Theologischer Verlag Zürich, 2009), 187–205; Stackert, "Innerbiblical Exegesis," 369–386; Baruch J. Schwartz, "'Profane' Slaughter and the Integrity of the Priestly Code," *Hebrew Union College Annual* 67 (1996): 15–42; Baruch J. Schwartz, *The Holiness Legislation: Studies in the Priestly Code* (Jerusalem: Magnes, 1999); Schwartz, "Reexamining the Fate," 151–170.
11. Stackert, "Innerbiblical Exegesis," 370.
12. Stackert, "Innerbiblical Exegesis," 371–372.
13. H refers to the Holiness Code authors; P to the Priestly authors; D to the Deuteronomistic School authors; E to the Elohist writers and CC represents the Covenant Code, while Pg refers to the first priestly document, the so-called 'Grundschrift'. See Thomas Römer, "The Exodus Narrative According to the Priestly Document," in *The Strata of the Priestly Writings: Contemporary Debate and Future Directions*, eds. Sarah Shectman and Joel S. Baden (Zürich: Theologischer Verlag Zürich, 2009), 159.
14. David M. Carr, *Reading the Fractures of Genesis: Historical and Literary Approaches* (Louisville: Westminster John Knox Press, 1996), 43; Philippe Guillaume, "Tracing the Origin of the Sabbatical Calendar in the Priestly Narrative (Genesis 1 to Joshua 5)," *The Journal of Hebrew Scriptures* 5, no. 13 (2005): 4; Konrad Schmid, "Genesis in the Pentateuch," in *The book of Genesis: Composition, Reception and Interpretation*, Vetus Testamentum Supplements 125, eds. Craig A. Evans, Joel N. Lohr, and David L. Petersen (Leiden: Brill, 2012), 34–37.

15. Konrad Schmid, "Genesis and Exodus as Two Formerly Independent Traditions of Origins for Ancient Israel," *Biblica* 93, no. 2 (2012): 197; Joel S. Baden, "The Continuity of the Non-Priestly Narrative from Genesis to Exodus," *Biblica* 93, no. 2 (2012): 161–186.
16. Schmid, "Genesis and Exodus," 198; cf. Baden, "Non-Priestly Narrative," 175.
17. Schmid, "Genesis and Exodus," 198.
18. Konrad Schmid, "The Late Persian Formation of the Torah: Observations on Deuteronomy 34," in *Judah and the Judeans in the Fourth Century B.C.E.*, eds. Obed Lipschits, Gary N. Knoppers, and Rainer Albertz (Winona Lake: Eisenbrauns, 2007), 236–245; Schmid, "Genesis and Exodus," 202; Baden, "Non-Priestly Narrative," 184.
19. Schmid, "Genesis and Exodus," 200; Joel S. Baden, *The Composition of the Pentateuch* (New Haven, CT: AB Reference Library, 2012), 248.
20. Schmid, "Genesis and Exodus," 201.
21. Stackert's definition of innerbiblical exegesis is remarkable. He views it as 'interpretive revision, reuse, expansion or application of biblical source material in subsequent biblical compositions'. See Stackert, "Innerbiblical Exegesis," 371. However, I would not restrict the definition to the compositional stage as he does, but also argue in favour of innerbiblical exegesis in the redactional phase, as will be shown below.
22. Stackert, "Innerbiblical Exegesis," 370.
23. Stackert, "Innerbiblical Exegesis," 373.
24. Schwartz, "Priestly Code," 15–16; Schwartz, "Reexamining the Fate," 165–170; Christophe Nihan, "The Holiness Code between D and P: Some Comments on the Function and Significance of Leviticus 17–26 in the Composition of the Pentateuch," in *Das Deuteronomium zwische Pentateuch und Deuteronomistischem Geschichtswerk*, eds. Eckart Otto and Reinhard Achenbach (Göttingen: Vandenhoeck & Ruprecht, 2004), 98–105; Nihan, *Priestly Torah*, 545–546; Stackert, "Holiness Legislation," 189; Stackert, "Innerbiblical Exegesis," 373–374.
25. Stackert, "Innerbiblical Exegesis," 371; Schwartz, "Priestly Code," 38–42.
26. Stackert, "Innerbiblical Exegesis," 371–386.
27. Stackert, "Innerbiblical Exegesis," 372; cf. Joel S. Baden, *J, E, and the Redaction of the Pentateuch* (Tübingen: Mohr Siebeck, 2009), 255–286.
28. Stackert, "Innerbiblical Exegesis," 372.
29. Stackert, "Innerbiblical Exegesis," 371.
30. Stackert, "Innerbiblical Exegesis," 374.
31. Stackert, "Innerbiblical Exegesis," 375; cf. Schwartz, *The Holiness Legislation*, 17–24; Schwartz, "Reexamining the Fate," 153; Baden, "Original Stratum of P," 13–29.
32. Nihan, *Priestly Torah*, 401.
33. Schwartz, "Reexamining the Fate," 153.
34. Schwartz, "Reexamining the Fate," 165–170; Baden, "Original Stratum of P," 13–29; Stackert, "Innerbiblical Exegesis," 375.
35. Schwartz, "Reexamining the Fate," 165–166; cf. Lev 18:28, 20:22–24.
36. Eckart Otto, "Deuteronomy between the Pentateuch and the Deuteronomistic History: Some Remarks about Thomas Römer, the So-called Deuteronomistic History," *Journal of Hebrew Scriptures* 9, no. 17 (2005): 22.
37. Otto, "Deuteronomy," 23.

38. Konrad Schmid, "The Persian Imperial Authorization as Historical Problem and as Biblical Construct: A Plea for Differentiations in the Current Debate," in *The Pentateuch as Torah: New Models for Understanding its Promulgation and Acceptance*, eds. Gary N. Knoppers and Bernard M. Levinson (Winona Lake: Eisenbrauns, 2007), 38; Thomas Römer, "How to Write a Literary History of the Hebrew Bible? A Response to David Carr and Konrad Schmid," *Indian theological studies* 50, no. 1 (2013): 9, 16; David M. Carr, *The Formation of the Hebrew Bible: A New Reconstruction* (Oxford: Oxford University Press, 2011), 124.
39. Schmid, "Genesis and Exodus," 198.
40. Madipoane Masenya (ngwan'a Mphahlele), "A bosadi (Womanhood) Reading of Proverbs 31:10–31," in *Other Ways of Reading: African Women and the Bible*, ed. Musa W. Dube (Atlanta and Geneva: Society of Biblical Literature and WCC Publications, 2001), 145–157; Ndikho Mtshiselwa, "Towards an Indigenous (Xhosa) South African Biblical Scholarship," *Old Testament Essays* 24, no. 3 (2011): 671.
41. Sangai Mohochi and Michae Wairungu. "Kiswahili," http://swahililanguage. stanford.edu/. (Accessed September 29, 2014).
42. Kalugila and Lodhi, *Methali Zaidi*, 82.
43. Kalugila and Lodhi, *Methali Zaidi*, 91.
44. Gerald O. West, "Biblical hermeneutics in Africa," in *African Theology on the Way: Current Conversations*, ed. Diane B. Stinton (London: SPCK, 2010), 30.
45. Somadoda Fikeni, "The Nature and Function of Izibongo-Panegyric Legends: The Case of the Xhosa People of South Africa," in *Indigenous People's Wisdom and Power: Affirming our Knowledge through Narrative*, eds. Julian Kunnie and and Nomalungelo Ivy Goduka (Burlington: Ashgate Publishing Company, 2006), 237; Vincent N. N. Mtshiselwa, "Leviticus 18: 22 and 20: 13 in Discussion with the Methodist Church of Southern Africa on Homosexuality," MA diss. (University of Pretoria, 2010), xi.
46. Nihan, *Priestly Torah*, 107–108.
47. Nihan, *Priestly Torah*, 520; cf. Gregory C. Chirichigno, *Debt-slavery in Israel and the Ancient Near East* (Journal of the Study of the Old Testament Supplement Series 141. Sheffield: Sheffield Academic Press, 1993), 317–321.
48. Nihan, *Priestly Torah*, 525–526.
49. José E. Ramírez Kidd, *Alterity and Identity in Israel: The rg in the Old Testament* (Beihefte zur Zeitschrift für die alttestamentliche Wissenschaft 283. Berlin/New York: Walter de Gruyter, 1999), 99–100; Nihan, *Priestly Torah*, 525–526, 534.
50. Mary Douglas, *Leviticus as Literature* (New York: Oxford University Press, 1999), 243; William H. Bellinger Jr., *New International Biblical Commentary: Leviticus and Numbers* (Peabody, Massachusetts: Hendrickson Publishers, 2001), 149.
51. Samuel E. Balentine, *Leviticus* (Louisville: Westminster John Knox Press, 2002), 193; Esias E. Meyer, *The Jubilee in Leviticus 25: A Theological Ethical Interpretation from a South African Perspective* (Vol. 15. Münster: LIT Verlag, 2005), 161–181; Jill A. Middlemas, *The Templeless Age: An Introduction to the History, Literature, and Theology of the "Exile"* (Louisville: Westminster John Knox Press, 2007), 128–129; Esias E. Meyer, "Returning to an Empty Land: Revisiting my Old Argument about the Jubilee," *Old Testament Essays* 27, no. 2 (2014): 503.
52. Meyer, "Leviticus 11," 505–507; cf. Robert P. Carroll, "The Myth of the Empty Land+ A Reflective Reading of Biblical Texts Focusing on Mythicized Sociopolitical Structuring during the 2nd-temple Period," *Semeia* 59 (1992): 83.

53. Meyer, "Empty Land," 516.
54. Carroll, "Empty Land," 83; Meyer, "Leviticus 11," 505–507.
55. Nihan, *Priestly Torah*, 537.
56. Klaus Grünwaldt, *Das Heiligkeitsgesetz Leviticus 17–26: Ursprüngliche Gestalt, Tradition und Theologie*, Vol. 271. (Berlin: Walter de Gruyter, 1999), 380–381; Meyer, *Jubilee in Leviticus*, 224.
57. Baruch J. Schwartz, "The Priestly Account of the Theophany and Lawgiving at Sinai," in *Texts, Temples, and Traditions: A Tribute to Menahem Haran*, eds. Michael V. Fox, Victor Avigdor Hurowitz, Avi Hurvitz, Michael L. Klein, Baruch J. Schwartz and Nili Shupak (Winona Lake, Indiana: Eisenbrauns, 1996), 123.
58. Christophe Nihan, "Forms and Functions of Purity in Leviticus," in *Purity and the forming of Religious Traditions in the Ancient Mediterranean World and Ancient Judaism*, eds. Christian Frevel and Christophe Nihan (Leiden: Koninklijke Brill NV, 2013), 313.
59. Nihan, *Priestly Torah*, 534–535.
60. Nihan, *Priestly Torah*, 520–521.
61. Eckart Otto, "The Holiness Code in Diachrony and Synchrony in the Legal Hermeneutics of the Pentateuch," in *The Strata of the Priestly Writings: Contemporary Debate and Future Directions*, eds. Sarah Shectman and Joel S. Baden (Zürich: Theologischer Verlag Zürich, 2009), 149.
62. Otto, "Holiness Code," 149.
63. Otto, "Holiness Code," 149.
64. Otto, "Holiness Code," 150; see also Esias E. Meyer, "From Cult to Community: The Two Halves of Leviticus," *Verbum et Ecclesia* 34, no. 2 (2013): 6.
65. Otto, "Holiness Code," 150.
66. Otto, "Holiness Code," 149; Thomas Römer, "How Many Books (Teuchs): Pentateuch, Hexateuch, Deuteronomistic History, or Enneateuch?," in *Pentateuch, Hexateuch or Enneateuch? Identifying literary works in Genesis through Kings*, eds. Thomas B. Dozeman, Thomas Römer, and Konrad Schmid (Atlanta: Society of Biblical Literature, 2011), 31. For Schmid, the Torah is established by the juxtaposition of P with JEP. Cf. Schmid, "Genesis," 236. Furthermore, he does not separate the Torah from the theme of land, but land is seen as one of Torah's conscious motifs, with reference to Deut 34. If one considers the minor reference to the law in Leviticus 25:8–55, Schmid's point would become weakened, that is, with regard to the Israelite Jubilee, even though Lev 25:8–55 is dominated by command statements.
67. Stackert, "Holiness Legislation," 188.
68. Nihan, *Priestly Torah*, 616–617.
69. Otto, "Holiness Code," 142.
70. Stackert, "Holiness Legislation," 189; cf. Schwartz, "Priestly Code," 15–16; Nihan, *Priestly Torah*, 545–546.
71. See Stackert, "Holiness Legislation," 189, for a detailed analysis of Numbers 18.
72. Stackert, "Holiness Legislation," 189–201.
73. Meyer, "Cult to Community," 6; cf. Eckart Otto, "Innerbiblische Exegese im Heiligkeitsgesetz Levitikus 17–26," in *Levitikus als Buch*, eds. Heinz-Josef Fabry and Hans-Winfried Jüngling (Berlin, Philo: Bonner Biblische Beiträge, 1999), 125–196; Nihan, *Priestly Torah*,

616; Mark Leuchter, "The Manumission Laws in Leviticus and Deuteronomy: The Jeremiah Connection," *Journal of Biblical Literature* 127, no. 4 (2008): 652–653; Michael Bartos and Bernard M. Levinson. "'This Is the Manner of the Remission': Implicit Legal Exegesis in 11QMelchizedek as a Response to the Formation of the Torah," *Journal of Biblical Literature* 132, no. 2 (2013): 353.

74. Otto, "Holiness Code," 136, 138, 142.
75. Schmid, "Torah," 239–240.
76. Erhard S. Gerstenberger, *Leviticus: A Commentary* (Louisville: Westminster John Knox Press, 1996), 377.
77. Gerstenberger, *Leviticus*, 377; cf. Guillaume, "Sabbatical Calendar," 4.
78. Jacob Milgrom, *Leviticus 23–27: A New Translation with Introduction and Commentary* (New York: Doubleday, 2001), 2322–2323; Meyer, "Dating the Priestly Text," 1–4.
79. Gerstenberger, *Leviticus*, 377–378.
80. See also Isaiah 61:1 for a similar use of the noun liberty.
81. Bartos and Levinson, "Manner of the Remission," 352.
82. Bartos and Levinson, "Manner of the Remission," 354.
83. Gerstenberger, *Leviticus*, 378.
84. Frank H. Gorman, *Divine Presence and Community: A Commentary on the Book of Leviticus* (Grand Rapids: Wm. B. Eerdmans Publishing Company, 1997), 138; Stephen Mott and Ronald J. Sider, "Economic Justice: A Biblical Paradigm," *Transformation* 17, no. 2 (2000): 58; Mark F. Rooker, *The New American Commentary, vol. 3A, Leviticus* (Nashville: Broadman and Holman Publishers, 2000), 306; Bellinger Jr., *Leviticus and Numbers*, 151; Balentine, *Leviticus*, 195; Tamara C. Eskenazi, and Andrea L. Weiss, eds. *The Torah: a Women's Commentary* (New York: URJ Press and Women of Reform Judaism, 2008), 750.
85. Schmid, "Genesis," 34–37.
86. Israel Knohl, *The Sanctuary of Silence: The Priestly Torah and the Holiness School* (Minneapolis: Fortress Press, 1995), 17–18; Jeffrey Stackert, "Compositional Strata in the Priestly Sabbath: Exodus 31: 12–17 and 35: 1–3." Journal of Hebrew Scriptures 11 (2012): 13–14; Jacob Milgrom, "HR in Leviticus and Elsewhere in the Torah," in *The book of Leviticus: composition and reception*, eds. Rolf Rendtorff, Robert A. Kugler, and Sarah Smith Bartlet (Leiden: Brill, 2003), 38–39.
87. Knohl, *Sanctuary of Silence*, 18; Stackert, "Compositional Strata," 9.
88. Stackert, "Compositional Strata," 9; cf. Knohl, *Sanctuary of Silence*, 196.
89. Baden, "Original Stratum of P," 24.
90. Baden, "Original Stratum of P," 23.
91. Baden, "Original Stratum of P," 23.
92. Milgrom, *Leviticus 1–16*, 649–652, 733.
93. Esias E. Meyer, "Divide and be Different: Priestly Identity in the Persian Period," *HTS Theological Studies* 68, no. 1 (2012): 57.
94. John J. Collins, *Introduction to the Hebrew Bible* (Minneapolis: Fortress Press, 2004), 139; Meyer, "Dating the Priestly Text," 2. The Priestly corpus includes both H and P materials. Cf. Stackert, "Holiness Legislation," 187.
95. Meyer, "Cult to Community," 1; cf. Knohl, *Sanctuary of Silence*, 175–180; Jacob Milgrom, *Leviticus—A Book of Ritual and Ethics: A Continental Commentary* (Minneapolis: Fortress

Press, 2004), 215–219; Christophe Nihan, "The Priestly Covenant, its Reinterpretations and the Composition of 'P,'" in *The Strata of the Priestly Writings: Contemporary Debate and Future Directions*, eds. by Sarah Shectman and Joel S. Baden (Zürich: Theologischer Verlag Zürich, 2009), 89.

96. Stackert, "Innerbiblical Exegesis," 374; cf. Knohl, *Sanctuary of Silence*, 201–203.
97. Carr, *Fractures of Genesis,* 43; Guillaume, "Sabbatical Calendar," 4.
98. Collins, *Hebrew Bible*, 146, 151; cf. Knohl, *Sanctuary of Silence*, 175–180.
99. Leigh M. Trevaskis, *Holiness, Ethics and Ritual in Leviticus*, Vol. 29. (Sheffield: Sheffield Academic Press, 2011), 4; cf. David P. Wright, "Holiness in Leviticus and Beyond: Differing Perspectives," *Interpretation* 53, no. 4 (1999): 352.
100. The Kings James Version (KJV) prefers 'perfect' whiles the New American Standard Bible (NAS) opts for 'blameless'. Even though one would translate תָּמִים as sound or complete or without defect, the NAS version appears attractive as it elevates the theme of integrity.
101. Stackert, "Compositional Strata," 4.
102. Knohl, *Sanctuary of Silence*, 8–14; Jacob Milgrom, *Leviticus 17–22: A New Translation with Introduction and Commentary* (New York: Doubleday, 2000), 1319–1443; Baruch J. Schwartz, "Introduction: The Strata of the Priestly Writings and the Revised Relative Dating of P and H," in *The Strata of the Priestly Writings: Contemporary Debate and Future Directions*, eds. Sarah Shectman and Joel S. Baden (Zürich: Theologischer Verlag Zürich, 2009), 5.
103. Thomas Römer, *The So-called Deuteronomistic History: A Sociological, Historical and Literary Introduction* (London: T & T Clark International, 2005), 178.
104. Louis Jonker, "The Exile as Sabbath Rest: The Chronicler's Interpretation of the Exile," *Old Testament Essays* 20, no. 3 (2007): 710–711; cf. Meyer, *Jubilee in Leviticus*, 161.
105. Jonker, "Exile," 710–711.
106. Römer, *Deuteronomistic History*, 116.
107. Konrad Schmid, "The So-called Yahwist and the Literary Gap between Genesis and Exodus," in *A Farewell to the Yahwist? The Composition of the Pentateuch in Recent European Interpretation*, eds. Thomas B. Dozeman and Konrad Schmid (Atlanta: Society of Biblical Literature, 2006), 39.
108. For a clear reference to P texts see Schmid, "So-called Yahwist," 39.
109. Römer, "Exodus Narrative," 162.
110. Collins, *Hebrew Bible*, 148; cf. Knohl, *Sanctuary of Silence*, 16; Milgrom, *Leviticus 17–22*, 1338–1339; Nihan, *Priestly Torah*, 567; Stackert, "Compositional Strata," 19.
111. Römer, "Exodus Narrative," 161.
112. Werner H. Schmidt, *Old Testament Introduction* (Trans. Matthew L. O'Connell with David J. Reimer. Berlin and New York: Walter de Gruyter & Co. and Louisville: Westminster John Knox Press, 1999), 91.
113. Nihan, *Priestly Torah*, 465, 468.
114. Baden, *Pentateuch*, 156, 158.
115. Baden, *Pentateuch*, 192.
116. Meyer, "Cult to Community," 1–7.
117. Meyer, "Cult to Community," 7.

118. Meyer, "Cult to Community," 7; cf. Lev 20:22–27; 26:1–2.
119. Otto, "Innerbiblische Exegese," 173.
120. Römer, *Deuteronomistic History*, 135, 136.
121. Bellinger Jr., *Leviticus and Numbers*, 154.
122. Bellinger Jr., *Leviticus and Numbers*, 150; cf. Balentine, *Leviticus*, 194.
123. Eskenazi and Weiss, *Torah*, 752.
124. Jonathan Warner, "Towards a Christian Economics?," *Pro Rege* 30, no. 1 (2001): 16.
125. Otto, "Holiness Code," 140.
126. Ross Kinsler, and Gloria Kinsler. *The Biblical Jubilee and the Struggle for Life. Maryknoll* (New York: Orbis Books, 1999), 15; cf. Eskenazi and Weiss, *Torah*, 753.
127. Douglas, *Leviticus*, 243; Rooker, *Leviticus*, 306; Bellinger Jr., *Leviticus and Numbers*, 151.
128. Milgrom, *Leviticus*, 298.
129. Römer, *Deuteronomistic History*, 116.
130. Schmid, "Torah," 239–240; Schmid, "Genesis," 32.
131. See also Gen 17:8 and 28:4.
132. Römer, "Exodus Narrative," 164.
133. Schmid, "So-called Yahwist," 43.
134. Knohl, *Sanctuary of Silence*, 217.
135. See also Num 5:5–8; Ruth 4:1–6; Jer 32:6–9.
136. Balentine, *Leviticus*, 195; cf. Gorman, *Divine Presence*, 139–140; Rooker, *Leviticus*, 307; Bellinger Jr., *Leviticus and Numbers*, 151–152.
137. Roland K. Harrison, *Leviticus: An Introduction and Commentary* (Leicester: Inter-Varsity Press, 1980), 229.
138. Graham J. Philpott and Mark Butler. "Land in South Africa: Gift for all or Commodity for a Few," *Occasional Paper* 1 (2005): 2.
139. Douglas, *Leviticus*, 243; Kinsler and Kinsler, *Biblical Jubilee*, 16; Bellinger Jr., *Leviticus and Numbers*, 150.
140. Douglas, *Leviticus*, 243; Kinsler and Kinsler, *Biblical Jubilee*, 17.
141. Douglas, *Leviticus*, 243; Bellinger Jr., *Leviticus and Numbers*, 149.
142. Bellinger Jr., *Leviticus and Numbers*, 149–150; cf. Harrison, *Leviticus*, 226; Douglas, *Leviticus*, 243.
143. Römer, *Deuteronomistic History*, 175.
144. Römer, *Deuteronomistic History*, 177.
145. Römer, *Deuteronomistic History*, 169, 171.
146. Baden, "Original Stratum of P," 23–25; Jan Joosten, *People and Land in the Holiness Code: An Exegetical Study of the Ideational Framework of the Law in Leviticus 17–26*, Vetus Testamentum Supplements 67 (Leiden: Brill, 1996), 194–195.
147. Baden, "Original Stratum of P," 24; Erhard Blum, "Issues and Problems in the Contemporary Debate Regarding the Priestly Writings," in *The Strata of the Priestly Writings: Contemporary Debate and Future Directions*, eds. Sarah Shectman and Joel S. Baden (Zürich: Theologischer Verlag Zürich, 2009), 33.
148. Römer, *Deuteronomistic History*, 116.
149. Douglas A. Knight, *Law, Power and Justice in Ancient Israel* (Louisville: Westminster John Knox Press, 2011), 203.

150. Gorman, *Divine Presence*, 140.
151. Römer, *Deuteronomistic History*, 175, 177.
152. Baden, "Original Stratum of P," 25.
153. Schmid, "So-called Yahwist," 43.
154. Otto, "Holiness Code," 140.
155. Nihan, *Priestly Torah*, 520–521.
156. Nihan, *Priestly Torah*, 520.
157. Nihan, *Priestly Torah*, 521.
158. Stackert, "Compositional Strata," 6; cf. Otto, "Innerbiblische Exegese," 125–196; Bernard M. Levinson, "The Birth of the Lemma: The Restrictive Reinterpretation of the Covenant Code's Manumission Law by the Holiness Code (Leviticus 25:44–46)," *Journal of Biblical Literature* 124, no. 4 (2005): 617–639; Nihan, *Priestly Torah*, 616; Leuchter, "Manumission Laws," 637; Otto, "Holiness Code," 139; Meyer, "Cult to Community," 6–7.
159. Leuchter, "Manumission Laws," 637.
160. Leuchter, "Manumission Laws," 641; cf. Bernard M. Levinson, "The Manumission of Hermeneutics: The Slave Laws of the Pentateuch as a Challenge to Contemporary Pentateuchal Theory," in *Congress Volume Leiden*, Vetus Testamentum Supplements 108, ed. André Lemaire (Leiden: Brill, 2004), 302; Baden, *Pentateuch*, 266–267.
161. Temba Rugwiji, "Appropriating Judean Post-exilic Literature in a Postcolonial Discourse: A Case for Zimbabwe," PhD diss. (Pretoria, University of South Africa, 2013), 44; cf. Neh 2:7; 3:7; Ezr 5:3; 6:6; 8:36
162. Eben Scheffler, *Politics in Ancient Israel* (Pretoria: Biblia Publishers, 2001), 139.
163. Nihan, *Priestly Torah*, 520–521, Carr, *Hebrew Bible,* 124; Römer, "How to Write," 9ff; cf. Schwartz, *Holiness Legislation*, 17–24; Schwartz, "Reexamining the Fate," 153; Baden, "Original Stratum of P," 13–29.
164. Schmid, "Genesis and Exodus," 198.
165. Meyer, "Leviticus 11," 509; cf. Eckart Otto, "The Pentateuch in Synchronical and Diachronical Perspectives: Protorabbinic Scribal Erudition Mediating between Deuteronomy and the Priestly Code," in *Das Deuteronomium zwischen Pentateuch and Deuteronomistischem Geschhichtwerk*, Frlant 206, eds. Eckart Otto and Reinhard Achenbach (Göttingen: Vandenhoeck and Ruprecht, 2004), 30–32; Otto, "Holiness Code," 139; Nihan, *Priestly Torah*, 545–559; Nihan, "Forms and Functions," 316.
166. Otto, "Pentateuch," 30–32; Otto, "Holiness Code," 139.
167. Meyer, *Jubilee in Leviticus*, 221–255.
168. Jacob Milgrom, "The Antiquity of the Priestly Source: A Reply to Joseph Blenkinsopp," *Zeitschrift für die alttestamentliche Wissenschaft* 111, no. 1 (1999): 10–22; Meyer, "Dating the Priestly Text," 1–6.
169. Meyer, *Jubilee in Leviticus*, 252–253; cf. Knohl, *Sanctuary of Silence*, 213, 223.
170. Joosten, *People and Land*, 203–207.
171. Meyer, *Jubilee in Leviticus*, 223; also see Schwartz, "Priestly Code," 15; Grünwaldt, *Leviticus 17–26*, 375–381; Otto, "Innerbiblische Exegese," 134; Otto, "Holiness Code," 139. Although one would have expected Meyer to probe the possibility of a late exilic dating of H, he does not move in that direction.

172. Grünwaldt, *Leviticus 17–26*, 380–381; Meyer, *Jubilee in Leviticus*, 224, 228; cf. Lev 26:13.
173. Meyer, *Jubilee in Leviticus*, 227.
174. Meyer, *Jubilee in Leviticus*, 224; cf. Grünwaldt, *Leviticus 17–26*, 380–381.
175. Jan Joosten, "The Distinction between Classical and late Biblical Hebrew as Reflected in Syntax," *Hebrew Studies* 46, no. 1 (2005): 328.
176. Joseph Blenkinsopp, "Abraham as Paradigm in the Priestly History in Genesis," *Journal of Biblical Literature* 128, no. 2 (2009): 225, 230; cf. Joseph Blenkinsopp, *The Pentateuch: an introduction to the first five books of the Bible* (New Haven: Yale University Press, 1992), 4–11; Erich Zenger, "Theorien Über die Entstehung des Pentateuch im Wandel der Forschung," in *Einleitung in das Alte Testament*. 5th edition, ed. Erich Zenger (Kohlhammer: Stuttgart, 2004), 90–91.
177. Schwartz, "Priestly Code," 36.
178. Walter Brueggemann, *An Introduction to the Old Testament: The Canon and Christian Imagination* (Louisville: Westminster John Knox Press, 2003), 113.
179. Meyer, "Empty Land," 510; cf. Nihan, *Priestly Torah*, 383; Jakob Wöhrle, "The Un-empty Land: The Concept of Exile and Land in P," in *The Concept of Exile in Ancient Israel and its Historical Context*, eds. Ehud Ben Zvi and Christoph Levin (Berlin: Walter de Gruyter, 2010), 189–206.
180. Nihan, *Priestly Torah,* 383; Christophe Nihan, "Resident Aliens and Natives in the Holiness Legislation," in *The Foreign and the Law: Perspectives from the Hebrew Bible and the Ancient Near East*, eds. Reinhard Achenbach, Rainer Albertz, and Jakob Wöhrle (Wiesbaden: Harrassowitz Verlag, 2011), 131.
181. Blenkinsopp, *Pentateuch*, 7–8; Nihan, *Priestly Torah*, 572–575; Reinhard Achenbach, "Das Heiligkeitzgesetz und die Sakralen Ordnungen des Numeribuches im Horizont der Pentateuchredaktion," in *The Books of Leviticus and Numbers*, ed. Thomas Römer (Leuven: Uitgeverij Peeters, 2008), 155; Meyer, "Divide," 57.
182. From this viewpoint, it is clear that the date of P is determined in relation to H, while P is more reliable and decisive than H, as argued above. Should one therefore not probe an H dating based on P's date? Having decisively identified the strata in Leviticus 25:8–55, with P being used as a base stratum, we can safely use H to date P. Here, the reason for using H and moving backwards is mainly that Leviticus 25 is viewed generally as belonging to H, which is not entirely convincing. Besides, we have already identified above the stratum with the help of P.
183. Joseph Blenkinsopp, "An Assessment of the Alleged Pre-exilic Date of the Priestly Material in the Pentateuch," *Zeitschrift für die alttestamentliche Wissenschaft* 108, no. 4 (1996): 514.
184. Milgrom, *Leviticus 1–16*, 5; Avi Hurvitz, "Once Again: The Linguistic Profile of the Priestly Material in the Pentateuch and its Historical Age. A Response to J. Blenkinsopp," *Zeitschrift für die alttestamentliche Wissenschaft* 112, no. 2 (2000): 180–191.
185. Milgrom, *Leviticus 1–16*, 5.
186. Meyer, "Dating the Priestly Text," 3.
187. Otto, "Deuteronomy," 24; cf. Römer, *Deuteronomistic History*, 67–106.
188. Martin Noth, *The Deuteronomistic History*, Journal of the Study of the Old Testament Supplement Series 15. (Sheffield: Sheffield Academic Press, 1991), 145; cf. Otto, "Deuteronomy," 23; Römer, *Deuteronomistic History*, 23–24.

189. Römer, *Deuteronomistic History*, 68.
190. Eckart Otto, "Torah and Prophecy: A Debate of Changing Identities," *Verbum et Ecclesia* 34, no. 2 (2013): 1–5; cf. Scheffler, *Politics*, 136; Deut 4:29; 30.
191. Römer, *Deuteronomistic History*, 72.
192. Scheffler, *Politics*, 135–137; Eben Scheffler, "The Exilic Literature (586–539 BCE)," in *Ancient Israelite Literature in Context*, eds. Willem S. Boshoff, Eben Scheffler, and Izak J. J. Spangenberg (Hatfield: Protea Bookshop, 2000), 142–167; cf. Jer 29:5–7.
193. Blenkinsopp, "Abraham," 230.
194. Römer, *Deuteronomistic History*, 72.
195. Römer, *Deuteronomistic History*, 175, 177.
196. David P. Wright, *Inventing God's Law: How the Covenant Code of the Bible Used and Revised the Laws of Hammurabi* (New York: Oxford University Press, 2009), 5.
197. Otto, "Deuteronomy," 22; Thomas Römer, "The Elusive Yahwist: A Short History of Research," in *A Farewell to the Yahwist? The Composition of the Pentateuch in Recent European Interpretation*, eds. Thomas B. Dozeman and Konrad Schmid (Atlanta: Society of Biblical Literature, 2006), 24–27; Schmid, "So-called Yahwist," 29–31.
198. Bernard M. Levinson, *Deuteronomy and the Hermeneutics of Legal Innovation* (New York: Oxford University Press, 1997), 11.
199. Bernard M. Levinson, "The Case for Revision and Interpolation within the Biblical Legal Corpora," in *Theory and Method in Biblical and Cuneiform Law*, Journal of the Study of the Old Testament Supplement Series 181, ed. Bernard M. Levinson (Sheffield: Sheffield Academic Press, 1994), 37–59; Eckart Otto, "Aspects of Legal Reforms and Reformulations in Ancient Cuneiform and Ancient Law," in *Theory and Method in Biblical and Cuneiform Law*, Journal of the Study of the Old Testament Supplement Series 181, ed. Bernard M. Levinson (Sheffield: Sheffield Academic Press, 1994), 160–196.
200. See the discussion of the stratification of Leviticus 25:8–55.
201. The manner in which the motif is re-used by D is illustrated above.
202. In this section, the reconstruction of the ancient Israelite society will interact minimally with the works of previous scholars. Most of the inferences will emanate from the study conducted so far in the present study. However, this does not mean that the inferences will not be qualified by evidence from other scholars.
203. Evidence of Jehu's possession of Naboth's vineyard is presented by Franklin. According to him, archaeological findings suggest that Jezreel's enclosure shows that someone else other than Ahab later occupied the land which was seized from Naboth, and that this was most likely a Jeroboam rather than a Jezebel initiative. See Norma Franklin, "Jezreel: Before and after Jezebel," in *Israel in Transition: from Late Bronze II to Iron IIa (c. 1250–850 B.C.E.)*. Volume 1. The Archaeology, ed. Lester L. Grabbe (New York/London: T & T Clark, 2008), 45, 51.
204. Meyer, "Empty Land," 505.
205. In this instance, the New International Version (NIV) is used.
206. Nihan, "Resident Aliens," 131.
207. Meyer, *Jubilee in Leviticus*, 189; cf. Otto, "Innerbiblische Exegese," 168.
208. Robert P. Carroll, *From Chaos to Covenant: Uses of Prophecy in the book of Jeremiah* (London: SCM Press, 1981), 108–124; Grünwaldt, *Leviticus 17–26*, 322–323.

209. Madipoane Masenya, "Struggling with Poverty/emptiness: Rereading the Naomi-Ruth Story in African-South Africa," *Journal of Theology for Southern Africa* 120 (2004): 46–59; Madipoane Masenya, "Is Ruth the 'ēšet hayil for Real? An Exploration of Womanhood from African Proverbs to the Threshing Floor (Ruth 3:1–13)," *Studia Historiae Ecclesiasticae* 36 (2010): 1–21.
210. Meyer, *Jubilee in Leviticus*, 253.
211. Meyer, *Jubilee in Leviticus*, 243.
212. Rugwiji, "Appropriating," 38.
213. Rugwiji, "Appropriating," 44.
214. Daniel L. Smith, *The Religion of the Landless: The Social Context of the Babylonian Exile* (Bloomington: Meyer Stone Books, 1989), 38–41; cf. Walter Brueggemann, *Cadences of Home: Preaching Among Exiles* (Louisville: Westminster John Knox Press, 1997), 115; Emmanuel O. Usue, "Restoration or Desperation in Ezra and Nehemiah? Implications for Africa," *Old Testament Essays* 20, no. 3 (2007): 843; Rugwiji, "Appropriating," 46.
215. Brueggemann, *Cadences of Home*, 115; Usue, "Ezra and Nehemiah," 843.
216. Knight, *Law, Power and Justice*, 202.
217. Rugwiji, "Appropriating," 89.
218. Rugwiji, "Appropriating," 90; cf. Lev 25:36–37.
219. Itumeleng J. Mosala, "Wealth and Poverty in the Old Testament—A Black Theological Perspective," *Journal of black theology in South Africa* 5 (1996): 21; cf. Itumeleng J. Mosala, "Reconstructing the Azanian mišp h t (Clans): Land, Class and Bible in South Africa Today," in *Text and Experience: Towards a Cultural Exegesis of the Bible*, ed. Daniel L. Smith-Christopher (Sheffield: Sheffield Academic Press, 1995), 239.
220. Mosala, "Wealth and Poverty," 138; cf. Terry Eagleton, *Walter Benjamin: Or Towards a Revolutionary Criticism* (London: Verso, 1981), 113.
221. Norman Gottwald, *The Tribes of Yahweh: A Sociology of the Religion of Liberated Israel 1250–1050 B.C.E.* (Sheffield: Sheffield Academic Press, 1999), 35.
222. Mosala, "Biblical Hermeneutics," 248.
223. Meyer, "Cult to Community," 7.
224. Bellinger Jr., *Leviticus and Numbers*, 150; Balentine, *Leviticus*, 194.
225. Eskenazi and Weiss, *Torah*, 752.
226. Kinsler and Kinsler, *Biblical Jubilee*, 15; Eskenazi and Weiss, *Torah*, 753.
227. Douglas, *Leviticus*, 243; Rooker, *Leviticus*, 306; Bellinger Jr., *Leviticus and Numbers*, 151.
228. Gorman, *Divine Presence*, 139–140; Rooker, *Leviticus*, 307; Bellinger Jr., *Leviticus and Numbers*, 151–152; Balentine, *Leviticus*, 195.

References

Achenbach, Reinhard. "Das Heiligkeitzgesetz und die Sakralen Ordnungen des Numeribuches im Horizont der Pentateuchredaktion." In *The Books of Leviticus and Numbers*, edited by Thomas Römer, 145–176. Leuven: Uitgeverij Peeters, 2008.

Baden, Joel S. "Identifying the Original Stratum of P: Theoretical and Practical Considerations." In *The Strata of the Priestly Writings: Contemporary Debate and Future Directions*, edited by Sarah Shectman and Joel S. Baden, 13–30. Zürich: Theologischer Verlag Zürich, 2009.

Baden, Joel S. *J, E, and the Redaction of the Pentateuch*. Tübingen: Mohr Siebeck, 2009.

Baden, Joel S. "The Continuity of the Non-Priestly Narrative from Genesis to Exodus." *Biblica* 93, no. 2 (2012): 161–186.

Baden, Joel S. *The Composition of the Pentateuch*. New Haven, CT: AB Reference Library, 2012.

Balentine, Samuel E. *Leviticus*. Louisville: Westminster John Knox Press, 2002.

Bartos, Michael, and Bernard M. Levinson. "'This Is the Manner of the Remission': Implicit Legal Exegesis in 11QMelchizedek as a Response to the Formation of the Torah." *Journal of Biblical Literature* 132, no. 2 (2013): 351–371.Bellinger Jr, William H. *New International Biblical Commentary: Leviticus and Numbers*. Peabody, Massachusetts: Hendrickson Publishers, 2001.

Blenkinsopp, Joseph. *The Pentateuch: an introduction to the first five books of the Bible*. New Haven: Yale University Press, 1992.

Blenkinsopp, Joseph. "An Assessment of the Alleged Pre-exilic Date of the Priestly Material in the Pentateuch." *Zeitschrift für die alttestamentliche Wissenschaft* 108, no. 4 (1996): 495–518.

Blenkinsopp, Joseph. "Abraham as Paradigm in the Priestly History in Genesis." *Journal of Biblical Literature* 128, no. 2 (2009): 225–241.

Blum, Erhard. "Issues and Problems in the Contemporary Debate Regarding the Priestly Writings." In *The Strata of the Priestly Writings: Contemporary Debate and Future Directions*, edited by Sarah Shectman and Joel S. Baden, 31–44. Zürich: Theologischer Verlag Zürich, 2009.

Brueggemann, Walter. *Cadences of Home: Preaching Among Exiles*. Louisville: Westminster John Knox Press, 1997.

Brueggemann, Walter. *An Introduction to the Old Testament: The Canon and Christian Imagination*. Louisville: Westminster John Knox Press, 2003.

Carr, David M. *Reading the Fractures of Genesis: Historical and Literary Approaches*. Louisville: Westminster John Knox Press, 1996.

Carr, David M. *The Formation of the Hebrew Bible: A New Reconstruction*. Oxford: Oxford University Press, 2011.

Carroll, Robert P. *From Chaos to Covenant: Uses of Prophecy in the Book of Jeremiah*. London: SCM Press, 1981.

Carroll, Robert P. "The Myth of the Empty Land+ A Reflective Reading of Biblical Texts Focusing on Mythicized Sociopolitical Structuring during the 2nd-temple Period." *Semeia* 59 (1992): 79–93.

Chirichigno, Gregory C. *Debt-Slavery in Israel and the Ancient Near East*. Journal of the Study of the Old Testament Supplement Series 141. Sheffield: Sheffield Academic Press, 1993.

Collins, John J. *Introduction to the Hebrew Bible*. Minneapolis: Fortress Press, 2004.

Douglas, Mary. *Leviticus as Literature*. New York: Oxford University Press, 1999.

Eagleton, Terry. *Walter Benjamin: Or Towards a Revolutionary Criticism*. London: Verso, 1981.

Eskenazi, Tamara C. and Andrea L. Weiss, eds. *The Torah: A Women's Commentary*. New York: URJ Press and Women of Reform Judaism, 2008.

Fikeni, Somadoda. "The Nature and Function of *Izibongo*-Panegyric Legends: The Case of the Xhosa People of South Africa." In *Indigenous People's Wisdom and Power: Affirming our Knowledge through Narrative*, edited by Julian Kunnie and Nomalungelo Ivy Goduka, 225–245. Burlington: Ashgate Publishing Company, 2006.

Franklin, Norma. "Jezreel: Before and After Jezebel." In *Israel in Transition: from Late Bronze II to Iron IIa (c. 1250–850 B.C.E.)*. Volume 1. The Archaeology, edited by Lester L. Grabbe, 45–53. New York/London: T & T Clark, 2008.

Gerstenberger, Erhard S. *Leviticus: A Commentary*. Louisville: Westminster John Knox Press, 1996.

Gorman, Frank H. *Divine Presence and Community: A Commentary on the Book of Leviticus*. Grand Rapids: Wm. B. Eerdmans Publishing Company, 1997.

Gottwald, Norman. *The Tribes of Yahweh: A Sociology of the Religion of Liberated Israel 1250–1050 B.C.E.* Sheffield: Sheffield Academic Press, 1999.

Grünwaldt, Klaus. *Das Heiligkeitsgesetz Leviticus 17–26: Ursprüngliche Gestalt, Tradition und Theologie*. Vol. 271. Berlin: Walter de Gruyter, 1999.

Guillaume, Philippe. "Tracing the Origin of the Sabbatical Calendar in the Priestly Narrative (Genesis 1 to Joshua 5)." *The Journal of Hebrew Scriptures* 5, no. 13 (2005): 1–19.

Harrison, Roland K. *Leviticus: An Introduction and Commentary*. Leicester: Inter-Varsity Press, 1980.

Hurvitz, Avi. "Once Again: The Linguistic Profile of the Priestly Material in the Pentateuch and its Historical Age. A Response to J. Blenkinsopp." *Zeitschrift für die alttestamentliche Wissenschaft* 112, no. 2 (2000): 180–191.

Jonker, Louis. "The Exile as Sabbath Rest: The Chronicler's Interpretation of the Exile." *Old Testament Essays* 20, no. 3 (2007): 703–719.

Joosten, Jan. *People and Land in the Holiness Code: An Exegetical Study of the Ideational Framework of the Law in Leviticus 17–26*. Vetus Testamentum Supplements 67. Leiden: Brill, 1996.

Joosten, Jan. "The Distinction between Classical and late Biblical Hebrew as Reflected in Syntax." *Hebrew Studies* 46, no. 1 (2005): 327–339.

Kalugila, Leonidas, and Abdulaziz Y. Lodhi. *Methali Zaidi za kiSwahili toka Afrika Mashariki: More Swahili Proverbs from East Africa*. Uppsala: Nordiska Afrikainstitutet, 1980.

Kaufmann, Yehezkel. *The Religion of Israel: From Its Beginnings to the Babylonian Exile*. Translated by Moshe Greenberg. New York: Schocken Books, 1972.

Kidd, José E. Ramírez. *Alterity and Identity in Israel: The rg in the Old Testament*. Beihefte zur Zeitschrift für die alttestamentliche Wissenschaft 283. Berlin/New York: Walter de Gruyter, 1999.

King, Greg A. "The Documentary Hypothesis." *Journal of the Adventist Theological Society* 12, no. 1 (2001): 22–30.

Kinsler, Ross and Gloria Kinsler. *The Biblical Jubilee and the Struggle for Life*. Maryknoll, New York: Orbis Books, 1999.

Knight, Douglas A. *Law, Power and Justice in Ancient Israel*. Louisville: Westminster John Knox Press, 2011.

Knohl, Israel. *The Sanctuary of Silence: The Priestly Torah and the Holiness School*. Minneapolis: Fortress Press, 1995.

Leuchter, Mark. "The Manumission Laws in Leviticus and Deuteronomy: The Jeremiah Connection." *Journal of Biblical Literature* 127, no. 4 (2008): 635–653.

Levinson, Bernard M. "The Case for Revision and Interpolation within the Biblical Legal Corpora." In *Theory and Method in Biblical and Cuneiform Law.* Journal of the Study of the Old Testament Supplement Series 181, edited by Bernard M. Levinson, 37–59. Sheffield: Sheffield Academic Press, 1994.

Levinson, Bernard M. *Deuteronomy and the Hermeneutics of Legal Innovation.* New York: Oxford University Press, 1997.

Levinson, Bernard M. "The Manumission of Hermeneutics: The Slave Laws of the Pentateuch as a Challenge to Contemporary Pentateuchal Theory." In *Congress Volume Leiden.* Vetus Testamentum Supplements 108, edited by André Lemaire, 281–324. Leiden: Brill, 2004.

Levinson, Bernard M. "The Birth of the Lemma: The Restrictive Reinterpretation of the Covenant Code's Manumission Law by the Holiness Code (Leviticus 25:44–46)." *Journal of Biblical Literature* 124, no. 4 (2005): 617–639.

Masenya (ngwan'a Mphahlele), Madipoane. "A *bosadi* (Womanhood) Reading of Proverbs 31:10–31." In *Other Ways of Reading: African Women and the Bible,* edited by Musa W. Dube, 145–157. Atlanta and Geneva: Society of Biblical Literature and WCC Publications, 2001.

Masenya, Madipoane. "Struggling with Poverty/emptiness: Rereading the Naomi-Ruth Story in African-South Africa." *Journal of Theology for Southern Africa* 120 (2004): 46–59.

Masenya, Madipoane. "Is Ruth the 'ēšet hayil for Real? An Exploration of Womanhood from African Proverbs to the Threshing Floor (Ruth 3:1–13)." *Studia Historiae Ecclesiasticae* 36 (2010): 1–21.

Meyer, Esias E. *The Jubilee in Leviticus 25: A Theological Ethical Interpretation from a South African Perspective.* Vol. 15. Münster: LIT Verlag, 2005.

Meyer, Esias E. "Dating the Priestly Text in the Pre-Exilic Period: Some Remarks about Anachronistic Slips and other Obstacles." *Verbum et Ecclesia* 31, no. 1 (2010): 1–6.

Meyer, Esias E. "Divide and be Different: Priestly Identity in the Persian Period." *HTS Theological Studies* 68, no. 1 (2012): 54–60.

Meyer, Esias E. "From Cult to Community: The Two Halves of Leviticus." *Verbum et Ecclesia* 34, no. 2 (2013): 1–7.

Meyer, Esias E. "Returning to an Empty Land: Revisiting My Old Argument About the Jubilee." *Old Testament Essays* 27, no. 2 (2014): 502–519.

Meyer, Esias E. "Leviticus 11, Deuteronomy 14 and Directionality." *Journal for Semitics* 23, no. 1 (2014): 71–89.

Middlemas, Jill A. *The Templeless Age: An Introduction to the History, Literature, and Theology of the "Exile."* Louisville: Westminster John Knox Press, 2007.

Milgrom, Jacob. *Leviticus 1–16: A New Translation with Introduction and Commentary.* New York: Doubleday, 1991.

Milgrom, Jacob. "The Antiquity of the Priestly Source: A Reply to Joseph Blenkinsopp." *Zeitschrift* für die alttestamentliche Wissenschaft 111, no. 1 (1999): 10–22.

Milgrom, Jacob. *Leviticus 17–22: A New Translation with Introduction and Commentary.* New York: Doubleday, 2000.

Milgrom, Jacob. *Leviticus 23–27: A New Translation with Introduction and Commentary*. New York: Doubleday, 2001.

Milgrom, Jacob. "HR in Leviticus and Elsewhere in the Torah." In *The book of Leviticus: Composition and Reception*, edited by Rolf Rendtorff, Robert A. Kugler, and Sarah Smith Bartlet, 24–40. Leiden: Brill, 2003.

Milgrom, Jacob. *Leviticus—A Book of Ritual and Ethics: A Continental Commentary*. Minneapolis: Fortress Press, 2004.

Mohochi, S Sangai and Michae Wairungu. "Kiswahili," http://swahililanguage. stanford.edu/.

Mosala, Itumeleng J. "Biblical Hermeneutics and Black Theology in South Africa." PhD diss., University of Cape Town, 1987.

Mosala, Itumeleng J. "Wealth and Poverty in the Old Testament—A Black Theological Perspective." *Journal of black theology in South Africa* 5 (1996): 16–22.

Mosala, Itumeleng J. "Reconstructing the Azanian *mišpāh□t* (Clans): Land, Class and Bible in South Africa Today." In *Text and Experience: Towards a Cultural Exegesis of the Bible*, edited by Daniel L. Smith-Christopher, 238–246. Sheffield: Sheffield Academic Press, 1995.

Mott, Stephen, and Ronald J. Sider. "Economic Justice: A Biblical Paradigm." *Transformation* 17, no. 2 (2000): 50–63.

Mtshiselwa, Ndikho. "Towards an Indigenous (Xhosa) South African Biblical Scholarship." *Old Testament Essays* 24, no. 3 (2011): 668–689.

Mtshiselwa, Vincent N. N. "Leviticus 18: 22 and 20: 13 in Discussion with the Methodist Church of Southern Africa on Homosexuality." MA diss., University of Pretoria, 2010.

Nihan, Christophe. "The Holiness Code between D and P: Some Comments on the Function and Significance of Leviticus 17–26 in the Composition of the Pentateuch." In *Das Deuteronomium zwische Pentateuch und Deuteronomistischem Geschichtswerk*, edited by Eckart Otto and Reinhard Achenbach, 81–122. Göttingen: Vandenhoeck & Ruprecht, 2004.

Nihan, Christophe. *From Priestly Torah to Pentateuch: A Study in the Composition of the Book of Leviticus*. Tübingen: Mohr Siebeck, 2007.

Nihan, Christophe. "The Priestly Covenant, its Reinterpretations and the Composition of 'P.'" In *The Strata of the Priestly Writings: Contemporary Debate and Future Directions*, edited by Sarah Shectman and Joel S. Baden, 87–134. Zürich: Theologischer Verlag Zürich, 2009.

Nihan, Christophe. "The Laws about Clean and Unclean Animals in Leviticus and Deuteronomy and their Place in the Formation of the Pentateuch." In *The Pentateuch: International Perspectives on Current Research*, edited by Thomas B. Dozeman, Konrad Schmid and Baruch J. Schwartz, 401–434. Tübingen: Mohr Siebeck, 2011.

Nihan, Christophe. "Resident Aliens and Natives in the Holiness Legislation." In *The Foreign and the Law: Perspectives from the Hebrew Bible and the Ancient Near East*, edited by Reinhard Achenbach, Rainer Albertz and Jakob Wöhrle, 111–134. Wiesbaden: Harrassowitz Verlag, 2011.

Nihan, Christophe. "Forms and Functions of Purity in Leviticus." In *Purity and the Forming of Religious Traditions in the Ancient Mediterranean World and Ancient Judaism*, edited by Christian Frevel and Christophe Nihan, 311–368. Leiden: Koninklijke Brill NV, 2013.

Noth, Martin. *The Deuteronomistic History*. Journal of the Study of the Old Testament Supplement Series 15. Sheffield: Sheffield Academic Press, 1991.

Otto, Eckart. "Aspects of Legal Reforms and Reformulations in Ancient Cuneiform and Ancient Law." In *Theory and Method in Biblical and Cuneiform Law.* Journal of the Study of the Old Testament Supplement Series 181, edited by Bernard M. Levinson, 160–196. Sheffield: Sheffield Academic Press, 1994.

Otto, Eckart. "Innerbiblische Exegese im Heiligkeitsgesetz Levitikus 17–26." In *Levitikus als Buch*, edited by Heinz-Josef Fabry and Hans-Winfried Jüngling, 125–196. Berlin, Philo: Bonner Biblische Beiträge, 1999.

Otto, Eckart. "The Pentateuch in Synchronical and Diachronical Perspectives: Protorabbinic Scribal Erudition Mediating between Deuteronomy and the Priestly Code." In *Das Deuteronomium zwischen Pentateuch and Deuteronomistischem Geschhichtwerk.* Frlant 206, edited by Eckart Otto and Reinhard Achenbach, 14–35. Göttingen: Vandenhoeck and Ruprecht, 2004.

Otto, Eckart. "Deuteronomy between the Pentateuch and the Deuteronomistic History: Some Remarks about Thomas Römer, the So-called Deuteronomistic History." *Journal of Hebrew Scriptures* 9, no. 17 (2005): 22–27.

Otto, Eckart. "The Holiness Code in Diachrony and Synchrony in the Legal Hermeneutics of the Pentateuch." In *The Strata of the Priestly Writings: Contemporary Debate and Future Directions*, edited by Sarah Shectman and Joel S. Baden, 135–156. Zürich: Theologischer Verlag Zürich, 2009.

Otto, Eckart. "Torah and Prophecy: A Debate of Changing Identities." *Verbum et Ecclesia* 34, no. 2 (2013): 1–5.

Philpott, Graham J., and Mark Butler. "Land in South Africa: Gift for all or Commodity for a Few." *Occasional Paper* 1 (2005): 1–21.

Römer, Thomas. *The So-called Deuteronomistic History: A Sociological, Historical and Literary Introduction.* London: T & T Clark International, 2005.

Römer, Thomas. "The Elusive Yahwist: A Short History of Research." In *A Farewell to the Yahwist? The Composition of the Pentateuch in Recent European Interpretation*, edited by Thomas B. Dozeman and Konrad Schmid, 9–28. Atlanta: Society of Biblical Literature, 2006.

Römer, Thomas. "The Exodus Narrative According to the Priestly Document." In *The Strata of the Priestly Writings: Contemporary Debate and Future Directions*, edited by Sarah Shectman and Joel S. Baden, 157–174. Zürich: Theologischer Verlag Zürich, 2009.

Römer, Thomas. "How Many Books (*Teuchs)*: Pentateuch, Hexateuch, Deuteronomistic History, or Enneateuch?." In *Pentateuch, Hexateuch or Enneateuch? Identifying Literary Works in Genesis through Kings*, edited by Thomas B. Dozeman, Thomas Römer and Konrad Schmid, 25–42. Atlanta: Society of Biblical Literature, 2011.

Römer, Thomas. "How to Write a Literary History of the Hebrew Bible? A Response to David Carr and Konrad Schmid." *Indian Theological Studies* 50, no. 1 (2013): 9–20.

Rooker, Mark F. *The New American Commentary, vol. 3A, Leviticus.* Nashville: Broadman and Holman Publishers, 2000.

Rugwiji, Temba. "Appropriating Judean Post-exilic Literature in a Postcolonial Discourse: A Case for Zimbabwe." PhD diss., Pretoria, University of South Africa, 2013.

Scheffler, Eben. "The Exilic Literature (586–539 BCE)." In *Ancient Israelite Literature in Context*, edited by Willem S. Boshoff, Eben Scheffler and Izak J. J. Spangenberg, 58–76. Hatfield: Protea Bookshop, 2000.

Scheffler, Eben. *Politics in Ancient Israel.* Pretoria: Biblia Publishers, 2001.

Schmid, Konrad. "The So-called Yahwist and the Literary Gap between Genesis and Exodus." In *A farewell to the Yahwist? The Composition of the Pentateuch in Recent European Interpretation*, edited by Thomas B. Dozeman and Konrad Schmid, 29–50. Atlanta: Society of Biblical Literature, 2006.

Schmid, Konrad. "The Persian Imperial Authorization as Historical Problem and as Biblical Construct: A Plea for Differentiations in the Current Debate." In *The Pentateuch as Torah: New Models for Understanding its Promulgation and Acceptance*, edited by Gary N. Knoppers and Bernard M. Levinson, 22–38. Winona Lake: Eisenbrauns, 2007.

Schmid, Konrad. "The Late Persian Formation of the Torah: Observations on Deuteronomy 34." In *Judah and the Judeans in the Fourth Century B.C.E.*, edited by Obed Lipschits, Gary N. Knoppers, and Rainer Albertz, 236–245. Winona Lake: Eisenbrauns, 2007.

Schmid, Konrad. "Genesis and Exodus as Two Formerly Independent Traditions of Origins for Ancient Israel." *Biblica* 93, no. 2 (2012): 187–208.

Schmid, Konrad. "Genesis in the Pentateuch." In *The Book of Genesis: Composition, Reception and Interpretation.* Vetus Testamentum Supplements 125, edited by Craig A. Evans, Joel N. Lohr, and David L. Petersen, 27–50. Leiden: Brill, 2012.

Schmidt, Werner H. *Old Testament Introduction.* Translated by Matthew L. O'Connell with David J. Reimer. Berlin and New York: Walter de Gruyter & Co. and Louisville: Westminster John Knox Press, 1999.

Schwartz, Baruch J. "'Profane' Slaughter and the Integrity of the Priestly Code." *Hebrew Union College Annual* 67 (1996): 15–42.

Schwartz, Baruch J. "The Priestly Account of the Theophany and Lawgiving at Sinai." In *Texts, Temples, and Traditions: A Tribute to Menahem Haran*, edited by Michael V. Fox, Victor Avigdor Hurowitz, Avi Hurvitz, Michael L. Klein, Baruch J. Schwartz, and Nili Shupak, 103–134. Winona Lake, Indiana: Eisenbrauns, 1996.

Schwartz, Baruch J. *The Holiness Legislation: Studies in the Priestly Code.* Jerusalem: Magnes, 1999.

Schwartz, Baruch J. "Reexamining the Fate of the 'Canaanites' in the Torah Traditions." In *Sefer Moshe—The Moshe Weinfeld Jubilee Volume: Studies in the Bible and Ancient Near East, Qumran, and Post-biblical Judaism*, edited by Chaim Cohen, Avi Hurvitz, and Shalom M. Paul, 151–170. Winona Lake, Indiana: Eisenbrauns, 2004.

Smith, Daniel L. *The Religion of the Landless: The Social Context of the Babylonian Exile.* Bloomington: Meyer Stone Books, 1989.

Stackert, Jeffrey. "The Holiness Legislation and its Pentateuchal Sources: Revision, Supplementation, and Replacement." In *The Strata of the Priestly Writings: Contemporary Debate and Future Directions*, edited by Sarah Shectman and Joel S. Baden, 187–205. Zürich: Theologischer Verlag Zürich, 2009.

Stackert, Jeffrey. "Distinguishing Innerbiblical Exegesis from Pentateuchal Redaction: Leviticus 26 as a Test Case." In *The Pentateuch: International Perspectives on Current Research*, edited by Thomas B. Dozeman, Konrad Schmid, and Baruch J. Schwartz, 369–386. Tübingen: Mohr Siebeck, 2011.

Stackert, Jeffrey. "Compositional Strata in the Priestly Sabbath: Exodus 31: 12–17 and 35: 1–3." *Journal of Hebrew Scriptures* 11 (2012): 1–21.

Trevaskis, Leigh M. *Holiness, Ethics and Ritual in Leviticus*. Vol. 29. Sheffield: Sheffield Academic Press, 2011.

Usue, Emmanuel O. "Restoration or Desperation in Ezra and Nehemiah? Implications for Africa." *Old Testament Essays* 20, no. 3 (2007): 830–846.

Warner, Jonathan. "Towards a Christian Economics?." *Pro Rege* 30, no. 1 (2001): 10–20.

West, Gerald O. "Biblical hermeneutics in Africa." In *African Theology on the Way: Current Conversations*, edited by Diane B. Stinton, 21–31. London: SPCK, 2010.

Wöhrle, Jakob. "The Un-empty Land: The Concept of Exile and Land in P." In *The Concept of Exile in Ancient Israel and its Historical Context*, edited by Ehud Ben Zvi and Christoph Levin, 189–206. Berlin: Walter de Gruyter, 2010.

Wright, David P. "Holiness in Leviticus and Beyond: Differing Perspectives." *Interpretation* 53, no. 4 (1999): 351–364.

Wright, David P. *Inventing God's Law: How the Covenant Code of the Bible Used and Revised the Laws of Hammurabi.* New York: Oxford University Press, 2009.

Zenger, Erich 2004. "Theorien Über die Entstehung des Pentateuch im Wandel der Forschung." In *Einleitung in das Alte Testament.* 5th edition, edited by Erich Zenger, 74–123. Kohlhammer: Stuttgart, 2004.

CHAPTER FOUR

An African Liberationist Reading of Leviticus 25:8–55

Introduction

On a hermeneutical level, the African liberationist reading of Leviticus 25:8–55 employed in this study draws on and simultaneously departs from Mosala's liberationist approach, as stated in Chapter 1. Thus, the importance of cultural resources which stand in continuity with postcolonial biblical studies has been shown. However, the postcolonial theory advanced by scholars such as Dube, Berquist and Sugirtharajah is consistent with Mosala's approach as it offers a reading of ancient texts that seeks transformative possibilities for oppressed people. It has been noted in Chapter 1 that the contributions of both Sugirtharajah and Masenya (ngwan'a Mphahlele) which employ indigenous narratives and proverbs adds an interesting dimension to the postcolonial theory and to African biblical hermeneutics, respectively. Thus, an African liberationist reading employed here draws on the second author's contribution. However, this study departs from Masenya (ngwan'a Mphahlele) whose contribution focuses mainly on African proverbs and stands in continuity with postcolonial biblical scholarship in the sense that three African liberation songs were considered as hermeneutical tools for constructing the theoretical framework for re-reading the Israelite Jubilee legislation. It is noteworthy that the African proverbs and liberation songs that are considered in the formulation of a theoretical framework in Chapter 1 are those, which are relevant to the socio-economic and political issues raised in the present study.

Furthermore, the African[1] liberationist reading employed here will build on the remarkable contribution of scholars in Africa and the African Diaspora in the volume, *The Africana Bible: Reading Israel's Scriptures from Africa and the African Diaspora*. Snyman rightly shows that *The Africana Bible* '… is about foregrounding the own context that provides an impetus for an understanding of the biblical text that differs from an understanding within what is known as the mythical norm'.[2] His observation resonates with the Swahili proverb, *Maji yaliyoko mbali hayakati kiu*, 'Water that is far away (unreachable) cannot quench one's thirst!' and the Setswana saying, *Mphemphe o a lapisa motho o kgonwa ke sa gagwe*, 'Borrowed water never quenches thirst'.[3] In the context of biblical interpretation, the tenor underlying the preceding saying is that non-African hermeneutics, which are conceived in non-African contexts, may prove to be unhelpful in the reading of the Bible in Africa. Snyman also mentions a mythical norm which refers to how white, Eurocentric, male, heterosexual, wealthy, middle class Christians created an 'Other' which is black, African/Asian/Latin, female, homo-/bi-/trans-/inter-sexual, poor, working class, non-Christian.[4] In that creation, the creator dominates the created—the 'Other'—which also includes any interpretation and epistemology conceived to be the 'Other'. Although there are several contributions made in *The Africana Bible*, for instance, on the socio-political context in South Africa and on the socio-economic analysis of the South African and biblical contexts, the focus here is on Masenya (ngwan'a Mphahlele)'s study.[5] Of Masenya (ngwan'a Mphahlele)'s chapter, Snyman writes:

> Employing a Northern Sotho proverb about disobedient children who refuse to take advice from others, and making congruent with wisdom in the Deuteronomistic History, she argues that the fall of the Afrikaner regime in 1994 illustrates the wisdom of the proverb: 'disobedience comes at a heavy price'.[6]

The proverb that Masenya (ngwan'a Mphahlele) considers is *Ngwan'a magana go botšwa o wetše dikomeng, a re dikoma ke tšešo*, 'A child who refused to listen [to advice] landed in "initiation schools" and claimed that the schools were part of his extended family'.[7] In addition to Snyman's interesting reading of Masenya (ngwan'a Mphahlele)'s chapter, the tenor underlying the proverb guides her to construct parallels between the South African context and the Israelite context. For instance, the elevation of the Babylonian returnees tallies with the elevation of members of the ANC who experienced 'political' exile during the apartheid era. The proverb, which is the interpretive resource, serves as a hermeneutical tool with which Masenya (ngwan'a Mphahlele) engages with the Old Testament text of Jeremiah.

The lack of in-depth relationship of the Israelite Jubilee legislation with the South African context from an African liberationist perspective is an area worth researching in Old Testament scholarship. Meyer, for example, does not discuss the South African context in depth.[8] Leviticus 25:8–55 has not been re-read from an African liberationist perspective in the South African context in which land redistribution and socio-economic justice are highly contested. If one draws on the exegesis of Leviticus 25:8–55, one could make a case for the liberating and empowering possibilities that the Israelite Jubilee offers poor African South Africans. Therefore, Leviticus 25:8–55 will be interpreted from an African liberationist point of view since the text contains liberating potential for poor African South Africans.[9]

As mentioned in Chapter 1, the term African South Africans is employed in this study to refer to the indigenous peoples of South Africa—the Xhosas, Ndebeles, Sothos, Tswanas, Zulus, Vendas and so forth.[10] The term refers to black people in South Africa who are of African descent, and it differs from Mosala who employs the designation 'black' to refer to the same people. Setiloane finds the designation 'African' more appealing mainly because of his methodological approach to theology and his reading of the Bible, which is based on African proverbs, idioms and liberation songs.[11] Rather than opting for the notion of Africanness in the place of Mosala's *blackness* as Setiloane does, it is helpful to examine the relationship between the two notions. Cone argues that the liberation of black people in America, for instance, may not be attained completely without accepting *blackness* and without loving Africa as a location of origin and meaning.[12] This argument shows that the notion of *blackness* is intrinsically related to Africanness since both notions are rooted in the values of black people who are of African descent.

Additionally, the African liberationist reading employed here is 'Africentric' in tenor because the socio-economic location of South Africa constitutes the primary context for interpreting the ancient text.[13] This implies that an African liberationist reading of Leviticus 25:8–55 in the light of socio-economic justice and land redistribution in South Africa will express solidarity with the poor. Thus, the situation of poor African South Africans in relation to the country's land redistribution discourse will be the location from which one reads Leviticus 25:8–55. The discussion of socio-economic justice and land redistribution in South Africa based on an African liberationist reading of Leviticus 25:8–55 will be guided by the following point:

- Re-reading Leviticus 25:8–55 in the post-apartheid South Africa—locating the discourse on land redistribution and socio-economic justice within the liberationist framework.

Re-Reading Leviticus 25:8–55 in Post-Apartheid South Africa—Land Redistribution Discourse and Socio-Economic Justice within the Liberationist Framework

Since poverty and economic inequality are persistent in South Africa, it will be helpful to consider the possible reception of a re-reading of Leviticus 25:8–55 in post-apartheid South Africa. Locating the discourse of land redistribution and socio-economic justice within the liberationist framework is a way of interpreting Leviticus 25:8–55 from an African perspective. The analysis of the Israelite Jubilee will therefore be carried out in line with the discussion of socio-economic justice and land redistribution. It is important also to consider whether Leviticus 25:8–55 and the discourse of land redistribution and socio-economic justice are relevant to the South African context given the key African liberationist values outlined above. On that point, as indicated in Chapter 1, one is mindful of Gottwald's caution that 'the reality that economic systems cannot be "imported" from the Bible to meet our needs', as well as of his claim that: 'the ethical force of the Bible on issues of economics will have to be perspectival and motivational rather than prescriptive and technical'.[14] In other words, this section will probe African liberationist values; first, in the discourse of land redistribution and socio-economic justice in South Africa; and second, in the interpretation of Leviticus 25:8–55 in post-apartheid South Africa. Such values emerged from the discussion of the methodological and theoretical framework in Chapter 1.

In Search of Liberation in South Africa's Discourse of Socio-economic Justice and Land Redistribution

In the critique of the South African political economy in Chapter 2, we have noted a 'winner takes all' situation in the country and the point that the white oligarchs namely the NP and ANC élites benefited from the negotiations and compromise(s) made in the negotiations for a democratic South Africa while the poor masses remain trapped in poverty. Bond claims that Cyril Ramaphosa (one of the ANC representatives in the negotiations), among others, unduly benefited from the negotiations.[15] When understood within a liberationist framework particularly with reference to the value of 'Refuting greed in favour of sharing of resources' which is critical of the current greed of the élites, such an argument would be compelling.

Both greed and the absence of equitable sharing of resources, which in fact, are refuted by the criticism of self-enrichment at the expense of the poor in the

Xhosa proverb *Ubophelele inja enkangeni*, 'He has fastened a dog to a shrub' would not fit within the liberationist framework. The fact that the rich are becoming richer and the poor poorer confirms the perturbing reality of greed and the lack of equitable sharing of resources especially of productive land. Thus, one may reasonably agree with Bond that the political élites benefited from the negotiations of the democratic South Africa at the expense of the poor. However, the search for liberation in terms of the discourse of socio-economic justice and land redistribution in the country may be realised when the tendency for self-enrichment on the part of the political élites is criticised in the light of the proverb *Ubophelele inja enkangeni*.

Furthermore, it is argued that the concerns and interests of the poor and landless African South Africans were silenced and neglected in the secret negotiations as well as in the Codesa negotiations.[16] That is, the political élites who negotiated the establishment of a democratic South Africa found it difficult to treat the issue of land redistribution and socio-economic justice as priority. The liberationist framework constructed above elevates such concerns as the call for political and economic liberation in the expression *Mayibuye iAfrika*, 'Let Africa return' is ignored. The rise of the political party the Economic Freedom Fighters (EFF) confirms that call. Worthy of note also is the observation that the tenor of the expression Mayibuye iAfrika, 'Let Africa return' which calls for equitable sharing of resources is set to grant the poor access to land. The verse line *Mabawuyeke umhlaba wethu*, 'They must leave our land alone' confirms that tenor. However, the need to grant the poor access to land was silenced and ignored in the negotiations for a democratic country. The notion is presented in the context of the protest for political and economic liberation implied in the liberation song *Thina sizwe esimnyama*, 'We, the black nation'.

The idea of equitable sharing of resources particularly of productive land is important in the liberationist framework, which is also affirmed in part by the Tshivenda saying *Lupfumo lu mavuni*, literally, 'Wealth is in the land'.[17] Wealth comes from the proceeds of the land and it is reasonable to view the call for redistribution of land as just means to redistribute wealth and to alleviate poverty. Based on the tenor underlying the Tshivenda proverb *Lupfumo lu mavuni* as well as the liberation song *Thina sizwe esimnyama*, the call to redress socio-economic injustice in terms of land redistribution is compelling.

At issue in the discourse of land redistribution and socio-economic justice is the view that white people entrenched land dispossession and poverty among black masses.[18] Thus:

> In our current South African context, the Promised Land is a contested space which will not easily be handed back to the previously dispossessed people. The white

> farmers and owners of large corporations who own the land will not just hand over the land without a fight or without further defrauding the poor in the process. The dispossessed poor are the victims of injustice.[19]

The view above is echoed in the clause *elathathwa ngabamhlophe* 'which was taken by white people' which captures the protest against landlessness and socio-economic injustice in South Africa. In addition, the statement *Mabawuyeke umhlaba wethu*, 'They must leave our land alone' in the song *Thina sizwe esimnyama* moves the discourse away from mere articulation of socio-economic injustice. The reading of the two clauses refutes the idea of land dispossession and poverty among the ordinary black folks. It is worth noting also that the seizure of land by the white people or the Boers prompted the verse line *Amabhulu azizinja*, 'The Boers are dogs' in the song *Senzeni na?* 'What have we done?' In light of the protest against the socio-economic injustice implied in the clause *elathathwa ngabamhlophe*, 'which was taken by white people' and against land dispossession in the protest song *Mabawuyeke umhlaba wethu*, the view that white people entrenched land dispossession and poverty among the African-South African masses is justified and could be placed within the liberationist framework proposed above.

Masenya (ngwan'a Mphahlele) and Ramantswana claim that the South African government has failed to address injustice in the country through the land reform program.[20] Yanou has also made a similar point from a historical and legal perspective arguing that the land reform program has failed essentially because it ignores the history of land dispossession of African South Africans under the colonial and apartheid regimes.[21] Second, Yanou claims that the land reform initiative would not succeed in a situation where property is protected.[22] Inspired by the persistent protest against land redistribution expressed in *Mabawuyeke umhlaba wethu*, one would be inclined to support the view of the scholars mentioned above. Moreover, in light of the song *Thina sizwe esimnyama*, 'We, the black nation', an African liberationist reading of the text in the South African context, which continues to search for liberation would call for socio-economic justice and land redistribution.

As a contested space, the discourse on land redistribution and socio-economic justice would be relevant in South Africa when discussed in the light of the subject of the politics of exclusion. Kwakye explains that the politics of exclusion refers to a trend in which the political élites alienate one another and ordinary citizens from decision-making processes.[23] In the South African context, some scholars have noted the presence of political exclusion. For example, Hertz argues that on an ideological level, dissenting voices were excluded in the rise of neo-liberal capitalism.[24] Similarly and more explicitly, Desmond rightly shows that the masses were not given the opportunity to articulate their voices at Codesa in the negotiations for a democratic South Africa.[25] The argument made in Chapter 2 of this study that the ideals of COSATU and SACP were excluded from the ideals on which the new democratic South Africa was founded resonates with the position of both Hertz and Desmond. Furthermore, the African liberationist reading employed in this study supports the view that the ANC élites excluded COSATU and SACP politically and subsequently compromised socio-economic redress in the area of land redistribution.

The Swahili proverb *Wapiganapo tembo nyasi huumia*, 'When elephants fight the grass gets hurt' illustrates a situation in which the political élites alienate one another and end up compromising certain values, as evident in the negotiations for a democratic South Africa.[26] With this Swahili proverb in mind, an African liberationist reader would be sensitive to the presence of the 'fighting elephants' particularly in the (South) African context. In the African liberationist reading, the ideological clashes and compromises made during and after the negotiations that resulted in the persistence of socio-economic injustice warrant a search for liberation in the form of redressing poverty and economic inequality.

On the compromise made during and after the negotiations, Hertz argues that a shift occurred from Marxism to neo-liberal capitalism, which was triggered by the rise of privatisation, deregulation and trade liberalisation, all of which are individualistic in character.[27] From the perspective of individualism, the rise of neo-liberal capitalism may be viewed as a non-issue. However, from an African liberationist perspective, the 'willing-seller, willing-buyer' approach relegated the poor black masses to the margins in the process of acquiring land and generating capital and wealth due to their lack of capital. Given that neo-liberal capitalism is individualistic in tenor, the 'willing-seller, willing-buyer' approach does not fit the liberationist framework.

For her part, Klein claims that 'the most persuasive argument' concerns the abandoning of the idea of redistribution on the part of the political élites within the ANC, SACP and COSATU.[28] Interestingly, the 'willing-seller, willing-buyer' approach is at the heart of that argument but the song *Thina sizwe esimnyama* renders individualism unattractive. The phrase *Thina sizwe* 'we, the nation' which is communal and collective in tenor rather than individualistic confirms that neo-liberal capitalism is irrelevant within the framework of liberation. Moreover, because Sub-Saharan Africa contains a growing share of the world's absolute poor who in turn have little power to influence the allocation of resources, the 'willing-seller, willing-buyer' approach may not be considered a suitable model in that context.[29] Clearly, communalism and the sharing of resources as opposed to individualism and capitalism that underpin the preceding approach would be attractive in a context, which is beset by poverty and economic inequality and where the rich are persistently becoming richer, while the poor are becoming poorer. In this case, the search for liberation through the discourse of land redistribution and socio-economic justice in South Africa would be merited.

In Chapter 2, evidence that the African-South African political élites accumulated wealth through the BEE and their political connections has been brought to light. It has been noted that as an economic model, the BEE generates wealth for few individuals and companies and legitimates the capitalist system.[30] In a situation where the ANC élites promote and enrich themselves, the BEE becomes unattractive in the liberationist framework proposed in this study. The trend of self-enrichment in the BEE initiative contrasts with the idea of equitable sharing of resources because it promotes greed and the individualistic approach to the accumulation of wealth. Furthermore, in view of the Northern Sotho proverb *Tlala ke a neka phefo ke ja nong*, which suggests that the wealthy continue to revel in their riches whilst the poor experience the scourge of poverty and hunger, the BEE initiative which promotes economic inequality would not fit into the liberationist framework. Again, the trend of self-enrichment which is evident in the BEE initiative contrasts with the Northern Sotho proverb *Noka e tlala ka melatswana*, 'A river is filled by other rivers'. The proverb approves the sharing of resources in order to elevate the poor from poverty while counteracting the tendency towards greed and self-enrichment in the BEE initiative.

Thus, an African liberationist reading is justified because the present land policies in South Africa impede land redistribution and the redress of socio-economic injustice. First, the interpretation of Section 25(2) of the South African constitution as a provision that requires payment of compensation for land expropriation and redistribution poses a challenge to the poor African South Africans.[31] That is, people who lost their land to white farmers in the colonial and apartheid South Africa find it difficult to retrieve such land without capital. Thus, the majority of the poor black people in South Africa remain trapped in the poverty cycle as the land policies which are influenced by the socio-economic model and neo-liberal capitalism impede socio-economic justice. The liberation overtones in this study, which oppose injustice, suggest that the land policies constitute an impediment to land redistribution and socio-economic justice.

Furthermore, the idea of sharing resources by literally giving them to the poor contained in the liberative statement *Mayibuye iAfrika* and in the song *Senzeni na?* 'What have we done?' shows that the requirement of the payment of compensation would not be justified especially in the light of the statement *Mabawuyeke umhlaba wethu* in the protest song *Thina sizwe esimnyama*, 'We, the black nation'. Thus, an African liberationist reading, which rejects the current South African land policies, would also tally with the tenor of liberation in the liberation songs under discussion.

Scholars have pointed out that the provision of capital and skills to access the market is critical in the face of climate change.[32] The adaptation to climate change is imperative as it is no longer easy to work the land as in the past when productivity depended mainly on rain. The provision of capital and skills in an attempt to alleviate the persistent poverty experienced by African South Africans is in order, but the return of land ownership to black people expressed in the call *Mayibuye iAfrika*, 'Let Africa return' does not translate to economic liberation. Land redistribution would lead to economic liberation if coupled with the provision of finance and farming skills to the poor African-South African farmers. In cases, which the government did not provide the necessary financial support and skills for the emerging poor African-South African farmers to whom land was redistributed, unproductiveness has been reported. It is reported that 90 percent of farms redistributed to South Africa's black population from white farmers have not been utilised productively.[33]

In the light of an African liberationist reading, the impediment to poverty alleviation caused by the unproductiveness which accrues from the lack of capital and skills is worrisome, as well as the failure to redress socio-economic injustice in terms of poverty alleviation and the redress of economic inequality. The tenor underlying the call *Mayibuye iAfrika*, 'Let Africa return' would be appreciated by the previously disadvantaged black people who do not have the financial capital and skills to use the land productively. Therefore, the search for liberation in the discourse of land and socio-economic justice would take into account the argument that the return of land to African South Africans suggested in the protest call *Mayibuye iAfrika* should be combined with the provision of the necessary financial capital and farming skills.

As shown in Chapter 2, the land issue in South Africa has been described broadly as 'only an agenda item'.[34] That description of the land issue as 'only an agenda item' is disturbing to an African liberationist reader and it shows that the call for political and economic liberation in *Mayibuye iAfrika*, 'Let Africa return' is not supported. Had the call been taken seriously, the protest against economic inequality in terms of the disproportionate benefits from land ownership and use would be translated to land redistribution instead of remaining 'an agenda item'. Furthermore, the expression of frustration by the black protesters at the injustice inflicted by the oppressive policy that is embedded in the song *Senzeni na?* 'What have we done?' would be justified. In a context which land policies impede the redress of socio-economic injustice, such frustration would be considered and addressed, as the subject of land in South Africa constitutes a contested space where an African liberationist reading is relevant.

An African Liberationist Reading of Leviticus 25:8–55

In his 2011 book *The Cross and the Lynching Tree*, James Hal Cone the pioneer of Black Liberation Theology throws light on how a biblical narrative and an African American narrative can interpret each other. He draws insight from both the narrative of the cross of Jesus and the stories of the African Americans, which illustrate how the lynching tree was used as a tool of injustice. On the hermeneutical level, Cone writes that:

> The cross and the lynching tree interpret each other. Both were public spectacles, shameful events, instruments of punishment reserved for the most despised people in society. Any genuine preaching of the Christian gospel must be measured against the test of the scandal of the cross and the lynching tree. Until we can see the cross and the lynching tree together, there can be no genuine understanding of Christian identity in America, and no deliverance from the brutal legacy of slavery and white supremacy.[35]

It has been pointed out that both the American context and the Bible interpret each other, that is, to the extent that one could possibly not understand one without the other. Cone's hermeneutical approach highlights points of convergence between the biblical text and the context of the modern readers of the Bible. However, he is also aware of the fact that 'the cross and the lynching tree are separated by nearly two thousand years'.[36] Similarly, the context of Leviticus 25:8–55 and the South African context are separated by many years. Thus, the question of the relevance of the biblical text to the context (or the inverse) is important. In line with Cone, the interaction between the Leviticus 25:8–55 and the South African context would also fit in with West's call for a dialogue between the modern context and the biblical text.[37]

However, somewhat unlike both Cone and West, the interaction between the biblical text and later context in this study will be carried out within the African liberationist framework that is proposed above. The framework promotes African liberationist values such as reaction to the role of white people in the entrenchment of land dispossession and poverty among black people; an argument for political and economic liberation in *Mayibuye iAfrika*, 'Let Africa return'; the value of sharing resources by literally giving away resources (land and financial capital) to the poor, among other values noted above. Therefore, this framework shows a feature of the approach of the present study that partly differs from that of Cone and West.

The *Sitz-im-Leben* of Leviticus 25:8–55 and the South African setting

Some South African scholars have argued that the starting point of the interaction with the biblical text—an interaction that seeks to impact modern contexts—is paying attention to the struggle of the exploited working-class people or the poor.[38] As such, the present discussion of an African liberationist reading of Leviticus 25:8–55 in South Africa will begin with an analysis of the interaction between the *Sitz-im-Leben* of Leviticus 25:8–55 and the South African setting. The social locations of both the Israelite Jubilee and the South African land redistribution discourse will be analysed critically in such a way that the one would interpret the other, as James Cone suggests.

(i) The Pre-exilic Setting

Against Noth's late exilic dating of D, Otto and Römer support the pre-exilic dating of the first layer of D.[39] As argued in Chapter 3, if D was probably active during Hezekiah's rule and his revision was later documented at the time of Josiah, then, Leviticus 25:10, 39–40 could be assigned to a pre-exilic setting. In this section, the pre-exilic situation of the addressees of the first layer of D will be held in conversation with the South African context. As shown in the preceding chapter, the noun 'remission' in Leviticus 25:10 is related to Deuteronomy 15:2 and to the noun 'slave' in Leviticus 25:39–40 which calls for the release of slaves. Thus, it has been argued that the first layer of D sought to address the issue of slavery during the time of Hezekiah as illustrated by 2 Kings 19:5–7 which reports that Hezekiah had slaves.

First, it should be mentioned that the majority of African South Africans would identify with the challenge of slavery. As Mosala has noted, the colonial and apartheid systems 'dispossessed the African of their land and created out of them a wage class with nothing but their labour power to sell'.[40] Mosala's observation implies that the system forced black people to work in the mines and farms as slaves. The deliberate use of the term 'slaves' here speaks to the way black people were treated in the workplace. With reference to Leviticus 25:8–55, can one identify the working-class people of the pre-exilic period? Given the argument made in Chapter 3 that Leviticus 25:39–40 is pre-exilic, the particle preposition כְּ 'but as' which is attached to an absolute noun שָׂכִיר 'hired worker' (NIV) in v.40 validates the view that in such a period, there were also working-class people. Further, the Qal verb יַעֲבֹד 'to work' supports this inference. Interestingly, vv.39–40 contain a distinction between slavery and employment, as D insists that the poor brother should not work as a slave but a hired worker. The presence of the working-class people in the pre-exilic period in Leviticus 25:40 reminds one of the working-class people of South Africa.

To date, the labourers in the South African mines and farms continue to protest against low wages. For instance, Masenya (ngwan'a Mphahlele) holds that some of the protesting miners—the so-called working-class 'slaves' in Marikana—are 'stuck in the perpetual cycle of poverty which was inherited from the inequities of the apartheid era'.[41] This view is convincing because it is confirmed by statistics as well as by the persistent protest of the working-class people in South Africa. Therefore, in the light of the South African situation, D's allusion to slavery in Leviticus 25:8–55 in the pre-exilic period may be viewed as a protest against the socio-economic injustice experienced by the so-called slaves, that is, the working-class people.

An African liberationist reading of the experiences of the working-class people both in the South African context and in the world of the biblical text insists on their liberation. For Hopkins, the discussion of liberation, that is, 'the freedom of the individual self and the interest of those structurally occupying the bottom of community (i.e., in particular citizens dwelling in systematic poverty as well as working-class people)' is inseparable from the themes of politics and economics.[42] In Hopkins' view, the convergence of politics which relates to the decision on the process of sharing and distribution of wealth, and economics which involves the actual sharing and distribution of resources are at the core of the discourse on liberation.

The idea that the liberation of the working-class people, that is, the so-called slaves in Leviticus 25:8–55 is attached to the return of land resonates with Hopkins' view that the liberation of the working class is linked to, if not dependent on, the actual sharing and distribution of resources. Such resources refer to productive land. The song *Lelizwe* shows that the working-class people linked the protest against their labour for the Boers to the claim of land ownership. The complaint *Kudala sisebenzel' amabhulu*, 'We have been working for the Boers far too long' is linked to the claim *Lelizwe ngelethu*, 'This land is ours'. Thus, at the centre of the protest of the working-class people is the contestation for land, and for this reason it may be justified to argue that the loss of land was probably also at the centre of the experience of the working-class people, that is, the so-called slaves in Leviticus 25:8–55.

At the time of the Omri Dynasty and the rule of Jeroboam II, for example, some of the Israelites lost their land and were subsequently relegated to the 'wage class with nothing but their labour power to sell'.[43] This is evident in the Naboth and Ahab narrative as well as the Jeroboam II and Naboth's land case which show that the élites often used their power to confiscate land from the owners particularly from poor land owners.[44] Such misuse of power is also evident in the history of South Africa. Mtshiselwa notes the perturbing reality that the land which was confiscated from African South Africans by the white (British) colonists is still owned mainly by white South Africans.[45] Interestingly, Mosala's reading of Naboth from a 'black perspective' shows that Naboth was 'rendered poor by the experience of land expropriation'.[46] In agreement with Mosala, an African liberationist reading of the pre-exilic setting of the first layer of D would insist that the land of the working-class people was expropriated by some members of the élite class such as Ahab. The expropriation of land therefore perpetrated the poverty of the working-class people or the so-called slaves.

Earlier, it has been argued that in the pre-exilic period, the poor unlike the rich élites who had money found it difficult to acquire productive land under the conditions of payment of compensation. Textual evidence shows that Omri purchased a parcel of land from a citizen named Shemer for two talents, and there he built the city of Samaria.[47] This evidence is confirmed by the argument that 'Political figures (e.g., Omri) enriched themselves by purchasing land for private ownership'.[48] On the interaction between the pre-exilic context in which the provision for the payment compensation to acquire land impeded land redistribution and the South African context, Mosala makes a valid point:

> The issues of wealth and poverty in South Africa today touch significantly on the role of the economic market. For those who have power and possess wealth the market forces of the economic system of 'free enterprise' should be left to determine the creation and distribution of wealth. The powerless majority of black people in South Africa have no faith in the market. They argue that the market is an instrument of competition among those who already own wealth which they, the blacks have produced. It is the basis for the further dispossession of the oppressed and exploited black people. The notion, therefore, of 'a fair price' as is enunciated by the ruling classes of biblical times (Ahab, etc.) as well as the economic bosses of our time are hoax.[49]

Therefore, an African liberationist reading of the pre-exilic setting shows that the requirement for the payment of compensation to acquire land in the Israelite economic system was an impediment to socio-economic justice. The system was on the one hand in favour of the rich élites and on the other hand costly to the poor. Thus, the argument made earlier that in the pre-exilic Israelite context, the poor such as Naboth were in a position of disadvantage mainly because of their poverty and the inability to offer money to recover land appears to be valid.

(ii) The Babylonian Exilic Society in the Light of the Notion of 'Exile-at-Home'—Making the Connections

On the interaction between the Bible and modern African as well as the African diaspora context, Masenya (ngwan'a Mphahlele) poses a fundamental question: 'Why do Africana peoples continue to cling to the Book which has been successfully used by the powerful for, among others, their humiliation, land dispossession, racial segregation, slavery, patriarchy/*kyriarchy*, domination/ imperialism and neo-imperialism?' The response to the question could be found in Okure's argument that 'they (African women), *for instance*, are close to life at the grassroots; they see themselves in the texts of scripture, sometimes too literally and in ways that oppress rather than liberate them'.[50] In the South African context, the system of apartheid elevated white people to the level of superiority over black people.[51] The level of elevation and privilege could be compared to the exilic context in which the Babylonians were in position of power and privilege, as will be argued below. However, before probing the exilic context, the notion of 'exile-at-home' as it is used in the South African setting is worth exploring.

In their conceptualisation of the notion 'exile-at-home', Maluleke and Nadar refer to the powerless state of the African-South African intellectuals in a predominantly white academy.[52] Masenya (ngwan'a Mphahlele) explains the notion of being an 'exile-at-home' with the Vashti character in Esther Chapter 1 who is said to experience being in exile in her own country.[53] However, this study will give the experience of Vashti the attention it deserves. In terms of the South African context, Masenya (ngwan'a Mphahlele), like Mofokeng, holds that the loss of land during the colonial and apartheid eras in South Africa perpetrated the so-called socio-economic exiles in the midst of political liberation.[54] In other words, landlessness in one's country can be likened to being in 'exile-at-home'. As such, the clauses *Thina sizwe esimnyama*, 'We, the black nation' and *sikhalela izwe lethu*, 'are crying for our land' in the liberation song *Thina Sizwe* articulate the persistent experience of being landless in South Africa. No doubt, the experience of the Israelites in the Babylonian exile tallies with the experience of landlessness in South Africa as in both settings the poor and the working-class people do not own productive land.

We have argued that the features of both P and D fit with the exilic setting. On P's addressees, the noun 'possession' and the theme of the 'return to the homeland' in vv.13, 24–25, 27–28 and 32–34 reasonably hint at a situation of exile in which people needed to return home. An African liberationist reading of the noun and the theme would contend that the addressees of P in this case were in need of liberation. Masenya (ngwan'a Mphahlele)'s observation that 'exile' is often marked by negative experiences such as lack of freedom, assimilation into foreignness, xenophobia and even death comes to mind.[55] The contestation for the 'return to the homeland' typifies the experiences of the 'exiled'. The exiled people had no land of their own and no independence. An African liberationist reading of the exilic experience that hints at the theme of the 'return to the homeland' would thus consider the contested idea of an 'empty land'.

For his part, Carroll decisively argues that in 2 Chronicles 36:21 and Leviticus 26:34, 35 and 53, the land is presented as 'empty' so that the exilic community could return to it.[56] The texts are set against passages such as 2 Kings 24:14; 25:12 and Jeremiah 39:10; 52:15 which mention the 'poorest of the land' left behind, causing Meyer to note a tension within the Old Testament.[57] However, the tension does not discredit Carroll's argument, which enjoys the support of several scholars.[58] From an African liberationist perspective, the idea of an 'empty land' not only acknowledges the 'poorest of the land' left behind but it also shows that the working-class Israelites who were in exile were in fact landless, that is, they did not own productive land. Thus, the idea of the 'empty land' was created with the hope of returning to claim the homeland.

To determine the interaction between the exilic addressees of D and the South African context, it is important to consider the noun 'liberty' which is related to D's reference to 'remission' and to the 'release of slaves' (cf. Lev 25:10, 39–40, 54). The situation of the Israelites in the Babylonian exile is unclear as some scholars argue that they were treated as slaves while others hold that the Israelites were actually slaves. Noth and Obed have already argued that the Israelites were not living under harsh realities in Babylonia, that is, they were not slaves or prisoners. Since there is no evidence of suppression, Obed argues that the exiles had 'a certain internal autonomy and that they enjoyed the freedom to manage their community life (Ezek 33:30–33)'.[59] However, Obed slightly departs from Noth who admits that the exiles were 'compelled to render compulsory services'.[60] In other words, Noth does not object to the idea that the exiles engaged in forced labour in Babylonia.

Similarly, Scheffler assumes that 'taking into account that the exiles to Babylonia were from the upper classes, it should be noted that they were not as a rule treated as slaves by the Babylonians (contra "Nabucco" of Verdi!)'.[61] He bases his argument, first, on the idea that the *Marashu inscription* discovered at *Nippur* reveals Jewish economic activity. Second, he claims that the letter sent to the Jews by Jeremiah, which encouraged them to be active economically, to multiply and to pray for the welfare of the Babylonian Empire points to some economic activity in exile.[62] He believes that the reference to the economic activity refutes the claims that the Israelites were slaves in Babylonia. In the light of the views of Noth, Obed and Scheffler on the exiles, a pertinent question to ask is what is it that an African liberationist reader could affirm or refute about the discourse of the exiles in Babylonia?

The issue of whether the exiles were slaves, prisoners, hard labourers or forced labourers reminds one of the liberation song *Lelizwe*, 'This Land'. In the song, the working-class men who work mostly for the white people are referred to as '*pikinini*'. Thus, verse line 7 says *Bambiz' upikinini, engadini*, 'They call him *pikinini* in the garden'. Interestingly, the word 'pikin' in Pidgin English also means 'child' or kid. It was borrowed from the Portuguese *pequenino* or *pequeno*. In addition, the word *pikinini* '... in Papua New Guinea, *pik man* "pig man" is a male pig, *pik merin* "pig woman" is a sow and *pikinini pik* "child pig" is a "piglet"'.[63] Thus, verse line 7 *Bambiz' upikinini, engadini* may be viewed as an expression that degraded the working-class black people to the level of a kid (animal or human). Therefore, the treatment that corresponds with the name *pikinini* would have been a harsh one coupled with hard labour. Based on the experiences of the working-class people in South Africa who were dehumanised and reduced to the level of animals, an African liberationist reading of the addressees of D in exile would identify with the argument that the exiles experienced either slavery or hard labour. In that reading, one would also ask why D would mention 'remission' and the 'release of slaves' in Leviticus 25:10, 39–40 and 54 if the exiles did not experience any harsh realities that necessitated a call for liberation.

Some scholars have also argued that the exiles were slaves in Babylonia. The strength of the Babylonian Empire was based on the exploitation of non-Babylonian populations for the benefit of the ruling elite. That is, the exploitation of the non-Babylonian exiles was inevitable in Babylonia. Similarly, the exploitation of the labour of the Judean exiles made them virtual slaves of the Empire.[64] Drawing from the biblical text, he correctly claims that the words 'chains' and 'bonds' do not only typify exilic experience but they also show that the exiles were slaves.

For instance, Nahum 1:13 says, 'Now I will break their yoke from your neck and tear your shackles away;' Isaiah 52:2 reads: 'Shake off your dust; rise up, sit enthroned, Jerusalem. Free yourself from the chains on your neck, Daughter Zion, now a captive;' Psalm 107:14 says, 'He brought them out of darkness, the utter darkness, and broke away their chains;' and Isaiah 45:14 reads, '... they will come over to you and will be yours; they will trudge behind you, coming over to you in chains. They will bow down before you ...'. Interestingly, Smith-Christopher notes that Jeremiah 40:1 'when he took him bound in fetters' in 'the Septuagint has *chairopedais* literally "foot shackle"'.[65] Thus, based on the biblical text, Smith-Christopher's argument that the exiles were slaves and captives who were in chains appears convincing.

Furthermore, Rugwiji affirms the view of Smith-Christopher on the experience of the exiles in the following words:

> Economic exploitation was at the heart of the experience of Judah in the Babylonian exile. ... The biblical text narrates that part of the ideology of subjugating the Judeans in Babylonia included some kind of 'cheap labour' provision as well as possibilities of other kinds of ill-treatment. (Is 52:5; Jr 51:6–7; Lm 3:1–9; Ps 137)[66]

In Leviticus 25:8–55, the exploitation of the working-class people would be a plausible typification of the experience of the exiles as there is a clear allusion to 'remission' the 'release of slaves' and the instruction to avoid oppressing the poor.

This counters the suggestion that the Israelite exiles were not slaves.[67] As such, an African liberationist reader would support the views of Smith-Christopher and Rugwiji that the exiles experienced slavery and hard labour. Based on D's reference to the term 'remission' and to the expression 'release of slaves', which presuppose a situation of captivity, a liberationist reading would insist that D's addressees in Babylonia experienced the need for liberation.

As shown above, the liberation song *Lelizwe*, 'This Land' helps one to identify with the experience of hard labour and oppression of the exiles. That is, from an African liberationist perspective, one tends to support the arguments backed by textual evidence that the Israelite exiles were in chains. This is informed by the experience of the so-called *pikinini*—the working-class men of South Africa—expressed in the song *Lelizwe.* However, based on the argument by Cone, West and Masenya (ngwan'a Mphahlele) that the biblical text needs to interpret the modern context the debate on the experience of the landless exiles who were D's addressees is relevant in South Africa. D's reference to 'remission' and the 'release of slaves' could be interpreted as experiences that would remind African South Africans of their 'exile-at-home' experiences of oppression.

A number of South African scholars have noted that the present socio-economic realities in South Africa are marked by the land dispossession, oppression and exploitation of African South Africans.[68] In other words, the present South African context is not free from oppression and injustice. Thus, 'a negotiation that seeks to redress the socio-economic injustice which is inherited from the land dispossession Act of the colonial and apartheid South Africa is of paramount importance', and will be discussed further below.[69] In the light of the demand for the 'release of slaves' by D, it is also reasonable to call for liberation from socio-economic injustice evident in the poverty-cycle in which many African South Africans are trapped.

Furthermore, the references in the biblical text to words such as 'chains', 'bound', 'remission' and the 'release of slaves' in the Israelite Jubilee prompt the question: could one consider the post-apartheid South Africa a completely free country? Besides, if H used D's exilic reference to 'remission' or the 'release of slaves' in the post-exilic setting, perhaps the Israelites were not completely free in the post-exilic Yehud. That possibility triggers a pertinent dialogue between the so-called post-apartheid South Africa and post-exilic Yehud especially within an African liberationist framework.

(iii) Post-apartheid South Africa in Dialogue with Post-exilic Yehud—The Search for Freedom

In his speech 'I Have a Dream', Martin Luther King, Jr. quoted an African American spiritual liberation song sung by slaves 'Free at last! Free at last! Thank God

Almighty, we are free at last!'[70] The fact that the song was sung in the context of oppression, that is, slavery, shows that it does not declare the freedom of the African American people. Rather, as James Cone has noted, the song is a resilient expression of the struggle for freedom.[71] An African liberationist reading would affirm such a struggle in the dialogue between post-exilic Yehud and post-apartheid South Africa.

The compromise of the property clause and the protection of land ownership against redistribution without compensation which is still an impediment to socio-economic redress bears a striking similarity to the protection of the rights of the Levites in Leviticus 25:32–33. In the South African context, it appears that the protection of land ownership does not address the statement *Thina sizwe esimnyama sikhalela izwe lethu elathathwa ngabamhlophe* 'We, the black nation, are crying for our land, which was taken by white people'. The protection of the rights to ownership of land that was taken initially from black people through colonialism and apartheid may be considered an impediment to socio-economic-redress. Viewed from the South African context, the protection of the rights of the Levites must have impeded the attempts to alleviate poverty through land redistribution. Stated differently, the protection of the ownership of land occupied by the Levites refutes the very same principle that the Israelite Jubilee seeks to uphold, that is, redistributing land in order to alleviate poverty. Therefore, the idea of protecting the rights of certain people would not be helpful in the South African context where the protection of land that was dispossessed from black people by their white counterparts still poses a challenge to socio-economic justice.

Furthermore, based on the argument that in the Persian period, power resided with the priestly and scribal élites from the Babylonian exile, it is useful to probe the accumulation and retention of power and control through the acquisition of productive land. Ilbury and Sunter have argued that the security of economic interest is directly linked to the accumulation and retention of power and control in South Africa.[72] The argument is relevant to the discussion of the protection of land rights of the Levites in Leviticus 25:32–33. It is also confirmed by the textual evidence which shows that the Levites continued to be the beneficiaries of the agricultural activities as well as the substantive argument presented above that power resided with the priestly and scribal élites from the Babylonian exile (cf. Neh 10:39). It would therefore mean that the protection of the land given to the Levites served to protect the economic and political interests as well as power at the cost of economic equality. No doubt, subjecting the land occupied by other people to the process of Israelite Jubilee while protecting the land occupied by the Levites shows inequality. An African liberationist reader would therefore be resolute in highlighting such inequality in the text as well as showing that it would not be a helpful model in the South African context.

The negative command 'you shall not oppress one another' (v.14) is set in the context of agricultural activity relating to the use of land as well as in the context of the statement, 'If your brother becomes poor' (v.25). Like the proverb *Marumo a ja mabekane ga se tlala e hlaolago*, 'When enmity sets in, it kills everybody, unlike hunger which comes to persecute only the poor' Leviticus 25:8–55 points to a situation in which hunger persecuted the poor.[73] Thus, from an African liberationist perspective, the link of the theme of oppression, land and poverty in a single legislation, that is, the Jubilee would be considered relevant in the South African context. It has been argued above that the Land Act of 1913 engineered the persistent poverty of black people in South Africa, which is still evident in the post-apartheid setting.[74] Therefore, the concern for the poor in the clause 'If your brother becomes poor' (v.25) would enjoy a positive reception within the African liberationist framework employed in this study.

However, the fact that the verse 25 exclusively focuses on men with its particular reference to 'brother' but it is silent about the poverty of women would pose a challenge in both ancient Israel and the South African context. Such exclusivity and bias would be unfriendly to the poverty of women in the South African setting which has 56 percent of women who live in poor households as opposed to 51.8 percent of men.[75] On the treatment of black women in the United States, Cone inquires: 'Why is it that the Black church can be so progressive on race and so conservative when dealing with patriarchy and homophobia?'[76] The question seeks to address the oppression of women under patriarchy and the silence regarding women's experiences of injustice. Since such a question affirms the liberation of women, it is worth considering in an African liberationist reading of the Israelite Jubilee.

Furthermore, the idea that the Israelite Jubilee legislation is silent on the poverty experienced by women in post-exilic Yehud reminds one of a question posed by Masenya (ngwan'a Mphahlele), 'Can she [Vashti] be a model for women of Africa in South Africa today?'[77] Following Masenya (ngwan'a Mphahlele), but not focusing on the character of Vashti, a critical question to ask is can the Israelite Jubilee legislation be employed as a legal model for the poor women of South Africa today? On the one hand, the silence of the Jubilee legislation on the experience of poverty by women would not be liberative in the South African context, as it may project an aspect of patriarchy, which is often inconsiderate of the plight of the women. On the other hand, highlighting the silence, that is, reading the Jubilee as being silent to the concerns of women would be liberative since it would remind South Africans that women equally need to own productive land, which could alleviate their poverty. Such a reading would insist on re-reading the liberations songs *Thina sizwe esimnyama*, 'We, the black nation;' *Senzeni na*? 'What have we done'; and *Lelizwe*, 'This Land' which are also silent about redistributing land to women. One may ask whether the plural pronoun 'we' in 'We the Black Nation' does not include women. The song *Thina sizwe esimnyam*a, 'We, the black nation' was sung by both male and female African-South African exiles in foreign lands.[78] Even if the song considered the plights of women, it does not mean that it effectively advocated for and accomplished land redistribution on behalf of women. The point that women experience poverty the most in South Africa confirms the view that the socio-economic redress which includes redistributing land to women has not yet been attained.

However, the song *Lelizwe* 'This Land' affirms the liberative reading of the Israelite Jubilee in relation to the concerns of women. The portrayal of the challenge experienced by female domestic workers who form part of the poor working-class group in the expression *Umama wami, ekhishini*, 'My mother, in the kitchen' in the song *Lelizwe* 'This Land' aims to alleviate the poverty of women. The song articulates the unpleasant experiences of the working-class people who historically have been dispossessed of their land and degraded to a wage class with nothing but their labour power to sell.[79] However, verse line 9 *Lelizwe ngelethu*, 'This land is ours' of the song *Lelizwe*, 'This Land' shows that women also expressed claims to productive land. That means the song may be viewed as liberative to women also as it empowers and challenges women in the present South African setting to claim their right to own and use productive land. In the light of the Israelite Jubilee and of the songs *Thina sizwe esimnyama*, 'We, the black nation' and *Lelizwe*, 'This Land' a deliberate position which argues that productive land needs to be equally redistributed to women would be both convincing and liberative.

Above, we have shown that some of the addressees of the Jubilee could not use the land productively but it is difficult to prove the exact cause of the unproductiveness. However, the textual evidence from Nehemiah 5:4 shows that the payment of taxes clearly caused a strain on the farming activities of the middle-class Israelites, as they eventually struggled to make profit. The consequence was indebtedness, loss of land and poverty among the working-class Israelites in the post-exilic Yehud. As argued above, the absolute noun שָׂכִיר 'hired worker' (NIV) and the Qal verb יַעֲבֹד 'to work' in Leviticus 25:40 which were re-used in the post-exilic Yehud setting refer to the class of people who were employees, that is, the working-class Israelites. On the surface, the lack of productivity on the part of some Israelites in post-exilic Yehud seems to have a striking similarity to the lack of productivity of African South Africans in the post-apartheid South African context. Although in both settings unproductivity is not helpful to the alleviation of poverty, the payment of taxes affected the profits of farmers in post-exilic Yehud while in post-apartheid South Africa this is not the case.

As the Vumelana Advisory Fund has shown, 'Transferred land becomes unproductive because the newly enfranchised land owners cannot raise the capital or acquire the skills needed to work the land …'.[80] That is, unlike the post-exilic Yehud context, the lack of skills, capital and resources strains productivity in post-apartheid South Africa. However, the argument that the lack of financial resources contributed to the unproductivity of the poor farmers in post-exilic Yehud would be considered valid since it is evident that the payment of taxes placed a heavy strain on their productivity. Thus, an African liberationist reading of the Israelite Jubilee would highlight the lack of financial resources as a contributing factor to unproductivity on the part of African-South African farmers and the nation's efforts to attain socio-economic justice.

Earlier, an important question was posed as to whether the Judeans in post-exilic Yehud were actually free. The theme of 'slavery' in the post-exilic Yehud community is worth exploring in the present dialogue between the context of the post-exilic Yehud and post-apartheid South Africa. As argued above, several scholars have criticised the nature of South Africa's freedom. For instance, it has been noted that African South Africans are still not free after the demise of apartheid and the dawn of democracy and that the nature of South Africa's freedom and democracy is not equally liberative to all the citizens of the country especially to the poor African South Africans.[81]

The above statements show that on the one hand South Africa is enjoying political liberation while on the other hand many South Africans are not economically free, as confirmed by the level of poverty in the country. Thus, due to the noticeable forms of oppression in South Africa today such as patriarchy and economic oppression which have trapped many black people in a persistent poverty-cycle the so-called freedom of the post-apartheid South African state has been questioned.[82]

The idea that Nehemiah 5:3–5 highlights the indebtedness of the working-class Israelites which led to poverty and slavery under the Persian rule validates the view that the post-exilic Yehud community was not economically free.[83] This is besides the view which will be examined later that the Persians did not allow the Judeans to have their own government, a pointer that the Judeans were not free.[84] Interestingly, the theme of indebtedness in the Israelite Jubilee legislation triggers the interest in the indebtedness of the working-class people of South Africa which may be linked to the lack of productive land, skills and capital.

In his *Ending Economic Apartheid*, Edozien argues that 'the end of political apartheid is ultimately meaningless without the end of economic apartheid' which South Africa is currently experiencing.[85] On the indebtedness of the working-class people, who are mostly African South Africans, he notes that:

> Today, most national money originates in a conceptually very simple process. The private banking system creates the money, most of it out of nothing, as a loan to be repaid with interest according to a set schedule. So: most money is introduced into circulation by those whom the banking industry considers to be creditworthy borrowers. You must already have money in order to get money easily.[86]

Edozien's insight above confirms that many working-class people are trapped not only in debt but also in an economic system which does not allow them to own resources. For instance, the so-called possessions, that is, the cars and houses of many middle-class workers which in fact belong to the banks because of loan conditions validate the view that this class of people are trapped in debt.[87] Moreover, the issue of financial credibility of the borrowers which demands evidence of a track record as a paying creditor from the poor is an impediment to socio-economic-redress particularly in light of South African history of black people being dispossessed of their assets (land). Therefore, an African liberationist critique of indebtedness in South Africa would insist on land redistribution as inspired by the theme of redistribution of land in the Jubilee legislation, which sought to address indebtedness.

The reference to walled cities in Leviticus 25:5–88 suggests that there was an élite class in post-exilic Yehud. Knight rightly argues that in post-exilic Yehud, large portions of agricultural land, which produced wealth were owned by the rich and powerful élites who resided in the walled cities.[88] The post-exilic text of Nehemiah also refers to the élite class. Nehemiah was an Israelite élite who was once appointed the governor of Yehud by the Persian Empire; hence, he served the interest of the Empire.[89] In fact, textual evidence confirms that Nehemiah built the חוֹמַת הָעִיר 'walls of the city' (Neh 2:8, 15, 17; 3:8. 13; 4:1, 3, 6). However, it should be considered also that Nehemiah did not receive a salary throughout his term but relied on his resources and fought for the oppressed (Neh 5:1–19; 13:10–11).

One could argue that Nehemiah did not rebuild the walls to separate the rich from the poor but for security reasons since his men had to arm themselves while building the walls of the city to defend themselves against Sanballat and Tobias. However, the possibility that the wall marked a distinction between the wealthy and the poor cannot be ignored as shown in Chapter 3. If Nehemiah contributed to the rebuilding of the walls of the city which served as a wall of separation between the people living in the villages and those in the walled cities, then, this prominent religious leader and élite figure did not help to redress economic inequality in Yehud. Instead, he enjoyed the royal treatment he received from the Persian Empire. If the Jewish leaders such as Nehemiah had taken seriously the challenge of economic inequality that is evident in the text of Leviticus 25:8–55 particularly with regard to the distinction between the villagers and city people, such a challenge would have been addressed, as an African liberationist reader would do.

The inability to address the gap between the rich and the poor in the post-exilic Yehud in the texts of Leviticus 25:8–55 and Nehemiah 2:8, 15, 17; 3:8. 13; 4:1, 3, 6 tallies with the post-apartheid South African situation in which such a gap that is confirmed by the high level of poverty continues to widen. Furthermore, the idea that the rich élites most of whom must have lived in walled cities accumulated wealth while the poor remained in the margins reminds one of the South African situation.

Degenaar has categorised South Africans into two classes—a ruling class of rich élites and a working class of impoverished South Africans.[90] As noted in Chapter 2, Bond has also disclosed that some black politicians, namely Cyril Ramaphosa, Nthato Motlana, Jonty Sandler, Dikgang Moseneke and Zwelakhe Sisulu have become wealthy through their association with the political élites—the NP and ANC politicians.[91] The gap between the poor and the wealthy élites in South Africa tallies with the post-exilic Yehud situation in which there was an élite class amidst the poor majority and shows that the ancient text does relate to the situation of the modern reader of the Bible. An African liberationist reader of the distinction between the people living in the villages and the walled cities in post-exilic Yehud would note first that some Israelite élites established close relations with the Persian Empire.

Second, most of those élites served the interest of the Empire. Third, the élites did not address the economic inequality which is evident in the different treatment meted out to the people in the villages and those in the cities. Similarly, the African-South African political élites including Cyril Ramaphosa, Nthato Motlana, Jonty Sandler, Dikgang Moseneke and Zwelakhe Sisulu established a close relation with the NP politicians who were in the position of power prior to the dawn of democracy in South Africa. As aforementioned, statistical data confirms economic inequality in South Africa, and the political élites in the country have not yet effectively addressed the gap between the poor and the rich. No doubt, there are resemblances between the context of post-exilic Yehud and the post-apartheid South African setting when it comes to the situation of the élites and the poor.

A dialogue between the *Sitz-im-Leben* of Leviticus 25:8–55 and the South African setting enables both the ancient text and the modern context to interpret each other. The text throws light on the modern South African context while the South African context offers a unique interpretation of the situation of the addressees of the Israelite Jubilee. Furthermore, it may prove helpful also to draw the meaning of the ancient texts from the interaction between the South African context and the intertextual relationship between Leviticus 25:8–55 and its surrounding texts.

The South African context and intertextual relationship between Leviticus 25:8–55 and its surrounding texts

At this point, the interaction between the intertextual relationship of the Israelite Jubilee to its surrounding text—the Sabbatical Year—and the South African context will be considered. Particularly noteworthy is the idea of seven years of the Sabbatical Year (Lev 25:1–7), which was supplemented in the Israelite Jubilee in vv.23–24 to highlight the idea that the land belongs to YHWH.[92] The idea could be compared in a sense to the belief in African tradition that the land is the property of the ancestors who control its fertility.[93] It was based on that belief that King Moshoeshoe refused to cede the land to the Boer Trekkers at the Caledon River and the Vaal River in 1858.[94] Given the African view that the land belongs to the ancestors, the idea that the land belongs to YHWH would enjoy a positive reception among African South Africans as it rejects the private ownership of land, which is to their disadvantage.

Nonetheless, in the unit of vv.23–24, we see that the land belongs to YHWH and not to the ancestors of the Israelites. Therefore, one could also say that YHWH's ownership of the land in Leviticus 25:8–55 is comparable to the view that the ancestors owned the land in Africa is not strong. However, the Sotho terms *Badimo* 'ancestors' and *Modimo* 'God' etymologically share the same root suggesting that the ancestors are regarded as gods.[95] Setiloane shows that etymologically the root of the word *Badimo*, 'ancestors', that is, *dimo* is derived from the stem *dzimu* which means 'spirit'.[96] The same root is also noticeable in the word *Modimo*, 'God'. Furthermore, the prefix *Ba* in *Badimo* is the plural of the singular prefix *Mo* in *Modimo.* As such, the argument that *Badimo*, 'ancestors or gods' is the plural for *Modimo* 'God' is justified.[97] Both *Badimo* 'the ancestors' and *Modimo*, 'God' share in the essence of *BoModimo*, the 'spiritual realm'.[98] The notions that *Motho ke Modimo* 'A human being is God' and that the realm of the ancestors is above that of human beings also support the argument that ancestors can be regarded as gods.[99] Therefore, in the light of the African understanding of *Badimo* 'ancestors' as gods, the comparison of the views that the land belonged to YHWH in Leviticus 25:8–55 and to *Badimo* 'ancestors or gods' in Africa is justified. Furthermore, as mentioned in Chapter 3, H's ideological standpoint on the centralisation of land in v.23 is liberating because it challenged the ideology of classism which commoditised and privatised land in favour of the rich élites. Thus, H's ideological stance would enjoy a positive reception among African South Africans.

As noted above, Leviticus 25 and 26 are closely related to each other.[100] However, Meyer has distanced himself from the argument he made a decade earlier that the close reading of Leviticus 25 and 26 alludes to the Babylonian exile returnees who sought to claim the so-called 'empty land'.[101] However, he does not reject the 'myth of the empty land'.[102] Textual evidence suggests that H presented the post-exilic Yehud land as being cleared of its occupants.[103] Significantly, the rejection of the argument that Leviticus 25 and 26 refer to the élites about to return from exile who wanted their land—the so-called 'empty land'—based on the post-exilic dating of Leviticus 25 is not convincing. As argued in Chapter 3, the attractive dating of various layers of Leviticus 25:8–55, for instance, P's discussion of returning to the homeland in the late exilic period, justifies the argument that the élites returned to Yehud to claim the so-called 'empty land'.[104] Furthermore, a late exilic dating of H (the second half of the sixth century BCE) cannot be ruled out as it supports the view that Leviticus 25 and 26 refer to the Babylonian exile returnees who sought to reclaim their land.[105] The dating of certain layers of P and H to the exilic period would make Meyer's initial argument about the élite returnees who sought the so-called empty land appealing.[106] One would therefore ask whether the 'myth of the empty land' could be used to relate the context from which Leviticus 25 and 26 emerged and the context of modern readers of the Bible?

In the history of land dispossession in South Africa, it is argued that the Boer (Afrikaner) Trekkers, for example, believed that a part of South African land was 'empty land'.[107] Hence, the Orange Free State Afrikaner Trekkers took the land that was first occupied by the Basotho people under the kingship of Moshoeshoe. However, the Afrikaner Trekkers' situation differs from that of the Babylonian élite returnees who sought to reclaim their land, that is, the so-called empty land in Yehud. The Afrikaner Trekkers were not returning to their homeland, but they sought the land that was first occupied by the Basotho people under the kingship of Moshoeshoe while in Leviticus 25 and 26 the élites sought the land, which they owned prior to their deportation to Babylonia. In both contexts, the construction of the 'myth of the empty land' was meant to legitimise access to the land. However, unlike the case of the Afrikaner Trekkers, the situation of the African-South African exiles who returned to South Africa during the transition from the apartheid to the democratic state strongly relates to the context of Leviticus 25 and 26.

Setiloane notes that while in foreign countries, the then African-South African exiles sang the liberation song *Thina sizwe esimnyama*, 'We, the black nation' which reminded them of their homeland.[108] Both the Israelite exiles and the African-South African exiles sought to retrieve their land while in exile, and this confirms the resemblance between the context of Leviticus 25 and 26 and the modern reader of the Bible in South Africa. Moreover, the African-South African exiles became the political élites who assumed leadership position under the ANC government as shown in Chapter 2. Similarly, the Babylonian exile returnees were part of the élite class in post-exilic Yehud. As argued above, both the élite class in post-apartheid South Africa and the post-exilic Yehud élites revel in their wealth, which was accrued from the use of productive land while many poor people remain trapped in the cycle of poverty. In the light of the value of sharing resources, an African liberationist reader would reasonably view the 'myth of the empty land' that emerges from the intertextual reading of Leviticus 25 and 26 as oppressive to the poor. Thus, it is important to probe the reality that the exile returnees in both the context of the text and the context of modern South Africa accessed productive land and accumulated wealth amidst the crunching poverty being experienced by the masses.

It has been argued that Leviticus 25:55 and Leviticus 26:1 are 'reminiscent of the Decalogue, which similarly opens with a reference to the exodus (Exodus 20:2; Deut 5:6)'.[109] Instead of reading the reference to the exodus as a focus on the theme of deliverance from Egypt in the intertextual relationship between Leviticus 25 and 26, an African liberationist reader would see a tenor of liberation. In his *Africa in need of an exodus? Perspectives on the theology of Exodus 15:1–21*, Human reads the theme of Exodus in conversation with the liberation struggles in Africa, which are actually struggles against oppression, poverty and unemployment, among others.[110] Therefore, from an African liberationist point of view, the reference to the Exodus in both Leviticus 25 and 26 may be re-read as a reference to the liberation narrative which when set in dialogue with the South African context can yield liberating possibilities, as will be argued below.

Given the intertextual relationship of Leviticus 17–27 (the Holiness Code) to Leviticus 1–16 (the P material), Leviticus 25:8–55 is viewed as a legislation.[111] Significantly, the statement 'this is the Torah' suggests that the Israelite Jubilee legislation became YHWH's law. The Torah was viewed by the Israelites as YHWH's law and this made the texts which contain the statement 'this is the Torah' to gain an authoritative status.[112] In other words, the Torah was viewed as authoritative by the Israelites since it represented the divine law from YHWH. The view that the authority of the Torah is inherent in it as a normative text supports the idea that the Torah became normative mainly because it was viewed as the law that came from YHWH through Moses.[113] The Torah functioned as a normative text, which demanded personal submission and obedience; therefore, the Torah served as a legal guide for the Israelites' behaviour and actions (cf. Deut 30:1–14). The way the Israelites were supposed to live and treat each other was guided by the Torah.

Interestingly, the subject of land and how the Israelite needed to deal with land was part of the Torah the divine law of YHWH.[114] For example, the motif and theme of the promise of land in the Torah is evident (cf. Gen 12:7; 13:15,17;

15:7,18; 17:8; 24:7; 28:4,13; 35:12; 48:4; 50:24; Exod 13:5,11; 32:13; 33:1; Lev 18:3; 19:23; 20:24; 23:10; 25:2,38; Num 11:12; 14:16,23; 32:11; Dt 1:8, 35; 6:10, 18, 23; 7:13; 8:1; 10:11; 11:9, 21; 19:8; 26:3,15; 28:11; 30:20; 31:7, 20; 34:4). No doubt, the promise of land in 'the Sabbatical Year' text (Lev 25:2) and in 'the Israelite Jubilee' text (Lev 25:38) which is found in the context of the Torah suggests that the Israelite Jubilee was in fact the law—a legal text. As such, Leviticus 25:8–55 was intended to guide the Israelites on how to deal justly and legally with the subject of land redistribution and socio-economic justice in both the exilic and the post-exilic contexts, as argued in Chapter 3.

In summary, first, the Torah represented YHWH's law; second, it was a normative text; and third, it functioned as a legal guide to the Israelites on how to live and treat each other. Lastly, in the context from which Leviticus 25:8–55 emerged, this text was intended to influence legally the people's approach to the subject of land redistribution and socio-economic justice. Like the Torah, the South African constitution serves as a normative text which legally guides the citizens of the country as to how they ought to live and treat each other, and like the Torah, the constitution upholds the principle of justice. Aspects of the South African law comparable to the Jubilee legislation in Leviticus 25:8–55 include the property clause in Section 25 of the 1996 Constitution of the Republic of South Africa; White Paper on Land Reform of 1991; Land Reform (Labour Tenants) Act, No. 3 of 1996; Green Paper on South African Land Reform of 2011. However, the difference between the law of Leviticus 25:8–55 and the South African land law is the fact that the Torah texts are regarded as divine law from YHWH and the South African land policies are not viewed as such. Nonetheless, in both contexts, a legal document was needed to guide the people in the process of dealing with land redistribution and socio-economic justice.

Dialogue between the South African context and the possible structure of Leviticus 25:8–55

The constitutive statement יֹובֵל הִוא תִּהְיֶה לָכֶם 'it shall be a Jubilee for you' (v.10) confirms that the unit of vv.8–13 is about the 'Institution of the Israelite Jubilee—Land Policy'. In the unit, the central word is דְּרוֹר 'liberty'. Gerstenberger views the word liberty as a comprehensive notion because it implies both the return of land and the release of debt-slaves.[115] Thus, the idea that the Israelite Jubilee sought to attain liberation for the poor Israelites through land redistribution as well as cancellation of debts and release from slavery would be a compelling view in the South African setting. In the two liberation songs *Thina sizwe esimnyama*, 'We, the black nation' and *Senzeni na*, 'What have we done?' the need for liberty (or liberation) is upheld. Furthermore, the call for political and economic liberation underlying the protest song *Mayibuye iAfrika*, 'Let Africa return' tallies with the idea of liberating the Israelites from poverty and inequality in Leviticus 25:8–55.

Thus, the view that the unit of vv.8–13 introduces a legislation that sought liberation with respect to land, debts and slavery could stimulate the South African discourse on land to include the subject of debts and hard labour, as will be discussed below. On the one hand, an interaction between the South African context and the unit of vv.8–13 shows that the discourse of land in South Africa could be enriched by the lesson from the text that the theme of land is inseparable from the subject of debts and slavery or hard labour. On the other hand, the South African context helps one to understand that the unit of vv.8–13 introduces a legislation that called for the political and economic liberation of the poor. Thus, the critical notion in the unit is דְּרוֹר 'liberty'.

Unlike Nihan, after him, Gerstenberger holds that vv.13–22 is a unit on 'economic praxis'.[116] First, Gerstenberger's position is interesting as the term 'praxis' suggests that the theory of the Israelite Jubilee is enacted and applied in the verses. However, this terminology may not enjoy a positive reception since there is no convincing evidence that the Israelite Jubilee was ever realised or implemented. Second, because the noun יוֹבֵל 'Jubilee' is said to link vv.12 and 13, one would be justified to place v.13 in the unit of vv.8–13 instead of in the unit of vv.13–22 as Gerstenberger has proposed. Therefore, rather than accept Gerstenberger's proposed structure of vv.13–22 as a unit, I submit that vv.14–22 be viewed as a unit, and as shown in Chapter 3, that unit focuses on the 'Trading of agricultural products and food security in the Israelite Jubilee'.

On the interaction between the unit vv.14–22 and the South African context, a critical question to ask is what would an African liberationist reader see and highlight in the unit which a non-African reader would readily overlook? African South Africans who have experienced economic injustice that was perpetrated by the colonial and apartheid systems would identify with the principle of fairness and justice which is expressed in the negative command 'therefore you shall not oppress one another' in v.17. Furthermore, Bellinger's interpretation of the phrase וְנָתְנָה הָאָרֶץ פִּרְיָהּ 'and the land shall yield her fruit' (v.19) as 'the land will on its own produce an abundance' would be contested by an African liberationist reader.[117] Since 90 percent of farms reclaimed from white farmers and redistributed to the South African black population are not productive, it is clear that the land does not produce abundance by itself. Moreover, African South Africans are presently faced with the challenge of lack of capital to purchase productive land or to sustain it, if they acquire such agricultural land. Thus, an African liberationist reader of the unit vv.14–22 would submit first, that the poor African South Africans would identify with the principle of fairness and justice. Second, both the poor Israelites in the text of Leviticus 25:8–55 and the African South Africans lose the benefits of owning and utilising productive land partly due to the lack of capital to purchase such land.

Nihan's simple captioning of vv. 23–24 as 'Introduction of the second part of Leviticus 25' appears unconvincing.[118] From an African liberationist perspective, v.23 could be read as alluding to the theme of Yahweh's entitlement to the land, which is set against the privatisation of land because poverty and inequality are perpetrated by the privatisation of productive land in South Africa, as argued in Chapter 2. The statement of entitlement כִּי־לִי הָאָרֶץ 'for the land is mine' (v.23) highlights the idea that YHWH is the only owner of the land, an idea which in my view rejects the private ownership of land by the élites in ancient Israel.[119] However, unlike Römer who does not refute explicitly and strongly the idea of private ownership of land, Gerstenberger notes that v.23 is set to 'decisively reject any private ownership claims to the land'.[120]

On the argument against the privatisation of land as it occurs in the texts of Leviticus 25:8–55 in relation to the Naboth narrative in 2 Kings 21 that has been noted in Chapter 3, Farisani's view is worthy of note. In his contextual reading of 1 Kings 21:1–29, Farisani rejects the idea of private ownership of land at the time of the Omri dynasty.[121] The reason is that the unfair treatment of Naboth which reflects the socio-economic injustice that poor Israelites often experienced cannot be justified. The land was lost mainly because the rich élites sought to acquire land privately at the expense of poor Israelites. Thus, following Farisani, Mtshiselwa holds that privatisation of land in the Omri dynasty, for example, intensified poverty among the small farmers.[122] In the light of the link between Leviticus 25:8–55 and 1 Kings 21 as well as the rejection of privatization of land in the Omri dynasty, Gerstenberger's claim that v.23 is set to reject privatization of land is compelling.

In terms of how the South African context relates to the text of Leviticus 25:8–55, first, the theme of Yahweh's entitlement to the land which is set against privatisation of land is related to the view that land belonged to *Badimo* 'ancestors or gods' in Africa. The argument of some South African scholars on land ownership supports this view.[123] Second, the argument that the rich political élites in ancient Israel sought land for private ownership at the expense of the poor in Israel resembles the situation of African South Africans.

In 1993, the political élites who belonged to the NP government entrenched the concept of privatization, which sustained their wealth.[124] Subsequently, the African South African political élites such as Cyril Ramaphosa, Nthato Motlana, Jonty Sandler, Dikgang Moseneke and Zwelakhe Sisulu benefitted from the privatisation of land and businesses. The élite class therefore became wealthy while many African South Africans remained trapped in poverty. Farisani's rejection of privatization of land in the Omri dynasty because the unfair treatment of Naboth caricatures the socio-economic injustice that the poor Israelites often experienced is compelling.

Third, privatization of land in the context of Leviticus 25:8–55 intensified the poverty of the small farmers as the situation at the time of the Omri dynasty shows. Similarly, some South African scholars have noted that the privatization of land has intensified the poverty of African South Africans. Thus, an African liberationist reader of the Israelite Jubilee legislation would reject the reality of private ownership of land in ancient Israel, which tallies with the notion of privatization of land in South Africa. In other words, the text of Leviticus 25:8–55 opposes the privatization of land, which perpetrates poverty and inequality in the South African context.

The idea that the land is owned only by YHWH and not the Israelites relates vv.23–24. Although the two verses are related, as argued in Chapter 3, v.24 is distinctively about the 'Provision for the payment of compensation'. The command גְּאֻלָּה תִּתְּנוּ לָאָרֶץ 'you shall grant a redemption for the land' supports the position on v.24. The idea that v.24 is set to subject land redistribution to the payment of redemption is accepted largely in Old Testament scholarship.[125] The process of the payment of redemption for the family property is in fact the 'repurchase' of land.[126] In other words, the poor Israelites who lost their land or their family members had to buy back the land. However, the poor who had no capital to repurchase their land could not retrieve such land until the Jubilee year. Since the poor Israelites had to wait for the Jubilee to repurchase the land mainly because they lacked the financial resources to retrieve their land, it is evident that the poor were disadvantaged by the command גְּאֻלָּה תִּתְּנוּ לָאָרֶץ 'you shall grant a redemption for the land' (Lev 25:24).

The argument that the poor Israelites who lost land needed to repurchase their land reminds one of the situation of the African South Africans. In South Africa, the reclamation of land was subject to the payment of compensation. Sections 25(2) and 25(3) of the 1996 Constitution of the Republic of South Africa stipulate that the poor African South Africans need to buy back the land that they lost during the colonial and apartheid systems. In Chapter 2, it is shown that the both Sections disadvantage poor people as they often do not have financial resources to repurchase their land.[127] Thus, the command גְּאֻלָּה תִּתְּנוּ לָאָרֶץ 'you shall grant a redemption for the land' in v.24 and the condition of payment of compensation for repossessing the land in Section 25(2) and 25(3) of the 1996 Constitution do not favour the poor in both contexts.

Interestingly, the idea that YHWH is the only owner of the land, which contradicts the idea of private ownership of land by the élites in ancient Israel in v.23

is undermined if not refuted by v.24 which protects private ownership of land. The fact that v.23 is refuted by v.24 could be explained by the view that v.24 was structurally inserted immediately after v.23 by a Pentateuchal redactor, as will be argued below. Nonetheless, it is clear that in this case, the South African context enables one to read the structural presentation of vv.23 and 24 in the light of the property clause in Section 25 of the 1996 Constitution of the Republic of South Africa, which supports land privatization and perpetrates poverty and inequality in South Africa. It is reasonable to argue from the liberationist viewpoint employed in this study that the tenor of land redistribution underlying the political slogan *Mayibuye iAfrika*, 'Let Africa return' is constricted by the said property clause. As such, the call for land redistribution and socio-economic justice is also constricted.

The unit of vv.25–28 which is about the 'Loss of land due to poverty' recalls the argument that the Natives Land Act of 1913 triggered the poverty of black people in South Africa.[128] For instance, poverty was perpetrated among the Hlubi people because of the expropriation of their land and cattle by the white farmers in the 1860s.[129] Thus, the South African situation is comparable to the situation of the addressees of the unit of vv.25–28. It has been argued above that the trend in which the rich became richer and the poor became poorer was perpetrated by the practice of usury, the private accumulation of land and slavery in Leviticus 25:8–55.[130] This argument is confirmed by v.25, which shows that the poor lost their מֵאֲחֻזָּתוֹ 'possession' to the rich in order to escape conspicuous and inevitable poverty. Specifically, the poverty of the addressees in the unit of vv.25–28 was perpetrated by the loss of land. The idea that the reference to poverty in the introduction of vv.25–28 (cf. v.25) links up with the subsequent content of vv.26–28 (loss of land) would be compelling in the South African setting in which historically, the loss of land entrenched the poverty of black people.

Furthermore, the link between poverty and the loss of land in vv.25–28 shows a clear preferential option and regard for the poor, noted above. This argument is influenced by the liberationist reading of the text which is rooted in Black Liberation Theology. Black theology as well as the ideology behind the unit of vv.25–28—at least as understood from an African liberationist perspective—insists on the preferential option for the poor. Since Black Liberation Theology 'stands with the poor and the marginalized in society', an African liberationist reading of vv.25–28 would take note of the commendable preferential option and regard for the poor in the ancient text which are evident in the consequential statement כִּי־יָמוּךְ אָחִיךָ 'If your brother becomes poor' (v.25).[131]

The provision that exempts houses in the city from redistribution (vv.29–30), and requires that the houses in the villages be returned to the original owner (v.31) in the Jubilee year has caught the attention of the Old Testament scholars.[132] The inconsistency in the provision reveals an ideology of inequality and segregation based on class. On the relationship between land, class and the Bible, Mosala remarks:

> The Bible is inseparable from the modem history of South Africa. It was there at the founding of modern South Africa when white colonizers dispossessed the Africans of their land and created out of them a wage class with nothing but their labour power to sell [...]. In the Bible and in the statements and programs of South African political organisations, the land question is undergirded by an underlying social class perspective. It is this social class perspective which readers of the Bible who are committed to a reconstruction programme along the lines of liberation, need to isolate and interrogate.[133]

In agreement with Mosala, Modise and Mtshiselwa write that:

> The implication of working for the white farmers was that black Africans lost the economic independence that they had enjoyed prior to the legislation of the Natives Land Act of 1913. To this end, their wealth possession was reduced to poverty for some and economic survival for others. Laboring for the white master also meant that black South Africans became dependent and controlled by their employers.[134]

Subsequently, the South African setting which has a history of prejudice based on social class leads one to probe the social class dynamics in vv.29–34. The claim that there was disparity between those who dwelt in the cities and those in the villages of Yehud, suggests that the villagers were mostly poor while the city dwellers were wealthier.[135] As such, an African liberationist reading of the unit of vv.29–34 highlights the inconsistency behind the socio-economic inequality between the poor (rural dwellers) and the rich (urban dwellers—even though not all were rich). It is noteworthy that the unit of vv.29–34 has been inserted abruptly between the unit of vv.25–28 which focuses on the 'Loss of land because of poverty' and the unit of vv.35–38 which is about 'Debt because of poverty'. From an African liberationist perspective, it would be reasonable to argue that the abrupt structural insertion of vv.29–30 which served to protect the interest of the people in the cities who were probably the wealthy class would not enjoy a positive reception in the South African setting which is still characterized by poverty and economic inequality. These verses encourage inequality and segregation based on social class which the addressees of the Israelite Jubilee legislation particularly the poor would have resented.

We have noted that a reading of the outline of the text, which is informed by the South African social location would identify with the references to poverty in the units of vv.39–46 and 47–54.[136] However, unlike Nihan's caption of the unit of vv.35–38 as 'Borrowing money to subsist', the unit is seen here as 'Debt because of poverty' mainly because it highlights the challenge of poverty. The proverb, *Tlala ke a neka phefo ke ja nong*, 'Death, unlike hunger which only chooses the poor, takes the rich who would still be revelling in their riches' highlights the indignity of victims of poverty. Thus, an African liberationist reading of the unit of vv.35–38 as 'Debt because of Poverty' would appeal to the South African poor. Moreover, since the phrase *sikhalela izwe lethu*, 'are crying for our land' in the song *Thina Sizwe* expresses distress and protests the act of land dispossession as well as the subsequent poverty, such a reading of vv.35–38 would relate well to the South African setting because it highlights the poverty of its addressees.

Interestingly, the unit of vv.39–54 is structurally linked to the theme of land in Leviticus 25:8–55. The first unit vv.39–46 addresses the issue of 'Hard labour—slavery as a result of poverty with an Israelite as the employer' while the second unit vv.47–54 is concerned about 'Hard labour—slavery as a result of poverty with a non-Israelite as the employer'. Again, the introductory formula וְכִי־יָמוּךְ 'And if he becomes poor' which links vv.35–38 and vv.39–54 to vv.25–28 calls to mind the proverb *Tlala ke a neka phefo ke ja nong*, 'Death, unlike hunger which only chooses the poor, takes the rich who would still be revelling in their riches'.[137] The proverb shows that economic inequality manifests along the lines of social class and that hunger is not a challenge for the wealthy class. The division of South Africa into two classes—a ruling class of wealthy white persons and a working class of impoverished people of colour during the apartheid regime has continued even in post-apartheid South Africa.[138] Inspired by the South African setting, that is, the social location from which one reads the Israelite Jubilee, the view that vv.39–54 is about the poor Israelites who were sold as slaves is convincing.[139] Furthermore, if the text of vv.39–40 refers to the hired workers, then, vv.39–54 probably also refers to the working-class.

The colonial and apartheid systems in South Africa dispossessed the African South Africans of their land and subsequently created out of them the working-class, as Mosala argues.[140] Therefore, the structural link between the land discourse and the experience of hard labour by the working-class work is plausible. An African liberationist reader recognises that the liberation of the working-class people who, according to Nihan, became slaves of both the Israelites and non-Israelites depends on the liberation of the land. That is, liberation without land redistribution and socio-economic redress will never be genuine and definite.[141] In the same vein, it can be said that without liberating the land through the Jubilee legislation the working-class people in Leviticus 25:8–55 would never have been genuinely liberated.

An African liberationist reading of the unit of vv. 39–54 could offer a liberative critique of the South African context. Masenya (ngwan'a Mphahlele) has rightly argued that all human beings are affirmed by God irrespective of their socio-economic class; both the rich and the poor are equal before God.[142] Consequently, the inseparability of the theme of land and the experiences of the working-class people in Leviticus 25:8–55 remind the working-class African South Africans that the contest for the land, which was unfairly seized, should in fact be prioritized in their discussion of poverty and inequality. Such a discussion should not be exclusively held by the poor but by all South African citizens. More importantly, the idea of land redistribution should be viewed as inseparable from the disturbing experiences of the working-class people.

In her discussion of the experience of poverty by the working-class people, Masenya (ngwan'a Mphahlele) concludes that God is the Maker of both the rich and the poor. In her words, 'One cannot but wonder if the exploiters of the weak, are aware that the Maker, who is the Maker of both the rich and the poor (*rāš*) (cf. Prov 22:2), pleads the cause (*sic*) of the poor'.[143] For Masenya (ngwan'a Mphahlele), the call for equality and for the redress of the exploitation of the poor is motivated by the fact that YHWH equally created both the rich and the poor irrespective of their social class. Masenya (ngwan'a Mphahlele) affirms the African wisdom in the Akan proverb *Nnipa nyinaa ye Onyame mma, obi nye asase ba*, 'All human beings are the children of God, none is a child of the earth'.[144] For Opoku also, equality is rooted in the idea that all human beings are children of the deity; they are created equally by God. The view of these two scholars resonates with the idea established in the concluding verse of Leviticus 25:8–55. The declarative and entitlement statement עֲבָדַי הֵם 'they are my slaves' (v.55) suggests that the Israelites, that is, all Israelites including the poor belong to YHWH. Since v.55 also refers to the liberation of the Israelites from Egypt, it may be assumed that the call for the liberation of the poor working-class people is made on the grounds that YHWH is the Maker of both the master and the slave—the rich and the poor. Thus, an African liberationist view of the structure of Leviticus 25:8–55 would insist that the Israelite Jubilee legislation be outlined in a way that articulates YHWH's preferential option for the poor, which sought their economic liberation.

Land and socio-economic policy in Leviticus 25:8–55 and the South African land policies

An African liberationist reading of the Israelite Jubilee legislation enables dialogue between the legal document in the ancient text and the land policies in the modern context of South Africa. In his reflection on biblical interpretation in Africa, Justin S. Ukpong states:

> The African context is used as a resource in the hermeneutic encounter with the Bible ... Biblical interpretation in Africa has made bold strides which can be said to place it

> at the threshold of maturity as we enter the third millennium. However, the real test of this maturity will be the extent to which it will sustain the African context as the *subject* of interpretation of the Bible so that the hitherto muted voices and concerns of ordinary readers will come alive in the academic forum.[145]

In line with Ukpong's view above, reading the land and socio-economic policy in Leviticus 25:8–55 in the light of South Africa's land policies speaks to the concerns of the poor—not only in the world of the ancient text but also in South Africa. Thus, the African liberationist reading will highlight not only elements and clauses that are liberative but also clauses that are viewed as not life affirming.

(i) Institution of the Israelite Jubilee—Land Policy (vv.8–13)

It is important to note the relationship between the nouns דְּרוֹר 'liberty' and יוֹבֵל 'Jubilee' and the noun שְׁמִטָּה 'remission' which suggests an element of liberation (cf. Lev 25:10; Deut 15:2).[146] In Leviticus 25:10, the substitution of 'liberty' and 'Jubilee' by H for the D noun שְׁמִט 'remission' would be accepted by an African liberationist reader, as it could be used to highlight the theme of liberation. The inclusion of the noun 'liberty' in the section on the institution of the Israelite Jubilee, which introduces legislation, issued to respond to the challenge of landlessness, poverty, indebtedness and slavery (hard labour) is significant in two ways. First, the poor in South Africa would identify with the need to address poverty, economic inequality and the effects of their being dispossessed of productive land. Second, the lyrics of the three liberation songs *Thina sizwe esimnyama*, 'We, the black nation'; *Senzeni Na?* 'What have we done?' and *Lelizwe*, 'This Land' which are sung often even in post-apartheid South Africa confirm the need for economic liberation in the country. Thus, a reading of the Israelite Jubilee legislation that highlights the element of liberation in the introductory verses, that is, the noun דְּרוֹר 'liberty' would enjoy a positive reception in South Africa particularly among the African South Africans. Furthermore, as argued in Chapter 3, H's contestation of the ideological position that the liberation of the poor could not only be attained through 'remission' in v.10 but also through the release of debt-slave and the return of land to the poor is appealing to the African liberationist reader of the ancient biblical t text in the South African context.

Interestingly, the descriptive command הִוא קֹדֶשׁ תִּהְיֶה 'it shall be holy to you' (v.12) which is distinctive of P does not describe a ritual, as P typically does. Thus, it has been argued that H broadens the conceptualization of holiness to accommodate the quest for social justice, that is, for poverty alleviation and the redress of economic inequality. The religious undertone in the song *Senzeni Na?* 'What have we done?' would cause the conceptualisation of the quest for justice as holy to be attractive in the South African setting. A religious undertone is detected in the word *sono*, 'sin' in verse lines 2 and 3 besides that the song was and is still often sung in the black churches as a prayer to *Qamata*, 'the deity'. During the singing, the cry for liberation and land redistribution almost carries a holiness dimension and tone. This shows that the cry for land redistribution and socio-economic justice in South Africa is not only a call or protest but it is also a prayer. Thus, the conceptualization of holiness to accommodate the quest for social justice by H would be compelling, and an African liberationist reading would equally highlight H's reconceptualization of holiness in Leviticus 25:8–55. As mentioned in Chapter 3, H's contestation of P's ideological conceptualization of holiness offers liberating possibilities to the oppressed people as it presents holiness as intrinsically inseparable from socio-economic justice issues. Thus, H's ideological position is appealing to an African liberationist reader of the Hebrew Bible.

Regarding v.13, Römer notes that the trend of permitting people to return to their homeland resembles Cyrus' edict that permitted the Golah community to return home.[147] Clearly, the returnees had the issue of הָאָרֶץ 'the land' on their minds as the discussion of the 'myth of the empty land' shows. An African liberationist reader of verse 13 would then probe the identity of those who were permitted to return to the homeland. It is generally accepted in Old Testament scholarship that most of the returning exiles were wealthy; that is, they were élites. Römer's claim that in the Persian period, power belonged to the Priestly and scribal élites from the Babylonian exile who in turn sought to secure productive land on their return to Yehud is significant at this point.[148] However, this view renders v.13 problematic because it has the interests of the rich élites from Babylonia in mind and not of the poor. Without doubt, the South African poor who need productive land to be able to overcome poverty would not identify with a clause in the Jubilee legislation, which supports the interests of the rich élites.

(ii) Trading of Agricultural Products and Food Security in the Israelite Jubilee (vv.14–22)

The use of CC by H in vv.14–15 shows the significant placement of the nouns שָׂדֶה 'field' (v.12) and תְבוּאת 'fruits' (v.15) within the context of the negative command אַל־תּוֹנוּ אִישׁ אֶת־ אָחִיו 'you shall not oppress one another' (v.14). If the placement of the nouns is understood first and foremost in the light of the liberationist framework employed in this study, the clause against oppression in the context of agricultural activities would be viewed positively. In fact, the nouns 'field' and 'fruits' call to mind the question of production and economic growth in the South African land policies.

The stipulation in the Land Reform (Labour Tenants) Act, No. 3 of 1996, which requires one to use the land productively after being allocated a farm stresses the importance of productivity. Thus, productivity and competitiveness take prominence in South Africa's economic stability and growth. In other words, the challenge of poverty and the protest expressed in the liberation songs above are not central to the Act but productivity is. In the Green Paper on South African Land Reform, Section 3.3 stresses the importance of investments while Sections 4.1(c), 4.2 and 6.3 emphasize production and economic growth.[149] In addition, any risk of disrupting agricultural productivity is vetoed in Section 6.1(a).[150] Since the Green Paper seeks to avoid or minimize land redistribution and restitution, the idea of redressing socio-economic injustice is subsequently refuted. The idea that the redistribution of land to the poor and the quest to enhance productivity and economic growth cannot co-exist as reflected in South African land policies offers an interesting element, which should be considered in interpreting Leviticus 25:14–15.

It appears that the connection of the nouns שָׂדֶה 'field' (v.12) with תְּבוּאֹת 'fruits' (v.15) and the negative command אַל־תּוֹנוּ אִישׁ אֶת־אָחִיו 'you shall not oppress one another' (v.14) by H poses a challenge. In the light of the South African context which is influenced by the global economic system and which gives priority to productivity, the theme of production implied by the nouns 'field' and 'fruits' refute the clause 'you shall not oppress one another'. The poor (who should not be oppressed) could not have been in a position to sustain themselves economically as they did not have the capital to do so. Instead, they were slaves to the rich élites mainly because they could not use the land productively and they were in debt. Verses 35–38 allude to the idea of borrowing money to subsist confirming the scarcity of the financial resources and the indebtedness of the poor Israelites.[151] Therefore, the theme of productivity in a legislation that pursued the redress of socio-economic injustice would defeat the purpose of the same legislation, as is arguably the case in South Africa. In this case, it appears that H did not help to address poverty, indebtedness, slavery and landlessness.

Like Otto, Meyer points out that H tended to utilize the motif of 'fields' as a carrot to motivate the Israelites to lead a sound ethical life in vv.18–19.[152] In Leviticus 25:18 'So you shall do my statutes, and keep my judgments, and do them; and you shall dwell in the land in safety' וִישַׁבְתֶּם עַל־הָאָרֶץ לָבֶטַח וַעֲשִׂיתֶם אֶת־חֻקֹּתַי וְאֶת־מִשְׁפָּטַי תִּשְׁמְרוּ וַעֲשִׂיתֶם אֹתָם, the fertility of the land seems to depend mainly on the people's faithfulness to the *Torah*, the law of YHWH. As noted above, H distinctively links the theme of productivity to the motif of ethical behaviour here. The issue of food security also appears to be subject to adherence to the *Torah*, that is, the motif of ethical behaviour and productivity.

The notion of land redistribution and of socio-economic justice highlighted above also triggered a debate on whether the land can produce fruit on its own and whether land redistribution alone can help alleviate poverty. We have argued above that land redistribution in South Africa will effectively redress socio-economic injustice only when it is coupled with the necessary capital, resources, skills and access to the agricultural market. Thus, the critical question posed above is still valid, that is, why did H use the statement וְנָתְנָה הָאָרֶץ פִּרְיָהּ 'and the land shall yield her fruit' (v.19)? H merely shows that agricultural productivity or fruitfulness was conditioned by adherence to Yahweh's command and legislation in vv.18–22, as noted above. However, the point that agricultural productivity depended on the availability of the capital, resources, skills and the market, at least in the South African context, exposes a flaw in the H clause 'and the land shall yield her fruit'. An African liberationist reading would show that the clause would make sense if the issue of capital, resources and skills to work the land were also highlighted in the Jubilee legislation. The land cannot yield fruit on its own without human and financial capital, and skill. The struggling farmers in post-exilic Yehud who were the addressees of H would have appreciated the provision of capital, skill and market to sell their agricultural products in the Jubilee legislation. Similarly, such a critical clause is also missing in the South African land policies.

The Economic Commission for Africa defines 'food security' as 'the capacity of households, communities and the state to mobilize sufficient food through production, acquisition and distribution, on a sustainable basis'.[153] Clearly, the issue of equitable access to productive land is critical when it comes to food security in South Africa. Food security is threatened among the poor black people because they have neither capital nor equal access to land as their white counterparts who already own land that was historically seized from Africans. Nonetheless, in the discourse on 'food security' issues of 'land grabs', that is, the purchase or lease of vast tracts of land by the wealthier and food-secure nations and private investors from mostly poor developing countries in order to produce crops for export have not gone unnoticed.[154] Scholars have noted that 'land grabs' by the private sector which comprises of rich élites threaten the development of rural economies, attempts to redistribute land and endeavours toward equitable access to food.[155] In other words, the purchase of land by the rich élites at the expense of the poor who do not have capital not only increases the threat to food security as the poor would have no productive land, access to capital to work the land or access to the markets. The land grabs also infringe on the human right to food in the developing countries.

Therefore, in the light of the debate on 'food security' and 'land grabs' in Africa, the threat to 'food security' among the poor could also have been a reality in the post-exilic Yehud. If the rich élites could dispossess the poor of their land and make them slaves in the process as implied in the Israelite Jubilee legislation, then, there was in fact a process of 'land grabbing'. There is evidence of the purchase or lease of vast tracts of land by the rich mostly from poor people.[156] In a situation of 'land grabs' where the rich access the land of the poor, the threat to the 'food security' of the poor becomes inevitable since there would be no equitable access to food. Unequal access to food is partly due to unequal access to capital, productive land, resources, skills and the market. Therefore, H's reference to 'fields', 'fruits' and the 'poor' in the Jubilee legislation would have been more meaningful to the poor in Yehud had it addressed the issue of 'land grabs' and 'food security'. No doubt, the rich grabbed the land of the poor through their access to capital, leaving the poor with unequal access to food or the 'fruits' of the land. The poor eventually became slaves to the rich élites.

(iii) Yahweh's Entitlement to the Land—Against the Privatization of Land (v.23)

The above debate on the privatization of the land 'which was taken by white people' (*elathathwa ngabamhlophe)* expressed in the song *Thina sizwe esimnyama*, 'We, the black nation' could offer clues to a liberationist reading of v.23. First and foremost, Section 3.1 of the 2011 Green Paper on South African Land Reform calls for the protection of property rights which are at the disposal of private companies and individuals.[157] The Green Paper increases the predominantly white ownership and control of private businesses including productive land at the expense of black empowerment and the redistribution of wealth in South Africa.[158] Thus, the protection of privately owned property in South Africa is comparable to the situation in post-exilic Yehud where the rich élites possessed the land, which was initially owned by the poor and where there were clear attempts to protect the private ownership of land.

In Leviticus 25:23, the reason statement כִּי־לִי הָאָרֶץ 'for the land is mine' explains Yahweh's entitlement to the land but it also exhibits an H feature, which refutes private ownership of land. In this case, an African liberationist reading which considers the protection of privately owned land in South Africa would argue that H's re-centralization of the ownership of land to Yahweh sought to refute private ownership of land by the rich élites because H had the interest of the poor in mind. It is assumed that H's statement כִּי־לִי הָאָרֶץ 'for the land is mine' was set to protect the private ownership of land by the élites at the expense of the poor who lost their land and became slaves of the rich due to their indebtedness. In this case, the poor in South Africa would appreciate the call by H to de-privatize land because YWHW owns the land.

(iv) Provision for the Payment of Compensation (v.24)

The idea of subjecting the expropriation of productive land to the payment of compensation in Sections 25(2) and 25(3) of the 1996 Constitution of the Republic of South Africa impedes land reform.[159] As such, the provision of the payment of compensation stifles the process of redressing socio-economic injustice which was inherited from the colonial and apartheid systems in South Africa in that the poor African South Africans find it difficult to access land because they have no capital or resources to do so. Similarly, the poor Israelites in post-exilic Yehud found it difficult to secure land and to become economically independent mainly because they had no capital. Thus, the Israelite Jubilee legislation cannot be viewed as flawless.

Furthermore, how could the poor who lost their land have obtained capital to pay the compensation to retain their land when they had already become slaves to the wealthy élites? An African liberationist reading of v.24 וּבְכֹל אֶרֶץ אֲחֻזַּתְכֶם גְּאֻלָּה תִּתְּנוּ לָאָרֶץ 'and in all the land of your possession you shall grant a redemption for the land' would note that it did not serve the interest of the poor as it unreasonably expects them to possess capital to pay for the redemption (compensation) of the land. Since the political slogan *Mayibuye iAfrika*, 'Let Africa return' which is used by the poor black protesters in the liberation song *Senzeni na*? 'What have we done' does not presuppose the need for payment of compensation; v.24 would therefore not be remarkable to a poor African South African. Furthermore, if v.24 legislated and required the payment of compensation from the poor, an African liberationist reader would assume that such a clause was not received positively by the poor in the post-exilic Yehud.

Furthermore, the argument that D influenced H in v.24 echoes the suggestion that the ANC was influenced by Oppenheimer in the formulation of the South African constitution. As noted above, the ANC élites reportedly submitted the party's economic program to Harry Oppenheimer for approval on the grounds that it contained no reference to nationalization or slogan connecting the government to Marxist ideology.[160] This move does not only show the ideological compromise by the ANC élites to accept Thatcherism but it also confirms the influence of Harry Oppenheimer on the African South African political élites which represented the ANC and sponsored the legislation of the payment of compensation for the expropriation of land in South Africa. An African liberationist reading would highlight the influence of D on H as H compromised the concern for the poor who did not have the capital to pay the redemption money, that is, the compensation that would enable them to retain land. Surprisingly, H also accepted D's position on the payment of compensation.

(v) Loss of Land Because of Poverty (vv.25–28)

Masenya (ngwan'a Mphahlele) draws her reader's attention to verse line 4 *Isono sethu ubulili bethu besifazane*, 'Our sin is our female sex' in the song *Senzeni na*, 'What have we done'.[161] The verse line highlights the fact that women experience the impact of both patriarchy and racism in Africa. In a setting where women are allocated secondary roles at the lowest rung of the socio-economic ladder as housewives and domestic workers while men worked on the farms and in mines, the protest by South African women in the song *Senzeni na*, 'What have we done?' is warranted.[162] Furthermore, the idea that women were relegated to the domestic sphere shows that land ownership and use were the exclusive preserve of their male counterparts.

On the domestication of women, Hazel confirms that 'ideologies of black female domesticity and motherhood have been constructed through their employment (chattel position) as domestics and surrogate mothers to white families rather than in relation to their own families'. Clearly, women were relegated to the lowest rung on the socio-economic ladder.[163] Even though many scholars denounce the idea of patriarchy particularly within the economic sphere, women remain poor and without productive land. Moreover, the South African land policies do not directly address the fact that women do not own productive land and they are the most affected by poverty as Statistics of South Africa has shown. The idea that the land policies do not directly address women's poverty and landlessness makes one to wonder whether the Israelite Jubilee legislation directly addresses women's experience of poverty and landlessness.

The section on 'Loss of land because of poverty (vv.25–28)' responds to the challenges of poverty and landlessness in post-exilic Yehud. One would have expected the clause in v.25 כִּי־יָמוּךְ אָחִיךָ 'If your brother becomes poor' to be gender inclusive. Instead, in its bias it assumes that sisters, that is, women were not poor. Furthermore, the clause assumes that the challenge of land dispossession did not affect women. Against the view that women did not own land, Eskenazi argues that in post-exilic Yehud, women could inherit property.[164] The phrase אֲחֻזַּת נַחֲלָה 'property as an inheritance' in Numbers 27:7 and 36:2 provides textual evidence for this argument. However, on account of the patriarchal nature of the post-exilic Yehud context, it is argued that women were viewed as men's property and were thus not allowed to inherit property.[165] Notwithstanding Eskenazi's position which is supported by textual evidence, in relation to Leviticus 25:8–55 Masenya (ngwan'a Mphahlele)'s view is compelling. Leviticus 25:8–55 is silent about women owning land and this fact confirms the argument that in the patriarchal post-exilic Yehud, women probably could not own land. Additionally, for the authors of Leviticus 25:8–55, only males could make claims to the land.[166] The insertion of 'sisters' by

H to render the clause as 'if your brother and sister become poor' would not only be a gender sensitive move but it would have addressed the reality of poverty as well. Poverty affects both men and women, and not just one's 'brother' as H presupposes in v.25. Thus, one can assume that the section on 'Loss of land because of poverty (vv.25–28)' particularly H's v.25 in its present form would not enjoy an affirmative reception among women in both post-exilic Yehud and post-apartheid South Africa. From an African liberationist perspective, the most compelling response by H to the challenge of poverty and landlessness should have been a gender sensitive one.

Furthermore, in, *Women and the Cry for Justice in Old Testament Court Narratives: An African Reflection*, Olojede shows her reader the case of a woman who not only experienced hunger, that is, poverty, but also loss of land.[167] The Deuteronomistic Historian (DH) recounts that the Shunemite woman cried out to the king for her land in 2 Kings 8:1–6. However, 'it is remarkable that the women approached the king (or the prophet) to state their case and to demand not only retributive but distributive justice'.[168] Eventually, according to the DH, the land that belonged to the Shunemite woman was redistributed to her. Olojede's contribution is valuable here because it confirms that in the history of the Israelites, women not only owned productive land they also experienced poverty. On the other hand, it is strange that in the Jubilee legislation, H in particular is silent about the poverty and landlessness of women as the text exclusively addresses the poverty of a 'brother' which means 'men'. In the context in which women like the Shunemite woman lost land and subsequently became poor, H's exclusion of women in the Israelite Jubilee legislation would be viewed as patriarchal. Thus, an African liberationist reader who is also concerned about the need for the liberation of women would appreciate a clause that is gender sensitive and that addresses the challenge of poverty justly.

(vi) City Property Versus Rural Land and the Élites Versus the Poor (vv.29–34)

The tension between the rich élites and the poor is often, if not at all times, evident in a number of African societies. Economic inequality—the disparity between the haves and the have nots—which is also evident in South Africa perpetrates such tension. The disparities in the ownership and use of as well as the benefits from the productive land are clearly not addressed by the South African land policies as argued above. Terreblanche confirms that privatization increases the predominantly white ownership of private businesses including productive land, leaving African South Africans entrapped in the poverty-cycle.[169] Furthermore, in view of the requirement of the payment of compensation in Section 25(8) of the 1996

Constitution of South Africa, the land policies do not only impede land redistribution to the previously disadvantaged poor African South Africans.[170] Land policies also fuel the tension between the rich élites and the poor because of the privatization of productive land, the enforcement of the principle of 'willing-seller, willing-buyer' and the policies which eventually keep the rich richer and the poor poorer.

The situation in which the poor are unable to access capital to purchase the land they lost under the colonial and apartheid regime brings to mind the 'walled cities and village houses' in Leviticus 25:29–34. The land in the walled cities was protected by the Jubilee legislation against redistribution (v.30). Likewise, the South African constitution also restricts the access to productive land that is mostly owned by white people by poor African South Africans. Just as the poor Israelites could not access the land that was owned by the élites in the walled cities, the poor black people who may never be able to raise the capital required for land repossession would also be unable to access productive land in South Africa. The similarity between the protection of the land owned by the rich élites in the post-exilic Yehud setting and in the post-apartheid South African context leads one to engage in a cautious reading of the clauses on 'City property versus rural land and the élites versus the poor (vv.29–34)'.

The view of vv.29–30 in Leviticus 25:8–55 as a later addition by the Pentateuchal redactor assumes that there was economic disparity, which was enforced by D. The disparity reminds one of the liberation songs *Thina sizwe esimnyama*, 'We, the black nation' and *Lelizwe*, 'This Land'. Noteworthy is the relationship between the expressions *sikhalela izwe lethu, elathathwa ngabamhlophe*, 'are crying for our land, which was taken by white people' (verse lines 2–3) in *Thina sizwe esimnyama*, 'We, the black nation' and *Kudala sisebenzel' amabhulu*, 'We have been working for the Boers far too long' (verse line 11) in *Lelizwe*, 'This Land'. In fact, Wilson's preferred version of the clause *elathathwa ngamabhulu*, 'which was taken by the Boers' in verse line 3 of *Thina sizwe esimnyama*, 'We, the black nation' is closer to verse line 11 of *Lelizwe*, 'This Land'. As such, the relationship between these two liberation songs shows the tension between the majority of the Afrikaner rich élites, and the working-class people who are mostly the poor African South Africans. The 'Boers' are also portrayed in these songs as those who dispossessed the working-class African South Africans of their land. Therefore, the masses who chant the liberation songs protest against the economic inequality between them and the rich élites who own productive land in South Africa.

Interestingly, unlike the masses or the late president Nelson Mandela who chant(ed) the liberation songs in South Africa, the Pentateuchal redactor did not denounce the economic inequalities and disparities that existed between the people in the walled cities and those in the village houses. However, an African liberationist reading of vv.29–34 would highlight the economic disparities and the silence of the Pentateuchal redactor on such disparities. An African liberationist reader would argue that the Pentateuchal redactor of the Jubilee legislation is not much different from the élites who wrote the constitution of South Africa. The two legal documents, that is, the Israelite Jubilee legislation and the South African constitution protect the interest of the rich élites instead of openly serving the interest of the poor. In the end, the two documents widen the gap between the rich and the poor. In Chapter 3, it is stated that the ideology of classism and economic inequality that is upheld in vv.29–34 is oppressive as it perpetuates socio-economic injustice.

(vii) Debt Because of Poverty (vv.35–38)

In his study *Ending Economic Apartheid*, Edozien argues that 'The end of political apartheid is ultimately meaningless without the end of economic apartheid'.[171] The statement implies that South Africa is not completely liberated. He argues that the poor in South Africa are prejudiced by the economic system as they often find it difficult to obtain loans from the bank since they have no credit record, that is, they are not creditworthy borrowers.[172] Those who already have some capital find it easier to access money from the bank. What this means in the context of the land discourse in South Africa is that the poor or the working-class people are unable to access loans from the bank to purchase productive land as the economic system is prejudiced against them.

Mtshiselwa also confirms that the working-class people in South Africa most of whom operate different loan accounts for clothing, housing (in form of bonds) and their cars among other items are 'perpetually trapped in debt'.[173] Such people may not be in the position to purchase productive land, and the working-class people who chant the song *Lelizwe* 'This Land' may probably never have sufficient capital to pay the compensation to expropriate land or to purchase productive land. The provisions of the South African land policies imply that black people who work as domestic workers and gardeners mentioned in the song are disadvantaged as they may never be able to purchase productive land. Interestingly, the subject of indebtedness, poverty and land is partly addressed in the Jubilee legislation.

As Nihan has shown, the indebtedness of the Israelites forced the poor man to 'sell a portion of his estate'.[174] Not only did indebtedness cause the loss of land, it also resulted in poverty and slavery. Since the clauses in vv.25–28 attempt to address the challenge of indebtedness, the reception of such a text by an African liberationist reader would be affirmative. Moreover, the fact that the challenge of indebtedness, loss of productive land and slavery are interconnected in the Israelite Jubilee legislation would be compelling within the African liberationist framework. The manner in which the Pentateuchal redactor edited, supplemented and combined different layers to create the present form of the Israelite Jubilee legislation is commendable. Thus, the poor African South Africans would identify with the challenge of loss of land, indebtedness and hard labour, and an African liberationist reader would argue that redressing the loss of land, poverty and indebtedness and hard labour through the South African land policies would be a positive step towards economic liberation.

As H has addressed the challenge of 'borrowing money to subsist' in vv.35–38, the clause on land in the constitution of South Africa needs to address the issue of the indebtedness of the working-class people and the poor in relation to the challenge of the loss of land.[175] Furthermore, the relational use of the liberation songs and the African proverbs as a point of reference in the critique of both the South African context and the context of the biblical text shows the importance of the interconnection between the challenges of loss of land, indebtedness, poverty and slavery as highlighted by H. In other words, redressing the loss of land may not be accomplished without addressing the issues of indebtedness, poverty and slavery. Further, the South African people need to recognize that the constitution of the country cannot address the issue of land redistribution without giving attention to the indebtedness of the working class. Similarly, the constitution cannot deal with poverty without addressing the issue of land redistribution. The issue of poverty cannot be successfully addressed without giving attention to the issue of land redistribution and the indebtedness of the poor and working-class people.

(viii) Hard Labor—Slavery Due to Poverty (vv.39–54)

In vv.39–54, H addresses the issue of land loss and poverty with the scenario in which the proclamation of the freedom of the working-class Israelites from slavery or hard labour played a fundamental role (cf. v.53). The freedom would also enable the Israelites to have their land restored to them. A critical question to ask is would H's proclamation of the freedom of the working-class people be accepted in present day South Africa? Would the South African government redistribute land to the working-class people to liberate them from hard labour or insufficient wages? Would people find it reasonable to leave their jobs to work in companies in which they hold shares? One doubts that the South African government would redistribute all the land that was seized from black people because the constitution of the country presently supports the payment of compensation. Hence, the South African government is making only slow progress with the purchase of land from white farmers with the aim of redistributing it to poor black people or the working-class group.

Furthermore, South Africa needs a land policy that would practically proclaim liberty for the working-class people. Such a policy could be inspired by the tenor of liberation in the conditional statement וְיָצָא בִּשְׁנַת הַיֹּבֵל 'then he shall go out in the year of Jubilee' (v.54) which expresses H's concern for social justice. Nihan has correctly noted that in vv.39–54 the poor Israelites were sold as slaves.[176] The proclamation of liberation shows that H sought to address the economic system which was not favourable to the poor in ancient Israel. In vv.47–54, H sought the redress of socio-economic injustice that was evident in post-exilic Yehud. Since the Israelite slaves were mostly people who lost their land and became poor as a result, the working-class people of South Africa would embrace the proclamation of such freedom. In fact, such a proclamation challenges the South African government to find ways of liberating the poor, that is, with regard to the issue of land, as the next chapter will show.

(ix) Conclusion (v.55)

Worthy of note is the observation that the Pentateuchal redactor concludes the Jubilee legislation with the tenor of liberation. The theme of deliverance from Egypt in v.55 becomes the highlight of Leviticus 25:8–55. The poor Israelites in post-exilic Yehud probably embraced the theme as they thirsted for liberation. Similarly, the theme of liberation that concludes the Jubilee legislation would enjoy a positive reception in post-apartheid South Africa. The liberation songs and African proverbs that have been discussed and used as a point of reference In this study attest to that possible reception.

Conclusion

The main question in the present research is if re-read from an African liberationist perspective in the context of land redistribution and socio-economic justice in South Africa, could the Israelite Jubilee legislation in Leviticus 25:8–55 offer liberating and empowering possibilities for the poor of South Africa?

First, the chapter has provided a framework for an African liberationist reading of the text which also engages in the debate of liberating *blackness* from *whiteness* and *Europeanness*. The importance of reading the ancient text from one's social location, that is, the South African context has been highlighted. Following African biblical scholars such as Masenya it is argued that the African proverbs constitute a relevant hermeneutical tool for an African liberationist reading.[177] In addition to the African proverbs, the three liberation songs which can also be employed as a relevant hermeneutical tool for an African liberationist reading of ancient texts serve as the voice of poor African South Africans and their contestation for liberation.

Second, in the light of established liberationist frameworks, the text of Leviticus 25:8–55 is read from an African liberationist perspective. The critique of the discourse of socio-economic justice and land in South Africa offers a unique understanding of the South African context as both the element of oppression and the quest for liberation are present in that discourse.

The chapter has also highlighted the interaction between the biblical text and the South African context, that is, in the sense of probing the relevance of the ancient text to a modern context and vice versa.[178] However, unlike both Cone and West, the interaction between the biblical text and the context was set within an African liberationist framework. In other words, on the hermeneutical level, the African proverbs and liberation songs were used as a point of reference in the interaction.

There is no doubt that when read from an African liberationist perspective the Israelite Jubilee of Leviticus 25:8–55 offers liberating and empowering possibilities for the poor in South Africa. Thus, practical recommendations will be made in the following chapter.

Notes

1. The word 'African' does not restrict one's reading to only the perspective of the people residing on the African continent, but extends it to people of African descent in both the African continent and the Diaspora. That is, instead of using the term 'Africana,' one has opted for an 'identical' term, which can be used to refer to both persons—from the diaspora and the African continent.
2. Gerrie Snyman, "'Looking into Black Eyes and Feel the Embarrassment.' A Selected and Selective Reading of the Africana Bible," *Old Testament Essays* 24, no. 2 (2011): 464–491
3. Kofi A. Opoku, "Cooking on Two Stones of the Hearth: African Spirituality and the Socio-cultural Transformation of Africa," *Journal of Christian Thought* 13, no. 1 (2009): 13; Kofi A. Opoku, *West African Traditional Religion* (Accra: FEP, 1978), 162; Kofi A. Opoku "Skinny but Imperishable Truth: African Religious Heritage and the Regeneration of Africa," *Studia Historiae Ecclesiasticae* 38, Supplement (2011): 5; Mokhele J. S. Madise. "Borrowed/begged Water Never Quenches Thirst," Inaugural lecture (Pretoria: University of South Africa, 2012), 1.
4. Snyman, "Black Eyes," 464–491; cf. Cheryl B. Anderson, *Ancient Laws and Contemporary Controversies: The Need for Inclusive Biblical Interpretation* (Oxford: Oxford University Press, 2009), 12, 135.

5. Madipoane Masenya (ngwan'a Mphahlele), "Jeremiah," in *The Africana Bible: Reading Israel's Scriptures from Africa and the African Diaspora*, ed. Hugh R. Page (Minneapolis: Fortress Press, 2010), 147–156; cf. Makhosazana K. Nzimande, "Isaiah," in *The Africana Bible: Reading Israel's Scriptures from Africa and the African Diaspora*, ed. Hugh R. Page (Minneapolis: Fortress Press, 2009), 136–146.
6. Snyman, "Black Eyes," 464–491; cf. Masenya (ngwan'a Mphahlele), "Jeremiah," 150.
7. Masenya (ngwan'a Mphahlele), "Jeremiah," 147.
8. Esias E. Meyer, "Returning to an Empty Land: Revisiting my Old Argument about the Jubilee," *Old Testament Essays* 27, no. 2 (2014): 512.
9. Justin S. Ukpong, "The Emergence of African Theologies," *Theological Studies* 45, no. 3 (1984): 501.
10. Madipoane Masenya (ngwan'a Mphahlele), *How Worthy Is the Woman of Worth? Rereading Proverbs 31:10–31 in African-South Africa* (New York: Peter Lang, 2004), 69
11. Itumeleng J. Mosala, "Wealth and Poverty in the Old Testament: A Black Theological Perspective," *Journal of black theology in South Africa* 5, no. 1 (1996): 20; Gabriel M. Setiloane, "Land in the Negotiations Chamber: An Afro-centric Approach," *Journal of Black Theology* 5, no. 2 (1991): 35–36.
12. James H. Cone, "Looking Back, Going Forward: Black Theology as Public Theology," in *Black Faith and Public Talk: Critical Essays on James H. Cone's Black Theology and Black Power*, ed. Dwight N. Hopkins (Maryknoll: Orbis Book, 1999), 256; cf. Malcolm X. *Malcolm X speaks: Selected Speeches and Statements* (New York: Grove Press, 1965), 165.
13. Na'Im Akbar, "Africentric Social Sciences for Human Liberation," *Journal of Black Studies* 14, no. 4 (1984): 404; Itumeleng J. Mosala, "Biblical Hermeneutics and Black Theology in South Africa," (PhD diss., Cape Town: University of Cape Town, 1987), 248.
14. Norman K. Gottwald, "How does Social Scientific Criticism Shape our Understanding of the Bible as a Resource for Economic Ethics?," *The Hebrew Bible in Its Social World and in Ours* (1993): 345.
15. Patrick Bond, *Elite Transition: From Apartheid to Neoliberalism in South Africa* (Pietermaritzburg: University of Natal Press, 2000), 31–32.
16. Setiloane, "Negotiations Chamber," 36–37; Bond, *Elite Transition*, 63, 75; Marinda Weideman, "Who Shaped South Africa's Land Reform Policy?," *Politikon* 31, no. 2 (2004): 219, 235; Sampie J. Terreblanche, *Lost in Transformation: South Africa's Search for a New Future Since 1986* (Johannesburg: KMM Review Publishing Company, 2012), 67.
17. Madipoane Masenya (ngwan'a Mphahlele) and Hulisani Ramantswana. "Lupfumo lu Mavuni (Wealth is in the Land): In Search of the Promised Land (cf. Exod 3–4) in the Post-Colonial, Post-Apartheid South Africa," *Journal of Theology for Southern Africa* 151 (2015): 96–116.
18. Leepo Modise and Ndikho Mtshiselwa, "The Natives Land Act of 1913 Engineered the Poverty of Black South Africans: A Historico-ecclesiastical Perspective," *Studia Historiae Ecclesiasticae* 39, no. 2 (2013): 365–366.
19. Masenya (ngwan'a Mphahlele) and Ramantswana, "Lupfumo lu Mavuni," 96–116.
20. Masenya (ngwan'a Mphahlele) and Ramantswana, "Lupfumo lu Mavuni," 96–116.
21. Michael A. Yanou, *Dispossession and Access to Land in South Africa: An African Perspective* (Mankon, Bamenda: Langaa Research & Publishing Common Initiative Group, 2009), 38.

22. Yanou, *Dispossession*, 38; cf. Aninka Claassens, "Compensation for Expropriation: The Political and Economic Parameters of Market Value Compensation," *South African Journal of Human Rights* 9, (1993): 424; Hans Binswanger, "The Political Implications of Alternative Models of Land Reform and Compensation," in *Agricultural Land Reform in South Africa: Policies, Markets and Mechanisms*, eds. Johan Van Zyl, Johann Kirsten, and M. P. Binswanger (Cape Town: Oxford University Press, 1996), 139.
23. John K. Kwakye, *Africa's Long Road to Development: It Is Not Just Economics, but Also History, Geography, Politics, and Leadership* (Accra: Frontiers Printing and Publishing Ltd, 2011), 127.
24. Noreena Hertz, *The Silent Takeover: Global Capitalism and the Death of Democracy* (London: William Heinemann, 2001), 22.
25. C. Desmond, "Overview," in *The Codesa File: Negotiating a Non-racial Democracy in South Africa*, ed. Fatima Meer (Durban: Madiba Publishers, 1993), 15.
26. Alfons Loogman, *Swahili Grammar and Syntax* (Pittsburgh: Duquesne University Press, 1965), 205; Julius K. Nyerere, *Freedom and Unity: Uhuru na Umoja—A Selection from Writings and Speeches, 1952–65* (London: Oxford University Press, 1966), 323; Joseph G. Healey, "When Elephants Fight the Grass (Reeds) Gets Hurt—Swahili (Eastern and Central Africa African Proverb of the Month November, 2001," http://www.afriprov.org/index.php/african-proverb-ofthemonth/27001proverbs /172nov2001.pdf. (Accessed August 27, 2013).
27. Hertz, *Silent Takeover*, 22.
28. Naomi Klein, "Democracy Born in Chains: South Africa's Constricted Freedom," in *The shock Doctrine: The Rise of Disaster Capitalism*, ed. Naomi Klein (New York: Metropolitan Books, Henry Holt and Company, LLC, 2007), 216; cf. Helena Dolny and Heinz Klug, "Land Reform: Legal Support and Economic Regulation," South African Review-SARS 6 (1992): 324; Ruth Hall, "Land Restitution in South Africa: Rights, Development, and the Restrained State," *Canadian Journal of African Studies/La Revue canadienne des études africaines* 38, no. 3 (2004): 654; Yanou, *Dispossession*, 77.
29. World Bank, *Africa Rainfall and Temperature Evaluation System (ARTES)* (Washington, DC: World Bank, 2010), 1.
30. Bond, *Elite Transition*, 33; Robert Dunnigan, Kevin Fazaeli and Jaco Spies, "Black Economic Empowerment—Difficulties and Opportunities in Making Right the Wrongs of the Past," http://faculty-course.insead.edu/dutt/emdc/projects/Sep-Oct05/Group_D.pdf. (Accessed January 20, 2014).
31. Binswanger, "Political Implications," 139; Andries J. Van der Walt, *The Constitutional Property Clause: A Comparative Analysis of Section 25 of the South African Constitution of 1996* (Kenwyn: Juta & CO. Ltd, 1997), 162.
32. James K. A. Benhin, *Climate Change and South African Agriculture: Impacts and Adaptation Options* (Vol. 21. CEEPA discussion paper, 2006), 10; Rashid M. Hassan, "Implications of Climate Change for Agricultural Sector Performance in Africa: Policy Challenges and Research Agenda," *Journal of African Economies* 19, no. 2 Supplement (2010): 2.
33. BBC News, "South Africa Black-owned farms 'failing,'" http://news.bbc.co.uk/2/hi/africa/8547621.stm. (Accessed January 20, 2014); Boyle, Brendon. "Massive Farm Failure in SA," http://www.timeslive.co.za/local/ 2010/03/02/massive-farm-failure-in-sa. (Accessed January 20, 2014).

34. Africa Research Institute, "Waiting for the Green Revolution: Land Reform in South Africa," *Briefing Note* 1301 (2013): 2; Jospeh Ochieno, "18 Years of Progress but ... Real Freedom Remains Elusive for Blacks in South Africa as the Structure of the Former Apartheid Economy Continues Largely Intact," *New African* 525 (2013): 36.
35. James H. Cone, *The Cross and the Lynching Tree* (Maryknoll, New York: Orbis Books, 2011), 160; cf. James H. Cone, "Strange Fruit: The Cross and the Lynching Tree," *Harvard Divinity Bulletin* 35, no. 1 (2007): 52.
36. Cone, *Lynching Tree*, xiii.
37. Gerald O. West, "Locating 'Contextual Bible Study' within Biblical Liberation Hermeneutics and Intercultural Biblical Hermeneutics," *HTS Theological Studies* 70, no. 1 (2014): 2.
38. Mosala, "Wealth and Poverty," 16; Madipoane Masenya (ngwan'a Mphahlele), "Eating the Louse and its Larva! The Indignity of Poverty as Embedded within Selected African and Old Testament Proverbs," *Scriptura* 111 (2013): 458.
39. Martin Noth, *The Deuteronomistic History*, Journal of the Study of the Old Testament Supplement Series 15. (Sheffield: Sheffield Academic Press, 1991), 145; Eckart Otto, "Deuteronomy between the Pentateuch and the Deuteronomistic History: Some Remarks about Thomas Römer, the So-called Deuteronomistic History," *Journal of Hebrew Scriptures* 9, no. 17 (2005): 24; Thomas Römer, *The So-called Deuteronomistic History: A Sociological, Historical and Literary Introduction* (London: T & T Clark International, 2005), 67ff.
40. Itumeleng J. Mosala, "Land, Class and the Bible in South Africa Today," *Journal of Black Theology in South Africa* 5, no. 2 (1991): 40.
41. Masenya (ngwan'a Mphahlele), "Eating the Louse," 453.
42. Dwight N. Hopkins, "Black Theology: The Notion of Culture Revisited," in *The Quest for Liberation and Reconciliation: Essays in Honour of J. Deotis Roberts*, eds. by James D. Roberts and Michael Battle (Louisville: Westminster John Knox Press, 2005), 68–81.
43. Mosala, "Land, Class and the Bible," 40.
44. Elelwani Farisani, "Land in the Old Testament: The Conflict between Ahab and Elijah (1 Kings 21:1–29) and its Significance for our South African Context Today," MA diss. (University of KwaZulu-Natal, 1993), 68–73; Elelwani B. Farisani, "A Sociological Reading of the Confrontation between Ahab and Elijah in 1 Kings 21: 1–29," *Old Testament Essays* 18, no. 1 (2005): 54; Makhosazana K. Nzimande, "Reconfiguring Jezebel: A Post-colonial Imbokodo Reading of the Story of Naboth's Vineyard (1 Kings 21:1–16)," in *African and European Readers of the Bible in Dialogue: In Quest of a Shared Meaning*, eds. Hans de Wit and Gerald O. West (Leiden/London: Koninklijke Brill NV, 2008), 237, 248–249; Norma Franklin, "Jezreel: Before and after Jezebel," in *Israel in Transition: from Late Bronze II to Iron IIa (c. 1250–850 B.C.E.)*. Volume 1. The Archaeology, ed. Lester L. Grabbe (New York/London: T & T Clark, 2008), 45, 51; Ndikho Mtshiselwa, "A Re-Reading of 1 Kings 21: 1–29 and Jehu's Revolution in Dialogue with Farisani and Nzimande: Negotiating Socio-economic Redress in South Africa," *Old Testament Essays* 27, no. 1 (2014): 206.
45. Mtshiselwa, "1 Kings 21," 211–212.
46. Mosala, "Wealth and Poverty," 16.
47. Cf. 1 Kgs 16:24; Farisani, "Sociological Reading," 48; Mtshiselwa, "1 Kings 21," 215.

48. Mtshiselwa, "1 Kings 21," 215.
49. Mosala, "Wealth and Poverty," 18–19.
50. Italics are my insertion. See Madipoane Masenya, "'For Better or for Worse?'—The (Christian) Bible and Africana women," *Old Testament Essays* 22, no. 1 (2009): 134; cf. Teresa Okure, "Invitation to African Women's Hermeneutical Concerns," *African Journal of Biblical Studies* 19, no. 2 (2003): 74.
51. Masenya, "'For Better," 132.
52. Tinyiko S. Maluleke and Sarojini Nadar, "Alien Fraudsters in the White Academy: Agency in Gendered Colour," *Journal of Theology for Southern Africa* 120 (2004): 5.
53. Madipoane Masenya (ngwan'a Mphahlele), "Sacrificing Female Bodies at the Altar of Male Privilege: A Bosadi (Womanhood) Reading of Judges 19," *Theologia Viatorium* 27, no. 1 (2003): 98–122; Madipoane Masenya (ngwan'a Mphahlele), "Their Hermeneutics was Strange! Ours is a Necessity: Rereading Vashti as African-South African Women," in *Her Master's Tools? Feminist and Postcolonial Engagements of Historical-critical Discourse*, ed. Caroline van der Stichele and Todd C. Penner (Atlanta: Society of Biblical Literature, 2005), 191; Madipoane Masenya (ngwan'a Mphahlele), "Invisible Exiles? An African-South African Woman's Reconfiguration of 'Exile' in Jeremiah 21:1–10," *Old Testament Essays* 20, no. 3 (2007): 756.
54. Masenya (ngwan'a Mphahlele), "Invisible Exiles," 761; cf. Takatso Mofokeng, "The Evaluation of the Black Struggle and the Role of Black Theology," in *The Unquestionable Right to be Free: Black Theology from South Africa*, eds. Itumeleng J. Mosala and Buti Tlhagale (Braamfontein: Skotaville, 1986), 113–128.
55. Masenya (ngwan'a Mphahlele), "Invisible Exiles," 756.
56. Robert P. Carroll, *From Chaos to Covenant: Uses of Prophecy in the Book of Jeremiah* (London: SCM Press, 1981), 247–248; cf. Masenya (ngwan'a Mphahlele), "Invisible Exiles," 768; Meyer, "Empty Land," 505–507.
57. Meyer, "Empty Land," 507.
58. Daniel L. Smith-Christopher, *A Biblical Theology of Exile* (Minneapolis: Fortress Press, 2002), 45–49; Masenya (ngwan'a Mphahlele), "Invisible Exiles," 768; Meyer, "Empty Land," 507.
59. Bustenay Obed, "Judah and the Exile," *in Israelite and Judean History*, eds. John H. Hayes and James M. Miller (Philadelphia: Westminster, 1977), 483.
60. Martin Noth, *The History of Israel*, Trans. Stanley Godman and Peter R. Ackroyd. (London: Adam and Charles Black, 1960), 296.
61. Eben Scheffler, *Politics in Ancient Israel* (Pretoria: Biblia Publishers, 2001), 136.
62. Scheffler, *Politics*, 137; cf. Jer 29:5–7.
63. Jean Aitchison, *The Seeds of Speech: Language Origin and Evolution* (Cambridge: Cambridge University Press, 2000), 11; Johanne Angeli, "'Mi no Whiteman, I Mean': Language Ideologies and Attitudes toward English and Pijin among Solomon Students, Between Social Mobility and National Consciousness," MA diss. (Concordia University, 2008), ix.
64. Daniel L. Smith, *The Religion of the Landless: The Social Context of the Babylonian Exile* (Bloomington: Meyer Stone Books, 1989), 38–41; Smith-Christopher, *Theology of Exile*, 71–73.

65. Smith-Christopher, *Theology of Exile*, 72.
66. Temba Rugwiji, "Appropriating Judean Post-exilic Literature in a Postcolonial Discourse: A Case for Zimbabwe," PhD diss., (Pretoria, University of South Africa, 2013), 48–49.
67. Noth, *The History of Israel*; Obed, "Judah," 483; Scheffler, *Politics*, 136–137.
68. Farisani, "Land," 68–73; Andile Mngxitama, "The Taming of Land Resistance: Lessons from the National Land Committee," *Journal of Asian and African Studies* 41, no. 1–2 (2006): 41; Ruth Hall, "The Politics of Land Reform in Post-apartheid South Africa, 1990 to 2004: A Shifting Terrain of Power, Actors and Discourses," PhD diss. (Oxford: St Antony's College, Oxford University, 2011), 18; Kirk Helliker, "Land Reform and Marginalised Communities in the Eastern Cape Countryside of Post-apartheid South Africa," in *Land Struggles and Civil Society in Southern Africa*, eds. Kirk Helliker and Tendai Murisa (New Jersey: Africa World Press, 2011), 43–44; Modise and Mtshiselwa "Natives Land Act," 367; Mtshiselwa, "1 Kings 21," 207.
69. Mtshiselwa, "1 Kings 21," 228.
70. Martin L. King Jr. "I Hhave a Dream," in *A Testament of Hope: The Essential Writings of Martin Luther King, Jr.*, ed. James M. Washington (San Francisco: Harper & Row, 1986), 217.
71. James H. Cone, *The Spirituals and the Blues: An Interpretation* (New York: The Seabury Press, 1972), 32; James H. Cone, "Martin, Malcolm and Black Theology," in *The Quest for Liberation and Reconciliation: Essays in Honour of J. Deotis Roberts*, eds. James D. Roberts and Michael Battle (Louisville, Kentucky: Westminster John Knox Press, 2005), 62.
72. Chantell Ilbury and Clem Sunter, *The Mind of a Fox: Scenario Planning in Action* (Cape Town: Human & Rousseau (Pty) Ltd, 2001), 100, 105.
73. Joseph R. D. Rakoma, *Marema-ka-dika: tša Sesotho sa lebowa* (Pretoria: Van Schaik, 1971), 162; Masenya (ngwan'a Mphahlele), "Eating the Louse," 457.
74. Modise and Mtshiselwa "Natives Land Act," 359–378.
75. Statistics South Africa. *Social Profile of Vulnerable Groups in South Africa 2002–2011* (Pretoria: Statistics South Africa, 2012), 71.
76. James H. Cone, "Loving God with our Heart, Soul, and Mind," in *Blow the Trumpet in Zion: Global Vision and Action for the 21st Century Black Church*, eds. Iva E. Carruthers, Frederick D. Haynes, and Jeremiah A. Wright (Minneapolis: Fortress Press, 2005), 62.
77. Masenya (ngwan'a Mphahlele), "Hermeneutics," 190.
78. Setiloane, "Negotiations Chamber," 36–36.
79. Mosala, "Land, Class and the Bible," 40.
80. Vumelana Advisory Fund, "Making Transferred Land Productive," http://vumelana.org.za/uploads/media/Vumelana_Advisory_Fund_Prospectus.pdf. (Accessed January 20, 2014).
81. Klein, "Democracy Born in Chains," 203–204.
82. Ndikho Mtshiselwa, "A Post-apartheid Nation in Chains? Relevance of Lucky Dube's Mickey Mouse Freedom in Reconfiguring Forms of Oppression in South Africa Today," *Studia Historiae Ecclesiasticae* 40, no. 1 (2014): 58.
83. Emmanuel O. Usue, "Restoration or Desperation in Ezra and Nehemiah? Implications for Africa," *Old Testament Essays* 20, no. 3 (2007): 843; Rugwiji, "Appropriating, 46; cf. Walter Brueggemann, *Cadences of Home: Preaching Among Exiles* (Louisville: Westminster John Knox Press, 1997), 115.

84. Rugwiji, "Appropriating," 44.
85. Joseph Edozien, "Ending Economic Apartheid," http://www.sane.org.za/docs/ eeashort-version.pdf. (Accessed February 20, 2014).
86. Joseph Edozien, "Ending Economic Apartheid," http://www.sane.org.za/docs/ eeashort-version.pdf. (Accessed February 20, 2014).
87. Mtshiselwa, "Post-apartheid Nation," 70–71.
88. Douglas A. Knight, *Law, Power and Justice in Ancient Israel* (Louisville: Westminster John Knox Press, 2011), 202.
89. Rainer Albertz, "The Controversy about Judean versus Israelite Identity and the Persian Government: A New Interpretation of the Bagoses Story (Jewish Antiquities XI.297–301)," in *Judah and the Judeans in the Achaemenid Period: Negotiating Identity in an International Context*, eds. Obed Lipschits, Gary N. Knoppers, and Manfred Oeming (Winona Lake, Indiana: Eisenbrauns, 2011), 485–486.
90. Johannes J. Degenaar, *Marxism-Leninism and Its Implications for South Africa* (Pretoria: H & R Academia (Pty) Ltd, 1982), 26.
91. Bond, *Elite Transition*, 31–32.
92. José E. Ramírez Kidd, *Alterity and Identity in Israel: The rg in the Old Testament* (Beihefte zur Zeitschrift für die alttestamentliche Wissenschaft 283. Berlin/New York: Walter de Gruyter, 1999), 99–100; Christophe Nihan, *From Priestly Torah to Pentateuch: A Study in the Composition of the Book of Leviticus* (Tübingen: Mohr Siebeck, 2007), 525–526, 534.
93. Motsoko Pheko, *Apartheid: The Story of a Dispossessed People* (London: Marram Books, 1984), 60; David Mosoma, "Restitution/reparation: A Commitment to Justice and Peace," *Journal of Black Theology in South Africa* 5, no. 1 (1991): 25–26.
94. Pheko, *Apartheid*, 60.
95. Mogomme A. Masoga, "A Critical Dialogue with Gabriel Molehe Setiloane: The Unfinished Business on the African Divinity Question," *Studia Historiae Ecclesiasticae* 38 (2012): 334; Jele S. Manganyi and Johan Buitendag, "A Critical Analysis on African Traditional Religion and the Trinity," *HTS Theological Studies* 69, no. 1 (2013): 2; Vuyani S. Vellem, "Modern Slavery in the Post-1994 South Africa? A Critical Ethical Analysis of the National Development Plan Promises for Unemployment in South Africa," *Koers—Bulletin for Christian Scholarship* 79, no. 2 (2014): 3.
96. Gabriel M. Setiloane, *African Theology: An Introduction* (Johannesburg: Skotaville Publishers, 1986), 24.
97. Masoga, "Critical Dialogue," 334; Manganyi and Buitendag, "African Traditional Religion," 2; Vellem, "Modern Slavery," 3.
98. Setiloane, *African Theology*, 17.
99. Masoga, "Critical Dialogue," 323–334; Vellem, "Modern Slavery," 3.
100. Samuel E. Balentine, *Leviticus* (Louisville: Westminster John Knox Press, 2002), 193; Esias E. Meyer, *The Jubilee in Leviticus 25: A Theological Ethical Interpretation from a South African Perspective*, Vol. 15. (Münster: LIT Verlag, 2005), 161–181; Jill A. Middlemas, *The Templeless Age: An Introduction to the History, Literature, and Theology of the "Exile"* (Louisville: Westminster John Knox Press, 2007), 128; Meyer, "Empty Land," 503.
101. Meyer, "Empty Land," 502.
102. Meyer, "Empty Land," 502–509.

103. Cf. Lev 26:34–35, 43; Robert P. Carroll, "The Myth of the Empty Land+ A Reflective Reading of Biblical Texts Focusing on Mythicized Sociopolitical Structuring during the 2nd-temple Period," *Semeia* 59 (1992): 83; Meyer, "Empty Land," 506.
104. Baruch J. Schwartz, "'Profane' Slaughter and the Integrity of the Priestly Code," *Hebrew Union College Annual* 67 (1996): 36; Walter Brueggemann, *An Introduction to the Old Testament: The Canon and Christian Imagination* (Louisville: Westminster John Knox Press, 2003), 113; Meyer, "Empty Land," 505; See also Lev 25:10.
105. Schwartz, "Priestly Code," 15; Klaus Grünwaldt, *Das Heiligkeitsgesetz Leviticus 17–26: Ursprüngliche Gestalt, Tradition und Theologie*, Vol. 271 (Berlin: Walter de Gruyter, 1999), 375–381; Eckart Otto, "Innerbiblische Exegese im Heiligkeitsgesetz Levitikus 17–26," in *Levitikus als Buch*, eds. Heinz-Josef Fabry and Hans-Winfried Jüngling (Berlin, Philo: Bonner Biblische Beiträge, 1999), 134; Eckart Otto, "The Holiness Code in Diachrony and Synchrony in the Legal Hermeneutics of the Pentateuch," in *The Strata of the Priestly Writings: Contemporary Debate and Future Directions*, eds. Sarah Shectman and Joel S. Baden (Zürich: Theologischer Verlag Zürich, 2009), 139; Meyer, *Jubilee in Leviticus*, 223.
106. Meyer, *Jubilee in Leviticus*, 38–58, 161–180.
107. Pheko, *Apartheid*, 61.
108. Setiloane, "Negotiations Chamber," 35–36.
109. Nihan, *Priestly Torah*, 537; cf. Grünwaldt, *Leviticus 17–26*, 380–381; Meyer, *Jubilee in Leviticus*, 224.
110. Dirk J. Human, "Africa in Need of an Exodus? Perspectives on the Theology of Exodus 15:1–21," in *A Critical Study of the Pentateuch: An Encounter between Europe and Africa*, eds. by Eckart Otto and Jurie Le Roux (Münster: LIT Verlag, 2005), 74–96.
111. Christophe Nihan, "Forms and Functions of Purity in Leviticus," in *Purity and the forming of Religious Traditions in the Ancient Mediterranean World and Ancient Judaism*, eds. Christian Frevel and Christophe Nihan (Leiden: Koninklijke Brill NV, 2013), 313.
112. See Konrad Schmid, "The Persian Imperial Authorization as Historical Problem and as Biblical Construct: A Plea for Differentiations in the Current Debate," in *The Pentateuch as Torah: New Models for Understanding its Promulgation and Acceptance*, eds. Gary N. Knoppers and Bernard M. Levinson (Winona Lake: Eisenbrauns, 2007), 36; Lev 7:37; 14:54; Num 19:2; Deut 1:5; Neh 8:2; 12:44; 13:3; Jer 2:8.
113. Konrad Schmid, "The Genesis of Normativity in Biblical Law: Historical and Theological Observations on the Development of the Canonical Notion of Law in the Hebrew Bible and its Applications on Nature," in *Concepts of Law in the Sciences, Legal Studies, and Theology*, eds. Michael Welker and Gregor Etzelmüller (Tübingen: Mohr Siebeck, 2013), 121; cf. Jeffrey Stackert, *A Prophet like Moses: Prophecy, Law and Israelite Religion* (Oxford: Oxford University Press, 2014), 34; Diana V. Edelman, "Introduction," in *Deuteronomy-Kings as Emerging Authoritative Books: A Conversation*, ed. Diana V. Edelman (Atlanta: Society of Biblical Literature, 2014), 5.
114. Konrad Schmid, "The Late Persian Formation of the Torah: Observations on Deuteronomy 34," in *Judah and the Judeans in the Fourth Century B.C.E.*, eds. Obed Lipschits, Gary N. Knoppers and Rainer Albertz (Winona Lake: Eisenbrauns, 2007), 243.
115. Erhard S. Gerstenberger, *Leviticus: A Commentary* (Louisville: Westminster John Knox Press, 1996), 378.

116. Gerstenberger, *Leviticus*, 379–382; cf. Nihan, *Priestly Torah*, 520–521.
117. William H. Bellinger Jr., *New International Biblical Commentary: Leviticus and Numbers* (Peabody, Massachusetts: Hendrickson Publishers, 2001), 150; Balentine, *Leviticus*, 194.
118. Nihan, *Priestly Torah*, 520–521; cf. Gerstenberger, *Leviticus*, 382.
119. Thomas Römer, "The Exodus Narrative According to the Priestly Document," in *The Strata of the Priestly Writings: Contemporary Debate and Future Directions*, eds. Sarah Shectman and Joel S. Baden (Zürich: Theologischer Verlag Zürich, 2009), 164.
120. Gerstenberger, *Leviticus*, 382.
121. Farisani, "Sociological Reading," 48; cf. Mordechai Cogan, *1 Kings* (New York: Doubleday, 2001), 419.
122. Mtshiselwa, "1 Kings 21," 215; cf. Roland K. Harrison, *Introduction to the Old Testament* (London: Tyndale Press, 1970), 215; Farisani, "Sociological Reading," 48.
123. Setiloane, *African Theology*, 24; Masoga, "Critical Dialogue," 334; Manganyi and Buitendag, "African Traditional Religion," 2; Vellem, "Modern Slavery," 3.
124. David Ginsburg, "The Democratisation of South Africa: Transition Theory Tested," *Transformation* 29 (1996): 75; James J. Hentz, "The Two Faces of Privatisation: Political and Economic Logics in Transitional South Africa," *The Journal of Modern African Studies* 38, no. 02 (2000): 205; Mngxitama, "Land Resistance," 41; Willem Saayman, "Being Human Together in Democratic South Africa: Umuntu Ngumuntu Ngabantu," *Journal of Gender and Religion in Africa* 17, no. 1 (2011): 170–188.
125. Gerstenberger, *Leviticus*, 383; Frank H. Gorman, *Divine Presence and Community: A Commentary on the Book of Leviticus* (Grand Rapids: Wm. B. Eerdmans Publishing Company, 1997), 139; Mark F. Rooker, *The New American Commentary, vol. 3A, Leviticus* (Nashville: Broadman and Holman Publishers, 2000), 307; Bellinger Jr., *Leviticus and Numbers*, 151; Balentine, *Leviticus*, 195; Nihan, *Priestly Torah*, 528.
126. Gerstenberger, *Leviticus*, 383–384.
127. Yanou, *Dispossession*, 77; Hall, "Land Restitution," 654; Dolny and Klug "Land Reform," 324.
128. Modise and Mtshiselwa "Natives Land Act," 359–378.
129. Paul Maylam, *A History of the African People of South Africa: From the Early Iron Age to the 1970s* (Cape Town: David Philip, 1986), 87; Modise and Mtshiselwa "Natives Land Act," 362–363.
130. Mary Douglas, *Leviticus as Literature* (New York: Oxford University Press, 1999), 243; Ross Kinsler, and Gloria Kinsler. *The Biblical Jubilee and the Struggle for Life. Maryknoll* (New York: Orbis Books, 1999), 17.
131. Rothney Tshaka, "Malcolm X's the Ballot or the Bullet Speech? Its Implications for Black Liberation Theology in Present Day South Africa," *Anais do Congresso Internacional da Faculdades EST* 1 (2012): 897.
132. Knight, *Law, Power and Justice*, 203; Römer, *Deuteronomistic History*, 175, 177.
133. Mosala, "Land, Class and the Bible," 40.
134. Modise and Mtshiselwa "Natives Land Act," 366.
135. Römer, *Deuteronomistic History*, 175, 177.
136. Nihan, *Priestly Torah*, 520–521.
137. Rakoma, *Marema-ka-dika*, 221; Masenya (ngwan'a Mphahlele), "Eating the Louse," 457.
138. Degenaar, *Marxism-Leninism*, 26.

139. Nihan, *Priestly Torah*, 520–521.
140. Mosala, "Land, Class and the Bible," 40.
141. Mosala, "Land, Class and the Bible," 45.
142. Masenya (ngwan'a Mphahlele), "Eating the Louse," 458.
143. Masenya (ngwan'a Mphahlele), "Eating the Louse," 456.
144. Opoku, "Cooking," 7; Opoku "Imperishable Truth," 6–7.
145. Justin S. Ukpong, "Developments in Biblical Interpretation in Africa: Historical and Hermeneutical Directions," in *The Bible in Africa: Transactions, Trajectories and Trends*, eds. Gerald O. West and Musa W. Dube (Leiden: Koninklijke Brill NV, 2000), 14, 26.
146. Michael Bartos and Bernard M. Levinson. "'This Is the Manner of the Remission': Implicit Legal Exegesis in 11QMelchizedek as a Response to the Formation of the Torah," *Journal of Biblical Literature* 132, no. 2 (2013): 352.
147. Römer, *Deuteronomistic History*, 178.
148. Römer, *Deuteronomistic History*, 116.
149. Department of Rural Development and Land Reform, "Green Paper on Land Reform," *Government Gazette* 34656 (2011): 11.
150. Department of Rural Development and Land Reform, "Land Reform," 11–12.
151. Nihan, *Priestly Torah*, 520–521.
152. Esias E. Meyer, "From Cult to Community: The Two Halves of Leviticus," *Verbum et Ecclesia* 34, no. 2 (2013): 7; cf. Lev 20:22–27; 26:1–2.
153. Economic Commission for Africa, *Land Tenure Systems and their Impacts on Food Security and Sustainable Development in Africa* (Addis Ababa: Economic Commission for Africa, 2004), 5.
154. Shepard Daniel and Anuradha Mittal. *The Great Land Grab Rush for World's Farmland Threatens Food Security for the Poor* (Oakland: The Oakland Institute, 2009), 1
155. Daniel and Mittal, *Great Land Grab Rush*, 1.
156. Daniel and Mittal, *Great Land Grab Rush*, 1.
157. Department of Rural Development and Land Reform, "Land Reform," 11.
158. Sampie J. Terreblanche, *The Need for a Transformation Period Towards a Post-apartheid South Africa* Vol. 3. (Stellenbosch: Stellenbosch Economic Project, 1991), 9.
159. Van der Walt, *Constitutional Property Clause*, 146.
160. Klein, "Democracy Born in Chains," 208; cf. Ken Wells, "US Investment in South Africa Quickens," *Wall Street Journal* 6 (1994): 1; Hein Marais, *South Africa: Limits to Change: The Political Economy of Transition* (Cape Town: University of Cape Town Press, 2001), 122.
161. Madipoane Masenya (ngwan'a Mphahlele), "An African-conscious Female's Reading of Steve Biko," in *The Legacy of Stephen Bantu Biko: Theological Challenges*, ed. Cornelius W. du Toit (Pretoria: Research Institute for Religion and Theology, University of South Africa, 2008), 114.
162. Mercy A. Oduyoye, "Women and Ritual in Africa," in *The Will to Arise: Women, Tradition and the Church in Africa*, eds. Mercy A. Oduyoye and Musimbi R. A. Kanyoro (Eugene: Wipf & Stock, 2005), 10; Masenya (ngwan'a Mphahlele), "African-conscious Female," 119–122; Gerrie Snyman, "The Ethics of Reading and the Quest for the Audience in the Book of Chronicles," *Old Testament Essays* 23, no. 3 (2010): 806.

163. Hazel V. Carby, "White Woman Listen! Black Feminism and the Boundaries of Sisterhood," in *Black British Feminism: A Reader*, ed. Heidi Safia Mirza (London: Routledge, 1997), 47.
164. Tamara C. Eskenazi, "Out from the Shadows: Biblical Women in the Postexilic era," *Journal for the Study of the Old Testament* 17, no. 54 (1992): 25–43.
165. Masenya (ngwan'a Mphahlele), "Eating the Louse," 452–459.
166. Meyer, *Jubilee in Leviticus*, 282.
167. Funlola Olojede, "Women and the Cry for Justice in Old Testament Court Narratives: An African Reflection," *Old Testament Essays* 26, no. 3 (2013): 764–767.
168. Olojede, "Women and the Cry," 767–768.
169. Terreblanche, *Transformation Period*, 9.
170. Binswanger, "Political Implications," 139; cf. Yanou, *Dispossession*, 77; Hall, "Land Restitution," 654.
171. Joseph Edozien, "Ending Economic Apartheid," http://www.sane.org.za/docs/ eeashortversion.pdf. (Accessed February 20, 2014).
172. Joseph Edozien, "Ending Economic Apartheid," http://www.sane.org.za/docs/ eeashortversion.pdf. (Accessed February 20, 2014).
173. Mtshiselwa, "Post-apartheid Nation," 71.
174. Nihan, *Priestly Torah*, 520.
175. Nihan, *Priestly Torah*, 520.
176. Nihan, *Priestly Torah*, 521.
177. Madipoane Masenya (ngwan'a Mphahlele), "A *Bosadi* (Womanhood) Reading of Proverbs 31:10–31," in *Other Ways of Reading: African Women and the Bible*, ed. Musa W. Dube (Atlanta and Geneva: Society of Biblical Literature and WCC Publications, 2001), 145–157, 186–199.
178. Cone, *Lynching Tree*, 160; West, "Locating," 2.

References

Africa Research Institute. "Waiting for the Green Revolution: Land Reform in South Africa." *Briefing Note* 1301 (2013): 1–4.

Aitchison, Jean. *The Seeds of Speech: Language Origin and Evolution*. Cambridge: Cambridge University Press, 2000.

Akbar, Na'im. "Africentric Social Sciences for Human Liberation." *Journal of Black Studies* 14, no. 4 (1984): 395–414.

Albertz, Rainer. "The Controversy about Judean versus Israelite Identity and the Persian Government: A New Interpretation of the Bagoses Story (Jewish Antiquities XI.297–301)." In *Judah and the Judeans in the Achaemenid Period: Negotiating Identity in an International Context*, edited by Obed Lipschits, Gary N. Knoppers, and Manfred Oeming, 483–504. Winona Lake, Indiana: Eisenbrauns, 2011.

Anderson, Cheryl B. *Ancient Laws and Contemporary Controversies: The Need for Inclusive Biblical Interpretation*. Oxford: Oxford University Press, 2009.

Angeli, Johanne. "'Mi no Whiteman, I Mean': Language Ideologies and Attitudes toward English and Pijin among Solomon Students, Between Social Mobility and National Consciousness." MA diss., Concordia University, 2008.

Balentine, Samuel E. *Leviticus*. Louisville: Westminster John Knox Press, 2002.

Bartos, Michael and Bernard M. Levinson. "'This Is the Manner of the Remission': Implicit Legal Exegesis in 11QMelchizedek as a Response to the Formation of the Torah." *Journal of Biblical Literature* 132, no. 2 (2013): 351–371.

BBC News. "South Africa Black-owned Farms 'Failing.'" http://news.bbc.co.uk/2/hi/africa/8547621.stm.

Bellinger Jr., William H. *New International Biblical commentary: Leviticus and Numbers*. Peabody, Massachusetts: Hendrickson Publishers, 2001.

Benhin, James K. A. "Climate Change and South African Agriculture: Impacts and Adaptation Options." *Centre of Environment Economics and Policy in Africa, Policy Note* 21 (2006): 1–8.

Binswanger, Hans P. "The Political Implications of Alternative Models of Land Reform and Compensation." In *Agricultural Land Reform in South Africa: Policies, Markets and Mechanisms*, edited by Johan Van Zyl, Johann Kirsten, and M. P. Binswanger, 139–146. Cape Town: Oxford University Press, 1996.

Bond, Patrick. *Elite Transition: From Apartheid to Neoliberalism in South Africa*. Pietermaritzburg: University of Natal Press, 2000.

Boyle, Brendon. "Massive Farm Failure in SA," http://www.timeslive.co.za/local/ 2010/03/02/massive-farm-failure-in-sa.

Brueggemann, Walter. *Cadences of Home: Preaching among Exiles*. Louisville, Kentucky: Westminster John Knox Press, 1997.

Brueggemann, Walter. *An Introduction to the Old Testament: The Canon and Christian Imagination*. Louisville: Westminster John Knox Press, 2003.

Carby, Hazel V. "White Woman Listen! Black Feminism and the Boundaries of Sisterhood." In *Black British Feminism: A Reader*, edited by Heidi Safia Mirza, 45–53. London: Routledge, 1997.

Carroll, Robert P. *From Chaos to Covenant: Uses of Prophecy in the Book of Jeremiah*. London: SCM Press, 1981.

Carroll, Robert P. "The Myth of the Empty Land+ A Reflective Reading of Biblical Texts Focusing on Mythicized Sociopolitical Structuring during the 2nd-temple Period." *Semeia* 59 (1992): 79–93.

Claassens, Aninka. "Compensation for Expropriation: The Political and Economic Parameters of Market Value Compensation." *South African Journal of Human Rights* 9, (1993): 422–427.

Cogan, Mordechai. *1 Kings*. New York: Doubleday, 2001.

Cone, James H. *The Spirituals and the Blues: An Interpretation*. New York: The Seabury Press, 1972.

Cone, James H. "Looking Back, Going Forward: Black Theology as Public Theology." In *Black Faith and Public Talk: Critical Essays on James H. Cone's Black Theology and Black Power*, edited by Dwight N. Hopkins, 246–260. Maryknoll: Orbis Book, 1999.

Cone, James H. "Martin, Malcolm and Black Theology." In *The Quest for Liberation and Reconciliation: Essays in Honour of J. Deotis Roberts*, edited by James D. Roberts and Michael Battle, 53–62. Louisville, Kentucky: Westminster John Knox Press, 2005.

Cone, James H. "Loving God with our Heart, Soul, and Mind." In *Blow the Trumpet in Zion: Global Vision and Action for the 21st Century Black Church*, edited by Iva E. Carruthers, Frederick D. Haynes, and Jeremiah A. Wright, 59–64. Minneapolis: Fortress Press, 2005.

Cone, James H. "Strange Fruit: The Cross and the Lynching Tree." *Harvard Divinity Bulletin* 35, no. 1 (2007): 46–55.

Cone, James H. *The Cross and the Lynching Tree*. Maryknoll, New York: Orbis Books, 2011.

Daniel, Shepard and Anuradha Mittal. *The Great Land Grab Rush for World's Farmland Threatens Food Security for the Poor*. Oakland: The Oakland Institute, 2009.

Degenaar, Johannes J. *Marxism-Leninism and its Implications for South Africa*. Pretoria: H & R Academia (Pty) Ltd, 1982.

Department of Rural Development and Land Reform. "Green Paper on Land Reform." *Government Gazette* 34656 (2011): 8–18.

Desmond, C. "Overview." In *The Codesa File: Negotiating a Non-racial Democracy in South Africa*, edited by Fatima Meer, 5–16. Durban: Madiba Publishers, 1993.

Dolny, Helena and Heinz Klug. "Land Reform: Legal Support and Economic Regulation." *South African Review-SARS* 6 (1992): 322–337.

Douglas, Mary. *Leviticus as Literature*. New York: Oxford University Press, 1999.

Dunnigan, Robert, Kevin Fazaeli and Jaco Spies. "Black Economic Empowerment—Difficulties and Opportunities in Making Right the Wrongs of the Past," http://faculty-course.insead.edu/dutt/emdc/projects/Sep-Oct05/Group_D.pdf.

Economic Commission for Africa. *Land Tenure Systems and their Impacts on Food Security and Sustainable Development in Africa*. Addis Ababa: Economic Commission for Africa, 2004.

Edelman, Diana V. "Introduction." In *Deuteronomy-Kings as Emerging Authoritative Books: A Conversation*, edited by Diana V. Edelman, 1–26. Atlanta: Society of Biblical Literature, 2014.

Edozien, Joseph. "Ending Economic Apartheid," http://www.sane.org.za/docs/ eeashortversion.pdf.

Eskenazi, Tamara C. "Out from the Shadows: Biblical Women in the Postexilic era." *Journal for the Study of the Old Testament* 17, no. 54 (1992): 25–43.

Farisani, Elelwani B. "Land in the Old Testament: The Conflict between Ahab and Elijah (1 Kings 21:1–29) and its Significance for our South African Context Today." MA diss., University of KwaZulu-Natal, 1993.

Farisani, Elelwani B. "A Sociological Reading of the Confrontation between Ahab and Elijah in 1 Kings 21: 1–29." *Old Testament Essays* 18, no. 1 (2005): 47–60.

Franklin, Norma. "Jezreel: Before and after Jezebel." In *Israel in Transition: from Late Bronze II to Iron IIa (c. 1250–850 B.C.E.)*. Volume 1. The Archaeology, edited by Lester L. Grabbe, 45–53. New York/London: T & T Clark, 2008.

Gerstenberger, Erhard S. *Leviticus: A Commentary*. Louisville: Westminster John Knox Press, 1996.

Ginsburg, David. "The Democratisation of South Africa: Transition Theory Tested." *Transformation* 29 (1996): 74–102.

Gorman, Frank H. *Divine Presence and Community: A Commentary on the Book of Leviticus*. Grand Rapids: Wm. B. Eerdmans Publishing Company, 1997.

Gottwald, Norman K. "How does Social Scientific Criticism Shape our Understanding of the Bible as a Resource for Economic Ethics?" *The Hebrew Bible in Its Social World and in Ours* (1993): 341–347.

Grünwaldt, Klaus. *Das Heiligkeitsgesetz Leviticus 17–26: Ursprüngliche Gestalt, Tradition und Theologie.* Vol. 271. Berlin: Walter de Gruyter, 1999.

Hall, Ruth. "Land Restitution in South Africa: Rights, Development, and the Restrained State." *Canadian Journal of African Studies/La Revue canadienne des études africaines* 38, no. 3 (2004): 654–671.

Hall, Ruth. "The Politics of Land Reform in Post-apartheid South Africa, 1990 to 2004: A Shifting Terrain of Power, Actors and Discourses." PhD diss., Oxford: St Antony's College, Oxford University, 2011.

Harrison, Roland K. *Introduction to the Old Testament.* London: Tyndale Press, 1970.

Hassan, Rashid M. "Implications of Climate Change for Agricultural Sector Performance in Africa: Policy Challenges and Research Agenda." *Journal of African Economies* 19, no. 2 Supplement (2010): 77–105.

Healey, Joseph G. "When Elephants Fight the Grass (Reeds) Gets Hurt—Swahili (Eastern and Central Africa African Proverb of the Month November, 2001," http://www.afriprov.org/index.php/african-proverb-ofthemonth/27001proverbs /172nov2001.pdf.

Helliker, Kirk. "Land Reform and Marginalised Communities in the Eastern Cape Countryside of Post-apartheid South Africa." In *Land Struggles and Civil Society in Southern Africa*, edited by Kirk Helliker and Tendai Murisa, 43–69. New Jersey: Africa World Press, 2011.

Hentz, James J. "The Two Faces of Privatisation: Political and Economic Logics in Transitional South Africa." *The Journal of Modern African Studies* 38, no. 2 (2000): 203–223.

Hertz, Noreena. *The Silent Takeover: Global Capitalism and the Death of Democracy.* London: William Heinemann, 2001.

Hopkins, Dwight N. "Black Theology: The Notion of Culture Revisited." In *The Quest for Liberation and Reconciliation: Essays in Honour of J. Deotis Roberts*, edited by James D. Roberts and Michael Battle, 63–81. Louisville: Westminster John Knox Press, 2005.

Human, Dirk J. "Africa in Need of an Exodus? Perspectives on the Theology of Exodus 15:1–21." In *A Critical Study of the Pentateuch: An Encounter between Europe and Africa*, edited by Eckart Otto and Jurie Le Roux, 74–96. Münster: LIT Verlag, 2005.

Ilbury, Chantell and Clem Sunter. *The Mind of a Fox: Scenario Planning in Action.* Cape Town: Human and Rousseau (Pty) Ltd/Tafelberg Publishers, 2001.

Kidd, José E. Ramírez. *Alterity and Identity in Israel: The rg in the Old Testament.* Beihefte zur Zeitschrift für die alttestamentliche Wissenschaft 283. Berlin/New York: Walter de Gruyter, 1999.

King Jr., Martin L. "I Have a Dream." In *A Testament of Hope: The Essential Writings of Martin Luther King, Jr.*, edited by James M. Washington, 217–220. San Francisco: Harper & Row, 1986.

Kinsler, Ross and Gloria Kinsler. *The Biblical Jubilee and the Struggle for Life.* Maryknoll, New York: Orbis Books, 1999.

Klein, Naomi. "Democracy Born in Chains: South Africa's Constricted Freedom." In *The Shock Doctrine: The Rise of Disaster Capitalism*, edited by Naomi Klein, 194–217. New York: Metropolitan Books, Henry Holt and Company, LLC, 2007.

Knight, Douglas A. *Law, Power and Justice in Ancient Israel*. Louisville: Westminster John Knox Press, 2011.

Kwakye, John K. "Africa's Long Road to Development: It is Not Just Economics, But Also History, Geography, Politics, and Leadership." Accra: Frontiers Printing and Publishing Ltd, 2011.

Loogman, Alfons. *Swahili Grammar and Syntax*. Pittsburgh: Duquesne University Press, 1965.

Madise. Mokhele J. S. "Borrowed/begged Water Never Quenches Thirst." Inaugural lecture. Pretoria: University of South Africa, 2012.

Malcolm X. *Malcolm X speaks: Selected Speeches and Statements*. New York: Grove Press, 1965.

Maluleke, Tinyiko S., and Sarojini Nadar. "Alien Fraudsters in the White Academy: Agency in Gendered Colour." *Journal of Theology for Southern Africa* 120 (2004): 5–17.

Manganyi, Jele S., and Johan Buitendag. "A Critical Analysis on African Traditional Religion and the Trinity." *HTS Theological Studies* 69, no. 1 (2013): 1–13.

Marais, Hein. *South Africa: Limits to Change: The Political Economy of Transition*. Cape Town: University of Cape Town Press, 2001.

Masenya (ngwan'a Mphahlele), Madipoane. "A *Bosadi* (Womanhood) Reading of Proverbs 31:10–31." In *Other Ways of Reading: African Women and the Bible*, edited by Musa W. Dube, 145–157. Atlanta and Geneva: Society of Biblical Literature and WCC Publications, 2001.

Masenya (ngwan'a Mphahlele), Madipoane. "Sacrificing Female Bodies at the Altar of Male Privilege: A *Bosadi* (Womanhood) Reading of Judges 19." *Theologia Viatorium* 27, no. 1 (2003): 98–122.

Masenya, Madipoane. "Struggling with Poverty/emptiness: Rereading the Naomi-Ruth Story in African-South Africa." *Journal of Theology for Southern Africa* 120 (2004): 46–59.

Masenya (ngwan'a Mphahlele), Madipoane. "Their Hermeneutics was Strange! Ours is a Necessity: Rereading Vashti as African-South African Women." in *Her Master's Tools? Feminist and Postcolonial Engagements of Historical-critical Discourse*, edited by Caroline van der Stichele and Todd C. Penner, 179–194. Atlanta: Society of Biblical Literature, 2005.

Masenya (ngwan'a Mphahlele), Madipoane. "Invisible Exiles? An African-South African Woman's Reconfiguration of 'Exile' in Jeremiah 21:1–10." *Old Testament Essays* 20, no. 3 (2007): 756–771.

Masenya (ngwan'a Mphahlele), Madipoane. "An African-conscious Female's Reading of Steve Biko." In *The Legacy of Stephen Bantu Biko: Theological Challenges*, edited by Cornel W. du Toit, 114–155. Pretoria: Research Institute for Religion and Theology, University of South Africa, 2008.

Masenya, Madipoane. "'For Better or for Worse?'—The (Christian) Bible and Africana women." *Old Testament Essays* 22, no. 1 (2009): 126–150.

Masenya (ngwan'a Mphahlele), Madipoane. "Jeremiah." In *The Africana Bible: Reading Israel's Scriptures from Africa and the African Diaspora*, edited by Hugh R. Page, 147–156. Minneapolis: Fortress Press, 2010.

Masenya (ngwan'a Mphahlele), Madipoane. "Eating the Louse and its Larva! The Indignity of Poverty as Embedded within Selected African and Old Testament Proverbs." *Scriptura* 111 (2013): 452–459.

Masenya, Madipoane. "The Dissolution of the Monarchy, the Collapse of the Temple and the 'Elevation' of Women in the Post-exilic period: Any Relevance for African Women's Theologies?." *Old Testament Essays* 26, no. 1 (2013): 137–153.

Masenya (ngwan'a Mphahlele), Madipoane and Hulisani Ramantswana. "Lupfumo lu Mavuni (Wealth is in the Land): In Search of the Promised Land (cf. Exod 3–4) in the Post-Colonial, Post-Apartheid South Africa." *Journal of Theology for Southern Africa* 151 (2015): 96–116.

Masoga, Mogomme A. "A Critical Dialogue with Gabriel Molehe Setiloane: The Unfinished Business on the African Divinity Question." *Studia Historiae Ecclesiasticae* 38 (2012): 323–344.

Maylam, Paul. *A History of the African People of South Africa: From the Early Iron Age to the 1970s*. Cape Town: David Philip, 1986.

Meyer, Esias E. *The Jubilee in Leviticus 25: A Theological Ethical Interpretation from a South African Perspective*. Vol. 15. Münster: LIT Verlag, 2005.

Meyer, Esias E. "From Cult to Community: The Two Halves of Leviticus." *Verbum et Ecclesia* 34, no. 2 (2013): 1–7.

Meyer, Esias E. "Returning to an Empty Land: Revisiting my Old Argument about the Jubilee." *Old Testament Essays* 27, no. 2 (2014): 502–519.

Middlemas, Jill A. *The Templeless Age: An Introduction to the History, Literature, and Theology of the "Exile."* Louisville: Westminster John Knox Press, 2007.

Mngxitama, Andile. "The Taming of Land Resistance: Lessons from the National Land Committee." *Journal of Asian and African Studies* 41, no. 1–2 (2006): 39–69.

Modise, Leepo and Ndikho Mtshiselwa. "The Natives Land Act of 1913 Engineered the Poverty of Black South Africans: A Historico-ecclesiastical Perspective." *Studia Historiae Ecclesiasticae* 39, no. 2 (2013): 359–378.

Mofokeng, Takatso. "The Evaluation of the Black Struggle and the Role of Black Theology." In *The Unquestionable Right to be Free: Black Theology from South Africa*, edited by Itumeleng J. Mosala and Buti Tlhagale, 113–128. Braamfontein: Skotaville, 1986.

Mosala, Itumeleng J. "Biblical Hermeneutics and Black Theology in South Africa." PhD diss., University of Cape Town, 1987.

Mosala, Itumeleng J. "Land, Class and the Bible in South Africa Today." *Journal of Black Theology in South Africa* 5, no. 2 (1991): 40–46.

Mosala, Itumeleng J. "Wealth and Poverty in the Old Testament: A Black Theological Perspective." *Journal of black theology in South Africa* 5, no. 1 (1996): 16–22.

Mosoma, David. "Restitution/reparation: A Commitment to Justice and Peace." *Journal of Black Theology in South Africa* 5, no. 1 (1991): 12–28.

Mtshiselwa, Ndikho. "A Re-Reading of 1 Kings 21: 1–29 and Jehu's Revolution in Dialogue with Farisani and Nzimande: Negotiating Socio-economic Redress in South Africa." *Old Testament Essays* 27, no. 1 (2014): 205–230.

Mtshiselwa, Ndikho. "A Post-apartheid Nation in Chains? Relevance of Lucky Dube's Mickey Mouse Freedom in Reconfiguring Forms of Oppression in South Africa Today." *Studia Historiae Ecclesiasticae* 40, no. 1 (2014): 57–76.

Nihan, Christophe. *From Priestly Torah to Pentateuch: A Study in the Composition of the Book of Leviticus*. Tübingen: Mohr Siebeck, 2007.

Nihan, Christophe. "Forms and Functions of Purity in Leviticus." In *Purity and the Forming of Religious Traditions in the Ancient Mediterranean World and Ancient Judaism*, edited by Christian Frevel and Christophe Nihan, 311–368. Leiden: Koninklijke Brill NV, 2013.

Noth, Martin. *The History of Israel*. Translated by Stanley Godman and Peter R. Ackroyd. London: Adam and Charles Black, 1960.

Noth, Martin. *The Deuteronomistic History*. Journal of the Study of the Old Testament Supplement Series 15. Sheffield: Sheffield Academic Press, 1991.

Nyerere, Julius K. *Freedom and Unity: Uhuru na Umoja—A Selection from Writings and Speeches, 1952–65*. London: Oxford University Press, 1966.

Nzimande, Makhosazana K. "Reconfiguring Jezebel: A Post-colonial *Imbokodo* Reading of the Story of Naboth's Vineyard (1 Kings 21:1–16)." in *African and European Readers of the Bible in Dialogue: In Quest of a Shared Meaning*, edited by Hans de Wit and Gerald O. West, 223–258. Leiden/London: Koninklijke Brill NV, 2008.

Nzimande, Makhosazana K. "Isaiah." In *The Africana Bible: Reading Israel's Scriptures from Africa and the African Diaspora*, edited by Hugh R. Page, 136–146. Minneapolis: Fortress Press, 2009.

Obed, Bustenay. "Judah and the Exile." In *Israelite and Judean History*, edited by John H. Hayes and James M Miller, 435–488. Philadelphia: Westminster, 1977.

Ochieno, Jospeh. "18 Years of Progress but … Real Freedom Remains Elusive for Blacks in South Africa as the Structure of the Former Apartheid Economy Continues Largely Intact." *New African* 525 (2013): 36–61.

Oduyoye, Mercy A. "Women and Ritual in Africa." In *The Will to Arise: Women, Tradition and the Church in Africa*, edited by Mercy A. Oduyoye and Musimbi R A. Kanyoro, 9–24. Eugene: Wipf & Stock, 2005.

Okure, Teresa. "Invitation to African Women's Hermeneutical Concerns." *African Journal of Biblical Studies* 19, no. 2 (2003): 71–95.

Olojede, Funlola. "Women and the Cry for Justice in Old Testament Court Narratives: An African Reflection." *Old Testament Essays* 26, no. 3 (2013): 761–772.

Opoku, Kofi Asare. "Cooking on Two Stones of the Hearth: African Spirituality and the Socio-cultural Transformation of Africa." *Journal of Christian Thought* 13, no. 1 (2009): 3–9.

Opoku Kofi Asare. "Skinny but Imperishable Truth: African Religious Heritage and the Regeneration of Africa." *Studia Historiae Ecclesiasticae* 38, Supplement (2011):141–151.

Otto, Eckart. "Innerbiblische Exegese im Heiligkeitsgesetz Levitikus 17–26." In *Levitikus als Buch*, edited by Heinz-Josef Fabry and Hans-Winfried Jüngling, 125–196. Berlin, Philo: Bonner Biblische Beiträge, 1999.

Otto, Eckart. "Deuteronomy between the Pentateuch and the Deuteronomistic History: Some Remarks about Thomas Römer, the So-called Deuteronomistic History." *Journal of Hebrew Scriptures* 9, no. 17 (2005): 22–27.

Otto, Eckart. "The Holiness Code in Diachrony and Synchrony in the Legal Hermeneutics of the Pentateuch." In *The Strata of the Priestly Writings: Contemporary Debate and Future Directions*, edited by Sarah Shectman and Joel S. Baden, 135–156. Zürich: Theologischer Verlag Zürich, 2009.

Pheko, Motsoko. *Apartheid: The Story of a Dispossessed People*. London: Marram Books, 1984.

Rakoma, Joseph R. D. *Marema-ka-dika tša Sesotho sa Leboa*. Pretoria: Van Schaik, 1970.

Römer, Thomas. *The So-called Deuteronomistic History: A Sociological, Historical and Literary Introduction*. London: T & T Clark International, 2005.

Römer, Thomas. "The Exodus Narrative According to the Priestly Document." In *The Strata of the Priestly Writings: Contemporary Debate and Future Directions*, edited by Sarah Shectman and Joel S. Baden, 157–174. Zürich: Theologischer Verlag Zürich, 2009.

Rooker, Mark F. *The New American Commentary, vol. 3A, Leviticus*. Nashville: Broadman and Holman Publishers, 2000.

Rugwiji, Temba. "Appropriating Judean Post-exilic Literature in a Postcolonial Discourse: A Case for Zimbabwe." PhD diss., University of South Africa, 2013.

Saayman, Willem. "Being Human Together in Democratic South Africa: Umuntu Ngumuntu Ngabantu." *Journal of Gender and Religion in Africa* 17, no. 1 (2011): 170–188.

Scheffler, Eben. *Politics in Ancient Israel*. Pretoria: Biblia Publishers, 2001.

Schmid, Konrad. "The Persian Imperial Authorization as Historical Problem and as Biblical Construct: A Plea for Differentiations in the Current Debate." In *The Pentateuch as Torah: New Models for Understanding its Promulgation and Acceptance*, edited by Gary N. Knoppers and Bernard M. Levinson, 22–38. Winona Lake: Eisenbrauns, 2007.

Schmid, Konrad. "The Late Persian Formation of the Torah: Observations on Deuteronomy 34." In *Judah and the Judeans in the Fourth Century B.C.E.*, edited by Obed Lipschits, Gary N. Knoppers, and Rainer Albertz, 236–245. Winona Lake: Eisenbrauns, 2007.

Schmid, Konrad. "The Genesis of Normativity in Biblical Law: Historical and Theological Observations on the Development of the Canonical Notion of Law in the Hebrew Bible and its Applications on Nature." In *Concepts of Law in the Sciences, Legal Studies, and Theology*, edited by Michael Welker and Gregor Etzelmüller, 119–136. Tübingen: Mohr Siebeck, 2013.

Schwartz, Baruch J. "'Profane' Slaughter and the Integrity of the Priestly Code." *Hebrew Union College Annual* 67 (1996): 15–42.

Setiloane, Gabriel M. *African Theology: An Introduction*. Johannesburg: Skotaville Publishers, 1986.

Setiloane, Gabriel M. "Land in the Negotiations Chamber: An Afro-centric Approach." *Journal of Black Theology* 5, no. 2 (1991): 29–39.

Smith, Daniel L. *The Religion of the Landless: The Social Context of the Babylonian Exile*. Bloomington: Meyer Stone Books, 1989.

Smith-Christopher, Daniel L. *A Biblical Theology of Exile*. Minneapolis: Fortress Press, 2002.

Snyman, Gerrie. "The Ethics of Reading and the Quest for the Audience in the Book of Chronicles." *Old Testament Essays* 23, no. 3 (2010): 804–821.

Snyman, Gerrie. "Looking into black eyes and feel the embarrassment: A selected and selective reading of the Africana Bible." *Old Testament Essays* 24, no. 2 (2011): 464–491.

Stackert, Jeffrey. *A Prophet like Moses: Prophecy, Law and Israelite Religion*. Oxford: Oxford University Press, 2014.

Statistics South Africa. *Social Profile of Vulnerable Groups in South Africa 2002–2011*. Pretoria: Statistics South Africa, 2012.

Terreblanche, Sampie J. *The Need for a Transformation Period Towards a Post-apartheid South Africa*. Vol. 3. Stellenbosch: Stellenbosch Economic Project, 1991.

Terreblanche, Sampie. J. *Lost in Transformation: South Africa's Search for a New Future Since 1986*. Johannesburg: KMM Review Publishing Company, 2012.

Tshaka, Rothney. "Malcolm X's the Ballot or the Bullet Speech? Its Implications for Black Liberation Theology in Present Day South Africa." *Anais do Congresso Internacional da Faculdades EST* 1 (2012): 882–898.

Ukpong, Justin S. "The Emergence of African Theologies." *Theological Studies* 45, no. 3 (1984): 501–536.

Ukpong, Justin S. "Developments in Biblical Interpretation in Africa: Historical and Hermeneutical Directions." In *The Bible in Africa: Transactions, Trajectories and Trends*, edited by Gerald O. West and Musa W. Dube, 11–28. Leiden: Koninklijke Brill NV, 2000.

Usue, Emmanuel O. "Restoration or Desperation in Ezra and Nehemiah? Implications for Africa." *Old Testament Essays* 20, no. 3 (2007): 830–846.

Van der Walt, Andries J. *The Constitutional Property Clause: A Comparative Analysis of Section 25 of the South African Constitution of 1996*. Kenwyn: Juta & CO. Ltd, 1997.

Vellem, Vuyani S. "Modern Slavery in the Post-1994 South Africa? A Critical Ethical Analysis of the National Development Plan Promises for Unemployment in South Africa." *Koers—Bulletin for Christian Scholarship* 79, no. 2 (2014): 1–8.

Vumelana Advisory Fund. "Making Transferred Land Productive," http://vumelana.org.za/uploads/media/Vumelana_Advisory_Fund_Prospectus.pdf.

Weideman, Marinda. "Who Shaped South Africa's Land Reform Policy?" *Politikon* 31, no. 2 (2004): 219–238.

Wells, Ken. "US Investment in South Africa Quickens." *Wall Street Journal* 6 (1994): 1.

West, Gerald O. "Locating 'Contextual Bible Study' within Biblical Liberation Hermeneutics and Intercultural Biblical Hermeneutics." *HTS Theological Studies* 70, no. 1 (2014): 1–10.

World Bank. *Africa Rainfall and Temperature Evaluation System (ARTES)*. Washington, DC: World Bank, 2010.

Yanou, Michael A. *Dispossession and Access to Land in South Africa: An African Perspective*. Mankon, Bamenda: Langaa Research & Publishing Common Initiative Group, 2009.

CHAPTER FIVE

Conclusion

Introduction

As stated in Chapter 1, the main question this study has tried to answer is: If re-read from an African liberationist perspective in the context of land redistribution and socio-economic justice in South Africa, could the Israelite Jubilee legislation in Leviticus 25:8–55 offer liberating and empowering possibilities for the poor in South Africa? Based on this question, the research hypothesis states that: 'The Israelite Jubilee in Leviticus 25:8–55, when re-read from an African liberationist perspective and in the context of the discourse on redistribution of land and socio-economic justice can contribute positively to the redress of inequality and consequently, to poverty alleviation in South Africa'.

Following this hypothesis, the present chapter presents the findings, that is, the concise statements from the analyses in this study.

Findings: Leviticus 25 in the Context of an African Liberationist Reading

The inferences that will be made in this section emanate from the chapters of this study. That is, the summary and findings will follow the chapter outline of the study with the deliberate exception of the introductory chapter.

Critique of Socio-economic Injustice and Land in South Africa—Inferences and Implications

Chapter 2 offers a critique of the reality of socio-economic injustice and land in South Africa. The inferences that can be made based on such a critique include the fact that first, South African land policies impede land redistribution and the redress of poverty among African South Africans; and second, the political élites do play a role in the present disproportionate benefits from land ownership and socio-economic injustice in the country.

It is suggested, based on statistics on poverty and data on the land discourse, that the land policies in South Africa impede efforts to redistribute land to previously disadvantaged black people who lost it during the colonial and apartheid regimes. Neo-liberal economic globalization has not only influenced and continued to shape land policies in South Africa but it also inhibits socio-economic justice. It has also been pointed out that the possession of land by emerging African-South African farmers who have no education, skills and sufficient funds does not warrant the redress of socio-economic injustice.

The trend of self-enrichment by the political élites impedes attempts to redress socio-economic injustice and to redistribute land equitably among the citizens that shows the role of the élites in fostering the present disproportionate benefits from land ownership and socio-economic injustice in South Africa. Evidence from the analyses of South Africa's political economy is used to argue that the ideological clash and compromise between the ANC, SACP and COSATU in the transitional and post-apartheid South Africa led to the apparent rise of a flawed capitalism. The chapter refers to Fukuyama's theory of the 'end of history', which suggests that there can never be an alternative ideological basis for governance other than neo-liberal capitalism. Against such a theory, it has been argued that the evidence of persistent poverty and inequality underscores the need for the discourse on alternative ideologies and economic policies especially in South Africa.

Analysis of the Israelite Jubilee in Leviticus 25:8–55—Summary and Findings

Chapter 3 not only shows that socio-economic justice was upheld in the Israelite Jubilee but it also attempts to reconstruct the Israelite policy on land ownership and socio-economic justice in Leviticus 25:8–55. Traditionally, the text of Leviticus 25:8–55 is assigned to the authors of the Holiness Code. However, the critical exegetical analysis of the text of Leviticus 25:8–55 show the verses that are dependent on each other and on other unrelated verses. The distinct features and layers of sources such as D, P, D and the Pentateuchal redactor are identified. It has been extensively argued that these layers may be located to either the compositional or the redactional stage of the formation of the Israelite Jubilee. Furthermore, existing literature on Jubilee shows that the dating of the sources as well as the *Sitz-im-Leben* of their addressees is set within the framework of the non-documentarian approach. That is, this study contradicts the documentary hypothesis and neo-documentary hypothesis which restrict the dating of sources to a given period as it is important to identify and stress the possibility of different historical and social locations of the text and redactional layers in the Pentateuch.

The interesting finding is that the pre-exilic D layer sought to address the misuse of power on the part of the rich élites to confiscate productive land from the poor Israelites. Thus, the poor found it difficult to acquire or regain productive land under D's requirement of the payment of compensation. In the exilic context, the D layers evident in Leviticus 25:8–55 continued to elevate the rich élites at the expense of the poor. Similarly, it has been argued that P's addressees were Israelites who were in captivity in Babylonia and with no land of their own. In the case of certain layers of P, the Levites were probably already favoured economically in the Babylonian period as there is evident preferential treatment of the Levites in Leviticus 25:8–55. However, unlike P, in the post-exilic Yehud setting when the Jews were faced with the challenge of loss of land, indebtedness and poverty, H addressed both the poor Judeans and the rich élites but showed special interest in the plight of the poor. It is suggested that the addressees of H were not free in Yehud, as elements of oppression and poverty continued to manifest in the post-exilic period.

Implications of an African Liberationist Reading of Leviticus 25:8–55 for the South African Context

In line with *The Africana Bible: Reading Israel's Scriptures from Africa and the African Diaspora*, Chapter 4 focuses on the South African context as it offers an impetus for understanding Leviticus 25:8–55 which to a large extent differs from an understanding of what is known as normative. If understood in the light of the treatment of *whiteness* and *Europeanness* as a norm in biblical interpretation, the analysis of Leviticus 25:8–55 from an African liberationist perspective would also embrace *blackness.*[1] In addition to the use of African proverbs as a hermeneutical tool in biblical interpretation, this study finds that the employment of selected South African liberation songs as a hermeneutical tool equally leads to a liberative interpretation of the ancient text. The African liberationist framework has certain implications for the interpretation of Leviticus 25:8–55.

Significantly, it has been pointed out that the statement כִּי־לִי הָאָרֶץ 'for the land is mine' (Lev 25:23) is set by H to refute the protection of the private ownership of land by the rich élites, which perpetrated indebtedness, poverty and slavery. However, the clause in v.24 וּבְכֹל אֶרֶץ אֲחֻזַּתְכֶם גְּאֻלָּה תִּתְּנוּ לָאָרֶץ 'and in all the land of your possession you shall grant a redemption for the land' did not serve the interest of the poor as it unreasonably expects them to possess capital to pay the redemption (compensation) for the land. The implication of that clause is that the provision of the payment of compensation which stifles the process of redressing socio-economic injustice in South African needs to be addressed.

That the Pentateuchal redactor did not contest or protest against the economic disparities between the people in the walled cities and those in the village houses in vv.29–34 shows that the verses are not helpful in the struggle for liberation in post-exilic Yehud. As such, one could view vv.29–34 as a clause that widened the gap between the rich and the poor. Furthermore, it is significant that the abrupt structural insertion of the unit of vv.29–34 served to protect the interest of the people in the cities who were probably the wealthy class. Thus, it may be argued that the Israelite Jubilee has flaws as it perpetrated inequality and segregation based on social class. The South African situation of economic inequality resonates with the economic disparities reflected in vv.22–34, as shown above which implies that all South Africans need to denounce the gap between the rich and the poor.

The inference from the clause in v.25 כִּי־יָמוּךְ אָחִיךָ 'If your brother becomes poor' indicates that H's redaction was not gender-sensitive. It has been suggested that in a context, which women such as the Shunemite woman lost land and subsequently became poor, the exclusion of women from the Israelite Jubilee legislation by H appears mischievous. Given the fact that poverty in post-exilic Yehud equally affected both women and men, a gender-sensitive clause would have been appropriate to the context of H. In the same way, a gender-sensitive reading of v.25 in the South African context demands of South Africans to address the fact that in terms of the statistics women make up the majority of the poor. Therefore, priority should therefore be given to women in issues of land redistribution and redress of socio-economic injustice.

Due to the evidence that the payment of taxes placed a strain on the productivity of the poor Jewish farmers, it has been suggested that the lack of financial resources probably contributed to the unproductivity of the poor farmers in post-exilic Yehud. Furthermore, the statement וְנָתְנָה הָאָרֶץ פִּרְיָהּ 'and the land shall yield her fruit' (v.19) suggests that the land cannot yield fruit on its own, that is, without human and financial capital and skill. Thus, the argument is warranted that the clause about the land yielding fruit would have made sense if the issue of capital, resources and skills to work the land had been included in the Israelite Jubilee legislation. In the South African context, the need for capital, resources and skills is crucial in the quest for land redistribution and socio-economic justice.

It has been suggested that the loss of land was probably at the centre of the experience of the working-class people, that is, the so-called slaves in Leviticus 25:8–55. We have noted that Naboth was 'rendered poor by the experience of land expropriation' and the expropriation of land perpetrated poverty among the working-class people or the so-called slaves as implied in the pre-exilic layer of D.[2] Thus, this study submits that the liberation of the working-class people who according to Nihan became slaves to both Israelites and non-Israelites is dependent on the liberation of the land. As Mosala has also argued, 'without liberating the land through the Jubilee legislation the working-class people in Leviticus 25:8–55 could not be genuinely liberated'.[3]

Vanderhooft, Smith-Christopher and Rugwiji all agree that D's reference to the word 'remission' and to the 'release of slaves' confirms that the exiles experienced slavery and hard labour. Thus, the need for liberation constitutes the experience of D's addressees in Babylonia.

Notes

1. Gerrie Snyman, "African Hermeneutics' 'Outing' of Whiteness," *Neotestamentica* 42, no. 1 (2008): 114.
2. Itumeleng J. Mosala, "Wealth and Poverty in the Old Testament: A Black Theological Perspective," *Journal of Black Theology in South Africa* 5, no. 1 (1996): 20.
3. Itumeleng J. Mosala, "Land, Class and the Bible in South Africa Today," *Journal of Black Theology in South Africa* 5, no. 2 (1991): 45.

References

Mosala, Itumeleng J. "Land, Class and the Bible in South Africa Today." *Journal of Black Theology in South Africa* 5, no. 2 (1991): 40–46.

Mosala, Itumeleng J. "Wealth and Poverty in the Old Testament: A Black Theological Perspective." *Journal of black theology in South Africa* 5, no. 1 (1996): 16–22.

Snyman, Gerrie. "African Hermeneutics' 'Outing' of Whiteness." *Neotestamentica* 42, no. 1 (2008): 93–118.

Index of Authors

A

B

C

D

E

F

G

H

I

J

K

L

M

N

O

P

R

S

T

U

V

W

X

Y

Z

Index of Subjects

A

B

C

D

E

F

G

H

I

J

L

M

N

O

P

R

S

T

U

V

W

X

Y

Z

Bible & Theology in Africa

Knut Holter, *General Editor*

The twentieth century made sub-Saharan Africa a Christian continent. This formidable church growth is reflected in a wide range of attempts at contextualizing Christian theology and biblical interpretation in Africa. At a grassroots level ordinary Christians express their faith and read the bible in ways reflecting their daily situation; at an academic level, theologians and biblical scholars relate the historical traditions and sources of Christianity to the socio- and religio-cultural context of Africa. In response to this, the Bible and Theology in Africa series aims at making African theology and biblical interpretation its subject as well as object, as the concerns of African theologians and biblical interpreters will be voiced and critically analyzed. Both Africans and Western authors are encouraged to consider this series.

Inquiries and manuscripts should be directed to:

Professor Knut Holter
Center for Mission and Global Studies
VID Specialized University
Misjonsmarka 12
N-4024 Stavanger, Norway
knut.holter@mhs.no

To order other books in this series, please contact our Customer Service Department:

(800) 770-LANG (within the U.S.)
(212) 647-7706 (outside the U.S.)
(212) 647-7707 FAX

Or browse online by series:

www.peterlang.com

www.ingramcontent.com/pod-product-compliance
Ingram Content Group UK Ltd.
Pitfield, Milton Keynes, MK11 3LW, UK
UKHW021827100926
8556IPUK00003B/199

9 781433 138935